D1715038

NASHVILLE

NASHVILLE

The Western
Confederacy's
Final
Gamble

James Lee
McDonough

The University of Tennessee Press • Knoxville

This book is printed on acid-free paper.

Frontispiece: Left, John Bell Hood. Courtesy of the Tennessee State Library
and Archives. *Right,* George H. Thomas. Courtesy of the Tennessee State
Library and Archives.

Library of Congress Cataloging-in-Publication Data

McDonough, James L., 1934–
Nashville : the western Confederacy's final gamble / James Lee
McDonough.— 1st ed.
   p. cm.
Includes bibliographical references and index.
ISBN 1-57233-322-7 (hardcover)

1. Nashville, Battle of, Nashville, Tenn., 1864
2. Tennessee—History—Civil War, 1861–1865—Campaigns.
3. United States—History—Civil War, 1861–1865—Campaigns.
 I. Title.
E477.52.M353 2004
973.7'42--dc22   2004009524

Dedicated to all the students at Auburn University who took my classes in U.S. military history, World War II, and the American Civil War, especially those who have served and are now serving in the armed forces of the United States.

CONTENTS

Figures

ILLUSTRATIONS

Maps

As a native Nashvillian I have fond memories of boyhood days in the late 1930s and the 1940s. I well remember watching the black smoke rolling as the Louisville & Nashville's "Pan American" came down the line "on her way to New Orleans," as Hank Williams sang. World War II made a distinct impression on me, and proud I was that my favorite twin-engined war plane, the P-38 Lockheed Lightning, was being produced in Nashville (even if, as I later learned, only in small quantity) and occasionally appeared in the sky around Berry Field and the city—a spectacle than which few events were more exciting for a boy ten years old in 1944. Upon several occasions I was present at the Ryman Auditorium for the Grand Ole Opry when legendary performers, such as Bill Monroe, Roy Acuff, Red Foley, Ernest Tubb, Eddy Arnold, Minnie Pearl, and of course, Hank Williams, were on stage in the late forties and early fifties. Nashville's full-size replica of the magnificent Parthenon made a tremendous impression on me, whetting my appetite to know more about the ancient Greek civilization. My earliest memory of the recently renovated and elegantly restored Hermitage Hotel, particularly its Capitol Grille Restaurant, which had long been a favorite spot to eat, goes back to sometime in the mid-forties. And I have some particularly good memories of high school years in the late forties and early fifties. Many other Nashville impressions could be mentioned. There were some negatives, of course, but always I have held a warm feeling for the city; particularly the Nashville of my younger years.

Perhaps most pertinent for my future interests, I remember the impressive statue, commemorating the Civil War Battle of Nashville, that stood undisturbed from 1927 to 1974 at the intersection of Franklin Road and Thompson Lane, a work now restored following tornado damage and relocated at Granny White Pike and Battlefield Drive. As a native Nashvillian, and after becoming seriously interested in the Civil War, I long considered writing a book that would focus on the fighting at Nashville. After the late Tom Connelly and I coauthored *Five Tragic Hours,* a work that centered on the Franklin engagement, the thought of writing a book about the Nashville battle appealed even more. It is satisfying to know the project has at last become a reality. While this account, appropriately I believe, develops the whole campaign, the fighting at Nashville is the focus of the book.

My knowledge of the campaign has benefited, in varying degree to be sure, from the work of earlier writers. The most extensive accounts have been penned by, in order of publication: Thomas R. Hay, *Hood's Tennessee Campaign* (1929); Stanley F. Horn, *The Decisive Battle of Nashville* (1956); Thomas Lawrence Connelly, *Autumn of Glory: The Army of Tennessee, 1862–1865* (1971); Shelby Foote, *The Civil War: A Narrative,* vol. 3 (1975); Wiley Sword, *Embrace an Angry Wind: The Confederacy's Last Hurrah: Spring Hill, Franklin, and Nashville* (1992); Don Lowry, *Dark and Cruel War: The Decisive Months of the Civil War, September– December, 1864* (1993); Winston Groom, *Shrouds of Glory: From Atlanta to Nashville* (1995); and Anne J. Bailey, *The Chessboard of War* (2000). (All these books have source notes except Foote and Groom, and all are concerned with the entire campaign except Horn.)

Fortunately my research has tapped a number of primary sources (some published; most unpublished) that were not employed by any of the earlier authors. Also, with the exception of Wiley Sword, most studies of the Battle of Nashville have dealt only briefly (and some not at all) with the fighting on the eastern flank where United States Colored Troops (USCT) attacked the Confederates on both days of the battle. In researching and analyzing that bloody aspect of the engagement, I discovered and utilized several primary sources that have not appeared in any previous history. Notably too, while researching the U.S. army's attack against the Confederate redoubts on the western flank, I realized that redoubt number four actually came under assault first, rather than number five. In most accounts, beginning with Stanley Horn, number five has been presented as coming under assault initially. (Hay and Connelly did not deal with the order in which the redoubts were attacked.) All in all, I found stimulating work, years after first studying the 1864 Middle Tennessee Campaign, in taking another look, more carefully and in greater depth, at this fascinating topic.

The following account, as in several of my earlier books, attempts whenever possible, to allow the participants, both common soldiers and officers, to present their stories in their own words, without any effort to correct their grammar and spelling. Their accounts from letters, diaries, memoirs, and formal presentations (such as for the Military Order of the Loyal Legion of the United States), have been accepted at face value, unless there seemed to be a good reason for doubting their record. While the author would readily acknowledge that some people have a highly active imagination and are strongly inclined toward embellishment—perhaps to glorify themselves; perhaps to entertain others with contrived tales and thereby monopolize the limelight; perhaps to discredit someone else—he has also observed over several decades that truth is sometimes incredible, indeed "stranger than fiction." Furthermore, Civil War soldiers often had an ability to express themselves impressively, exhibiting an engaging writing style. Such ability is true even of some whose spelling and grammar is crude. I would venture a guess that a higher percentage of the population was then capable of such skill than would be the case today.

Another matter deserving comment is the choice of terminology for the armies. A half-dozen or more designations have been employed for each of the contending forces. The purpose was to avoid monotonously using Confederate and U.S., my terms of preference, every time I referred to the armies. It is likely that somebody objects to whatever word is chosen. For instance, I have heard it suggested that the word Rebel might be offensive to descendents of Confederate soldiers. It is a fact, however, that Confederate soldiers sometimes called themselves Rebels, even taking a bit of pride in the term. Certainly Yankees often referred to Rebels.

As for the word Yankee, often employed by Confederates to reference anyone in the opposing forces, U.S. troops from the Old Northwest region would have considered a Yankee as a Northeasterner, particularly a New Englander. Northern army is less than satisfactory because many Southerners, probably thirty to fifty thousand from Tennessee, for instance, served in the U.S. forces. Also, most African Americans who served with the U.S. were from Southern states. The designation Southern army leaves something to be desired, since large numbers of Southerners from the Upper South were not sympathetic to the Confederacy. There are Southerners who object to the term Federal army, claiming the Confederacy was actually more federalized than the Federals.

Still others are inclined to complain about the use of Union army, contending that the designation became common only in the latter stages and after the war. As for U.S. army, there are Southerners who do not relish being reminded that their ancestors once fought the United States Army. Fighting "the Yankees," for them seems not so bad. When it comes to Confederate, the official U.S. position was that no such organization actually existed. Some folks in Southern states were simply in rebellion. While I have no desire to offend anyone by my use of terms, I concluded years ago to spread the various designations all around. At least it avoids monotony.

Perhaps too it should be noted that this book was not written solely for Civil War specialists, nor even for history specialists. It was written for the educated general public as well. The general reader may find it helpful to keep in mind that military organization varies from time to time and country to country. In the American Civil War a regiment theoretically consisted of a thousand men. Several regiments composed a brigade, several brigades a division, and several divisions made up a corps. Late in the war, a regiment's strength typically was far less than a thousand men. During the Middle Tennessee Campaign of 1864, the typical U.S. regiment might number some 350 to 450 or 500. A Confederate regiment was normally smaller, often much smaller. In fact, some times at Nashville a Confederate brigade was no larger than a Union regiment.

I wish also to applaud the Battle of Nashville Preservation Society. Thanks to a generous investment of time, effort, and money, additional portions of the battleground have been identified and saved from destruction as the city has continued to expand. Finally, a word of caution to all readers who visit the battle sites: Be careful! Nashville is a rather large city now and, as in most big cities, unfortunately there are people who drive impatiently, carelessly, and irresponsibly.

James Lee McDonough
April 2003

ACKNOWLEDGMENTS

Many people have assisted me with the preparation of this book. First I must acknowledge Nat C. Hughes and James A. Ramage, who read the manuscript for the University of Tennessee Press, making comments and suggestions that helped this manuscript become a better book. Also reading the chapters on the fighting at Nashville and offering valuable suggestions was Ross Massey, currently historian of the Battle of Nashville Preservation Society.

Marylin Bell Hughes of the Tennessee State Library and Archives, who has assisted my research many times over the years, again proved very helpful. Vicki Gaw of Nashville typed the narrative on disk and Nancy McDonough typed the notes, bibliography, and army tables of organization on disk. Nancy was also a great help assisting my research at the United States Army Military History Institute; at the National Archives; at the University of North Carolina, Chapel Hill; and at Vanderbilt University.

Others who have contributed, in various ways, are: Jerry Gaw, Mary Glenn Hearne, Ross V. Hickey Jr., John Hursh, Jenny Johnson, Tim Johnson, James D. Kay Jr., James Lewis, James L. Moon Jr., Martha Riedl, Rudy Sanders, Jim Summerville, and Ridley Wills II. The assistance of all the above is greatly appreciated.

The staffs of many libraries, archives, and historical societies have rendered invaluable help. These include the Alabama Department of Archives and History, the Atlanta Historical Society, the Auburn University Archives, the Filson Club Historical Society, the Florida State University Special Collections, the Georgia Department of Archives and History, the Illinois State Historical Library, the Indiana Historical Society, the Library of Congress, the Mississippi Department of Archives and History, the Missouri Historical Society, the National Archives, the Ohio Historical Society, the Tennessee State Library and Archives, the Southern Historical Collection of the University of North Carolina, the Du Pont

Library at the University of the South, the Jean and Alexander Heard Library at Vanderbilt University, and the United States Army Military History Institute.

For well over two decades, in various capacities, Jennifer Siler, Director of the University of Tennessee Press, has been of great assistance with my books published by the press. This book is no exception. I greatly appreciate the work of all the staff at the UT Press, as well as Ms. Siler.

Finally, to research and write a history book of this size and scope without making any mistakes is an impossible task. Because Confederate officers' reports are relatively few, this work was a somewhat more difficult challenge than my previous books. I hope my mistakes are few and trivial. However that may be, I alone am responsible for all statements of fact, interpretations, analyses, and conclusions presented herein.

1

Making Georgia Howl

Wednesday, August 11, 1880, more than fifteen years after the Civil War ended, was a warm, overcast day in central Ohio. Along the banks of the Scioto River, at the state capital of Columbus, there probably had never been a more notable occasion in the sixty-eight years of the city's history. It was the second day of the Grand Reunion of Federal Army veterans.[1]

"The people are here and bent on having a Reunion," crowed the *Ohio State Journal*. The paper reported that three hundred packed railway coaches, with many people standing, arrived in Columbus on August 11. There were more visitors than Columbus ever before experienced. "There is no doubt," recorded the *Journal*, "that the number of people arriving at the Columbus depot . . . surpassed by thousands the influx at that place on any other day in the history of the city." Estimates of the number of visitors packing the streets of Columbus ranged between fifty and sixty thousand. "The streets were almost impassable," declared the paper, noting also that "many of the veterans have grown old" and that thousands were broken in health and disabled.[2]

Among the vast multitude of visitors some were very special. The President of the United States, Rutherford B. Hayes, a former Brigadier General of Union volunteers, would be on hand for the occasion; as well as Lieutenant General William Tecumseh Sherman, then General-in-Chief of the United States Army. Both men were natives of the Buckeye State. The president's arrival, accompanied by General Sherman and several other dignitaries—among them Major General William B. Hazen; Colonel Emory Upton; and Lieutenant Johnny Clem, the celebrated "Drummer Boy of Shiloh"—was anxiously anticipated. As it turned out, the train was forty minutes late, but that only seemed to add to the drama. When the president's train pulled into the Columbus depot during the late morning of August 11, a large crowd had assembled to hail the chief executive and his party. The car in which President Hayes and his companions were traveling was uncoupled from the train and run out to High Street where the men settled into carriages. Then began a procession, with people lining the streets to see and applaud the president and his entourage.[3]

By mid-afternoon, the old Ohio State Fair Grounds (later Franklin Park) was the focus of the celebration. A twenty-one-gun salute was fired and a military band struck up a wartime selection, with President Hayes scheduled to address the veterans. Unfortunately, the unpromising weather had worsened and rain was falling by the time the president spoke. The bad weather discouraged many visitors, as well as residents of the city, who stayed away from the afternoon's open air festivities. Nevertheless, perhaps ten thousand veterans were on hand, according to the reports in the newspapers. Because of the rain, President Hayes decided to cut short his speech. After all, it was written and would be published in its entirety. He thought the audience could seek shelter from the inclement weather and read his message later. As Hayes concluded his brief remarks, the veterans applauded him warmly, but most were not inclined to leave, regardless of the rain.[4]

As the applause for the president died away, shouts of "Sherman!" "Sherman!" and "Speech!" "Speech!" began to sound from the huge crowd. "Let's hear from Uncle Billy!" some shouted, recalling the name by which the soldiers fondly acclaimed him during the war. The effect was contagious and more and more men took up the cry for Sherman to speak. The crowd began to clap, the intensity of the applause building steadily. General Sherman was not on the schedule to speak. Soon, however, it became obvious that the sea of Union veterans would not be satisfied until the general responded.

At last Sherman arose, strode to the speaker's stand, and the roar of applause was described as "tremendous and deafening." The general gazed upon the crowd, waiting for the applause to subside. When he started to speak, the veterans were not disappointed.

"Fellow soldiers," he began. "My speech is not written, nor has been even thought of by me. It delights my soul to see so many of the good old boys left yet. They are not afraid of rain; we have stood it many a time." Sherman proceeded to note that he had come to Columbus, not for the purpose of speaking, but as a part of the president's escort, intending "simply to look on and let the boys look at old Billy again." Proclaiming that "Uncle Billy loves . . . as his own flesh and blood . . . every soldier here today," the general avowed that "could I command the language I would like to speak to you an hour." At this point of his extemporaneous remarks Sherman spoke the words for which he has been longest remembered: "The war now is away back in the past and you can tell what books can not. When you talk you come down to the practical realities just as they happened. You all know this is not soldiering here. There is many a boy here today who looks on war as all glory, but boys it is all hell. You can bear this warning voice to generations yet to come. I look upon war with horror, but if it has to come, I am here." This remark was received by the audience with long applause and vigorous, lusty hurrahs. Then Sherman concluded: "I wish to again congratulate you. Those who were at the rear in the war would have been gone from here covered with umbrellas before now. The country is now peaceful and long may it so remain. To you soldiers they owe the debt of gratitude."[5]

Obviously Sherman was a man of great popularity. No American of his era, except for Lincoln, has been more widely quoted. Speaking before a crowd, Sherman could be electrifying. Probably he could have been President of the United States. Certainly he could have had the Republican nomination in 1884. Sherman often professed, however, that he disliked, even despised politics, and it was when the Republican Party tried to persuade him to be a presidential candidate that he declined with another of his famous statements: "If nominated, I will not run; if elected, I will not serve."[6] But none of his often-quoted remarks— not "Atlanta is ours and fairly won"; not "I present Savannah to the country as a Christmas present"; not "War is Cruelty, and you cannot refine it"; nor any other—has come close to matching the pronouncement that "War is all hell."[7]

If indeed war is all hell, Sherman's critics have alleged that the general surely ought to have known it, because, they say, he did more than anyone else to make it hell. Whatever one concludes on that issue, sixteen years before Sherman's famous assertion at the grand reunion in Ohio, the general was conducting the campaigns for which his name will live always in American history. On August 11, 1864, Sherman's army was deep into Georgia, having laid siege to Atlanta, the Confederacy's last major rail and manufacturing center.

William Tecumseh Sherman—his father selecting the name Tecumseh in honor of the Native American Shawnee chief whose courage and military prowess he admired—was then forty-four years old. The war had physically

William T. Sherman.
Library of Congress.

worn the tall, lean, red-haired but rapidly graying Ohioan who wore a grizzled, short-cropped beard. Sherman was a restless man and a heavy cigar smoker, troubled by asthma all his life. One of his staff officers, John C. Gray, remarked on Sherman's rather unkempt appearance, noting that the general sometimes wore "a black felt hat slouched over the eyes . . . brown field officer's coat with high collar and no shoulder straps, muddy trowsers and one spur." He also said Sherman "talks continually and with immense rapidity."[8]

Except for the very early days of the war, when Sherman saw action leading a brigade at First Bull Run, all his service came in the western theater. There he proved his mettle at Shiloh, Vicksburg, and Chattanooga, and became a friend of U. S. Grant. Sherman had great confidence in Grant and the feeling was mutual. The victories of Grant and Sherman in the West elevated Grant to three stars and command of all the U.S. forces. When Grant went east to assume his new responsibilities, he placed Sherman in command of all Federal troops in the western theater.

The two generals, by then personally very close, soon planned a coordinated campaign, for the spring of 1864, against the Confederacy's two major armies. Their strategy, they believed, would win the war. Grant would travel with the Army of the Potomac (that army under the immediate command of George Gordon Meade, the victor at Gettysburg) and advance against Robert E. Lee's Army of Northern Virginia. Simultaneously, Sherman would move against Joseph E. Johnston's Army of Tennessee, deployed in north Georgia just south of Chattanooga. The campaigning was to be unrelenting, applying continual pressure with superior numbers and equipment, thus denying either Confederate army any opportunity to send reinforcements to the other. Much smaller, auxiliary campaigns also were projected for the purpose of further pressuring the Southerners, but all of them resulted in failure. Grant and Sherman, of course, ultimately succeeded.

By early May the stage was set and the Union armies began to move out toward the enemy. Sherman had approximately one hundred thousand men advancing against Johnston's fifty thousand (soon reinforced to sixty-five thousand). The city of Atlanta lay 120 miles south of Chattanooga. An obvious target, Atlanta would become, eventually, the objective of the campaign. The immediate goal, however, was the Rebel army. Sherman intended to force a battle, if possible, and inflict major damage. "Neither Atlanta, nor Augusta, nor Savannah, was the objective," explained Sherman years later in his memoirs, "but the 'army of Joseph Johnston,' go where it might." At the time of the campaign Sherman bluntly wrote his concept of the plan: "I am to knock Joseph Johnston, and to do as much damage to the resources of the enemy as possible."[9]

This mission would not be easy, even if Sherman did have more soldiers than the Confederates. Deep in enemy territory, he had to rely for supplies on a long railroad line from Louisville to Nashville to Chattanooga and southward. But "Uncle Billy" proved equal to the great logistical challenge. Carefully planning for the hundreds of necessary railroad cars; scores of locomotives to power them; thousands of garrison troops to guard the many vulnerable points, like bridges, trestles, and tunnels; as well as work crews when accidents or enemy attack necessitated repairs, Sherman kept the huge volume of supplies—130 cars transporting thirteen hundred tons a day on average—coming south without significant interruptions.[10] Employing well-executed flanking movements, except for the one time he grew impatient at Kennesaw Mountain and ordered a costly frontal assault, Sherman steadily compelled Johnston to give ground, falling back closer and closer to Atlanta. As the Confederate army retreated, criticism mounted against Johnston in Richmond. When Johnston, smarting from another of Sherman's well-designed turning movements, pulled back from the elaborate defenses prepared along the Chattahoochee, the last of the three major rivers between Chattanooga and Atlanta, Jefferson Davis, president of the Confederacy, decided that Johnston must be replaced.

The president's telegram reached Johnston's headquarters on Monday, July 18, 1864. It removed Johnston from command of the Army of Tennessee. "As you have failed to arrest the advance of the enemy to the vicinity of Atlanta, far in the interior of Georgia, and express no confidence that you can defeat or repel him, you are hereby removed from command of the Army and Department of Tennessee." Davis replaced Johnston with the young, aggressive-minded John Bell Hood. The well-formed, six-feet-two-inches-tall Kentuckian had risen rapidly through the ranks, advancing from a captain in 1861 to a division commander by 1862 and then to corps command in the Army of Tennessee. He had proven himself as a fighter and a brave warrior, but Hood was also weakened and maimed. He lost his right leg at Chickamauga and the use of his left arm at Gettysburg. There was another problem, well expressed by General Robert E. Lee's now well-known suggestion that Hood, relative to command, possessed too much of the lion and not enough of the fox. The Kentuckian was a controversial choice to lead the Army of Tennessee, both at the time and down through the years.[11]

When the news reached Sherman that the thirty-three-year-old Hood was now facing him, the Union commander at once asked General John M. Schofield, who had been Hood's classmate at West Point, what the man was like. Schofield answered that Hood was bold, rash, and "courageous in the extreme." James B. McPherson, another of the top-ranking Federal officers, and a member of the same West Point class, agreed with Schofield's assessment, as did George H. Thomas, who had been one of Hood's instructors at the military academy, and later served with him in the United States Army in Texas. General Oliver O. Howard knew Hood too. His estimate, penned in a letter to his wife, was brief and pointed: "Hood was a classmate of McPherson. He is a stupid fellow, but a hard fighter." Hood did exactly what the Northern officers expected him to do: attack. Also, and as they expected, he did not wait long to do it.[12]

July 20 was the day Hood struck. "God defends the right," declared the *Atlanta Appeal* on that day. "His hand is the buckler and shield of the soldier who bravely maintains such a cause as ours."[13] Whatever one may wish to make of God's part in it all, the battle waged along Peachtree Creek went decidedly in favor of the Yankees. Two days later Hood again struck at the Blueclads in the vicinity of Decatur, east of Atlanta (an engagement often called the Battle of Atlanta), and suffered some 5,500 casualties, more than twice the total of his effort at Peachtree Creek.[14] Attacking yet again at Ezra Church, only a few days later, Hood's forces were thrown back once more with heavy casualties. Sherman had inflicted terrible punishment on the Army of Tennessee, more than 13,000 casualties in the three battles, while Federal casualties totaled less than half as many.[15] Southern morale plummeted and desertion became more frequent. Hood would not attack again. In fact, Jefferson Davis cautioned him not to risk another assault.

Meanwhile, Sherman proceeded to put Atlanta under siege. Thus far, in a campaign of three months, he had forced the Southerners to fall back some one hundred miles while inflicting considerably more casualties than he took. "No other strategic offensive of the war except Grant's Vicksburg campaign," declared historian James M. McPherson, "accomplished so much at such relatively low cost."[16] By the first of September, Hood, about to be trapped in Atlanta, pulled out of the city, which the Federals quickly entered in triumph.

And suddenly, William Tecumseh Sherman (Cump to his friends, the nickname derived from Tecumseh) was truly famous, and about to become more so. He need never recall again those newspaper reports early in the war, when he served in Kentucky, claiming that he was insane. He had captured Atlanta. The news electrified the nation. No longer could intelligent people claim the Union war effort was a failure when one hundred thousand Federal soldiers occupied that major rail center in the Deep South. The victory carried the added bonus of contributing enormously to Lincoln's campaign for reelection, the realization of which would virtually guarantee the ultimate doom of the Confederacy. General Henry W. Halleck called Sherman's achievement the most brilliant of the war, and Charles Francis Adams ranked "Uncle Billy" with Napoleon and Frederick the Great, while the praise from newspapers, telegrams, and letters kept pouring in.[17]

But Sherman was not satisfied. Far from it. He was planning a bolder stroke, something that had been in his mind for a long time. He had seen vast numbers of people killed and wounded. The loss of life seemed to have no end and the war went on and on. While campaigning earlier in Mississippi, Sherman had destroyed property as a means of waging psychological warfare against the South. Sherman became more and more convinced that inflicting casualties, however horrendous the numbers, would never be as effective in achieving Federal victory as assaults on the Confederate psyche through the destruction of property.[18]

At the opening of his spring campaign in north Georgia, Sherman had been asked what he would do after capturing Atlanta and reportedly replied: "Salt water. Salt water."[19] Mulling over the possibility of marching into the interior of Georgia, Cump began to correspond with Grant in early September about his future operations. Sherman recognized that Grant, since becoming general-in-chief of the armies of the U.S. with responsibility for the strategic direction of the war, was actually the only person he needed to convince of the wisdom of his plans in order to get what he desired. At every opportunity Sherman pursued the topic. On September 20 he wrote Grant: "If you can whip Lee, and I can march to the Atlantic, I think Uncle Abe will give us twenty days leave of absence to see the young folks."[20]

Then in late September, General Hood moved around Sherman's right, striking the Western & Atlantic Railroad south of Chattanooga. Sherman followed, stating that "it was absolutely necessary to keep General Hood's infantry off our main route of communication and supply."[21] When Hood next marched westward toward Alabama, Sherman said that Hood could "turn and twist like a fox," and declared that he could "wear out my army in pursuit."[22] Hood was an enigma, complained Sherman: "I cannot guess his movements as I could those of Johnston, who was a sensible man and only did sensible things." His movements began to look to some, especially General Thomas, tending to affairs of the Department of the Cumberland in Nashville, as if Hood were going to invade Tennessee. The truth was that Sherman had no intention of following Hood to find out what the Confederate commander might do next.[23]

On October 1 Sherman asked Grant, "Why will it not do to leave Tennessee to the forces which Thomas has, and the reserves soon to come to Nashville, and for me to destroy Atlanta and then march across Georgia to Savannah or Charleston, breaking roads and doing irreparable damage?"[24] Grant and Sherman would exchange telegrams for several weeks, discussing Cump's proposal and considering various aspects of the strategic situation. On October 11, Sherman wrote that he "would infinitely prefer to . . . move through Georgia, smashing things to the sea." While Hood might turn into "Tennessee and Kentucky, . . . I believe he will be forced to follow me." Instead of being on the defensive, "I will be on the offensive," Sherman said. "Instead of my guessing at what he means to do, he will have to guess at my plans. . . . I can make Savannah, Charleston, or the mouth of the Chattahoochee (Appalachicola)."[25]

He told General Henry Halleck that the proposed march would not be "purely military or strategic, but it will illustrate the vulnerability of the South. They don't know what war means," he claimed, "but when the rich planters . . . see their fences and corn and hogs and sheep vanish before their eyes, they will have something more than a mean opinion of the 'Yanks.'" And to General James H. Wilson he vowed: "I am going into the very bowels of the Confederacy, and propose to leave a trail that will be recognized fifty years hence."[26]

Grant raised the issue of preparing a coastal base to supply the army, but Sherman responded that his troops would need no supplies, and no base. What they required would simply be taken from the countryside. "I can make the march and make Georgia howl!" asserted Sherman.[27] Another concern of Grant's was that Sherman might be "bushwhacked by all the old men, little boys, and such railroad guards as are still left at home." Sherman, however, intended to be very strong, planning as he worded it, to take none but "the best fighting material" on his march. Meditating on the matter in Washington, D.C., were Lincoln, Secretary of War Stanton, and Halleck, as well as Grant. President Lincoln was very concerned, but ultimately willing to accept Grant's decision on the matter.[28]

After weeks of Sherman's arguments and pleadings, Grant's concerns for Cump's safety and success somewhat subsided. Sherman got what he wanted. Grant advised the president that he considered the proposed march to be fundamentally sound. He telegraphed Sherman that his plan was approved and that he enjoyed the "confidence and support of the government." General George H. Thomas, at Nashville in command of the Department of the Cumberland, was to oppose General Hood's advance should the Confederates turn northward into Tennessee instead of following Sherman.[29]

Sherman then proceeded to force the evacuation of Atlanta, after which he burned all its war-producing facilities. He did not burn the city to the ground, as so often has been alleged. In mid-November the general "took his concept of destructive war to its next level," moving out of Atlanta and "sallying forth to ruin Georgia," as he phrased it.[30] Marching from Atlanta to the sea, with sixty thousand soldiers, Cump cut a sixty-mile swath, clearly marked with enormous property damage. John F. Marszalek, whose biography of Sherman has been called "the Sherman biography for our generation" by one reviewer and "the essential [Sherman] biography" by another, after acknowledging the tremendous destruction of property, succinctly summarizes the march: "Casualties on both sides were light, however, and personal violence against Georgia civilians was slight. Sherman did not pursue a scorched earth policy, but he used purposeful destruction to plant uncertainty and fear in the hearts and minds of the Confederate populace. Confederate soldiers, deserters, civilians, and fugitive slaves did their share of damage, too, and their activities added to the psychological drama."[31]

Generally, Sherman's soldiers destroyed what they did not consume. The troops looted and torched vast areas of the countryside and, as one historian expressed Sherman's role: "Although he did not condone wanton acts of violence and devastation, he certainly tolerated them."[32] By December 21, Sherman had forced the Rebels to evacuate Savannah, after which the general made his

"Christmas present" of the city to the president and the nation. Soon he was making plans to take his march of destruction into the Carolinas, while the morale of Southerners waned. Confederates may not have believed the Northern cause to be right or just (indeed few of them ever did), but a sullen dread of Northern power settled and spread over the region. There was no denying that Sherman was bringing the war home, grinding Southerners into the dirt, demonstrating the consequences of fighting "to the last ditch." And there was nothing they could do to stop him.

Meanwhile, as Sherman was "Marching through Georgia," as the popular tune said—a song incidentally that Cump never cared for—Confederate General John Bell Hood proceeded to move into Middle Tennessee, advancing toward Nashville, where General Thomas had the assignment to stop him. Undoubtedly, Major General George Henry Thomas—born in Southampton County, Virginia, in 1816 and graduated from West Point in 1840, twelfth in a class of forty-two and six behind Sherman, with whom he roomed for a time— was one of the best corps commanders in the U.S. army. Sent to Florida soon after graduation from the military academy, Thomas served with distinction in the Second Seminole War. In the Mexican War he was under the command of General Zachary Taylor, fighting at Resaca de la Palma, Monterey, and Buena Vista, again serving with distinction. Three times within a period of seven years Thomas was recognized for meritorious conduct. With experience in garrison and frontier duty, serving in California at Fort Yuma and with the elite Second Cavalry, as well as an artillery and cavalry instructor at The Point, Thomas had been an army man all his adult life. A severe wound in the face from an Indian arrow seemed to accentuate that fact.[33]

When, at the secession of Virginia, Thomas remained loyal to the U.S. army, his family was so deeply incensed that they reportedly turned his portrait to the wall. Thereafter his three sisters, at the mention of their brother's name, are said to have announced, "We have no brother!" The sisters never reconciled with him. Many of Thomas's peers, however, admired the Virginian who refused to serve with the Confederacy. General William S. Rosecrans called Thomas "a man of extraordinary character" and claimed that even when they were cadets together at West Point he had recognized a strong resemblance between Thomas's character and that of George Washington. Rosecrans remarked: "I was in the habit of calling him General Washington."[34]

Having fought at Logan's Crossroads (Mill Springs), Perryville, and Stones River (Murfreesboro)—where he allegedly responded to General Rosecrans at the midnight council of war following the first day of battle: "General, this army does not retreat" and "I know of no better place to die than right here," which statements, even if apocryphal, are representative of

George H. Thomas.
Courtesy of the Tennessee
State Library and Archives.

the kind of man he was—Thomas had never failed in an operation. As a defensive fighter he was probably unsurpassed in either army.[35]

Thomas's greatest moment as a military commander had come at Chickamauga. In the heavy and decisive fighting of September 20, 1863, the last day of that battle, the Confederates penetrated the Federal line, driving the troops south of Thomas in disorder, along with two corps commanders and the army commander, General Rosecrans. Brigadier General James A. Garfield, Rosecrans's chief of staff and future president of the United States (until an assassin's bullet ended his life on the eighteenth anniversary of Chickamauga), rode up, bringing Thomas reliable information that the right and part of the center of the army had been driven from the field, and no ammunition, so far as Garfield knew, was closer than Chattanooga. Garfield said of Thomas: "I shall never forget my amazement and admiration when I beheld Thomas holding his own with utter defeat on each side and wild confusion in the rear."[36]

Although Thomas's line was bent back severely while straining to arrest the Rebel troops surging forward and sensing victory, General Thomas and about half of the Yankee army continued to hold strategic Snodgrass Hill throughout much of the afternoon. Finally, around four thirty or a little later, perhaps an hour before the sun would set, Thomas began pulling back and retiring toward Chattanooga.[37] Thomas's stand on Snodgrass Hill saved the U.S. army from destruction. At West Point, Thomas had been dubbed "Old Tom" while a cadet and "Slow Trot" as an instructor (the latter because during cavalry exercises he often checked cadets who anticipated a gallop with the order "slow trot!"). But after the fight of September 20, Thomas was known ever after as "the Rock of Chickamauga." His leadership at that battle, more than any other action, elevated him to the top tier of Union generals, where he usually is ranked with Grant, Sherman, and Phil Sheridan as the best that the Union army developed. And two months after Chickamauga, the Army of the Cumberland, under Thomas's command, stormed up Missionary Ridge and drove Braxton Bragg's Confederates from the field.[38]

Close to, if not fully six feet tall, Thomas was formidably built, weighing about two hundred pounds, and is described in the *Dictionary of American Biography* as "studious in his habits, deliberate but decided in action, and fastidious to the point of exasperation." A contemporary newspaper reporter, David Conyngham, one of that stripe that Sherman disliked intensely, saw General Thomas as "quite the reverse of Sherman, both in manners and appearance. He is tall, stout, with brawny frame and shoulders. His head is slightly bent forward, as if drooping with thought and care. His hair and beard, which he wears cut pretty short, are rather dark, and slightly sprinkled with gray. He is about fifty years of age, . . . is very reserved; speaks little . . . [is] calm and cautious; does everything by rule; leaves nothing to chance."

After the Federal occupation of Atlanta, General Thomas would have preferred a campaign south from that city, with his own Army of the Cumberland—which had composed about two-thirds of Sherman's total force in the spring advance from Chattanooga—doing the work. He was opposed to Sherman's campaign of marching to the Atlantic coast while Hood was still moving westward, along the south bank of the Tennessee River. But once Grant approved Sherman's plan for the destructive march, Sherman wrote to Thomas in late October, arguing that simply to pursue Hood would wear out his army. "I know I am right," Sherman stated. Cump also said: "I think Hood will follow me, at least with his cavalry. . . . If, however, he turns on you, you must act defensively on the line of the Tennessee."[39]

Thomas, if he could mobilize all available troops rapidly, certainly possessed adequate strength at his command to handle the Confederate threat. Already he had some eight to ten thousand soldiers under arms in Nashville, as well as about that many more personnel in the quartermaster's department, who were available to man the city's fortifications if an enemy assault were launched. Too, Thomas had the authority to marshal various regional detachments. There were Gordon Granger's four thousand men at Decatur, Alabama; Lovell H. Rousseau's five thousand at Murfreesboro; and James B. Steedman's five thousand at Chattanooga. A number of smaller garrisons, several hundred or a thousand strong—like at Spring Hill and Gallatin—could also be pulled into Nashville. Two divisions in Missouri under Andrew Jackson Smith, numbering about fourteen thousand, were ordered to Nashville. And Sherman sent the Twenty-third Corps, under Major General John M. Schofield, numbering about ten thousand, and the Fourth Corps, led by David S. Stanley, numbering twelve thousand, to further augment Thomas's strength. A cavalry command of some ten thousand was also being assembled in the Tennessee capital. Altogether, Thomas could expect to eventually command nearly seventy thousand men.[40]

Of course Sherman did not think that Hood was in any condition to march on Nashville, which, in truth, he actually was not. Cump clearly was irritated when the Confederates began crossing the Tennessee River. And Grant and Thomas were alarmed as Hood started making the move that, only a few weeks earlier, all had thought highly improbable. Thomas did feel confident, however, that with Stanley's and Schofield's troops added to those already at hand, and if Smith hurried forward from Missouri, he would be able to defeat Hood.

While Thomas exercised overall command of Union soldiers massing in Nashville, actual field command of the forces that Thomas deployed seventy-five miles to the south, at the little town of Pulaski, was handled by General Schofield. Schofield's mission entailed delaying the Confederate advance south of the Duck River as long as feasible, thus providing Thomas additional time to marshal all the Federal troops in route for the defense of the capital. In fact, the ensuing campaign saw Schofield managing the Yankee movements until the battle at Nashville.

Major General John McAllister Schofield was a native of Gerry, New York, who spent his teen years in Illinois. Graduating from West Point in the class of 1853, Schofield compiled an enviable record academically, ranking seventh overall in a class of fifty-four graduates, and first in the study of infantry tactics. Articulate, calm, and reflective, "a gentleman of fine address and elegant manners," according to one observer, Schofield was a man who worked hard, paid attention to details, and kept up with his paper responsibilities. Even his memoranda were precise and thorough. Probably he realized that success may sometimes be achieved through striving to avoid mistakes, not necessarily from brilliance.[41]

General John Pope once remarked that Schofield "could stand steadier on the bulge of a barrel than any man who ever wore shoulder straps."[42] Perhaps so, but another observer likely had a better sense of Schofield, the man, when he said the general impressed him with the feeling that he was "in the presence of a statesman, rather than a soldier. Perhaps Schofield partakes of the character of both."[43] Certainly Schofield was not a fighter, in the manner of a Phil Sheridan or John Bell Hood—both former classmates. Essentially he was an organizer and administrator. For better or worse, Schofield was a fitting symbol of the machine-like efficiency to which the United States Army increasingly aspired and he was the type of man who was coming to dominate America, politically and economically.

In appearance, the thirty-three-year-old general was a little too short and a bit too heavy, even as a very young man in his prime, for his general image to be impressive. One historian said Schofield "looked the part of perhaps a rogue banker with the glint of evil in his eye."[44] (In later years his graying hair, Burnside whiskers, and military regalia would create a distinguished presence.) Although Schofield did see action early in the war at the Battle of Wilson's Creek, where a newspaper reporter observed him "ever in the lead, the foremost, coolest soldier in all that bloody fight,"[45] the long conflict proved to be a frustrating experience for the highly ambitious young man. His career did not keep pace with his expectations, and in fact seemed stagnated in the months following Wilson's Creek. Schofield confronted some very ordinary tasks in Missouri. Organizing and disciplining militia, and attempting to suppress bands of guerrillas, Schofield sometimes pursued seemingly phantom Confederate forces, and was dragged down physically by an attack of typhoid fever.[46]

He became deeply discouraged, engaging in petty quibbling with his department commander, General Samuel R. Curtis, before at last writing to then General-in-Chief Henry W. Halleck, excoriating Curtis as "the cause of all my troubles." He was also upset because "my juniors [are] promoted over me for meritorious conduct, while I, the only officer who has tried to do anything in this department, am tied down and condemned to almost obscurity." Schofield pleaded with Halleck to transfer him to some other command; anywhere, he said, that he would not be compelled to endure such "endless sloth" and "imbecility." At last he concluded: "I am sick—scarce able to leave my bed. . . . I have broken myself down in the service—and all for nothing."[47]

Schofield's ambition was outracing his opportunities and the "green-eyed monster" was vexing the young officer. There was some truth, however, in his complaints about Union operations in Missouri. For a while in 1863 Schofield was elevated to command the vast Department of Missouri, encompassing Missouri, Kansas, the Indian Territory, and part of Arkansas. Yet the assign-

John M. Schofield.
National Archives.

ment did not bring Schofield the chance to distinguish himself, resulting only in more frustration as he contended with Rebel guerrillas and struggling political factions.

Politicking heavily through Halleck, Senator John Henderson of Missouri, and others in an effort to gain an assignment in a major military campaign, Schofield at last became one of Sherman's army commanders for the advance into Georgia. As promising as the Atlanta campaign seemed at its inception, Schofield's Army of the Ohio constituted no more than a small corps in numbers, and the critical flanking movements against the enemy usually were performed by James B. McPherson's Army of the Tennessee (Sherman's old command). Schofield acquitted himself well enough throughout the Georgia operations, but any glory for which he may have longed proved elusive in the end.[48]

By late 1864 "the portly and bewhiskered"[49] Schofield found himself in southern Middle Tennessee, where he would finally gain a measure of fame, although ironically, much of the eventual publicity must have been less than satisfying. While Schofield later professed to consider the ensuing military maneuvers an excellent demonstration of his tactical skill, and proudly lectured about the lessons of military science that young officers might learn therefrom, in the twentieth century the Spring Hill–Franklin campaign often was cited for wrongheaded blundering by Schofield, from which he achieved extrication only by a combination of luck and the even greater bungling of the Southern commander.

More than likely Schofield was still capable of dealing with people whom he did not like, or who stood in the way of his ambition, in the same underhanded vein that he demonstrated in Missouri. There would be allegations that he intrigued to replace General Thomas as the Union commander at Nashville; that he sent reports to Grant criticizing Thomas for being too slow in attacking the enemy. Considerable circumstantial evidence supports the accusation.[50] Whatever the truth of this matter, the war never brought the aspiring Schofield the degree of recognition, fame, and glory that he sought.

The essence of Schofield's instructions from Thomas was that he should slow Hood's advance as much as possible in order to gain time for the concentration of all available troops in Nashville, particularly the arrival of General Smith's command coming from Missouri.[51] Thomas never intended that Schofield should attempt to defeat Hood by himself. General Stanley was already present at Pulaski with the Fourth Corps. Once Schofield's corps arrived, the total Bluecoat infantry force would number approximately twenty-two thousand. A small section of cavalry, about thirty-five hundred, also was at hand, under the command of Brigadier General Edward Hatch.[52]

While the Confederates would be approaching with some forty thousand men, numbers on both sides would not hold constant as the campaign developed.[53] The Yankee force would increase a bit as Schofield retired northward toward Nashville, acquiring garrison troops and additional cavalry when Major General James H. Wilson, the newly chosen cavalry commander, joined up. Hood's strength, on the other hand, would diminish somewhat. There were casualties of course. The cavalry, spearheading the Southern advance, particularly suffered. Also harsh, cold weather took its toll, striking the poorly equipped Confederates worse than the Federals. The enticement of home and family beckoned to many Rebels, proving irresistible for some. By the time of the legendary Spring Hill episode and the blood bath at Franklin, the Grayclads actually engaged numbered not many more than the Union forces.[54]

Just as with the Confederates, concerns of home and family weighed upon the U.S. soldiers too. A Federal at Pulaski who made his home in Hickman County, Tennessee, wrote his wife on November 8 that he "did not know how to take [her] last letter." Realizing that she desperately needed him at home, he reminded her: "You know that I am in the Federal service and I can't come home to you without desertion and I don't intend to do that." Vowing to send her more money (previous mailings apparently having gone astray), John

Wesley McDonough offered his opinion that the war would not last much longer "and I hope and trust to God that my life will be spared through this rebellion for I want to return home to you again." If, in the meantime, she could get help from anyone, he promised to repay the money, because "I do not want you to get anything for nothing." Remarking that he had been "guarding a bushwhacker" while writing the letter, he finally admonished Ecloey to "take good care of my little babies and kiss them for me. . . . Kiss the one that I have never seen 40 times for me." John was fortunate; surviving the war (later telling his children that a comrade directly in front of him at the Battle of Franklin was killed by a missile that otherwise would have struck him), he and Ecloey both lived into the twentieth century.[55]

When Schofield assumed command at Pulaski on November 14 (the day before Sherman set forth from Atlanta to "make Georgia howl"), David Stanley greeted him with disconcerting news. The U.S. troops occupied an isolated position, he said, vulnerable to an enemy turning movement, especially on their right flank. David Sloane Stanley grew up in Cedar Valley, Ohio. Schofield had known him since their days together at The Point, where Stanley had graduated in the class of 1852, a year ahead of Schofield, and ranking ninth among his forty-three classmates. A veteran of the Indian wars in Texas, he served at frontier posts in California and Kansas. Like Schofield, Stanley first saw action in the Civil War at Wilson's Creek, afterward promoted to Brigadier General of Volunteers. Under the command of John Pope in early 1862, Stanley led a division at New Madrid and Island Number Ten. For a while he commanded the cavalry corps of the Army of the Cumberland and then an infantry division during the Atlanta campaign, where he was wounded at Jonesboro, but recovered to return to action in Tennessee.[56]

Feelings between Schofield and Stanley left something to be desired. Years afterward, in his memoirs, General Stanley wrote of Schofield that he could "pick [Schofield's] chapter on Jonesboro to pieces," but did "not think it worthwhile." And of the campaign upon which the two were embarking at Pulaski, Stanley would record that "all said in Schofield's book as to his foreseeing and providing to meet the events as they unfolded, is the merest bosh." He "assumes a grand superiority and wisdom, in each case at variance with the facts, and appropriates circumstances entirely accidental and the run of luck in our favor as a result of his wise foresight."[57]

Stanley was a man of ability and he was not exaggerating the exposed position of the Blueclads at Pulaski. The little village was thirty miles south of

Columbia and the crossings of the Duck River. From Columbia to Nashville, connected by both a turnpike and the Nashville & Decatur Railroad, was a distance of about forty-five miles. The Yankees at Pulaski were most vulnerable to the west. The town of Lawrenceburg lay only eighteen miles away as the crow flies, with a direct road to Columbia through Mount Pleasant. The superior Rebel force might take Schofield by surprise, making a rapid march to the bridges at Columbia, which were defended by fewer than eight hundred men, and cut him off from Nashville. This was the greatest danger. But Hood might elect instead to move directly on the Federals at Pulaski. With any Southern movement being screened by a strong cavalry command, some seven thousand in number and led by the aggressive veteran Nathan Bedford Forrest, accurate information of Confederate movements would be difficult for the Federals to come by—until it was too late.[58]

Upon hearing Stanley's remonstrances, Schofield, as yet unfamiliar with the terrain, ordered General Jacob D. Cox's division to halt four miles north of Pulaski. There he was in position to cover a road from Lawrenceburg until Schofield could weigh his options.[59] Soon aware of his vulnerable locale, Schofield, on Sunday afternoon, November 20, suggested to Thomas at Nashville that he would like to withdraw his main force to Lynnville, halfway between Pulaski and Columbia. His dispatch well summarized the Union situation:

> If Hood advances, whether his design be to strike this place or
> Columbia, he must move via Lawrenceburg, on account of the
> difficulty of crossing Shoal Creek. Under cover of his cavalry he can
> probably reach Lawrenceburg without our knowledge and move
> his forces a day's march from that point toward Columbia before
> we could learn his designs, and thus reach that point ahead of us;
> or, he might move upon this place, and, while demonstrating against
> it, throw his forces onto the pike north of us, and thus cut us off from
> Columbia and from our reinforcements. Lynnville would be free from
> these objections as a point of concentration for our forces.[60]

Thomas replied that there was little hope of Smith's troops arriving from Missouri before Friday (actually Smith would not be on hand until December 1). While Thomas hoped that Pulaski might be held until then, he acknowledged that Schofield must withdraw to Columbia if Hood attempted to cut him off from the crossings of Duck River. Schofield clearly believed that he would be wise to leave Pulaski. In deference to Thomas, however, he said that he would "consider the move more maturely before deciding." Also, he mistakenly thought that Hood, due to the heavy rains in recent days making the roads difficult to traverse, could not reach the vicinity of Pulaski any earlier than Tuesday "at best."[61]

Believing that he had adequate time to make his troop dispositions, and thinking too that it would "be well to avoid the appearance of retreating when it is not necessary," Schofield started Cox's division back to Lynnville on the morning of Tuesday, November 22, and planned to move Stanley's forces back the next day. Stanley marched about two o'clock in the afternoon of the 23rd, bivouacking at Lynnville late that night. Meanwhile, Cox had moved to within seven miles of Columbia where he called a halt for the night.[62]

But on this day, Hood's advance nearly kept pace with Schofield's. The Confederate general, moving much more rapidly than the Bluecoat commander anticipated, was striking for the river crossings at Columbia. Suddenly, Schofield faced a very dangerous situation and, worse yet, several hours would pass before he fully realized it.

2

My Face
Is towards
Tennessee

The Confederate advance into Tennessee had developed in a strange manner. In late September the Army of Tennessee lay encamped around Palmetto, Georgia, about twenty miles southwest of Atlanta. Disheartened both by the fall of Atlanta and the heavy casualties suffered in trying to defend the Gate City, as that turntable of the Confederacy was also known, some soldiers had slipped away and headed for home. Those who remained with the army, which was the vast majority, of course, were not only discouraged and pessimistic; many were angry. When Governor Joseph Brown of Georgia appointed September 15 as a day of fasting and prayer, and in an ill-advised, insensitive decision, called upon the army to observe it, an Alabama soldier recorded in his diary: "We have been fasting most of the time for two years," and added that he feared not enough prayers would be associated with the "fast" to avail anything.[1]

Some of the men had not been paid for the better part of a year. All manner of supplies, from shoes and clothing to weapons and ammunition, were sorely needed. Above all, the men were rankled by the loss of Atlanta and, as they saw the matter, the incompetence of Hood. Having disapproved when General Johnston was removed from command of the army in mid-July, ensuing events had convinced them by early September that they had been right. Directing their wrath at Hood, many blamed him for the recent defeats and the loss of the symbolic city. General Hood had some defenders, but not a great many of them were in the Army of Tennessee.

A Texas soldier said in a diary entry that Hood "is in a bad fix. And more, he has virtually murdered near 10,000 men around Atlanta, trying to do that which Joe Johnson said could not be done." The Yankees, he continued, "should thank Jeff Davis for removing General Johnson and appointing Hood in his place." A Mississippian wrote to his sister after the fall of Atlanta, saying "Hood is no general and the worst of all is the soldiers all know it." Three days later, directing another letter to her, the same soldier declared: "Our army is considerably demoralized. . . . Hood has not, nor ever had, the confidence of a single soldier in the army. . . . I can say to you that Hood is no more a general than is your negro girl [presumably a reference to a household slave] and all this disaster is caused by his blunders." A Tennessee infantryman bitterly claimed that if Hood "had been in command from Dalton to Atlanta the most of us would have been killed," while a Floridian told his wife that the men were swearing "they will not fight under Hood."[2]

Another Confederate thought "Sherman is more than a match for Hood, and has completely out-generaled him," while a Louisiana soldier said, after the loss of Atlanta, that the army "is so weakened and demoralized that it will never be worth a curse again." The troops were also fatigued and lonely. A Georgia soldier told his wife that if he should be fortunate enough to survive the war he would need a year to rest, and added that he had "heard some men swear that if they live to get home, they never intend to get out of sight of their wife again." Yet another Confederate declared that "nothing was accomplished by this great slaughter" in battles around Atlanta. Many of "the best soldiers" had been lost; soldiers "Johnston . . . protected so long from unnecessary exposure. . . ." He said the men had "lost confidence in Hood as a wise leader."[3]

According to an Alabama infantryman, "the situation was desperate," and he thought "something must be done" because the army had become "greatly displeased with General Hood. . . ." Another soldier thought that dissatisfaction, both with Hood and the army's condition, had become "quite manifest"; while still another stated that "the terrible losses sustained in the hard fought but fruitless battles; and at the loss of Atlanta; had produced a feeling of distrust and discontent that was not favorable in its promises." Years later, a Tennessee veteran would acknowledge that Hood was a brave man, and even claimed he "was a good man," but summarized that the Kentuckian was "a poor general in the capacity of commander-in-chief, . . . a failure in every particular."[4]

In September of 1864 Jefferson Davis was heavily pressured by the circumstances he faced in Georgia. The loss of Atlanta, the supply and morale problems of the Army of Tennessee, the bitter criticisms leveled at Hood, together with calls for a new commander of the army, demanded the attention of the Confederate president. Politically speaking, as well as militarily, Jefferson Davis knew the situation must be addressed quickly. He determined to personally visit the army. The trip proved eerily reminiscent of earlier occasions when the president had evaluated the army firsthand: at Murfreesboro, Tennessee, in December 1862, and near Chattanooga in October 1863.

Davis's trip to Murfreesboro had followed the failure of the longest Southern campaign, in miles traversed, that the war saw: the great endeavor to claim Kentucky for the Confederacy. The Kentucky dream, enchantingly vivid to many Graycoats in the late summer of 1862, had rapidly faded, undermined from the first by a divided command, as Edmund Kirby Smith drastically altered the plan of campaign agreed upon with Braxton Bragg at Chattanooga. "Kentucky Fever" continued to wane, weakened by the blundering at Munfordville and the frustrating retreat from the Perryville battlefield, and finally destroyed in the campaign's manifest truth that the Bluegrass State would not rise en masse to support the Confederacy.[5]

A disillusioned Butternut force made the long, tough trek back from Kentucky, a portion of the men vehement in criticism of their commander, General Bragg. According to historian Allan Nevins, some of the soldiers "would gladly have burned [General Bragg] at the stake." Generals too, were angry and disgusted with Bragg. The most vocal of all—ironically when the major difficulties that he caused Bragg are recalled—was Kirby Smith. He wrote to the War Department, bitterly complaining about Bragg's conduct of the campaign. He asked to be transferred, preferably to the Gulf Coast, but to anywhere, he said, if staying in his present capacity meant further cooperation with Bragg.[6]

Although, despite the uproar within the army and elsewhere, President Davis sustained General Bragg in command, Bragg's ability to lead the army had suffered grave damage in the perception of many officers and soldiers, whether deservedly or not. Unfortunately, Davis's Murfreesboro trip did not permit him to attend the wedding, with Bishop General Leonidas Polk officiating, of twenty-one-year-old Mattie Ready and General John H. Morgan, which certainly was the social highlight of the Christmas season. As to overall western command, Davis assigned General Joseph E. Johnston to the oversight of a large theater encompassing all territory between the Appalachian Mountains and the Mississippi River. Johnston's duties, however, were never clearly defined, especially his command authority over the armies of Bragg in

Middle Tennessee and John C. Pemberton on the Vicksburg front. Johnston was said to have supervisory authority, but Bragg and Pemberton actually maintained the same prerogative they exercised before Johnston's appointment.

And then Davis, without consulting Johnston, made a strategic decision, possibly a fateful one. Believing that Pemberton's Mississippi army was in a more seriously threatened position than Bragg's force, Davis detached Carter Stevenson's three-brigade division of seventy-five hundred officers and men, ordering it to Mississippi to reinforce Pemberton. Bragg protested that the move, sure to be found out by the Federals, would encourage the U.S. army in Nashville to march against him (which indeed occurred within a short time), but Bragg's effort was to no avail.

The decision to send Stevenson's troops to Mississippi seemed to disturb Johnston even more than Bragg. When Davis, after his visit to Murfreesboro, informed Johnston about the transfer of the division, Johnston became quite upset. He had long experienced a poor relationship with Davis and already suspected that the president had simply given him a nominal command with little power, but heavy responsibilities, in order to make him look incompetent. Johnston asked that he be transferred to another command, a request that Davis denied.[7]

The president's efforts did not relieve the dissension within the Army of Tennessee, which mounted again after the Battle of Stones River. Once more, as in the Kentucky endeavor, many Southerners believed a great opportunity had been frittered away in the bloody Murfreesboro struggle along the banks of Stones River. Recriminations and blame placing abounded, enveloping the high command of the army. The situation became even worse following the Battle of Chickamauga. The Army of Tennessee then faced near mutiny in the high command. A terrible sacrifice of manpower, in fact the heaviest casualties the army ever suffered, had been the price of victory in northwest Georgia—a triumph that seemed to promise much, though virtually nothing, in the strategic sense, would be realized. As was his habit, General Bragg claimed others were to blame for his failures, while at the same time, several of his generals strove to rid themselves of their commander.

James Longstreet's chief of staff well summarized the tension: "The tone of the army among its higher officers toward the commander was the worst conceivable," wrote G. Moxley Sorrel. "Bragg was the subject of hatred and contempt, and it was almost openly expressed. His great officers gave him no confidence as a general-in-chief."[8] Dissension was so pronounced that Jefferson Davis, aboard a special train, headed south from Richmond on October 6, 1863, to again inspect the army.

The Confederate president did not handle the situation well. Davis was in a particularly difficult bind due to his longtime friendship with both Bragg and Leonidas Polk. The breach between the two generals was irreparable, as Polk unequivocally balked at ever serving again under Bragg's command, saying he would resign from the army first. Bragg was equally adamant to be rid of Polk. Fortunately for Davis, Polk was willing to accept a transfer to another department. Davis, however, then proceeded to conduct a meeting (some have called it a council of war) at which he compelled Bragg's critics, such as Longstreet, D. H. Hill, Simon Bolivar Buckner (a general who participated in "a mutinous assemblage," as Bragg later expressed his view of Buckner's actions), and Frank Cheatham, to voice their objections in their commander's presence. Awkward as the setting must have been, they all expressed their lack of confidence in Bragg. Davis nevertheless chose to sustain the North Carolinian as commander of the army. The president emerges from the bizarre episode as, at the least, lacking in perception and tact, and at the worst, lacking in ability to evaluate and resolve the problems of the army.[9]

By September 1864, Jefferson Davis's history with the Army of Tennessee strongly foreshadowed his likely decisions at Palmetto, Georgia. The circumstances were as dire as after Chickamauga; actually worse, for the overall problems of the Confederacy were worse. Certainly the military situation had greatly deteriorated during the eleven months since Davis was with the army near Chattanooga. Bragg, commander of the Army of Tennessee longer than any other general, had finally departed following the defeat at Chattanooga. Joe Johnston, however, who succeeded Bragg, had been relieved in mid-summer, as previously noted, despite his widespread popularity with the troops. Having steadily withdrawn in the face of Sherman's continual pressure, which had forced the army back to the northern outskirts of Atlanta—and failing to keep Davis satisfactorily informed of his plans—Johnston suddenly found himself replaced by General Hood. Then within a short time Atlanta was gone, occupied by Sherman's host. Gone too were the lives of a great many Confederates, after which some influential people demanded that Davis remove Hood and name still another commander for the army. There were even those who said Joseph Johnston should be reinstated, a thought totally repugnant to the president.

Meanwhile Hood pleaded for reinforcements, especially after Georgia Governor Joseph E. Brown withdrew the state's militia from Confederate service in the wake of Atlanta's fall. The Kentuckian overstated the army's casualties while Joseph Johnston had commanded, and grossly understated his own losses ("about 8,000 in fifty-four days"), while claiming "the army is in good spirits," and wondered what reinforcements he could expect "within the next month." Also, like Bragg before him, Hood was blaming his troubles and failures on others, particularly General William J. Hardee. "In the battle of July 20 [Peachtree Creek] we failed on account of General Hardee," declared Hood in a message to Davis on September 13. "Our success [an interesting choice of term for the battle at Decatur] on July 22 was not what it should have been, owing to this officer. Our failure on August 31 I am now convinced was greatly owing to him." Hood claimed that "It is of the utmost importance that Hardee should be relieved at once. . . . I must have another commander." General Hardee, who considered Hood incompetent to command an army, was equally resolved to serve no more under the rash Kentuckian. For President Davis, the Hardee-Hood tension, like the earlier clash of Polk and Bragg, presented an especially distasteful problem, because Davis was on friendly terms with both generals.[10]

The president arrived at Palmetto on September 25. Besides deciding if Hood would continue as commander of the army (which Davis may have already determined before reaching the little Georgia town), the president intended to exert a major influence in defining the next move of the Army of Tennessee. Davis realized too that the Southern populace needed a morale boost. Thus he planned to deliver several speeches which he hoped would inspire faith that the Confederate cause would yet triumph. Recognizing that the morale of the army required bolstering as well, the president decided to review the troops.[11]

The most pressing issue obviously involved who would command the army, with demands widely voiced that Hood should be replaced by Johnston or Beauregard. (Robert E. Lee was out of the question, for everyone knew Davis would not allow him to leave Virginia.) Davis held conferences with the three corps commanders Hardee, Stephen D. Lee, and A. P. Stewart. According to a correspondent of the *Augusta Chronicle*, on September 26, all the generals told the president that some other commander than Hood would be better for the army—better both for the rank and file, as well as the officers. When Davis inquired who the new commander should be, they spoke of Johnston and Beauregard.

That Davis might restore Johnston to command was highly unlikely, to say the least. In fact, the choice of Johnston to replace Bragg in early 1864 must have been a shock to many Richmond insiders, because of the ill feeling long existing between Johnston and Davis. And the animosity was no secret. Some said the trouble between the two went back to their West Point days, involving an alleged fistfight over the daughter of Benny Haven, owner of the famous tavern down the street from the military academy. Supposedly Johnston bettered Davis in the fight and also won the affections of the young lady. Johnston's biographers, however, Gilbert E. Govan and James W. Livingood, claim no contemporary source supports the story. They concluded the tale is a fabrication.[12]

P. G. T. Beauregard.
Library of Congress.

If the rumored fight over the girl is untrue, then the tension between the general and the president apparently stemmed from incidents beginning in the early 1850s. Some eight or ten clashes, occurring over a decade or so, fueled the development of a bitter relationship between the two men. If Davis should restore Johnston to command only two months after removing him in favor of Hood, the president clearly would be perceived by virtually everyone as admitting that he had made a mistake. Back in 1862, when Davis appointed Johnston as commander of the Department of the West, he "swallowed gall," observed Frank Vandiver in his book *Rebel Brass*.[13] To reappoint Johnston commander of the Army of Tennessee in late September of 1864 would have been worse than a double dose of gall for Davis. Such a thing was not going to happen.

Then there was Beauregard. His relationship with the president had worsened as the war progressed. The breach between the two men would never be healed. Their enmity, in a sense, went even beyond the grave. When Davis died while in New Orleans in 1889, he was laid to rest in the Crescent City's Metairie Cemetery. Beauregard, long a leading citizen of New Orleans, confided to family members that he was not sorry that Davis was dead, because the two had "always been enemies." Four years later, when Beauregard himself died and also was placed in Metairie, the body of Davis was removed within a few weeks and reinterred in Richmond. "The timing of the removal," wrote William I. Hair, ". . . shortly after Beauregard's body was taken there, probably was not coincidental." Mrs. Jefferson Davis made the decision to remove her husband's body, and she knew, continued Hair, "that her husband and Beauregard could not stand being near each other while alive, and it surely occurred to her that they would not want to be near in death."[14]

Following the loss of Atlanta, some of Richmond's politicos who proclaimed that Hood must go, confidently prophesied that Davis would never appoint Beauregard to the command. "The President was sometimes a smarter politician than his enemies credited him with being," wrote T. Harry Williams. Jefferson Davis "realized now that he would have to do something," continued Williams, "to allay the storm of criticism and raise popular morale. If he had to make use of a general he detested, he would do it."[15] And, a cynical observer might wonder, did Davis take a cruel pleasure in setting up the "Napoleon in Gray," as Williams liked to call the general, encouraging Beauregard to believe that he was about to gain field command of the Army of Tennessee, the army from which he had been removed after Shiloh, and to which he always wanted to return?

Because of the long animosity between Davis and Beauregard, Davis asked Robert E. Lee to explore with Beauregard the prospect of serving in Georgia. To serve in Georgia, of course, did not necessarily indicate that Beauregard might be replacing Hood. Without question though, such a possibility must have entered Beauregard's mind. General Lee evidently took Davis to mean that Beauregard was being considered for the command of the Army of Tennessee, and so broached the matter to the Creole. Reporting back to Davis, General Lee wrote from Petersburg on September 19, "I have had a conversation with General Beauregard with reference to the army and operations in Georgia." Lee well may have thought that the Creole would be a better commander for the army than Hood, and probably believed he was conveying good news to the president as he wrote that Beauregard "says he will obey with alacrity any order of the War Department placing him in command of that army [clearly a reference to the Army of Tennessee], and do his best to expel the enemy." Lee continued, telling Davis that should he deem "a change in the commander of the army in Georgia advantageous, and select General Beauregard for that position, I think you may feel assured that he understands the general condition of affairs, the difficulties with which they are surrounded, and the importance of exerting all his energies for their improvement."[16]

But General Lee, in writing to Davis, was addressing a man who, two years earlier, when Beauregard's congressional friends requested that the

Creole be reinstated after Davis removed him following Shiloh, had angrily replied: "If the whole world were to ask me to restore General Beauregard to the command [of the army] I would refuse it."[17] It seems rather doubtful that the passing of two years appreciably diminished Davis's dislike of Beauregard, whom the president believed, with reason, had both misled him about the results of Shiloh and then left the army for several days without any real justification.

Probably Jefferson Davis never seriously considered replacing Hood with Beauregard. But the handsome Creole, desperately wanting a major field command and highly appreciative as always of his own talents, perhaps naively believed his old enemy had buried the hatchet and was about to grant the general that which he most desired. Instead, Davis offered Beauregard an impressive-sounding assignment, although one embodying little actual power. (Shades of Joe Johnston's command earlier in the war which had resulted only in confusion.) Beauregard would direct a new department, designated the Military Division of the West. Extending from Georgia to the Mississippi River, and encompassing all or part of five states, Beauregard's responsibility would include overseeing the armies under both Hood and Richard Taylor, the latter's force then in Alabama.

Essentially, however, Beauregard would be little more than an adviser; certainly not a commander of troops. Davis explicitly, in writing, made that fact plain. "The commander of a department like this," observed T. Harry Williams, "could exercise no direction of the forces under him unless he assumed command of an army, which he was not supposed to do." Particularly, Davis did not want Beauregard interfering with the army led by Hood.[18]

Why did Davis establish such a department? "Perhaps," suggested Williams, "the reason was to lay on the shelf a general who was out of favor [with the president]."[19] Perhaps also Davis sought to pacify friends of Beauregard, some of whom were critics of the administration as well, through creating a position that, superficially considered, seemed to encompass far-reaching responsibilities and authority, but truly was of no real consequence.

Davis played well the political game, both to get his opponents off his back about the army's commander, and simultaneously make life a touch more frustrating for a general whom he despised. As for that other general whom the president abhorred, Joe Johnston, Davis told Beauregard, in the context of praising Hood (and according to Beauregard), that Johnston "would have retreated ere long" all the way to the Gulf of Mexico, if Sherman had been inclined to pursue him that far.[20] Beauregard longed to be away from Virginia, and likely supposed that he could exert some control over Hood's maneuvers, for he had little personal experience with the Kentuckian. Thus Beauregard accepted the assignment Davis offered, though he surely must have been disappointed.

29

If Beauregard thought he could influence Hood he badly misjudged his man. While Hood had been proving, and would continue to demonstrate that he was not competent to command an army, he did possess some political instincts, particularly realizing that his successful flattery of Davis basically rendered unnecessary any accounting for his actions to anyone other than the president. And at Palmetto, the two men seem to have had a meeting of their minds. Davis was fully in sympathy with the plan of campaign that he and Hood outlined.

Hood knew as well as Davis that the army must not continue simply resting in camp and waiting to see what Sherman might do next. Sherman would only get stronger as time passed. Thus Hood intended to lead the Army of Tennessee west and north of Atlanta and strike the Western & Atlantic Railroad, threatening the destruction of Sherman's line of communications. He believed the maneuver would compel the Yankee commander to pull back from Atlanta, with a major portion of his army, in order to defend his supply line. Hood then hoped for a battle on grounds and circumstances favorable to the Confederates, where Sherman could be beaten. If, instead of giving chase, Sherman marched south of Atlanta, Hood would pursue him. Both Hood and Davis believed, however, that the Union commander would most likely follow the Confederate army.[21]

Satisfied after his conversations with the Kentucky general, the president proceeded to relieve Hardee from corps command, just as Hood had wished, and ordered him to take command of the lower Atlantic Coast, a department including Florida, part of Georgia, and South Carolina. Davis also busied himself with reviewing the troops. He ignored the shouts of soldiers who called for Johnston to be returned to command; shouts erupting in spite of orders to some units warning the men to keep quiet about their sentiments.[22] Many of the troops did receive the president respectfully, and politely cheered his remarks. General Howell Cobb of Georgia and Governor Isham Harris of Tennessee were also present at Palmetto and joined in the speechmaking. "There were speeches galore," wrote Stanley Horn, "but the soldiers in the ranks knew that the time had passed for speeches, and they were little affected."[23]

Many of the soldiers were naturally thinking of home. S. J. McMurry, of the Twenty-fourth Tennessee Infantry, addressed a letter to his cousin, Miss Frances A Kidd, on September 28. Telling her that he had "passed through a great deal of hardship" since last he saw her, and could only expect more of the same, McMurry marveled that he had been "very fortunate so far," for he had "neither been wounded nor sick enough to go to a hospital." After mentioning some less lucky comrades, McMurry's thoughts turned to the young women of his acquaintance, several of whom reportedly were getting married. "Ann," he ordered, "you must put an end to this at once." Asserting that "I have got to have a girl . . . when I get back," McMurry feared that if so many "continue to marry I will be compelled to take a goobergrabler." He then instructed his cousin to "pick me out a nice sweetheart," because "I will be getting too old to hunt her up after the war is over." Closing with a reference to "those thievish yankies," he vowed the enemy would yet be whipped, promising "we will do it or die." McMurry would be killed two months later at the Battle of Franklin.[24]

When the reviewing of troops came to a conclusion at Palmetto, Jefferson Davis journeyed to his Augusta meeting with Beauregard, as well as delivering more speeches at several places, such as Macon, Augusta, and Columbia, South Carolina. The speeches had an intriguing aspect. While the president made some critical remarks about Joseph Johnston, Governor Joseph Brown, and others whom he considered military and political liabilities, the most memorable statements concerned future operations of the army. Davis prophesied that Sherman soon would be forced into a withdrawal from Atlanta that would be "more disastrous" than Bonaparte's retreat from Moscow. Hood shortly would lead his troops, claimed Davis, in a strike "upon Sherman's line of communications."[25] In his address to Frank Cheatham's division, primarily composed of Tennessee troops, the president told the men to "be of good cheer, for within a short while your faces will be turned homeward and your feet pressing Tennessee soil." Upon another occasion Davis spoke of planting the Southern banners on the banks of the Ohio River: "We must march into Tennessee . . . and . . . push the enemy back to the banks of the Ohio."[26]

Critics of Davis have claimed that the Confederate president irresponsibly gave away significant information about the coming campaign of the Army of Tennessee. Sherman professed surprise at Davis divulging such facts. The president's messages obviously were intended to revive sagging Confederate spirits both in and out of the army. How better to accomplish that goal than with proclamations of offensive campaigning and victory? Probably something else shaped his speech as well. Certainly Davis knew his words conceivably would find their way to Sherman. He clearly wanted Sherman to pursue Hood. His remarks likely were uttered with that objective in mind.

And then Davis entrained once more for Richmond. Meanwhile, Hood had been preparing to lead the Army of Tennessee northwest of Atlanta for a strike against Sherman's railroad. One Confederate captain was not at all impressed by the president's visit, apparently considering it a bad omen. "This army is

Patrick Cleburne.
Courtesy of the Tennessee
State Library and Archives.

going to . . . undertake something that will not be a success, if the future is to be judged by the past," he wrote. Captain Samuel T. Foster recalled that "just before the battle of Murphreesboro . . . Jeff Davis was at Army Headquarters advising with General Bragg, and the result was our army was defeated. . . ." Then after the Battle of Chickamauga, "Jeff Davis came around again," said Foster, "and again . . . the army was defeated and fell back to Dalton, Georgia." Somewhat bitterly the captain concluded: "Now . . . he comes here just after the fall of Atlanta to concoct some other plan for our defeat and display of his Generalship."[27]

As for General Hood, the Kentuckian had made his reputation in Virginia, where he was known for his aggressive, inspiring leadership of men on the brigade and division levels. As an army commander, he already had been proven wanting. Hood was a bad administrator. He was particularly poor in dealing with logistics. In fact, he gave a disconcerting hint of coming problems in the message that regimental commanders were to deliver on his behalf to their units. On the morning of October 2, each regimental commander addressed his men as the general had instructed. General Hood proclaimed that the Army of Tennessee was taking the offensive immediately, with the objective of flanking Sherman out of Atlanta. He acknowledged that the army "might be short of rations occasionally," but the general promised to do his best to alleviate sacrifice.[28] The prospect of effective offensive action was well received, but the thought of inadequate food, not to mention inadequate clothing as colder weather would be coming on, was not encouraging.

The observations of the Texan Foster, as the Confederate maneuvering began, are again arresting. "Rain, Rain, Mud, Mud, March, March, is all we see . . . and do now," he wrote in his diary. Cynically, within a short time, he reported: "One of Old Hood's promises is coming to pass already. Our rations are very short." Foster said he had had neither meat nor bread since noon of the previous day, and then only ate "a beef rib with not enough meat on it to feed a cat." He also noted that the men were running short on tobacco, which he declared was worse for some of them than not having enough to eat.[29]

As the army marched north, intent on tearing up railroad track, Major General B. Franklin Cheatham led Hardee's old corps. Cheatham was a Tennessean, approaching the mid-forties in age, whose reputation combined fierce fighting with frequent swearing and heavy drinking. (One of the worst tales alleged that he was drunk at Stones River and fell from his horse while attempting to lead his men.)[30] Cheatham had no experience at the level of corps command. As a division commander his performance had been inconsistent, but many of his men seemed to like him, and few questioned his complete dedication to the Confederate cause. Yet there was no escaping the fact that the army's most experienced (and some would have said best) corps commander, Hardee, had been replaced by an officer with no experience at that level.

Patrick R. Cleburne would have been a better choice to replace Hardee. Many soldiers in Hardee's corps disliked seeing their longtime commander removed, and none more so than Cleburne. The two men were close friends and Cleburne had been the best man at Hardee's wedding back in the winter. (It was at Hardee's wedding that Cleburne met Susan Tarleton, a young lady from Mobile, who soon after became his fiancé.) Hardee considered Cleburne not only the outstanding division commander in his corps, but the best in the army. Probably a majority of the soldiers would have concurred. Hood's pronounced animosity toward Hardee, however, perhaps carried over to the Irish general, whom Hood likely knew had sympathized with Hardee.

There was another factor against Cleburne being elevated to corps command. Back in early January, Cleburne presented to the high command of the Army of Tennessee a plan to solve the South's military manpower problem. Slaves, he advocated, should be enlisted in the Confederate army, and in return for faithful service, should be granted freedom. Most slaveholders, as Captain Irving Buck, one of Cleburne's loyal aides, warned the general, were not at all prepared to consider such a measure. Some in the army's high command were offended, even incensed, by the proposal, with Brigadier General W. H. T. Walker—ambitious, high-tempered and proslavery—leading an attack on the proposal. Somehow Jefferson Davis and the executive branch of government in Richmond managed to keep the matter secret from all but a few powerful insiders. Braxton Bragg, serving as the president's chief military advisor since resigning from command of the army, considered Cleburne, and others sympathetic with his proposal, as "abolitionist men" who required watching.[31]

General Cleburne grew up in Ireland, a non-slaveholding society; did not own slaves after coming to the United States; and although he lived in the South for a decade before the Civil War, possibly did not fully grasp how sensitive an issue he had raised. Perhaps because of all the obscurant rhetoric generated by slave state leaders concerning states rights and constitutional issues, Cleburne failed to understand the true depth of Southern determination, based on economics, power, prestige, and race (though not necessarily in that order), to preserve slavery whatever the cost. Almost certainly because of this episode, originating from the best of intentions on the part of Cleburne, the general never rose above the level of division command.

In addition to Frank Cheatham, the two other corps commanders as the Army of Tennessee headed northward were Alexander P. Stewart and Stephen D. Lee. Like Cheatham, Stewart was a Tennessean. His experience as a corps commander dated from mid-June, when Leonidas Polk, atop a hill called Pine Mountain, had been killed by a cannon shot. Both during and after the war, some Southerners spread the absurd claim that Sherman himself sighted the gun and actually fired the shot that killed Polk. While there is no truth whatsoever to that story, the death of the Episcopal bishop–general did not displease the Federal commander, who had little time for organized religion, particularly Catholicism or anything akin to it. "We killed Bishop Polk yesterday, and made good progress today," was Sherman's telegraphic summary for General Halleck. To Joe Johnston, then still commanding the Graycoat army, fell the responsibility of naming a replacement for Polk. A. P. Stewart enjoyed a reputation as a solid division commander, a reputation recently enhanced by an impressive performance in the fighting at New Hope Church. Johnston thus awarded the Tennessean permanent command of Polk's old corps after the bishop-general was killed.[32]

As for Stephen Dill Lee, he was the youngest lieutenant general in the Confederate army, only thirty-one years of age. Recently arrived from Alabama, Lee was placed in charge of Hood's old corps in late July. Besides having been with the army only a short time, Lee had not seen major combat action for well over a year. In terms of experience, the high command of the Rebel army clearly left much to be desired as the Graycoats marched to strike Sherman's railroad.[33]

Like Davis and Hood anticipated, the Confederate movement soon got Sherman's attention. On October 3 and 4 the Union commander, with about forty-five thousand troops, moved out of Atlanta (having left one corps in the city) and gave chase to Hood, who already had some of his men "working on the railroad" in the vicinity of Big Shanty. After ripping up about ten or twelve miles of Western & Atlantic track, the Butternuts pushed on northward toward Allatoona Station. There large stores of U.S. army supplies reportedly awaited the hungry Southerners, as rumors spread of rations enough to feed the whole army. Hood ordered Major General Samuel G. French's division, about three thousand strong, to the attack. The New Jersey–born Mississippi planter first sent in a demand for the Federals to surrender. But Brigadier General John M. Corse, recently arrived from Rome to reinforce the Allatoona Pass garrison, and commanding approximately two thousand men, at once refused and a fierce fight ensued, with heavy casualties, as each side lost over seven hundred men, killed, wounded, or missing.

While the battle raged at Allatoona, General Sherman arrived atop Kennesaw Mountain, some fifteen miles distant, from which he heard the sound of the guns and saw the smoke rising from the engagement. There too Cump supposedly instructed a signal officer to wig-wag an inspiring message to General Corse. In response to Corse's bravado wire—"I am short a cheek-bone and an ear, but am able to whip all hell yet!"—Sherman allegedly signaled: "Hold the fort! for I am coming." Another famous Sherman "quote" had been born.

Actually, the episode was not quite like that. For his part Corse had only been grazed by a bullet, leaving his cheekbone and ear fully intact. And what Sherman really signaled was "Hold On, I am coming." Furthermore, Corse's message was not received by Sherman until the day after the Union commander sent his long-remembered signal. Legends, however, by definition are usually composed of something more than fact and, ironically, the press for which Sherman so often expressed disdain, seems to have embellished and glorified his signal into "Hold the Fort! for I am coming." Then a clergyman, in another touch of irony considering Cump's indifference toward organized religion, seized upon the message and composed an inspiring hymn that became a Christian standard. The last verse of "Hold the Fort" is especially striking: "Fierce and long the battle rages, But our help is near; Onward comes our great Commander, Cheer, my comrades, cheer! 'Hold the Fort, for I am coming,' Jesus signals still; Wave the answer back to heaven, 'By Thy grace we will.'"[34]

Meanwhile, in that 1864 real world of north Georgia carnage, Confederate General French had received reports that the Yankees were moving up fast from the South. Fearing his men might be trapped between the two enemy forces, French pulled back from Allatoona. The episode was a "most depressing failure," said one Graycoat. Disappointed Rebels were compelled to forget the supplies they had hoped either to appropriate for themselves or destroy. About this time a young Union soldier from Middle Tennessee came upon Sherman "walking back and forth abstractedly smoking his cigar and looking as ordinary and homely as ever." Lieutenant Marcus Woodson enjoyed a brief conversation with the general. "Uncle Billy" said the Rebels were "whipped . . . yesterday at Altoona Pass," and declared that "they have only 4 days' rations from this morning and that they intended to chew our crackers at Altoona but didn't do it. Also, he says they fight like Indians now. 'Don't make any fires, but they han't got any coffee to make no how.'"[35]

Eventually the Confederates worked their winding path northward until they arrived at Dalton, a familiar setting where the army had spent the preceding winter preparing to defend Rocky Face Ridge. Rocky Face was a rugged eminence named from the rocky outcropping on its western face, which runs from a point a few miles north of Dalton southward almost to the Oostanaula River. This time though the Graycoats came upon something with which they were not at all familiar: African Americans wearing U.S. army uniforms. The Federal army had been recruiting black soldiers for some time, of course. Blacks had seen combat in several locales, such as Fort Pillow, Tennessee; Fort Wagner, South Carolina; Port Hudson, Louisiana; and the Battle of the Crater at Petersburg, Virginia.

The Army of Tennessee, however, confronted black troops for the first time in the garrison at Dalton. Probably the army already would have experienced such a clash except for General Sherman's refusal to place African Americans in a combat role. Like many Northerners, as well as Southerners, Sherman considered blacks inferior, and would only consent to their use as cooks, teamsters, manual laborers, etc. Thus the Atlanta campaign had been strictly a white man's war—in so far as the actual fighting was concerned.

Sherman finally came around to testing some African Americans on garrison duty where, in protecting the railroad, for example, they need only fight defensively, from behind fortified positions. This is how the Forty-fourth United States Colored Troops (USCT), a regiment organized in Chattanooga, came to be at Dalton in October of 1864. The scene which ensued was ugly. About six hundred of the eight hundred–man garrison were African Americans. At first the garrison soldiers were defiant, shouting profane insults at the Butternuts. For their part, the Grayclads were incensed that former slaves, as they supposed most of the blacks to be, were poised to fight them. And while General Hood demanded the surrender of the garrison, an Arkansas private said the word was being passed down the line, as if it came from the division commander, to "kill every damn one of them" in the event the garrison refused to surrender.[36]

Hood told Colonel Lewis Johnson, commanding the Dalton garrison, that if the Confederates had to carry the position by assault there would be no way he could restrain his men, nor would he attempt to do so—a clear warning that no prisoners would be taken. When Johnson realized he was overwhelmingly outnumbered, the colonel agreed to surrender. "It was a very exciting scene when those negroes came marching out," said an Alabama soldier. "The boys were anxious to massacre those fellows," he continued, "and the officers had a hard time to keep the men from falling on them. The negroes were greatly excited and alarmed."[37]

Another Confederate helped fill in the story. He wrote that the African Americans "were disarmed, marched out in a field, strung out in a single line. Most probably," he speculated, "they had been told that they would be shot. . . ." Actually, the purpose was "to give masters who might be in the army an opportunity to identify and recover their slaves. Many did so." This was consistent with the Confederate government's official policy which recognized African American captives as runaway slaves, rather than prisoners of war.[38]

Allegedly, Confederate General William Bate did not approve of parole for the white officers who led the black troops. It was said that he favored executing them. Whether true or not, Hood had agreed to parole and that is what occurred. There is no doubt that the Southerners took what they wanted from the blacks, particularly shoes. Philip Stephenson said: "I was barefooted myself and made one of the Negroes give me his shoes." According to Stephenson's explanation, "we would wear their shoes," but not their "headgear or clothes." Such an observation speaks to the depth of racial prejudice and ignorance characterizing many white men.[39]

Next the prisoners were forced to tear up the railroad track. "One of the negroes protested against the work, as he was a sergeant," remembered Private William Bevens. "When he had paid the penalty for disobeying orders," Bevens continued, leaving the sergeant's fate to the reader's imagination, "the rest tore up the road readily and rapidly." All evidence points to the African Americans being badly treated, and several, perhaps a half-dozen, being executed within a very short time.[40]

It is impossible to know how many of the six hundred blacks survived the war. The chances are that relatively few did. Less than two weeks after the Dalton event, the *Charleston Mercury* struck an ominous note, claiming most men in the army preferred to see the prisoners hanged, and asserted that it was doubtful if many lived very long after their capture. Whatever the fate of the unfortunate members of the Forty-fourth USCT, the Confederate army soon moved on. But before leaving Dalton, a Confederate climbed to the height of Rocky Face Ridge, where the scenery was "majestic and wild," he wrote, as "vivid memories" of the past brought "a rush of profound melancholy and the whole [Atlanta] campaign came back to me." The campaign was, he said: "All for nothing. All the slaughter, all the toil, all the self denial, all the heroism, all the faithfulness, all for nothing. This was the conviction crushing the life out of my heart as I looked around me. And what I felt, all the rest of the army felt."[41]

Another Graycoat, at the same time, expressed quite a different concept, as he wrote in his diary that "The whole army are in high spirits. We have torn up the R.R. 100 miles in rear of the Yankee army and cut off their supplies—and their only chance now to live is to disband and . . . make their way back north as best they can."[42] The soldier was certainly right about the Southerners tearing up a mass of railroad track, but he far overestimated its impact on Sherman's army. For one, the Yankees had mastered the intricacies of railroad repair, much as they understood everything else about railroad communications. In marvelously short periods they would have the iron horses functioning once more, despite all the damage that the Butternuts might inflict. And Cump, of course, soon would be embarking upon a strategy foreign to the thoughts of most Rebels, a strategy totally negating all their destructive work on the Western & Atlantic Railroad. Still, for the time being, the morale of most Confederates seems to have improved with the northward march and the havoc they wreaked.

Then Hood turned westward and led the army toward Alabama. He could not remain long in northwest Georgia, even if he had wished to do so. For months, the blue and gray men of war had picked over the area until the region was virtually bare. In Alabama there would be more opportunity for successful foraging. Also it would be possible in that state to reestablish railroad communication to support the army. Above all, something else now dominated the mind of General John Bell Hood: To move north into Middle Tennessee, heading toward Nashville.

On October 21, in a meeting with Beauregard at Gadsden, Alabama, Hood gave the Creole his "astounding news." No one could fault the maimed Hood for not thinking big. (Never mind the numerous problems presented thereby.) He announced to Beauregard that he planned to march into Tennessee, "with a hope to establish our line eventually in Kentucky." The Creole, who had officially assumed command of the new Military Division of the West only a few days earlier, was taken completely by surprise. He had first conferred with Hood less than two weeks before, at Cave Spring, Georgia. There the Kentuckian had spoken of drawing Sherman farther north by wrecking the railroad

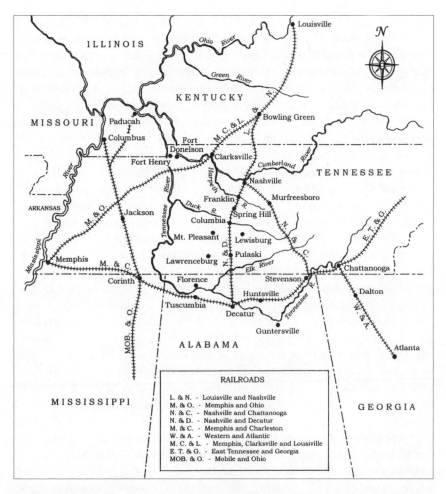

Area map. By Jim Moon Jr.

around Dalton, asserting that he intended to give the Yankees battle if a favorable situation developed. While Beauregard thought Hood's plans were rather carelessly formulated, he did sanction the operation, afterward traveling to Jacksonville, Alabama, where he conferred with General Richard Taylor and began working to build a supply depot for Hood. To Beauregard it was evident that Hood's northward movement from Palmetto had been "hastily undertaken, and without proper provisions being first made for a change of base . . . and that a great deal had been left to future determination, and even to luck."[43]

Beauregard was then amazed at Gadsden to find how quickly Hood had changed his plans. Once the Creole got beyond his initial shock at Hood's revelation, he possibly was impressed by the very boldness of the proposed maneuver. After all, Beauregard himself, saturated with Napoleonic concepts, had certainly conceived some ambitious campaigns in his time, as in 1862 when he called upon Earl Van Dorn to join him in an advance which, he claimed, would not only overrun Cairo, Paducah, and the mouths of the Cumberland and Tennessee Rivers, but "most probably be able to take St. Louis. . . ."[44] Perhaps with the passage of two years, and the hatching of several such plans that were never adopted, the Creole thought Hood, who enjoyed the support of the president, just might be able to pull off a grandiose campaign; if (and the "if" was big) he moved rapidly, before the U.S. army could concentrate sufficient forces at Nashville to oppose him.

And so Beauregard gave his blessing to Hood's invasion plans and, fully intending to support the campaign as best he could, began working to establish a new supply base on the Memphis & Charleston Railroad in the Tuscumbia area of western Alabama. Meanwhile, Hood headed north toward Guntersville, where he had told Beauregard that he would cross the Tennessee River, "continuing to tear up the railroad from Stevenson to Nashville" and compelling Sherman "to follow him into Middle Tennessee, in order to protect his line of communication and his large supplies at Nashville." Instead, Hood moved on westward, not bothering to inform the Creole that he had again changed his plans. As T. Harry Williams wrote, Hood "seemed to regard Beauregard almost as a figurehead." All of Hood's significant reports were sent directly to Richmond.[45]

An incensed Beauregard finally caught up with Hood at Decatur, where the Kentuckian claimed the river approaches at Guntersville had been too heavily defended to cross. Alleging the same at Decatur, and saying the army did not yet have enough supplies to move into Tennessee anyway, Hood soon marched still farther west, all the way to Tuscumbia. By this time Beauregard, who had believed Hood's success wholly dependent upon moving fast, was thoroughly frustrated. Not only had Hood tramped some one hundred miles west of Guntersville, with no specific promise of when he would march into Tennessee; he also twice responded to the Creole's request to see some specific plans with evasive, noncommittal language. Too, the army commander no longer seemed concerned about General Sherman. Beauregard had seen enough. He was compelled to face facts: He could exert no influence on the erratic Kentuckian, and his efforts on Hood's behalf were seemingly unappreciated. Learning that General Sherman had moved out of Atlanta and headed southeastward, the disheartened Creole returned to Georgia, hoping to aid the resistance against Cump's onslaught.[46]

Meanwhile, life for the men in the ranks of the Army of Tennessee went on much as usual, a life quite different from that of the generals. The Thirty-seventh Georgia's Hezekiah McCorkle, who thought the army was "bound for Tennessee," wrote in his diary that as the men crossed from Georgia into Alabama, "apples [are] thrown out liberally by citizens at many places while we pass." He said that "a young lady placed herself by the gate [of her house in Cherokee County] as our brigade passed and sang the Bonnie Blue Flag and Hurrah for Southern Rights. The boys cheer as they pass in real Rebel style." Philip Stephenson also recalled the young girl, presumably the same person, noting in his memoir that she played "an old cracked accordion" with an "energetic enthusiasm," although he thought she "had no voice worth speaking of. . . ." Nevertheless, looking back years later, Stephenson said that if given another chance, he would "take [his] hat off to her and start a rousing yell in her behalf."[47]

On October 21, the same day that Hood and Beauregard were meeting in Gadsden, William Barry of the Fourteenth Mississippi Infantry, penned a letter to his sister. Headed "Near Gadsden," Barry declared the last month was "the hardest time" that had yet "fallen to my lot." Claiming to have "marched over 250 miles . . . over rocks and mountains," until he was "completely worn out," Barry added that "the worst of it is [I] have had scarcely nothing to eat," and said he was "as poor as a snake and the hardest looking rebel in this army." Also, he told her "Madam rumor says we are on our way to Tennessee." There is no doubt that many of the soldiers desperately needed food, one man remarking that "the army was all but destitute of provisions. . . ."[48]

While trekking through the countryside, the Eighteenth Alabama's Edgar Jones remembered that General Beauregard came riding along with his staff, "and the soldiers began to hallow 'bread' in a thousand and more voices and oft repeated." The general responded, reining up his horse, facing the men and delivering "a speech in which he, with great feeling, told the men that they were insulting their general about a matter over which he had no control." Before Beauregard had finished, concluded Jones, "the men felt that they ought to apologize for their rudeness."[49]

Far down in Georgia, on the east bank of the Chattahoochee River at Columbus, Chaplain Charles Todd Quintard, a favorite with many of the men and officers, was anxious to rejoin the Army of Tennessee. Suffering from a long bout with influenza, the forty-year-old physician and Episcopal clergyman did enjoy the company of friends and family, including his wife, the former Katherine Isabella Hand of Roswell, Georgia. Partaking of a "very sumptuous" dinner on October 25, with "port, sherry, and maderia wines and champaign," Quintard remarked that "such a thing I have not met since the war began." A few days later, he noted a "most agreeable" time spent with family and friends, as a fifteen-year-old black pianist called "Blind Tom" entertained the group for several hours with "marvelous" selections.

Finally recovering a sufficient measure of health, Quintard departed on November 9, intent on overtaking Hood and the army as quickly as possible. "Leaving Columbus on a freight train, in a miserable box car with fellow passengers of the most disagreeable character," wrote Quintard, "the way seemed very long, and the hours very weary." As if to accentuate the torturous trip, the chaplain said "a boy three years old last May was puffing a full-sized cigar with great apparent gusto and I was not at all surprised . . . later in the day to hear him curse his mother." Slowly making his way across Alabama, northward through Mississippi, and then eastward into Alabama once more, Quintard at last reached the Tuscumbia-Florence region. It was three weeks into November.[50]

While most Confederates made their way into the Florence-Tuscumbia area from the east, there were some men, just as Chaplain Quintard had done, who approached from the west. A Confederate trooper of the Fourteenth Tennessee Cavalry, while waiting at Corinth, Mississippi, watched some Texas troops "aboard a train of flat cars, headed eastward, which stood for sometime on the track. . . ." John Johnston said they were "a very hardened, ill-clothed, dirty-looking set of fellows—but they were laughing and jeering and cursing as if there were nothing serious in life—or death." In his memoirs, Johnston wrote that "as I . . . looked at those fellows, so hardened, so Godless, and probably so soon to die, I felt oppressed with a feeling of pain and sadness, which comes back to me in some degree even to this day [1900] when I think of them."[51]

Some Confederates probably experienced Johnston's "feelings of pain and sadness," and perhaps bitterness and revenge as well, when they viewed the north Alabama countryside; a "desecrated land," as one soldier said, dotted with "blackened ruins, solitary chimneys, remnants of walls, . . . fragments of fences, . . . and half burnt houses, . . . a paradise blasted and abandoned." Hezekiah McCorkle observed that "Florence, like all the towns of this section of the country, has been used up by the wasting hand of war." Nevertheless, the Thirty-fourth Alabama's John Crittenden wrote his wife that the ladies of Florence "received us with rapturous applause, and many were the 'God Bless You's,' bestowed upon us as we filed through the streets. Young women, old women, and little girls thronged the streets."[52]

When William Barry, who earlier told his sister that he was "as poor as a snake" from lack of food, arrived at Florence, he wanted to visit an acquaintance. "If I had some [suitable] clothes," said Barry as he again wrote to his sister, "I would certainly . . . call on Mrs. Judge Walker"; but then he stated that "there is not much danger of her recognizing me in my present plight—indeed I think it extremely doubtful whether you or any of the family would know me. . . ." Clearly Barry was in no better condition than a month earlier and the same was true for most of the Grayclads. One of them described "our half-clothed, shoeless, and half-fed men," while another wrote that "the ladies [of Florence] were all out on the streets waving their handkerchiefs and appearing to be very glad to see us . . . ," but at the same time he observed that "they had on Yankee goods. Fine furs and silks purchased in Nashville." Still another Confederate said he did not think the army would go much farther north to winter, for "we are not prepared for it. The men are poorly clad and a great portion are without shoes. . . ."[53]

The last was John Crittenden, Notasulga, Alabama, who wrote his wife again in mid-November, telling her he was experiencing "as bad a time as I have seen during the war. . . . We have heard that Lincoln has been re-elected. If so we may make up our minds for another four years of war." Many a Confederate had hoped for the defeat of Lincoln and upon hearing the Illinoisan had won again, found the news very discouraging. Doubtless some Rebels, perhaps most of them, realized Lincoln's re-election meant the chances of Confederate success had become long indeed. Crittenden now realized too that the army would not winter in north Alabama. He reported to his wife that "we will start to Tennessee [soon and] I expect to be barefooted when I get back—if I am so fortunate as to do so. My shoes are nearly worn through now and the leg of one pair of pants rubbed out." John Crittenden would not be "so fortunate." It is believed that he was killed at Nashville on December 15 and buried somewhere on the battlefield.[54]

On Sunday, November 20, General John Bell Hood at last marched north from the Tennessee River. Texan Sam Foster would long remember General Hood's message, delivered by the regimental commanders, as the army prepared to move out for Tennessee. Hood said, according to Foster, that he was "not going to risk a chance for a defeat in Tennessee. That he will not fight in Tennessee unless he has an equal number of men and choice of the ground. . . ." Foster considered this "very nice talk," because the Graycoats were confident they "could always whip an equal number of men with the choice of ground. . . ." The captain claimed the army was "anxious to go" after such assurances from their general.[55]

About the same time, Hood was telling Jefferson Davis, in rather less qualified terms, "You may rely upon my striking the enemy whenever a suitable opportunity presents itself, and that I will spare no effort to make that opportunity," a message Shelby Foote branded "so characteristic that it was practically superfluous." The aggressive tone of Hood's communiqué to the president seems far removed from the reassuring words reported by Foster. Whatever Hood's frame of mind, many men marched northward in an optimistic mood. "The army left Florence with bright hopes for victory and success," wrote J. W. Harmon of the Thirty-fifth Alabama Infantry. "Onward for Tennessee" was the spirit of the army, according to Harmon. Chaplain Thomas H. Davenport of the Third Tennessee, who had recently observed in his diary that "there seems to be no deed too base or cruel for a Yankee," now reported that "many of [the soldiers] marched barefoot, both officers and men." Nevertheless, Davenport claimed "every eye is toward Tennessee. Oh, may she soon be free."[56]

Perhaps some were not quite so enthusiastic. The general feeling, claimed an Arkansan, was "We are marching to certain ruin. We will fall back in less than a month, or Hood will have us all captured!" Acknowledging that the cheering Tennesseans constituted an exception, he made a pertinent observation that their spiritedness probably stemmed as much from the fact they were going home, "many of them for the first time in years," and hoping to see loved ones, as from patriotism and assurance that victory would crown their march.[57] Whatever, precisely, the various soldiers may have been pondering, they were once more on the advance.

After three weeks in the Tuscumbia-Florence area, the army certainly needed to be moving north, if indeed it was not already too late for any realistic hope of success. Long after John Bell Hood lay in his New Orleans tomb, some Confederates continued to blame the campaign's failure on the delay in north Alabama; a delay that rewarded General Thomas in Nashville with considerably more time to marshal his forces. Several reasons have been alleged for the time lost by the Southerners: repairing the railroad from Corinth where one section of thirty miles had been abandoned; lack of supplies; waiting for Nathan Bedford Forrest's cavalry to join up after a spectacular raid resulting in the capture and destruction of gunboats on the Tennessee River at Johnsonville; and the bad weather.

Obviously the Confederate commander should not be faulted for failure to control the weather, and Forrest's seventy-five hundred troopers were indispensable to spearhead the Rebel advance. Supplies however, were something else again, and there were no significant logistical improvements to show for the time expended. Also, Hood was armed with only scant information about the strength and positioning of the enemy. But the general was not inclined to be overly concerned with Federal whereabouts, nor additional wagons, horses, clothing, food, and ammunition. Upon seizing Nashville he would resupply the army from its rich stores; Tennessee volunteers would swell the ranks of his depleted regiments; and the expanding Butternut forces would move through the Kentucky bluegrass to the Ohio. Thus Hood marched, as Tom Connelly liked to express the matter, "in one last dream of Glory."[58]

The Confederate columns soon met a prematurely early onslaught of snow and sleet, alternating with rain. One day roads would be mud holes, the next frozen sheets of ice. The army's three corps of infantry, roughly thirty thousand men in total, marched on separate routes, Cheatham's command on the left, moving on the road to Waynesboro. On the right advanced Stewart's corps, marching toward Lawrenceburg, while Lee was in the central position, tramping across the country roads. All moved in a generally northeastern direction, heading for Columbia, a small town lying on the south bank of the Duck River some forty miles south of Nashville.

Many men were desperate for shoes, as the story recorded by the Twenty-seventh Mississippi's Robert A. Jarman well indicates. Noting that Forrest's cavalry had recently joined the army, Jarman wrote: "They had a few days before taken some Federal transports on the Tennessee River, and many of the men had two or three pairs of extra shoes tied to their saddles, and at first they gave them away to the barefooted infantry until they had only those on their feet. Then at night the barefooted infantry stole those they wore; for they said it was no harm for a cavalryman to be barefooted, as he had a horse to ride."[59]

On Tuesday, November 22, Chaplain Charles T. Quintard, after his long trek from Columbus, Georgia, and accompanied by a small party of acquaintances, headed north into Tennessee. "The ground is frozen hard and a sharp, cold wind is blowing," Quintard recorded in his diary, "but as my face is towards Tennessee, I heed none of these things." By midday the sky had clouded and "a driving snow" was coming down, while the temperature dropped. Nevertheless, the chaplain covered some seventeen or eighteen miles and "crossed the line into Tennessee at 4:30 P.M. Bless the Lord O my soul. . . ." The next day Quintard at last caught up with the army, overtaking General Hood, and enjoying "a long and pleasant chat with him."[60]

Meanwhile many of the soldiers were fascinated by the countryside through which they were passing. Once the army "struck the beautiful country which is known as Middle Tennessee," wrote Philip Stephenson, a marked contrast from the destruction in north Georgia and north Alabama was immediately evident. Confederates were in awe of the beauty, wealth, and prosperity that seemed ubiquitously manifest, especially as they marched through the region from Mount Pleasant to Columbia. Georgian Hezekiah McCorkle said

*John Bell Hood.
Courtesy of the
Tennessee State
Library and
Archives.*

he was "in the midst of some of the finest country I ever saw," while Tennessean John Johnston spoke of "a country of surpassing beauty . . . , occupied by well-to-do people, who lived, many of them, in elegant homes." Texan Sam Foster, enamored by the several Polk homes, wrote that one of them was "the prettiest place I have ever seen in my life." (One wonders if he had reference to "Rattle and Snap.") And Arkansan Philip Stephenson pronounced the area a "paradise."[61]

However breathtaking the region—and the area to this day remains a magnificent pastoral setting—the pressing business of the Army of Tennessee was war. As earlier noted, the Confederates were advancing toward Columbia at a faster pace than Union General John Schofield had anticipated. Fortunately for the Bluecoat commander, his men had a shorter, more direct route to Columbia than did the Butternuts. Schofield's advance, led by Jacob Cox, got back to Columbia in the nick of time. About seven thirty on the morning of November 24, Cox arrived at a crossroad about two miles south of Columbia, which led westward to a junction with the pike from Mount Pleasant. Sending his wagon train on into Columbia, Cox turned his infantry off to the west, striking at a double-quick pace for the Mount Pleasant Pike, which he had learned was approximately a mile away. Cox's infantry arrived just in time to check the advance of Forrest's troopers, who had been rapidly driving the Union cavalry before them, and otherwise possibly would have pushed right on into the town.[62]

Schofield, at the head of General Stanley's command, rode into Columbia about ten o'clock. As fast as the Federals arrived at Columbia, they were detailed to throw up earthworks covering all approaches from the South, while the wagons were sent across the river. Schofield had no intention of dallying on the south bank of the Duck, and began preparations at once to transfer his forces across the stream as soon as possible. This he did on November 27, afterward destroying the railroad and pontoon bridges. By then the Army of Tennessee had completed its deployment in front of Columbia.[63]

At least one Columbia resident seemed to think the arrival of the Confederates proved even more oppressive than had the presence of the Yankees. Nimrod Porter wrote in his diary that the Rebels were trying to conscript any male between eighteen and forty-five, even if the person had already provided a substitute, which by law he was allowed to do. He thought soon they would be taking everyone from sixteen to fifty, and predicted "They may get me yet, at 74." Porter said that the Confederates destroyed "everything in the way of provender before them," and a few days later, he summarized his own losses: "The Southern army has done me great damage" he charged. "They have taken 150 acres of corn, burned 30,000 rails, mostly cedar, cut and destroyed over 25,000 trees that will average over 2 feet across the stump, took 30 fattening hogs that would average 250 pounds each, took two horses and the Otey filly worth $1,000 in gold, and took off 5 or 6 head of cattle."[64]

While Porter and other Columbia citizens suffered significant losses as the Graycoats supplied themselves with all manner of sorely-needed provisions, the army's commander pondered his next move. On the night of November 27, at Confederate headquarters three miles south of Columbia in Amos and Cornelia Warfield's tastefully elegant, Greek revival home known as "Beechlawn," General Hood, looking more the part of a long-bearded, Old Testament patriarch, formulated a bold plan to cross the Duck, move around the left flank of the Yankees and strike northward. The maneuver would result in one of the war's most famous and enigmatic episodes: Spring Hill.

3

A Run
of Luck in
Our Favor

*Spring Hill was a pleasant little town. Situated thirty miles south of
Nashville, and about halfway between Columbia and Franklin, the
village lay in the midst of a classic agrarian community. From its
beginning in the early nineteenth century, the rich soil attracted
settlers who planted cotton and tobacco and raised livestock. The
rolling hills of bluegrass pastureland presented a panorama that
Vanderbilt's Agrarians well might have found inspirational. A
longtime friend who lives in Spring Hill once was fond of saying
that "if the Civil War soldiers could return to Spring Hill today, the
town would look to them just as it did in the 1860s."*

This statement, of course, was B.S. (Before Saturn). In the mid-
1980s General Motors brought progress (corporate America's common euphemism for such upheaval) to Spring Hill, building its
new automobile plant in the midst of some of Tennessee's finest
farm acreage and changing forever the pastoral setting once taken
for granted. Spring Hill's population, for years holding steady at
approximately one thousand, grew at an astonishing pace that
would have seemed unbelievable only a few years earlier. Within
days of the announcement that Saturn was coming, even overnight

in some cases, land prices escalated spectacularly. The general response was giddy. Speculation ran rampant. And the continuing expansion of the Nashville-Franklin metropolitan region has further contributed to Spring Hill's burgeoning citizenry and cultural metamorphosis.

Why General Motors selected Spring Hill (thirty-some odd sites were reportedly considered), once the shocking reality of the choice began to sink in, became a question of immediate interest to a great many people—whether residents of Spring Hill or inhabitants of neighboring communities. What it all might mean to their lives was of even greater concern. Some citizens welcomed heartily the prospect of change, rapid growth, and perhaps even a personal El Dorado, which they were convinced lay at their doorstep. Others, content with the status quo, were appalled by thoughts of far-reaching fluctuations, the long-term results of which no one could clearly foresee—although, as always, a few gifted souls proclaimed the future with the ringing certainty of an ancient prophet speaking on behalf of Jehovah. But whether for better or worse, and advocates of both persuasions frequently declared themselves in impassioned tones, the vast transformation of Spring Hill surged forward.

And, as trumpeted in a front page article of *The Tennessean* newspaper on July 29, 2002, the people "just keep coming." Spring Hill, gushed the writer, "is now hot, Hot, HOT, and some say the town may become the next Franklin—a fashionable, sought-after, status-symbol place to live."

Fortunately, despite such euphoria and wholesale change, the great antebellum mansions built by a few of the wealthy citizens still survive. Among them none is more memorable than Rippavilla, Nathaniel Cheairs's truly majestic home, with its tall, perfectly proportioned Corinthian columns. The arresting exterior detail is highlighted by two white-pillared porticoes, while the elegant interiors are enhanced by a grand hall and a fine staircase. Located two miles south of Spring Hill and east of the Columbia–Spring Hill Pike, Rippavilla was the house at which General Hood and several Confederate officers breakfasted on the fateful morning of November 30.[1]

Also notable is the red-brick, four-columned home of the William McKissacks, situated slightly west of the pike in the center of Spring Hill. This house was the girlhood home of the former Susan McKissack, wife of Nathaniel Cheairs, and her sister Jessie McKissack, the latter described by one writer as "a real flesh and blood Scarlett O'Hara." Jessie, said to have been a beautiful brunette, was married to Dr. George B. Peters. The doctor had been married twice before, was twenty-four years Jessie's senior, and the union reportedly took place "to keep the money in the family," the bride and groom being cousins. However, when Confederate General Earl Van Dorn, who had a reputation as "a ladies' man," came to town in 1863, he and Jessie apparently developed a mutual attraction. Jessie's widely rumored trysts with Van Dorn led her jealous husband to assassinate the general.[2]

Dr. Peters shot Van Dorn while he worked at his headquarters desk in Ferguson Hall, another of Spring Hill's magnificent mansions. Standing only a few hundred yards south of the McKissack house, on the east side of the pike, Ferguson Hall was built by Dr. John Haddox, who sold it several years before the war to Martin Cheairs, the brother of Nathaniel Cheairs. The architecture of Ferguson Hall and Nathaniel's Rippavilla are strikingly similar. The former is the older and evidently inspired Nathaniel Cheairs, when he constructed his own house, to even greater achievement, albeit in the same style.

As for Dr. George Peters, he achieved a sort of minor celebrity status, coming to be known in some circles, and seemingly in part due to his own publicizing endeavors, as the man who slew "the infamous Rebel, Earl Van Dorn." He and Jessie divorced after the war, then remarried a few years later. Jessie outlived her husband, who died in 1889. The story is told that when Dr. Peters died, Jessie stood over his grave, dressed appropriately in widow's clothes, and was heard to murmur: "I never loved George, but I guess I owe him this much."[3] There is an old saying, fitting for their relationship, that "marriage without love, means love without marriage."

Another Spring Hill home, often thought to go back to Civil War days, actually dates from a couple of years after the conflict. Appropriate it would have been, however, if the structure were antebellum. Located a short distance west of Spring Hill, on the crest of a hill at the end of Depot Road, this is the fine house, appointed with exquisite mahogany interiors, where General Richard S. Ewell, one of Lee's three corps commanders at Gettysburg, spent his last years. Only weeks before the great battle in Pennsylvania, bachelor Ewell had married Russian-born and once-widowed Lyzinka Campbell Brown, a wealthy, intriguing woman with whom Ewell is said to have been in love for years. (The rather eccentric Ewell, after the marriage, sometimes referred to his spouse as "the widow Brown," or "my wife, Mrs. Brown.") They spent five years together in the new house at Spring Hill, death coming to both at very nearly the same time.[4]

Spring Hill was a place that enjoyed no particular distinction in the fall of 1864. A touch of unpleasant notoriety came from the Van Dorn murder. (Dr. Peters, incidentally, immediately fled from Spring Hill and was never brought to trial for the slaying.) Yet the town, following the unsavory incident, generally had proceeded with life as usual. But now the relentless and unpredictable march of history—its ways so often strange and surprising— prepared to forever place the name "Spring Hill" among the famous and enigmatic legends of the war.

The Confederate army at Spring Hill, led by General Hood on November 29, 1864, has long been credited with a marvelous opportunity, somehow bungled, to ensnare the Federal forces under Schofield and administer a mortal blow. Presenting a typical interpretation of the campaign was Bruce Catton, the twentieth century's single greatest popularizer of the war. Catton wrote that General Schofield allowed Hood to steal a march on him, "and by the afternoon of November 29 had his army in position at Spring Hill, ten miles in Schofield's rear. By everything in the books, Hood now had a winning advantage. Schofield had to retreat, his escape route ran right past Hood's front, and one hard blow might obliterate him."[5]

What went wrong in the Graycoat army has been a puzzle ever since that day. Long after the voices of the last veterans were silenced in death, the perplexing mystery continued to puzzle innumerable students of the conflict. Explanations of Confederate failure have run the gamut from divine intervention to the intrigues of Union spies. An elderly black preacher, once a slave on Absalom Thompson's Spring Hill plantation, offered a simple, straight-forward analysis: "God," he declared, "just didn't want that war to go on no longer."[6]

Some longtime residents of Spring Hill, as well as old war veterans, claimed that General Hood was intoxicated. Some said the same of General Benjamin F. Cheatham, the commander of Hood's lead corps. John Gregory, for example, Hood's local guide who grew up near Columbia and was present at Spring Hill on the night of November 29, later claimed that "a long time" was spent by some Confederate officers "in eating and drinking and 'toasting'" and that "Cheatham was full drunk."[7] Suspicions have even focused upon the vivacious Jessie Peters, with rumors alleging a romantic dalliance involving her and one or more Grayclad officers. (She was in town and her husband was not.) Also, there was the fantastic story told by a Union soldier named J. D. Remington, Company I, Seventy-third Illinois Volunteers. Claiming in 1913 to be "the only person living who knew the real cause of Hood's failure . . . at Spring Hill," Remington said that "the Confederate generals allowed themselves to be deceived by taking orders from two Federal spies." The soldier referred to himself and a cousin who supposedly wrecked Southern attempts to coordinate effective action by spreading countermanding, confusing, and contradictory orders to various officers.[8]

On the other hand, not every student of the campaign has credited the Confederates with a clear-cut opportunity to destroy the Yankees at Spring Hill. Stanley Horn wrote that the Union force at Spring Hill simply "got there first with the most men," and General Hood never had much chance to hurt Schofield's army.[9] Thomas Hay acknowledged that the Confederate commander faced a major challenge: "Hood undertook to perform a difficult feat in attempting to cut off Schofield at Spring Hill," wrote Hay. Though Hood marched "at dawn" from Columbia and "crossed the Duck River some five or six miles above Columbia, he had only muddy, dirt roads over which to travel. The day was short and the distance long."[10]

What occurred at Spring Hill, and why, possibly will never be completely explained—in the sense of a generally accepted consensus. Much of the confusion about the whole campaign, however, began with General Hood himself. The United States Army today recognizes nine principals of generalship. The first is a clearly defined objective. Hood's long-range objectives were clouded, and he apparently was not certain of his immediate objective either. Spurred by thoughts of "the immortal Jackson," as Hood later praised his Virginia idol, and driven by the chance to make one of those "beautiful moves upon the chessboard of war," Hood had laid out a plan to execute a flank movement on the Union left.[11] The goal of the flanking march is something else.

The maneuver later would be represented (and Hood himself contributed to the idea by his subsequent claims) as a brilliantly conceived march to entrap Schofield's Federals at Spring Hill. Hood would lead the main body of his army, so it would be alleged, along rough country roads to the little village twelve miles north of Columbia. There he would position it across the pike to Franklin and Nashville, ready to attack the Yankee force as it retreated. Turning on his West Point classmate at that point would certainly be an option. Hood's favored plan, however, may well have been another matter.

What the Confederate commander actually seemed to desire, based on primary evidence, was to gain the pike in Schofield's rear and outrace the Bluecoats to the Tennessee capital. On Sunday, November 27, General Hood spoke to Chaplain, later Bishop, Charles Quintard, who recorded in his diary that Hood "detailed to me his plan of taking Nashville, calling for volunteers to storm the key of the works about the city." Quintard considered the volunteers a suicidal force, writing that "700 men will fill the graves of 700 heroes and receive the laurel crown." The next day Quintard recorded that General Hood "told me just now confidentially that he would either beat the enemy to Nashville or make him go there at a double-quick pace." And long before daylight on the morning of the ill-fated march, Hood "came to tell me goodbye," said Quintard, remarking that "The enemy must give me fight, or I will be at Nashville before tomorrow night."[12]

Evidently the Confederate commander, concluded one historian, knew little about potential Union strength at Nashville. Thomas Connelly thought that maybe Hood "even still considered Schofield's army the only real obstacle" to capturing the Tennessee capital. If Connelly's speculation is correct, it was unfortunate for the Southerners, considering the great number of Federals eventually marshaled at Nashville behind some of the strongest fortifications in America. An intention to plunge straight ahead for the city, outracing Schofield to Nashville, might at least help to explain the rather slipshod planning for the episode which developed at Spring Hill. "Hood's corps commanders, Stewart and Cheatham, marched without any specific orders," wrote Connelly, and "without most of the army's artillery," and without the bulk of their ammunition.[13]

That the Confederate objective was general and somewhat vague is reflected in the reports of key officers: General Stewart wrote that "we made a forced march to get in rear of the enemy." General Lee said the movement was "to the rear of the enemy in the direction of Spring Hill." General Carter Stevenson, division commander under Lee, simply said the Confederates "pushed for the enemy's rear," and General Edward Walthall, leading a division in Stewart's corps, mentioned nothing about an objective, merely noting that the movement was "without artillery or any wagons, except a few to carry a small supply of extra ammunition."[14] Unfortunately, several important officers did not survive to compose a report.

General Hood determined to ride with the advance of his army. Perhaps because of this decision, he may have concluded that written orders or detailed oral explanation of his plans would not be necessary. Maybe he thought he could personally issue specific orders when the appropriate time and place was at hand. Then again, perhaps murky planning and clouded objectives constitute a better explanation of the non-specific orders. Whatever the truth of the matter, General Hood was once more strapped to his saddle, hungering for victory and dazzled with dreams of glory, as he led the infantry of the Army of Tennessee in person, riding with Cheatham near the head of the column. Stewart's corps followed Cheatham's, reinforced by Ed Johnson's division from Lee's corps. The remainder of Lee's command and most of the army's artillery stayed in Columbia where they could mount a demonstration, hopefully to freeze a puzzled Schofield in place on the north side of Duck River.[15]

As commander of the lead corps, Cheatham's role was highly important, second only to Hood's, in the success or failure of the flanking maneuver. Cheatham was a native Nashvillian, descended on the maternal side from James Robertson, one of the founders of the city. A veteran of both the Mexican War and the California Gold Rush, he had returned to Tennessee and prominently participated in the state militia in the years prior to the Civil War. Commissioned a major general shortly before commanding a division at Shiloh, Cheatham served in most of the Army of Tennessee's great battles, winning a reputation as a formidable fighting man. Standing five feet, eight or nine inches tall, he was powerfully built, with light blue eyes, light brown hair, and a heavy moustache. He "presents the appearance of a soldier," declared one of his men; being a "quite

*Benjamin F. Cheatham.
Courtesy of the Tennessee
State Library and Archives.*

commanding figure." Cheatham's physical strength (which he took pleasure in demonstrating) and cursing were legendary. So too, as previously noted, was his consumption of alcohol. Upon Cheatham and Hood, primarily, depended the coordination of the Southern movement.[16]

The Confederate infantry certainly got off to a good start, crossing the Duck River unopposed, thanks to the spearheading efforts of General Forrest's horse soldiers. On the night of November 27 Forrest had met with Hood at Beechlawn, the Warfield home three miles south of Columbia, to which Hood had just moved his headquarters. Forrest was ordered to force a crossing of the Duck, cover the construction of a pontoon bridge for the passage of the infantry, and screen the northward march from the eyes of the Yankee troopers. All of this he proceeded to accomplish with his customary efficiency, beginning early the next morning.[17]

Forrest's assignment was made easier by the actions of his Federal counterpart. James Harrison Wilson had recently arrived to command the Union cavalry. Only five years out of West Point, he had recently been elevated to the rank of brevet major general. Standing about five feet, ten inches in height, Wilson's slim frame and erect carriage made him appear a trifle taller. His bearing commanded attention. Never one to be bashful about claiming success, while equally adept at glossing over his failures, the young general came very close to losing a division in his first independent operation in Virginia, a fact that Schofield may or may not have known. The slightly younger George Armstrong Custer, obviously envious of Wilson's rapid advancement, wrote his wife about "the upstart and imbecile" Wilson, whose defeat had come from "total ignorance and inexperience. . . ." But most importantly, Wilson had succeeded in impressing General Grant. Praising Wilson to Sherman, who generally thought little of the mounted arm, Grant claimed Wilson could add 50 percent to the effectiveness of a cavalry command. Wilson's biographer suggested that "perhaps his strongest point was an energetic, get-things-done style."[18]

Undoubtedly Wilson was a man of considerable ability. He was also inclined to be pompous and self-righteous. "His massive conceit," as Bruce Catton wrote of Wilson, led him to later depict "both Grant and Thomas as being strangely inert" at Missionary Ridge, Wilson taking credit for conceiving the attack that won the battle. More than once "a most unreliable witness," to again borrow a Catton phrase, Wilson would write in the same vein of Thomas and Schofield at Nashville, leaving an impression that if not for Wilson, neither would have attacked on the last day of the battle.[19] Although Wilson had just joined Schofield with additional horsemen, and wrote that "our force is now getting to be very respectable,"[20] he possessed neither the experience nor sufficient veteran troopers to deal with the hardened Southern cavalry led by a general who arguably was the single best commander of mounted men that the war produced.

Early on the morning of November 28, Forrest prepared to force a crossing of the Duck River at several points: farthest to the east at Hardison's Mill on the Lewisburg-Franklin Pike, some ten miles from Columbia; and at three other points closer to Columbia. Wilson initially operated under the impression that the river was "impassable, or nearly so, everywhere."[21] This concept, when facing an aggressive commander like Forrest, placed Wilson at a disadvantage from the start. At last learning differently about the river passages, the young general decided not to seriously contest the crossings. Perhaps he concluded that concentration of one's force in the face of the enemy, a frequently emphasized military concept, was the best part of valor.

Actually, Wilson probably stood a better chance of stopping Forrest at the river crossings than of dealing with the Confederates once they concentrated on the north bank of the Duck. (This is not to say that Wilson had any really good option.) Forrest took him by surprise. Only at Hardison's Mill, at the Lewisburg-Franklin Pike crossing, did the Union have respectable numbers to oppose

James H. Wilson. National Archives.

Forrest. Learning that the Southerners were across the River at Huey's Mills, which meant they could soon strike his troopers at Hardison's Mill in flank, Wilson determined to pull everybody back, massing his entire command at Hurt's Crossroads on the Lewisburg-Franklin Pike. The site was approximately five miles north of the river, where the Federals quickly assembled rough barricades across the pike.[22] Wilson's decision, however, awarded Forrest with the opportunity to immediately take the offensive—the offensive, as well as surprise, also recognized among the United States Army's nine principals of generalship—a chance which the Confederate commander, as was his habit, seized at once. Wilson, "in his eagerness to withdraw," wrote Edward Longacre, "made the most serious tactical error of his military career." Instead of retreating along routes "which would enable him to fulfill his primary job [of serving] as the eyes . . . of the army, he led his troopers up the Lewisburg Pike in a direction that carried them far from Schofield's main force above Columbia." Thus Wilson placed himself "in a position from which he could not readily inform Schofield about the enemy's movements. . . ."[23]

With Forrest pressing him, Wilson eventually despaired of holding Hurt's Crossroads, fearing that the Rebels would soon be enveloping his position. He proceeded to pull back about five more miles to the north, still on the Lewisburg-Franklin Pike, and took up a new position at Mount Carmel. Once again barricades were erected across the pike and on the morning of November 29 a fierce clash ensued. Some of the Federal troopers were armed with Spencer repeating carbines, which served them well in the fight. But Wilson, fearing that Forrest was again maneuvering to gain the pike in his rear, decided to retreat still farther toward Franklin. Early in the morning he had sent a dispatch to Schofield saying that he thought Hood was "aiming for Franklin." He advised Schofield to retire northward along the Columbia-Franklin Pike and "get back to Franklin without delay." Wilson then, instead of riding to help secure the infantry's line of retreat at Spring Hill, continued to pull back toward the town on the Harpeth River.

By noon Wilson was only three or four miles southeast of Franklin. Forrest had succeeded in taking the Federal cavalry out of the campaign altogether. Detaching a brigade of his troopers to keep up the pressure on the retreating Yankees, (but not too much pressure because he hoped to confuse Wilson), Forrest turned the bulk of his cavalry westward and rode for Spring Hill. Wilson was completely befuddled. He had no idea where Forrest might be, thinking it most likely that the Confederate cavalry had gotten around him and was striking for Nashville. He even sent a message to General Thomas saying "You had better look out for Forrest at Nashville." Later, from Franklin, Schofield would dispatch a telegram to General Thomas saying, "I do not know where Forrest is. . . . Wilson is entirely unable to cope with him."[24]

Nathan Bedford Forrest. Courtesy of the Tennessee State Library and Archives.

While Forrest made Wilson look rather like an amateur, Schofield himself was not looking particularly impressive. The Federal commander was not at all convinced that Hood was marching for Franklin or Spring Hill—or any other place along the pike to Nashville. The Confederate maneuver might be only a feint, he thought, designed to cause him to retreat from Columbia, leaving open the macadamized road to Nashville for the advance of Hood's infantry and artillery. If, on the other hand, Hood was actually crossing Duck River with the greater part of his infantry, the Rebel commander might drive down the right bank to attack the Union left flank. This is apparently what Schofield assumed was most probable, especially after the Southerners opened a heavy artillery fire against the Bluecoat lines from Columbia, indicating that most of Hood's guns were still in the town.

Thus Schofield made his decision. He would hold his ground at Columbia, at least for a while. Deploying the troops to counter either an enemy movement to get on the pike to his rear or a strike down the north bank of the river against his left flank, Schofield positioned General Nathan Kimball's division east of the pike, between Duck River and Rutherford's Creek, supported with General Thomas J. Wood's division, thereby protecting the Federal left flank. Sidney Post's brigade of Wood's division, already moving eastward, was to continue its reconnaissance to learn what Hood was doing. General Thomas H. Ruger's division was positioned just north of Rutherford's Creek, on the pike about halfway to Spring Hill, poised to march either north or south as might prove necessary, while General Stanley continued to Spring Hill with George D. Wagner's division. Also, the army's supply train of some eight hundred wagons and most of the artillery went with Stanley. The remainder of the Union force, under Cox, stayed in the lines at Columbia.[25]

Schofield calculated, or so he later claimed, that if he had to race for Spring Hill he could beat Hood, who would be marching a greater distance and on a rougher road. "I decided to hold on to the crossing of Duck River until the night of the 29th, thus gaining twenty four hours more for Thomas to concentrate his troops," said Schofield. "I did not apprehend any serious danger at Spring Hill, for Hood's infantry could not reach that place over a wretched country road much before night, and Stanley, with one division and our cavalry [which was not there] could easily beat off Forrest."[26] William M. Wherry, Schofield's assistant adjutant general, later testified that the matter "was fully considered and the decision deliberately made not to retreat at all that day—November 29. The important point to hold was the crossing of Duck River at Columbia," explained Wherry, so as to "delay Hood's use of the turnpike, by which alone he could move any large amount of artillery and trains."[27]

General Schofield, somewhat like Wilson in one respect, was never inclined to minimize his talents for making the necessary dispositions to meet all contingencies. In fairness to Schofield, however, no Socrates would have been required to identify Spring Hill as a possible Southern objective. That Schofield would estimate the marching time required to cover the distance is hardly surprising. It would, in fact, be remarkable if he had not done so. The accuracy of his calculation is something else altogether.

The Duke of Wellington famously remarked of the monumental Battle of Waterloo that it was the "damned . . . nearest run thing you ever saw in your life."[28] Perhaps the duke, as well as Napoleon—and probably Blucher also for that matter—would be unappreciative of even the mention of Spring Hill in the same paragraph with Waterloo. Nevertheless, Wellington's words are quite fitting: Spring Hill too was a damned near run thing—much more so than Schofield ever anticipated. Possibly the greatest danger for the Union army came at noon. If the Federal infantry had been a few minutes later in arriving at Spring Hill, Forrest's cavalry might have taken the town from its small garrison of infantry and a portion of the Twelfth Tennessee Cavalry, a green regiment recently arrived from Nashville. General Stanley was approximately two miles south of town, riding with the head of Wagner's division, when "a cavalry soldier who seemed badly scared," rode up and informed him that Forrest's troopers were fast approaching from the east. Forrest was galloping toward Spring Hill on the Mount Carmel Road "and estimated to be only about four miles out."[29]

Decisively responding with "the biggest day's work I ever accomplished for the United States," Stanley brought the Union infantry into Spring Hill at a double-quick pace, Colonel Emerson E. Opdycke's brigade in the lead, arriving at approximately twelve thirty. The Confederates then could be seen, said General Wagner, "in full view and moving upon the place from the east and not over half a mile distant."[30] Opdycke's Bluecoats were in the nick of time to reinforce the garrison defenders and stop General Abraham Buford's division of Forrest's cavalry from seizing the village. Following the bloody repulse of this initial attack by Forrest's leading division, Stanley rushed to strengthen his position. The wagon train was parked west of town, between the turnpike and the railroad, where it was both out of the way and in position to be protected. Wagner's three brigades, led by Opdycke, General Luther P. Bradley, and Colonel John Q. Lane, were deployed to form a long, semicircular line covering the highest ground available. The Federals were located, at the farthest point to the east, approximately a quarter to a third of a mile from Spring Hill, with both flanks refused to cover the pike north and south of the village. (To refuse a flank is to angle it back, a military tactic commonly employed to make an enemy's envelopment of a flank more difficult.) Opdycke was on the left, protecting the wagons, Bradley in the center facing east, and Lane on the right, looking south.[31]

Forrest, whether he recognized the fact or not, had come very near to capturing Spring Hill. By the time the Southern commander could deploy his troops for a massed attack, however, Stanley had 6,000 to 6,500 infantry positioned on good ground behind a quickly constructed breastwork of rail fences. He also held something of an ace: thirty-four artillery pieces, facing east and south, in support of the infantry.[32] If not a commanding position, it certainly was not a bad position.

Forrest had not expected to find such formidable resistance. Refusing to believe the Union defenses were manned by infantry, Forrest had ignored James Chalmers's protesting warning, ordering Chalmers to send a regiment against the Yankees. The hail of fire that greeted the assault and quickly stopped it, clearly demonstrated an infantry presence in strength. "They was in there sure enough, wasn't they Chalmers?" remarked a surprised Forrest.[33]

David S. Stanley. Library of Congress.

At this point the vagueness of Hood's planning becomes apparent. If Hood's objective really was to seize the pike and trap Schofield—and if Hood had made this goal clear to Forrest—there was little to prevent the cavalry chieftain from sweeping around Spring Hill and seizing the pike to the north. Instead, Forrest lost some men in assaults on the town until nearly three o'clock, when his ammunition ran low.[34]

About that time General Hood, riding at the head of the Confederate infantry column, reached the crossing of Rutherford's Creek, two and one-half miles southeast of Spring Hill. There the Davis Ford Road intersected the Rally

Hill Road, which led to the town. Hood had expected to be there earlier. The general had been riding since long before daybreak, but the march had consumed considerably more time than he anticipated. All went well initially. Between nine and nine thirty, the entire Gray column, nearly twenty thousand strong, was across the Duck River and heading north. The Davis Ford Road, however, soon proved a wretched passageway. Narrow, muddy, and badly rutted, it had actually been abandoned in some places and was poorly kept up in others. General Hood was expecting a better road and a shorter one. Instead he was advancing on one of the worst routes in the region.[35]

A mile or so north of the river the general's concern became pronounced. The map he was relying upon for guidance "differed materially" from the road the army was traveling.[36] Only then did Hood confer with John Gregory, his local guide earlier mentioned. In a later memorandum, Gregory himself described events, using the third person: "Gregory drew a rough sketch on the ground showing the relative distances, and positions of the roads, and explained it to Hood. Gregory's distances and locations were corroborated by another guide with Cleburne, Jim Smith [who had also grown up in the Columbia region] and General Pat Cleburne made a rough copy on a piece of paper of the sketch that had been made by Gregory on the ground." Hood obviously had been relying upon an imperfect and highly misleading map. The upshot of it all was that Hood thought the distance from the river to Spring Hill via the Davis Ford Road would be about twelve miles; after consulting with Gregory and Smith he realized it would be significantly more—another five or six miles.[37]

The situation soon became worse. Around mid-morning, some Union skirmishers were discovered off to the west, causing Hood to reform his lead corps under Cheatham into two parallel columns, the better to form battle lines if the Federals should appear in force and attack. Graycoat skirmishers were also thrown out on the left flank of the marching columns. This maneuver, plus the narrow and difficult road, resulted in a great many Confederates trudging through the woods and fields alongside the bad road. By midday Hood was not in a very good mood and John Gregory claimed that during a halt for a brief lunch "at a late hour," there was a "misunderstanding between General Hood and General [Hiram] Granberry [Granbury]," resulting in harsh words being exchanged. Finally, at some point during the trek to Spring Hill, General Hood suffered a fall from his horse, adding more misery to his painful wounds. For both Hood and his men the march to Spring Hill proved long and tiring.[38]

Arriving at Rutherford's Creek, Hood was completely ignorant of the strength of Stanley's position at the village. Without consulting Forrest—probably thinking he could not spare the time after arriving so late in the day—Hood sent forward his leading division under General Cleburne, a division enjoying

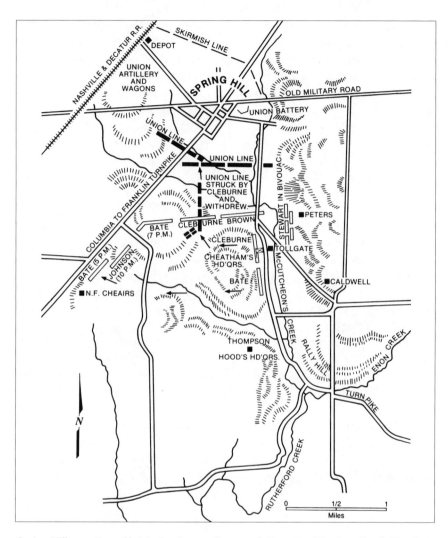

Spring Hill map. From Christopher Losson, Tennessee's Forgotten Warriors: Frank Cheatham and His Confederate Division.

the distinction of being the hardest-hitting unit in the Army of Tennessee. Cleburne was ordered to confer with Forrest and then seize the pike. Corps commander Cheatham was to remain at Rutherford's Creek until the arrival of William B. Bate's division, coming on after Cleburne. Cheatham would then lead Bate's division forward to the support of Cleburne. Hood himself would await the arrival of Cheatham's last division, that of General John C. Brown, and send it forward immediately upon arrival.[39]

From this time onward hardly anything went right for the Confederates at Spring Hill. Cleburne failed to make personal contact with Forrest and thus knew little, or nothing, of Stanley's position. Veering west from the Rally Hill Road toward the Columbia-Franklin Pike, Cleburne's right brigade stumbled into the Yankee line southeast of the village. Cleburne then swung his entire division northward toward the town and, supported by Tyree H. Bell's dismounted brigade from Forrest's cavalry, launched an assault on Stanley's position. The time was approximately four o'clock, barely half an hour before sunset. The Federals gave ground, falling back from their fence-rail breastworks. But Cleburne's pursuing command suddenly was swept by an artillery barrage from three Yankee batteries, a total of eighteen guns, massed on the southern outskirts of Spring Hill in anticipation of just such a situation. Cleburne had no satisfactory options. All he could do was retreat and reform. Only then could he possibly attack again. As to the cavalry, Bell's men had expended the remainder of their ammunition. Although the disarranged attackers had fallen back in the face of the Union guns, General Stanley was worried. He had recognized the Rebel division. He warned General Wagner to brace his men for another attack, probably with substantial reinforcements.[40]

Meanwhile, Hood and Cheatham were working at cross-purposes. While Hood attempted to seize the pike, Cheatham planned an assault on Spring Hill. Rapidly the Confederate effort went to pieces as Hood and Cheatham reversed each other's orders. (No Federal spies were required for the job; not at this point anyway.) First, Cheatham did not personally conduct Bate to the front as Hood had instructed. Bate proceeded north on the Rally Hill Road until he met Hood. The Confederate commander, consistent with his plan to take the pike, instructed Bate to move his division west to the pike and then "sweep toward Columbia." Darkness had almost enshrouded the countryside when Bate approached close to the pike on the Nathaniel Cheairs farm, north of the mansion and perhaps a mile and one-half south of Spring Hill. At that instant a Federal column was spied marching northward toward the town. A hail of skirmish firing ensued as Bate made ready to advance and seize the road. Before he could do so, Bate received an order from Cheatham telling him to pull back from the pike. Cheatham instructed him to march northeast and form on Cleburne's left flank facing Spring Hill.[41]

Bate reported his contact with the Union troops, probably Thomas Ruger's division, the lead element of Schofield's main body. Cheatham apparently did not concern himself, however, his attention then focused on Stanley's forces at the village. And thus another good chance to block the pike went for naught. Cheatham had moved to Cleburne's front, learned of the Irishman's difficulties, and ordered Bate to his support. Then, as John Calvin Brown's division moved up, Cheatham ordered it to form on Cleburne's right flank. Cheatham planned a full-scale assault on Spring Hill with his corps. General Hood, by this time, probably knew little about what was occurring. He did not remain on the field, going instead to his headquarters at the Absalom Thompson farm, a couple of miles south of the village. John Gregory said Hood sat for a time on a log between the Thompson house and the fishpond, while various couriers came and went, presumably reporting events as ranking Confederates at Spring Hill perceived them (which was not very clearly). Eventually Hood, according to Gregory, went to the house where he remained for the night.[42]

The Confederate effort continued to deteriorate. Cheatham's attack never materialized. Brown's division, deployed on the right, was scheduled to begin the assault. Cleburne was to attack when he heard Brown's guns, with Bate then going forward in coordination with Cleburne. Around five thirty, with darkness totally covering the scene, Brown was in position, ready for an attack on that moonless night. However, discovering some enemy troops to his right, Brown claimed he was badly outflanked and declined to move forward. "Inevitable disaster" awaited him if he advanced, said Brown. Cheatham later claimed that he ordered Brown to refuse his threatened right flank and attack anyway. Precious time continued to pass as Brown remained motionless. Brown later claimed he was instructed to await the arrival of Stewart's corps, holding his division in readiness for further orders at that time. Presumably some misunderstanding of orders—or a pronounced case of stubbornness—had occurred. Brown never did attack. Consequently, neither did Cleburne nor Bate.[43]

Yet more bungling soon foiled both the effort to seize the Columbia Pike and the assault on Spring Hill. By Hood's orders, General Stewart's corps, which had been following Cheatham's, was halted a short distance south of Rutherford's Creek. No reason was given. Puzzled, Stewart rode to Hood's headquarters to learn why his corps was not being deployed. Hood told Stewart that his command was being held in reserve for the purpose of pursuing any Yankees who might attempt to escape on the Rally Hill Road. This surely must have impressed Stewart as a strange and very optimistic explanation.[44]

While Stewart conferred with Hood, a courier arrived with a message for the army's commander from Governor Isham Harris, then serving on Hood's staff. The note reported that Brown's division was outflanked. The governor recommended (as reported after the war by Major Campbell Brown, son-in-law of Richard S. Ewell, in what Brown called "a remarkable conversation" with Harris) that Stewart should march to General John C. Brown's right flank and seize the pike north of Spring Hill. Hood seemed to think this a splendid idea and, again according to Harris as reported by Campbell Brown, ordered Stewart: "Put yourself across that road if it costs you every man of your command."[45]

Probably Hood supposed that Brown faced westward near the pike. Actually Brown was several hundred yards east of the pike and angled toward

The Absalom Thompson House. Photograph by Rudy E. Sanders.

the north. Whatever Hood believed about Brown's division, he ordered Stewart to proceed on a road east of and parallel to the Rally Hill Road, a route that would enable him to intersect the pike north of Spring Hill. The time was approximately six o'clock when Stewart left Hood's headquarters to begin the march.[46]

The going was slow. Total darkness prevailed and Stewart was not familiar with the area. Proceeding with a guide provided by Hood, "a young man of the neighborhood," Stewart seems to have been on the proper road—the route which intersected the pike north of town. At last the Confederates appeared on the verge of sealing off the pike. But once more their effort failed. Informed that Forrest's headquarters was close at hand, Stewart dismounted "to get such information as Forrest could give me." According to Forrest, as recalled by Stewart, "the enemy had left the direct road from Spring Hill to Franklin and taken the Carter's Creek Pike," farther to the west.[47]

Despite Forrest's rather startling information, Stewart mounted up to continue his mission of getting onto the pike north of the village, when a staff officer from Hood approached. Stewart was on the wrong road, the man said, and General Hood had sent him to show the corps commander the right route. (How Hood could have known what road Stewart was on is a mystery.) After some discussion, Stewart concluded to follow the staff officer's lead. He was eventually directed to an alignment with Brown's right flank. There Stewart soon realized his new position would not achieve Hood's order to make a lodgment on the turnpike. Perplexed and unsure what to do, Stewart once again rode to Hood's headquarters.[48]

In fact, several of Hood's generals, puzzled and confused, made their way to the commander's headquarters. Cheatham, Forrest, Cleburne, and Bate, in addition to Stewart, are all known to have visited Hood at least once that night. For Stewart the trip was his second, of course. This time he found General Hood in bed. Stewart asked if Hood "had changed his mind . . . as to what [Stewart] was to do." When the commander replied that he had not, Stewart said that he explained the situation. Then, evidently for the first time, Hood understood the actual Confederate position at Spring Hill, at least in general terms, and realized that no one had seized the Columbia-Franklin Pike, either north or south of the village.

Surprisingly, however, Hood did not seem particularly concerned. Nor did Stewart. When Stewart reported that his position did not control the pike, Hood simply asked if he could send a brigade to block the road. Stewart protested. His men were tired and hungry he said. Hood then granted permission for Stewart to bivouac his corps for the night. "Let the men rest and take the advance to Franklin in the morning," said Hood, according to Stewart's version of events.[49]

What little is known of Hood's conversations with other officers only generates more confusion. Hood supposedly inquired of General Forrest if he could seize control of the pike north of town. Two of Forrest's divisions were out of ammunition and the third possessed only a small supply appropriated from the Yankees. The cavalry commander said something to the effect that he would do what he could. If not a forlorn hope, successful action by the cavalry obviously faced very long odds. Not surprisingly, Forrest was unable to accomplish anything.[50]

Governor Harris's record conveys a rather different perspective, and is again striking. He claimed Hood was "annoyed" because Stewart had not placed his troops across the pike, "and said with emphasis" that it was of "great importance" that a lodgment should be made "on the road tonight"; then bluntly asking Stewart "Can you send [a brigade]?" When Stewart spoke a second time of his men being hungry and tired, Harris declared that Hood cut Stewart off, turned to Nathan Bedford Forrest and asked "General, can *you* [original emphasis] put a brigade there?" When the cavalry commander responded with a "yes," only to qualify his reply with "if I can get ammunition," Hood at once ordered Stewart to furnish Forrest with ammunition, and the two rode off together. So said Isham Harris.[51]

But as General Cheatham later recounted, Hood told Cheatham that he "had concluded to wait until morning, and directed me to hold my command in readiness to attack at daylight." Apparently William B. Bate was the last general to confer with the Southern commander that night. Bate informed Hood, according to Bate, of the conflicting orders he had received earlier in the evening when he pulled his men back from the pike at the Nat Cheairs farm. Hood's reply was that "It makes no difference now, or it is all right, anyhow, for General Forrest, as you see, has just left, and informed me that he holds the turnpike with a portion of his forces north of Spring Hill, and will stop the enemy if he tries to pass toward Franklin, and so in the morning we will have a surrender without a fight. We can sleep quietly tonight."[52]

Not all of Hood's visitors that night were generals, or even officers. Some time around midnight, a barefoot Confederate private made his way to General Hood's headquarters. He said Union infantry columns were moving northward on the pike in large numbers. Exasperated because nothing was being done to stop them, the private, thinking the army's commander must not realize what was happening, had trekked across the fields by starlight to personally inform the general. Hood's blasé reaction to this highly commendable initiative—and alarming news—was to rouse himself briefly, telling his adjutant, Major A. P. Mason, to instruct General Cheatham to "advance a line of skirmishers" and "confuse" the Yankees by firing into their column. Then Hood went back to sleep, not bothering to further disturb his rest and check on the matter himself, or even send a staff officer to observe the pike.[53]

Hood's response to the private may be viewed as consistent with the general's belief that the pike north of Spring Hill already was in Confederate hands and the halting of the enemy's movement thus assured. It may also be interpreted as further evidence of Hood's poor condition physically and mentally. By the night of November 29, Hood probably was in no shape to make military decisions. The stump of his leg likely was irritated by the long ride over rough roads. The chances are that exhaustion overwhelmed him. "There seems to have been a most definite impairment of Hood's mental processes," observed the editor of *Blue & Gray Magazine*. "A man in great pain, as Hood was, probably had a supply of pain-killing drugs on hand." As previously noted, the general took a spill from his horse on the ride to Spring Hill and, again quoting from *Blue & Gray*, "may well have turned to his pain-killers early in the day. Laudanum, a tincture of opium which induces euphoria, was a commonly used drug of the period. At the time of the Civil War little was known of its addictive effects."[54]

One consistent thread running through much of the confusing and contradictory evidence that has survived over the years is that General Hood seemed optimistic, groggily assured of success, on the night of November 29. If he took laudanum for his pain, and it seems highly likely that he did, his desire to believe that everything was working out as he hoped could well have been obsessive. The drug probably is the key to the general's behavior, for Hood was known to use it, rather than the possible use of whiskey, or alcohol of whatever kind.

Like Hood, Cheatham did not bother to investigate for himself whether the Federals were moving north on the pike, instead passing Major Mason's instruction from the commander to General Edward Johnson. Johnson's division had finally come up behind Stewart, taken position near Cheatham's left flank, and was actually camping in the area originally occupied by William Bate near the Cheairs home. The division commander proceeded to examine the pike, only to find the road empty. Perhaps Johnson encountered a gap between segments of the Union force on the march. Perhaps some of the Federals filed off the pike on a road to their left, mentioned by General Bate in his report, and came into Spring Hill by a less direct country road. Possibly too, because the time is very unsure and conceivably might have been long past midnight (one soldier so testified), the last of the Yankees had just passed. Johnson soon returned to his headquarters, while Schofield's troops continued to trek northward and the Confederates slept in the fields east of the pike at Spring Hill.[55]

One of the Southern generals, Samuel G. French, memorably summarized the situation: "Schofield . . . passed by us while we were dreaming—artillery and wagons, infantry and horse, all gone on to Franklin!" French apparently was also the source of an oft-repeated Spring Hill myth. When he met General Hood the next morning, French said the disgusted Hood exclaimed, "Well General French, we have missed the great opportunity of the war." French wrote that he responded, "Yes," and noted he had been told that "the Yankees passed along all night and lit their pipes at our camp fires." French then explained: "Of course my answer was a *little* [the general's emphasis] figurative, but some soldiers heard it, and taking it literally, it soon spread through the ranks."[56]

The many contradictions and confusions of accounts by participants are perhaps nowhere better illustrated than in the conflicting stories of General Cheatham and Governor Harris, regarding the note that Hood instructed Major Mason to send Cheatham. Cheatham later wrote that he received a note "about midnight" by courier from Mason. Harris, however, recorded that the following day Mason pulled him aside and confessed that he never sent Cheatham the order—the very order Cheatham claimed he received. "I fell asleep again before writing it," revealed the major, as he explained that General Cheatham should not be held accountable for failing to make a night attack. Did an exhausted Mason manage to write the note to Cheatham and then completely forget that he had done so? Did Cheatham somehow imagine that he had received a note that never existed? Such are the enigmas of Spring Hill.[57]

The hands of the clock reached about three in the afternoon before General Schofield became satisfied that he would not be attacked in force at Columbia. Instead, he decided, Hood was marching to seize the pike somewhere to the north. The Federal commander then led Ruger's two brigades in a rapid march to Spring Hill, leaving staff officers to give orders to the other division commanders to follow shortly. Schofield rode into Spring Hill about six thirty.[58]

Conferring with General Stanley, he learned that no help could be expected from Wilson's cavalry and, worse, that some of Forrest's troopers had been seen at Thompson's Station, about three miles to the north on the road to Franklin. Quite possibly, the Rebels had the road to Franklin completely blocked. Thousands of Union soldiers—the divisions of Kimball, Wood, and Cox—were on the march in the darkness, somewhere south of Spring Hill and would require four or five hours before all could reach the village. (The last troops did not come into Spring Hill until about one o'clock on the morning of November 30.) Meanwhile, just east of the pike, massed enemy forces were presumably poised, awaiting only their commander's signal to strike the Federals in flank.[59]

It was a nerve-wracking night march for Yankees who watched Confederate campfires flickering all over the nearby fields and pastures. "Every minute of those anxious hours we were looking for [the Rebels] to awake to the opportunity that was slipping through their fingers," wrote Captain J. K. Shellenberger of the Sixty-fourth Ohio, "and grab hold of it by advancing and opening fire on the congested mass of troops and trains that choked the pike." And General Bradley, wounded as his men helped turn back Cleburne's late afternoon attack, said: "It was the most critical time I have ever seen. If the enemy had shown his usual boldness, I think he would have beaten us disastrously." Little wonder that Lieutenant Colonel Joseph H. Fullerton's entry in the journal of the Fourth Corps reads: "Take it all together, we are in a very bad situation."[60]

Stories have come down through the years describing Schofield at his temporary headquarters at the McKissack house, wringing his hands in despair. While such extraordinary behavior by the young general is rather difficult to imagine, Schofield undoubtedly was nervous, probably very, very nervous. Fearing that the Confederates had occupied a favorable position dominating the pike north of Spring Hill, Schofield led Ruger's division out from town, hoping to force an opening and resume the retreat on the main road. To his surprise (and no doubt profound relief), no evidence of the enemy was found at Thompson's Station except for smoldering campfires. Lacking sufficient numbers and ammunition, the Rebel cavalry had pulled out and the Federal infantry took possession of the crossroads without opposition.

Schofield said he ordered his headquarters troop, under chief engineer Captain William J. Twining, to go at full gallop down the pike toward Franklin. If they got through, Schofield instructed that the situation be telegraphed to

General Thomas at Nashville. Twining was also ordered to examine the means of crossing the Harpeth River. Schofield then sat on his horse and listened until he could no longer discern the clatter of hoofs on the pike in the distance, thus satisfied that the road to Franklin was actually clear.[61]

He turned and rode back to Spring Hill with the good news, arriving shortly after General Cox came in with his division, representing the rear of the army. The time was then midnight, or somewhat later, and the weather was frosty. Ordering Cox to take the advance immediately and march to Franklin, Schofield told Stanley to again take charge of the trains and follow behind Cox. From about one o'clock until five o'clock of the morning of November 30, General Stanley was busy with getting about eight hundred wagons, one at a time, across a single bridge at Spring Hill. About three o'clock Confederate cavalry attacked "in considerable force," but were driven away after a dozen wagons were lost. A little later, some of the Rebel troopers attacked a second time but once more were repelled. The march continued all through the night. Cox had taken "an easy gait" to avoid outmarching the trains, which strung out for approximately five to seven miles. The head of his column approached the outskirts of Franklin about four thirty in the morning.[62]

A "run of luck" had gone in favor of the Union. Schofield took far too great a risk in holding on at Columbia. The chances of placing his army, as Colonel Fullerton observed, "in a very bad situation"—very possibly a disastrous situation—were too great when compared with gaining a little more time for the massing of General Thomas's troops at Nashville. Just as Hood, convinced that the Union commander was trapped, underestimated what Schofield could do, so Schofield assuredly underestimated what Hood could do. Schofield was deceived by Lee's demonstration at Columbia, and lacking reliable information from his cavalry, stayed much too late on the north bank of the Duck River before retreating. Consequently, for several long hours during the evening, until midnight or after, the Confederates could have captured and held the pike in force either north or south of Spring Hill. That such a lodgment would have presented Schofield with problems is a marked understatement.

When Hood awoke on that Wednesday morning to learn that the Yankees had slipped by while he slept, he was infuriated. "Wrathy as a rattlesnake" was General Brown's oft-quoted phrase to describe the Confederate commander's rage. Hood is "striking at everything," said Brown. He "is mad about the enemy getting away last night, and he is going to charge the blame of it on somebody."[63] Several of the ranking Southern generals ate breakfast at Major Nathaniel Cheairs's Rippavilla, and tempers quickly flared as the failure of the previous night dominated everyone's thoughts. Accounts of a near violent quarrel have come down in local tradition. The appeal of a fine meal of "fried ham, hot biscuits and steaming coffee" was eclipsed by angry accusations, demands for apology, and a very tense atmosphere.[64] Furiously addressing his officers, General Hood blamed them rather than himself for not halting Schofield's army.

Primarily he blamed General Cheatham. According to Hood, as later written in his memoirs, he rode up to Cheatham at twilight of November 29 and exclaimed: "General, why in the name of God have you not attacked the enemy and taken possession of that pike?" Cheatham bitterly stated in reply that any such theatrical scene "only occurred in the imagination of General Hood." For the remainder of his life, Hood claimed that the flanking march to Spring Hill was "the best move of my career as a soldier." However, because of the alleged mistakes of Cheatham and others, Hood dramatically declared that "I was thus destined to behold [it] come to naught."[65]

But Hood himself made mistakes, major ones. Because he commanded the Army of Tennessee he was basically responsible for the failure. The general's planning was vague. The breakdown of command responsibility and communication is a textbook lesson in how not to run an army. His failure to remain on the field to see that his orders were implemented is inexcusable. He seemed depleted of energy and aggressiveness. Also, at the same time, he was comfortably and strangely optimistic. Undoubtedly his bodily ills played a considerable role in Hood's failings. His experience manifestly demonstrates the folly of any general commanding an army in the field who is not in excellent physical condition.

Cheatham too was at fault. Whether because of a misunderstanding of Hood's plan or some other reason, the corps commander failed to follow Hood's order to seize the pike, focusing instead on trying to take Spring Hill, only to cease his attempt shortly after six o'clock. Just what Cheatham did afterward is a mystery. Strange indeed was his inertia toward possible Yankee movements along the pike. One of Hood's staff officers even claimed he saw Cheatham talking with Hood after dark, "remonstrating with General Hood against a night attack." Before Hood's midnight order to advance and fire on anyone marching on the pike, Cheatham had already heard from one of his own staff officers that enemy troops were on the road. Apparently responding personally to neither warning, Cheatham contented himself with only passing Hood's order on to Edward Johnson. When Johnson reported that all was quiet, Cheatham seems to have laid the matter to rest.[66]

There is also the intriguing story that bachelor Cheatham, who "apparently did have an eye for the ladies," spent some time at the home of Jessie Peters. This rumor came to the attention of Union General James Wilson, who later reported it in his memoir *Under the Old Flag*. "Perhaps," as Cheatham's biographer wrote, the general "did avail himself of [Jessie's] charms," but to establish any probability on this issue "is virtually impossible, given the uncertain time sequence of events during the late afternoon and night."[67] Probably the tale is another of those Spring Hill mysteries that seems fated to be forever unresolved.

Strangely too, General Stewart appeared somewhat nonchalant about blocking the pike. But was Stewart actually ordered to do so? Sam Elliott's recent biography of Stewart suggests that Hood did not request the Tennessean to place his men across the road. Elliott points out that after the war, Stewart consistently defended himself, remarking that "as Hood was present on the field, he should have made sure his orders were obeyed," and if Hood gave an order to Stewart to block the pike, Hood should have charged the corps commander with insubordination for not obeying. According to J. P. Young's account, however, General Stewart told him in a letter of April 1895, that Hood had instructed the corps commander to "put my right across the turnpike beyond Spring Hill."[68]

And where were the division and brigade commanders while the Federals were marching northward? They too must shoulder some measure of responsibility for permitting the enemy to slip by. As for General Forrest, Captain H. A. Tyler of Forrest's command said that he and the general sat on their horses about dark near Spring Hill and observed the Bluecoats passing along the pike. Tyler claimed a frustrated Forrest threw up a clenched fist and exclaimed: "——— Hood! Had he supported me here as he promised, that whole army would have been our prisoners!"[69] Perhaps such a memorable scene did occur, but even the usually energized cavalry commander did little to control the pike north of Spring Hill that night. Some of his troopers were on the road briefly but soon fell back. Likely Forrest thought it useless to waste any more men at such a late hour—even if he did find more ammunition—knowing Hood had long before retired for the night.

Despite the many Confederate mistakes, the contest for Spring Hill was so close (if Forrest had been only a few minutes earlier at noon for example) that a slight change could easily have brought about a different outcome. Surely a more capable Southern commander—perhaps even a more healthy Hood— could have eliminated some of the confusion and time wasted in organizing the Grayclad ranks for an assault to drive Stanley from the village before Schofield could reinforce him. Once it was obvious that Confederate efforts against Stanley were not succeeding, the best move for Hood was to make a lodgment on the pike north of Spring Hill. Early on, such would have been an insurance move against Schofield's possible escape. Later, it was patently the priority maneuver. This was what Schofield most feared, and rightly so.

But the pike was not blocked and Schofield had escaped. Twenty years ago the author wrote the following, and it still seems applicable: "The strange inertia of key Confederate officers remains a puzzle. Attempts to unravel what happened and why never quite seem to explain. The suspicion of something more lingers. Were the rumors of wild parties merely spice to the Spring Hill legend? Or might there have been some germ of truth therein?"[70]

Captain H. A. Tyler, who was quoted above, also said that "as the sun was setting," he observed a woman standing on the front porch of her house. "Struck by her great beauty," the captain reported that he rode up to the gate of the house and "she came out and joined me." After she answered his questions, Tyler claimed the woman asked if General Forrest was present. When Tyler pointed the general out to her, according to Tyler, she then said "she would like to meet him and speak to him. I said, 'Who are you madam?' and she replied: 'Mrs. Peters. General Forrest will know me.' I, of course, knew her too," said Tyler, who immediately galloped back and "told General Forrest that Mrs. Peters wished to see him. I took him to her and left them talking. . . ."[71]

From accounts such as Captain Tyler's, tales of improprieties are sometimes concocted. The captain's story may well have contributed to some of the rumors about the love life of Jessie Peters. The situation, however, assuredly could have been totally innocent—and probably was. Any number of explanations for a conversation between Mrs. Peters and General Forrest are possible. Even if Jessie Peters sought more than polite conversation, it seems rather unlikely that Forrest, who had intensely disliked Earl Van Dorn—once declaring to friends in Columbia that he would like to cut Van Dorn's heart out and "stomp" it[72]—would have been at all interested in a woman whom people generally believed had found Van Dorn intimately attractive. Presumably, too, Forrest might have set up his headquarters at the home of Mrs. Peters. Instead, he picked a house about half a mile distant.

Then there was the damning account of Colonel Henry Stone, assistant adjutant general on the staff of George H. Thomas. Attempting to explain the Spring Hill failure of the Confederates a few years afterward, Stone said that "there were queer doings in the rebel lines among some of the leading officers. Nearly two years before," Stone explained, "the rebel General Van Dorn had been shot to death by the infuriated husband of a fascinating woman who lived in a large mansion near Spring Hill. As the rebel army now approached, he left for Nashville, but she remained behind." The Union colonel proceeded to claim that "there was music and dancing and feasting, and other gods than Mars were worshipped. During the sacrificing at their shrines," concluded Stone, "the whole of Schofield's . . . force moved silently . . . by. . . . But in the morning there was much swearing. . . . Cheatham and Forrest and the others who had given themselves up to the charms of society the night before were more chagrined at the disappearance of the enemy than at their own lapse from duty."[73]

That a Federal colonel in Nashville could have known what the Confederate officers in Spring Hill were doing that night is clearly suspect. The fact that Cheatham liked his whiskey (once praising fellow Tennessean Jack Daniel's product with a widely circulated ringing endorsement as "beyond compare and without a doubt the finest whiskey I ever tasted," going on to declare that "Once one has sampled his first sip, it is impossible to refuse a second.")[74] makes the general an easy target for anyone seeking to place blame, or anyone who is inclined to play fast and loose with rumors. It is unlikely, however, that Cheatham could so long have retained a high position of command if he was a habitual drunkard. (Of course the key word here is "habitual" and does not mean that Cheatham did not get drunk on occasion.) As for Forrest, he was never known, through four years of war, to allow any human frailty—not greed, not alcohol, not women, not gambling, not anything—to interfere with the performance of his duty as a Confederate officer.

Another soldier's story, focusing on the possible role of whiskey, deserves to be taken more seriously than Colonel Stone's account. This is Confederate scout John Gregory's claim of "a big feast" at Absalom Thompson's plantation. In fact, Gregory said "there had been a good deal of drinking among the officers (and some of the soldiers) during the day." As noted earlier, Gregory claimed that "Cheatham was full drunk." He also said "Cleburne and Granberry [doubtless Granbury] drank quite freely" and was of the opinion that Walthall "had too much liquor." Gregory thought the hour was "eleven or twelve at night before the eating and drinking stopped." Relative to Forrest, under whom the scout had served for some time, Gregory reported that the general "did not like at all the drinking and carousing going on among the higher officers." When Forrest, and again according to Gregory, told Hood that the Federals were "getting through" on the pike, Hood said, allegedly punctuating his reply with "cussing," that "he'd find the Yankees in the morning."[75]

Interestingly, the editor of *Blue & Gray Magazine* remarked that "local Spring Hill residents claim Absalom Thompson was a fanatic teetotaler and would have permitted no one, not even a Confederate general, to drink under his roof." On the other hand, granting that Thompson did not set a sumptuous table abundantly stocked with alcohol, he perhaps had little control over "what may have happened behind his back," as *Blue & Gray* also noted. Besides, it is not certain that Thompson was continuously present that evening.[76]

But John Gregory's claim that Cleburne "drank quite freely" seems unlikely. Captain Irving A. Buck, Cleburne's assistant adjutant general, who knew the Irishman well, wrote that Cleburne "abstained from the use of tobacco and liquor." Buck said the general "feared the possible effect of intoxicants" upon his ability to properly discharge his duties as a leader of men in the army. Cleburne, continued Buck, "said that a single glass of wine would disturb the steadiness of his hand" in firing a pistol, for example, or "effect his calculations in playing chess. . . ."[77] It is doubtful that a general who felt his responsibilities so keenly drank anything alcoholic on the night of November 29—and extremely doubtful that he would have been drinking "quite freely." Perhaps Gregory, whose knowledge of Cleburne could only have been superficial, assumed that all Irishmen drank heavily. The comment about Cleburne creates a touch of skepticism concerning all said by Gregory relative to alcohol. On the other hand, November 29 witnessed a few strange and unusual occurrences and Gregory's account just might have contained some truth.

Yet another soldier in Forrest's command, John Johnston, focused on the role of whiskey as the basic cause of the Confederate failure at Spring Hill. "Some blame Cheatham, others John C. Brown, some even Hood," said Johnston. "I think probably the fault lay between all of them and that *whiskey—whiskey* [Johnston's emphasis] that accursed thing—had a great deal to do with it."[78] (Johnston was in college preparing for the Presbyterian ministry when the war began, a fact that might be pertinent when evaluating what he said about whiskey.)

Before bidding adieu to the subject of "demon rum," it is interesting to note that corps commander Stephen D. Lee weighed in with his opinion after the war, placing the blame for failure to attack at Spring Hill upon John C. Brown, who "either lacked nerve on that day or was drunk (no doubt the latter)."[79] Lee, of course, was back at Columbia during the events in question. The general was hardly in the best location to know about happenings in Spring Hill.

For the Southern army, the tragic significance of the fiasco at Spring Hill was its impact on General Hood. Far worse than criticizing his corps and division commanders, the Confederate general blamed the men in the ranks too. Hood wrote that "grave concern" troubled him upon discovering that the army, "after a forward march of 180 miles, was still seemingly unwilling to accept battle unless under the protection of breastworks." Worst of all possible conclusions, the young general, totally unable to face the fact that he lacked the capacity to command an army, somehow imagined that for purposes of discipline and élan the men needed to launch a frontal assault against a prepared enemy position. Other than Hood's biased rendition of events, there is no reason to think the miserable episode of the Grayclads at Spring Hill revealed any lack of courage on the part of the soldiers in the Army of Tennessee.[80]

Quite the contrary, such evidence as exists indicates the men in the ranks were appalled by the way their officers botched a rare opportunity to strike a devastating blow at the Yankees. A veteran of the Twenty-seventh Alabama Infantry kept a diary in which he wrote that, "having accomplished the very thing which General Hood asked us to do, it was provoking to . . . lie still and let the golden opportunity slip away from us. . . ." As J. P. Cannon continued to write, he said "Every private was impressed with the idea that a fearful blunder had been made, and many remarks were made uncomplimentary to those in command. . . ." A Mississippian recalled that he had "never seen more intense rage and profound disgust than was expressed by the weary, foot-sore, battle-torn Confederate soldiers when they discovered that their officers had allowed their prey to escape."[81]

What then may be said in summary of the Spring Hill affair? To quote a key actor from each side seems felicitous. A Confederate general deeply involved in it all, corps commander Alexander P. Stewart, wrote: "There is a Divinity that shapes our ends. . . . If in the next life we are permitted an insight into the events of this life and their causes, we shall . . . find how much Providence, and how very little human agency and planning have to do with all really noble and grand achievements. And how little credit is due to many who pass among us as great."[82] Stewart's Divine Providence explanation probably satisfied many. On the other hand, a Union general who was even more intensely engaged at Spring Hill than Stewart, set forth a quite different concept. Major General David S. Stanley, while sarcastically downplaying General Schofield's proud account of the campaign and especially Spring Hill, wrote that, as quoted in the opening chapter, "all said in Schofield's book as to his foreseeing and providing to meet the events as they unfolded, is the merest bosh." For Stanley, "circumstances entirely accidental and the run of luck in our favor" were the true determinants at Spring Hill.[83] And, it seems essential to add, the incapacity of the Confederate commander.

4

General Hood
Has Betrayed Us

Thus the armies came to Franklin. The Federal force was well in the lead, of course. If General Schofield had had his way, the Northerners would have been across the Harpeth River and marching for Nashville before the Graycoats approached Franklin's southern outskirts. He neither intended nor wanted to fight at Franklin. Circumstances at the Harpeth River, however, changed everything.

After issuing his final orders at Spring Hill, Schofield mounted up once more, rode to the front of the slow-moving, long Blue column, and overtook General Cox. Topping the Winstead–Breezy Hill range, which formed the southern border of the plain of Franklin, they descended from the high ridge toward the town. The time was still too early for the sun to appear in the east. As they approached one of the outermost houses, the home of Fountain Branch Carter as fate would have it, Schofield ordered Cox to mass his troops on both sides of the turnpike, leaving the road clear for the wagons to come through.

Exhausted soldiers settled down for a short nap or boiled coffee, while Schofield rode on into town seeking Captain Twining from whom he expected to learn about the condition of the river crossings.

The Harpeth had been abnormally high, swollen by recent rains. The Union commander hoped to find a pontoon bridge spanning the stream. Twice, on November 28 and shortly after noon on the 29th, he had requested a bridge from Nashville. If it were in place, the artillery, wagons, and infantry could all be safely on the river's north bank before the Rebels arrived in force. But—the bridge was not there.[1]

Quickly riding to the Carter house, where General Cox had established his headquarters, Schofield roused his division commander from a doze into which he had drifted. Schofield spoke, as Cox recalled, with "a deep earnestness of feeling which he rarely showed."[2] He said the pontoons were not there, the turnpike bridge had been wrecked by the rising river, a second bridge partially destroyed by fire, and the ford hardly passable. Nevertheless, Schofield had made a decision to fight, if he must, with the river at his back, thus hoping to save the wagon train (not to mention the embarrassment attendant to losing such a huge quantity of supplies).

Cox was placed in charge of the front line and ordered to entrench astride the Columbia Pike, choosing the best defensive ground available. Cox's own Third Division, temporarily commanded by General James W. Reilly, would dig in on the left and Thomas H. Ruger's Second Division on the right, awaiting the arrival of the three divisions still on the march from Spring Hill. When the artillery of the Twenty-third Corps came in, it was to be crossed to the north bank of the Harpeth as soon as the ford could be made passable. The Fourth Corps artillery would be positioned along the front line. The wagons, already beginning to rumble in, were to be parked in the cross streets of town, leaving open the main pike.

Schofield then rode back to the Harpeth, anxiously seeking to devise and implement any means of crossing that might be possible. First, attention focused on the approaches to the ford. The banks on both sides of the river required scraping because the grade was too steep for the heavily loaded army wagons. Since the railroad bridge was sound, planks could be laid across the rails. A detail of men was ordered to ransack the town for wood to put that structure in condition for crossing. They also had to construct wagon approaches to the railroad bridge.

A bridge built for the passage of wagons had been burned earlier in the year, during a skirmish, but fortunately it was not completely destroyed. Sawing off the bridge's support posts at the water's edge, the men attached new cross beams and stringers, then proceeded to plank over the hastily rigged framework. This bridge, intended only for the passage of soldiers, turned out to be suitable for wagons as well. Not until noon, however, was any other crossing than the ford practicable for wagons. And the ford, once it had been satisfactorily scraped, still entailed a slow and laborious process to get the wagons over to the north bank.[3]

As soon as possible, Schofield wanted artillery across the Harpeth and placed in Fort Granger, atop a high bluff overlooking the river just east of the railroad bridge. Built in 1862 by Major General Gordon Granger—a heavily bearded, profane-talking, West Point career man, distinguished for reinforcing General Thomas in the nick of time at Chickamauga with a three-brigade division—the fort once had quartered over eight thousand men and twenty-four guns. Abandoned for some time, the fort now came alive. Captain Giles J. Cockerill's Battery D, First Ohio Volunteer Light Artillery, a powerful battery of three-inch rifled guns, was positioned in the fort. Fort Granger lay approximately a mile, as the crow flies, from where the Union front line was being formed. Its rifled guns could readily command an enemy approach from the south and east. Other artillery pieces would be placed on both sides of the Harpeth, on the extreme left of Schofield's line.[4]

The general was finally in touch with his cavalry again. James Harrison Wilson was some two and one-half miles away, off to the east on the road to Triune. Orders were dispatched instructing Wilson to protect the army's immediate (left) flank and rear. Schofield was very worried about the Confederate cavalry. He had little confidence that General Wilson could help. Schofield wrote General Thomas that he had no idea where Forrest and the Rebel cavalry might be. He also said, as noted earlier, that Wilson was "entirely unable" to cope with Forrest.[5] Meanwhile, work progressed rapidly at the river crossing.

Franklin lies in a bend of the Big Harpeth River, with the opening to the south. In the late 1700s white settlers began an all-too-familiar process, wresting the rich land from the Native Americans who for many centuries had lived and roamed the region. Usually credited with being the first white man to build a house on the site of the town was a settler named Ewen Cameron. Soon a number of log cabins composed a little village named in honor of Benjamin Franklin, with the town officially recognized by the Tennessee General Assembly on October 26, 1799. By the Civil War, Franklin boasted about a thousand residents and was the county seat of Williamson, the third wealthiest county in Tennessee. The money was derived from cotton-growing, timber, and livestock. The Tennessee & Alabama Railroad certainly helped the town's affluence, connecting the village with Nashville and the Memphis & Charleston Railroad in north Alabama. Franklin and its close neighbor Triune, were also known for their private male and female academies. Further touches of sophistication were evidenced

The William Harrison House. Photograph by Rudy E. Sanders.

by a local newspaper, the *Franklin Review and Journal,* several churches, and some fine homes.[6]

Among the more notable of the impressive residences was a two-storied, white-columned, brick structure, known as the Harrison House. It was built around 1848 by William Harrison, one-time sheriff of Williamson County. The imposing edifice still stands on the west side of the Columbia-Franklin Pike, gracing the valley just south of the Winstead-Breezy Hills. Destined to be forever linked with the war's carnage, the Harrison house was where the mortally wounded cavalryman John H. Kelly was brought to die only a few weeks earlier. Struck down in a nearby fight, the Alabama native is said to have been the youngest general in the Confederate army. On November 30, General Hood selected the Harrison house as his headquarters, there meditating upon an attack plan that would send more than seventeen hundred Confederates to their death that afternoon. And that same night, two of Hood's wounded generals, William A. Quarles and John C. Carter, were transported to the Harrison place. Quarles would survive a shattered left arm, but Carter, after suffering for ten days, finally succumbed to his injuries, the youngest of six Confederate generals who died at Franklin.[7]

The Fountain B. Carter House. Photograph by Rudy E. Sanders.

Even today, if one approaches the Harrison house from the south—and if favored by an Indian summer afternoon in the latter days of November— thoughts of Civil War generals astride their mounts, sweaty soldiers marching on the pike, the crippled and angry Hood in the library of the house contemplating an attack, seem not so long ago and far away. That is, until one ascends the Winstead–Breezy Hill range to gaze upon Franklin's present-day development. Then the spell cast by the Harrison house quickly slips away.

Also among the large and magnificent homes adorning the Franklin community was Randall McGavock's Carnton. McGavock was a former mayor of Nashville, whose extensive landholdings along the Harpeth River (lands that rumors held were acquired through "a one-sided Indian trade for a pony and a second-hand shotgun") led him to take up permanent residence near Franklin. Southeast of the town and a few hundred yards west of the Lewisburg Pike, McGavock completed his great house with its formal gardens in the late 1820s, and called it Carnton in honor of his ancestral home in Ireland. Andrew Jackson, James K. Polk, John Overton, Sam Houston, and other notable personages are said to have been guests at the McGavock home. Carnton, however, like the Harrison house, was fated to become associated foremost with the tragedy of war, although its builder died several years before the conflict. When the slaughter of the awful struggle at Franklin ceased at last, Carnton became a hospital where hundreds of wounded men were brought, many dying with their blood sometimes staining the floors, and the bodies of four dead Confederate generals laid on the back veranda.[8]

Yet another significant home, still bearing the marks of shots fired that day, was Fountain Branch Carter's simple but impressive brick structure fronting on the west side of the Columbia-Franklin Pike. The house, as previously noted, was commandeered by General Cox for his headquarters. With a double door in the center front, flanked by columns, the entrance was further adorned by a fanlight transom. Large windows, equally distant on each side of the door, and stepped parapet walls at both ends of the house, topped with a chimney, convey an overall sense of balance and proportion. A fine home, although not on the scale of Carnton or the Harrison house, its location destined it to be in the midst of the fiercest and bloodiest action of the day.

Long before Schofield led the Federals into Franklin early on the morning of November 30, the town had experienced a number of war-related episodes. One of the more memorable came on April 10, 1863, when Earl Van Dorn led the Twenty-eighth Mississippi Cavalry in a charge into the town. Approaching by the Lewisburg Pike, Van Dorn's foray resulted in a sharp skirmish, even a small-scale battle said some. Aided by the guns of Fort Granger, the Union garrison forced the Graycoats to retreat. The attack came less than a month before Dr. Peters shot and killed Van Dorn.[9]

By late 1864, the Civil War had gone on for more than three and one-half years. But in Franklin, nothing to compare with what was now about to happen had yet occurred. The town's previous war experiences would soon pale into relative insignificance when contrasted with the bloodletting of November 30.

Although General Schofield did not want to fight at Franklin, he could hardly have asked for a better defensive position from which to repel a frontal assault. From the river southward, the land rises steadily for a mile or more to the site of the Carter house, an elevation about forty feet above the heart of Franklin at "the square." South of the Carter house a plain slopes ever so slightly away, while appearing almost flat. In General Cox's words, the open fields slant "very gently from the [Union] line," and "along the whole front of the Federal position," continuing for more than a mile and a half to the Winstead-Breezy Hills, which form a southern enclosure. Only a few farm buildings, with orchards here and there in the distance, obscured vision in any direction. "Very few battlefields of the war," wrote another Union officer, "were so free from obstruction to the view."[10] If the Confederates should elect to try a frontal assault, they would have to advance some twenty-five hundred yards across largely open, gradually ascending ground.

Schofield's men enjoyed yet another advantage. They did not have to construct an entirely new line of fortifications. The greater part of their entrenchments had been erected in 1862–63. In many places the soldiers needed only to improve and strengthen these works. Other defenses had become partially obliterated and did require considerable labor. The thud of the pick and the clink of the shovel sounded steadily through the morning. Tired men toiled, mostly in silence, for several hours as they strove to secure their position.

The Union line stretched from the river on the east to the river on the west, crossing the Columbia-Franklin Pike slightly south of the Carter house. Perhaps the best way to visualize the overall position is to use the Columbia-Franklin Pike as a divider separating the two strongest portions of the Federal line. East of the pike, the Bluecoats found a substantial line of entrenchments already in place and proceeded to improve it. This part of the fortifications originated on the far left flank, where the river and the tracks of the Nashville & Alabama Railroad ran closely parallel for approximately a quarter of a mile. The line led west from the river, bearing south, on a rough arc that passed across the Lewisburg Pike and continued to the Columbia Pike.

A Southern attack against this portion of the line, regardless of numerical strength, would have little chance of success. Besides marching across generally flat and open terrain to face the powerful guns of Fort Granger, the Confederates nearing the railroad and the Lewisburg Pike sector would be raked by enfilading fire from artillery stationed across the river on their right flank. Also, much of the Federal line across the entire front from the Harpeth to the Columbia Pike was covered with a thick hedge of Osage orange. Soldiers cut down as much as they could in the time available, and sharpened the branches to make an abatis (an obstacle formed of trees felled toward the enemy). The remainder of the hedge was so strong that it too served as a major obstruction to an enemy assault. Colonel Israel N. Stiles, commanding the Union brigade closest to the river on the far left, said that "substantial works" were at once erected, and "such portions of our front as were not already obstructed by a well-grown and almost impenetrable hedge were covered with a strong abatis made of the hedges which ran at right angles with the works."[11]

While not the hedgerows of World War II Normandy, these barriers were certainly formidable. They were used too by Colonel John S. Casement's brigade, next in line from left to right, to construct an abatis across its front. "Jack" Casement's entrenchments were additionally topped by head logs with a three-inch space through which rifles could be fired. And, one of Casement's units, Company A of the Sixty-fifth Ohio, possessed a considerable advantage in weaponry, armed with the sixteen-shot Henry repeating rifles. Head logs were also placed atop the earthworks along the front of Brigadier General James W. Reilly's brigade, which extended the Bluecoat line westward to the

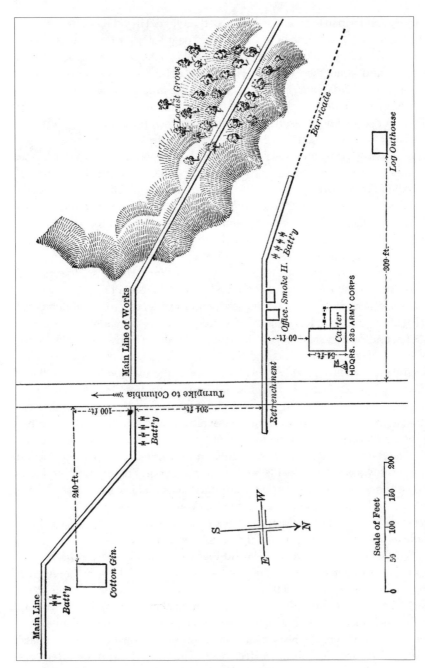

Carter Hill map. From Jacob D. Cox, The Battle of Franklin.

Columbia Pike. Finally—not that the Federal infantry actually required any more strength in this sector—salient angles for cross-firing existed at intervals, in addition to embrasures for artillery pieces.[12]

As for the Columbia-Franklin Pike itself, which had been left open for the passage of wagons and artillery, that point might have appeared vulnerable when viewed by the Confederates from a distance. Such a conclusion would have been an unfortunate misapprehension. Although no breastworks topped with head logs and fronted by an abatis blocked the road, nevertheless the position was quite stout. Part of the strength came from three artillery batteries that had been stationed close to the pike. One battery was positioned west of the road and slightly to the right of Fountain Branch Carter's smokehouse. Two more batteries took position east of the pike. One of these rested only a few feet from the road at the point where the main line of works crossed the pike. It was situated to fire straight down the road. The third battery, slightly more advanced and located some three hundred feet east of the pike, was stationed in front of Mr. Carter's cotton gin.[13]

In addition to the three, four-gun batteries, the Federals had another advantage at the pike. About 240 feet east of the road, according to General Cox's measurement, the Union line of entrenchments, which in that area had been extending directly west, suddenly slanted sharply northwest, continuing on a diagonal line until almost reaching the pike, and then turned due west again. Thus any Rebels advancing up the road toward the Carter house would find their right flank exposed to an enfilading fire from both infantry and artillery. Bluecoat infantry along the slanted portion of the line already faced partially toward the pike, while the artillery pieces readily could be turned due westward if necessary.[14]

"The cotton gin formed a marked salient in the line," explained General Cox in a detailed description that helps to visualize the scene. "A little to the right of [the gin] the works made an angle toward the rear, coming back to join the epaulement of four guns on the left of the turnpike, ninety yards south of the Carter house." To the west of the pike the line extended, continued Cox, "at right angles to the road for fifty yards on level ground, and then bent to the rear, descending the slope somewhat as it did so. This was the purpose of placing a battery on the summit at the right of the brick smokehouse, which could fire over the heads of the infantry in the front line. . . ."[15]

The Bluecoats at the pike could play yet another ace. About two hundred yards inside the breastworks, and north of the Carter house, was located the seven-regiment brigade of Colonel Emerson Opdycke. Opdycke was a thirty-four-year-old Ohioan with a well-deserved reputation as a fierce fighter. His brigade, strategically positioned, could provide quick reinforcement at the pike if necessary.[16]

The other major sector of strong Union fortifications extended westward from the Columbia-Franklin Pike to the Carter's Creek Pike, a distance in a straight line of nearly half a mile. Of course the Federal entrenchments did not follow a straight line, instead forming a rough and slight crescent shape, generally bending northwestward. Here were located the two brigades of General Thomas Ruger, with Colonel Silas A. Strickland's command on the left, its flank resting on the Columbia Pike, and Colonel Orlando H. Moore's brigade extending the line westward. Moore's right flank was on the Carter's Creek Pike. Strickland's brigade was in a two-line formation and Moore's smaller command in single-line formation.

General Ruger said that "a small locust grove" fronted a portion of the division's line near the left, "which was felled, forming a fair abatis" protecting Strickland's brigade. Fronting part of Moore's brigade was "a row of fruit trees," which was also cut down to make an abatis for the earthworks on the division's right. As to the general development of the position, "I caused the line of breastworks to be made in the form of a broken line," reported General Ruger, "thus . . . providing a cross-fire on portions of the ground" along the division front. The battery slightly west of the Carter house was well positioned to strengthen Ruger's line, as were guns located at other places along the entrenchments to the west.[17]

The final sector of the Yankee defenses, stretching on a rough arc from the Carter's Creek Pike to the Harpeth River northwest of Franklin, was a pronounced contrast to the rest of their position. It was surely the weakest portion of the Union line. Here three brigades were assigned to cover approximately three-quarters of a mile. Brigadier General William Grose's seven regiments held the left, the brigade's flank resting on the Carter's Creek Pike. On the right, with its flank on the Harpeth River, was another seven-regiment brigade, commanded by Brigadier General Walter C. Whitaker. Stationed in the middle were the four regiments of Colonel Isaac M. Kirby's brigade.[18]

No previously constructed defensive works existed anywhere along this section. "In position by 1 P.M.," reported General Grose, "all hands went vigorously to work making barricades, preparing for the reception of the enemy. . . ."[19] There was not sufficient time, however, and General Whitaker said his brigade's line of works was "but half finished" when the Graycoats attacked.[20] One of Grose's regimental commanders reported that he "kept [the men] hard at work making rifle pits until about 4 P.M.," when the enemy attack began. "I ordered the men," continued Colonel John E. Bennett of the Seventy-fifth Illinois, "to drop their intrenching tools . . . and take their places behind the uncompleted works. . . ."[21] Another regimental commander referred to the "hasty breast-works [that] were thrown up," but noted also that "no time was given to construct works of sufficient strength. . . ."[22]

Other reports from Federal officers hint at further weaknesses in this part of the line. An Indiana captain said his regiment was "composed mostly of new levies or drafted men, and entirely ignorant of the use of arms. . . ."[23] Colonel Kirby told of "a gap between [his] brigade and that of General Grose." Two companies were being shifted to close the gap when the Southerners attacked.[24] More confirmation of the Northern vulnerability west of Franklin came from the Confederates. General William Bate reported that "The works to the left of the Carter's Creek turnpike were not strong, and with a vigorous assault should have been carried; a fact, however, not known until the next day."[25]

The weakness of the Yankee position west and north of the Carter's Creek Pike proved of no consequence. Conditions in that sector could not be evaluated from atop the Winstead-Breezy Hills. The distance in a straight line from Hood's command post to that portion of the Union line was fully three miles, with a series of hills, knobs, and ridges additionally complicating any attempt with field glasses to examine the Federal defenses in that direction. General Hood had no intention of taking the time to conduct a proper reconnaissance before attacking. Thus the vast weight of Southern manpower would be massed between the Lewisburg and Carter's Creek Pikes, advancing against the strongest portions of the Union fortifications.

Still another factor favored Schofield's position. The Graycoats forming for attack would be spread out across a distance of some two miles. As they marched toward the Federal line, however, the Confederate units would be constricted into less and less space, finally converging to a front of less than a mile. Such compacting of their forces meant that the advance would be slowed, and probably, to some degree, disorganized and confused.

By noon much of the apprehension of the Blueclad troops subsided. Not only had they slipped free from the impending trap at Spring Hill, now they had strong fortifications in front of them, from the river on their left to the Carter's Creek Pike on their right. All the men were then inside the line, with the single exception of George Wagner's rear guard, still sniping at the Rebels, from their position atop the Winstead-Breezy Hills. The Columbia Pike was empty and relative quiet prevailed, after hours of noisy wagons lumbering along the road, the shouting of orders intermixed with a bit of cursing, and the clattering of tools. Troops at the breastworks rested or prepared a little food. Many of them, too tired to get dinner, and thankful for a little respite, simply lunched on crackers and raw bacon, and dozed. "There was now a period of rest and refreshment for the officers and men of the main line," recalled

General Cox.[26] The day had developed bright and warm—a good example of Indian summer. Certainly the weather was not a typical last day of November.

"Nothing appeared so improbable as that [the Confederates] would assault," said General David Stanley in his campaign report.[27] General Cox later wrote, "None of us were quick to believe that a *coup de main* would be attempted."[28] Many of the general officers held the same opinion. The Union position was formidable. By this late stage of the war everyone knew that rifled weapons had dramatically strengthened those who defended a fortified position. One soldier behind breastworks and armed with a rifled musket was the equal of two or three—maybe even, dependant on circumstances, four or five—attackers advancing in the open.

With the trains and artillery in and the troops entrenched, an attack seemed highly unlikely. Schofield was in town at the home of a Union sympathizer, where he ate dinner with the doctor and his wife. When the Rebels did move again, Schofield thought Hood would try to turn his position by crossing the river, most probably on the east flank. All of the day's correspondence between Schofield and General Thomas in Nashville conveys this expectation. Clearly another flanking maneuver was the most sensible course for the Southern commander.[29]

Meanwhile, around two o'clock in the afternoon, the last of the Federal troops coming in from Spring Hill were moving up the pike toward the entrenchments manned by their comrades. These men were General Wagner's rear guards. Rather than being allowed to march on into the main works, however, Wagner was halted and ordered to take position astride the pike a quarter of a mile or so south of the Union line. The purpose was to better observe Hood's movements. In the seemingly unlikely event of an enemy attack they were expected to fall back within the main works. But only two of Wagner's three brigades deployed in that advanced position. Joseph Conrad's brigade filed off east of the pike, except for one regiment that deployed with John Lane's brigade west of the road.[30]

The third brigade of Wagner's division, and the last to come up the pike, was the unit commanded by Colonel Emerson Opdycke. When General Wagner rode forward to meet Opdycke, and ordered him to deploy his men in the advanced position, the colonel forcefully objected. Prophetically he declared that "troops out in front of the breastworks were in a good position to aid the enemy and nobody else!" Tired from the Spring Hill fight, then an all-night watch against an attack, followed by a morning skirmish-march as rear guard of the army, Opdycke said his brigade was "worn out" and entitled to rest. While Opdycke and Wagner talked, the two officers rode along the pike together, with the brigade marching behind, until they reached the main line.

Emerson Opdycke.
Library of Congress.

About two hundred yards inside the breastworks and north of the Carter house, as previously noted, the brigade came to a large, clear space and finally came to a stop. At that point, Wagner turned to ride away, calling out one last remark: "Well, Opdycke, fight when and where you damn please; we all know you'll fight!" The men of the brigade stacked arms and fell out on the ground.[31]

Of course neither Opdycke nor his men, like virtually all of the Federals, expected to fight that afternoon. General Schofield was anticipating transferring the troops across the river at dark. Already the general had moved his headquarters north of the Harpeth to the home of Alpheus Truett, located on the east side of the pike to Nashville. The Truett home was less than a half-mile north of the river and within easy riding distance of the vantage point at Fort Granger. Around three o'clock Schofield issued orders for the soldiers to be withdrawn from their positions at nightfall.[32]

The Union commander's primary concern at mid-afternoon was protecting the army's flanks. Dispatches from General Wilson indicated Hood was attempting to cross the river with infantry, about two or three miles to the east. Just before two o'clock Wilson reported that "rebel infantry" were approaching a ford "three miles above Franklin, apparently with the intention of crossing." Nearly an hour later Wilson said the Confederate movement "has not yet developed itself into anything more than the appearance of the enemy's infantry in the neighborhood of the river." But, added the cavalry commander, "citizens say they can cross anywhere." Shortly after this message, another dispatch from Wilson reported that "the enemy charged the picket at Hughes' Ford and he [bearer of the dispatch] thinks they crossed."[33]

Upon receiving the message Schofield immediately ordered a brigade of infantry to Hughes' Ford, "to check the crossing of the enemy at that point." At the same time he sent a dispatch to General Thomas saying that Hood "now has a large force, probably two corps, in my front, and seems prepared [so recorded in Schofield's telegrams-sent book, but in Thomas's telegrams-received book, the words are "preparing" and "above"] to cross the river above and below [the town]. I think he can effect a crossing tomorrow . . . and probably tonight, if he attempts it. A worse position than this for an inferior force could hardly be found. . . . I have just learned that the enemy's cavalry is already crossing. . . ."[34]

Assuredly Schofield was worried. Some type of flanking attack was the reasonable move for Hood to make. It was to counter such a maneuver that Schofield had placed Thomas J. Wood's infantry division on the north bank of the river, as well as positioning batteries in the fort. Toward his flanks the nervous Schofield continually cast his eyes. But he was wrong. John Bell Hood had no plans for a turning movement. "I cannot guess his movements," Sherman earlier complained about Hood, as he contrasted him with Joe Johnston who, according to Sherman, "was a sensible man and only did sensible things."[35] Schofield well might have echoed Cump's words. He was about to learn, for the second time in two days, that he too could not guess the movements of the Confederate general.

Through the morning of November 30 the ragged Confederates tramped northward. The pike on which they marched wound over the hills and through the bluegrass valleys of a picturesque countryside. The sun rose higher in the sky and the temperature grew pleasantly warmer, promising the most agreeable day in some time. Nevertheless, the mood of the men was somber. The effect of the Spring Hill failure "was bad on our men," wrote a Southerner from Arkansas. "The thing was looked upon as a terrible blunder," with some blaming Hood, some Cheatham, as the dismal episode "cast a shadow. . . ."[36] It was a long shadow and, as if accompanied by a cold wind blowing, chilled the confidence and enthusiasm of recent days.

Stewart's corps was in the lead, followed by Cheatham's. Lee's corps, with most of the army's guns, marched far in the rear, some of the column having not yet cleared the Columbia area. Somewhere ahead of Stewart's infantry Nathan Bedford Forrest had his cavalry harassing the Yankee rear guard as the morning wore on. And somewhere back with Cheatham's corps rode a troubled and aroused Patrick Cleburne. He sent a message ahead to General Brown, requesting him to hold up while Cleburne came forward to talk. "When he came up we rode apart from the column," remembered Brown. Cleburne told him "with much feeling" that he had learned that Hood "was endeavoring to place upon him [Cleburne] the responsibility of allowing the enemy to pass our position" at Spring Hill. When Brown replied that he hoped Cleburne was mistaken, the latter responded: "No, I think not; my information comes through a very reliable channel."

Brown said Cleburne declared that "he could not afford to rest under such an imputation" and intended to have the matter fully investigated as soon as there was opportunity. "General Cleburne was quite angry," continued Brown, "and evidently . . . deeply hurt. . . ." Brown said he then asked Cleburne who he believed to be responsible for the Federals' escape, to which the general replied that "of course the responsibility rests with the commander-in-chief, as he was upon the field during the afternoon and was fully advised during the night of the movement of the enemy." Shortly thereafter the conversation was interrupted and Cleburne, as he prepared to leave, told Brown, "We will resume this conversation at the first convenient moment."[37]

General Hood meanwhile rode at the head of Stewart's corps. The sights he saw along the road surely impacted his thinking. All manner of debris from the Yankees' night march littered the pike. Scores of dead horses and mules lay beside the road, some shot by the Federals when the exhausted animals could no longer pull the wagons; others killed by enemy fire when Graycoat cavalry had swept in to attack. Also, abandoned wagons, about fifty, according to J. P. Cannon of the Twenty-seventh Alabama, were burned to prevent the Confederates from looting them, and still smoked and smoldered along the pike. Many civilians, mostly older men, women, and boys too young for military service, lined the fences along the pike, cheering the Southerners onward and claiming the Yankees had just passed "on the dead run," or something to that effect.[38]

Hood well may have interpreted such scenes as evidence of a Yankee retreat in panic. Perhaps as the ugly spectacles of destruction along the pike assaulted his eyes, coupled with the encouraging shouts of people along the way, Hood concluded that Schofield's forces were demoralized and vulnerable to a frontal assault.

The time was approaching noon when Hood at last rode up to the Harrison house, hobbled through the front door with his crutch, and rested for a time at the mansion he had claimed for his headquarters. The morning ride had done nothing to cool his anger, only allowing additional time for it to fester. His wrath continued to focus upon both his generals and the men in the ranks, all of whom he held responsible for the blundering at Spring Hill. Perhaps it was then, at the Harrison house, that the seething general made his decision to attack—a frontal assault to discipline men who, Hood believed, had become too cautious, accustomed to the protection of breastworks while under the command of General Joe Johnston.

Perhaps the decision came even later. Sometime after one o'clock Hood got his first view of the Union entrenchments south of Franklin. He rode up on the high slope of Winstead Hill and there gazed northward across the Franklin plain. Maybe Hood heard the exhilarating cheers raised by many of the Tennesseans when they topped the range of hills and saw the valley of the Harpeth in their immediate front. Perhaps, as one historian speculated, Hood "was inspired by the Federal retreat from Winstead Hill." It was George Wagner's troops, of course, who had held the eminence until the Southerners appeared, then falling back in obedience to orders. Once more the Yankees, as the situation might have seemed to Hood, "had not stood and fought; instead they had run away at the direct approach of the massed gray ranks." Maybe, as Hood saw it, the Federals were so intent on escaping a fight that they would not stand even when protected by entrenchments.[39]

Obviously no one knows with certainty what thoughts passed through the mind of John Bell Hood on that tragic afternoon. What is known, from more than one primary account, is that the general dismounted—"painfully, as always, with the help of an orderly who passed him his crutches once he was afoot"[40]—removed his field glasses from their case and trained them on the Union works. He was then positioned a short way down the northern slope of Winstead Hill, on or near the site of the commemorative battlefield map usually visited by present-day Civil War tourists. Having briefly examined the enemy defenses in silence, the Confederate commander returned the glasses to the leather case, rode back to the top of the hill where several officers were gathered and simply announced: "We will make the fight!"[41]

One wonders, when Hood explained that the Confederates were to prepare for a frontal assault, if there was a moment of stunned silence. Those officers who actually heard Hood's words, as well as those who soon learned of the general's decision, surely recognized, as did the soldiers of every regiment in the army, that such an attack would be a very bloody affair with little chance of success. Most of Stephen Lee's corps was still on the march from Columbia, accompanied by the bulk of the army's guns, and could not possibly arrive soon enough to participate in an afternoon attack. The Federals would probably have as many men fighting from behind entrenchments as the Confederates would have advancing in the open. And Hood had not taken time for a proper reconnaissance of the Yankee position to determine any possible weak points. Soon objections were voiced by some, the sequence of which is difficult to determine because of conflicting accounts. General Forrest, who was usually not hesitant to express his mind, was one of the first, quite possibly the very first, to offer his counsel.

The cavalry commander strongly opposed a frontal assault. Like Hood, Forrest too had examined the Union defenses with his glasses. He also had seen them up close earlier in the war. Unlike Hood, he thought the entrenchments were too strong to be taken by a direct attack. If per chance they could be carried, the feat would only be achieved through great and unnecessary bloodshed. The Southerners could not afford such a waste of manpower. Hood replied to the effect that Schofield had no intention of fighting: the Federal general was only making a show of force while working to secure his retreat. Whatever Schofield's intentions, Forrest contended the Union position was too formidable to attack. Such a gamble made no sense to Forrest. Particularly so when, as the cavalryman knew, the Harpeth River could be forded at more than one place east of the town. He said to General Hood: "Give me one strong division of infantry with my cavalry . . . and within two hours' time I can flank the Federals from their works." Hood, however, obsessed with the Spring Hill failure, seemed to have no interest in a flanking maneuver.[42]

Cheatham also was among those generals who were bold enough to voice their opposition to a frontal assault. After examining the terrain for himself, "he was struck by the open expanse confronting the Confederates," as well as the strength of the enemy position. He concluded the Graycoats would be taking "a desperate chance" if they attacked head-on. He told Hood: "I don't like the looks of this fight. The Federals have an excellent position, and one well fortified."[43]

But General Hood's eyes seemed blinded to what was clearly apparent to others. He responded to Cheatham with a cavalier put-down—rather like a politician confronted by an unwelcome question, who offers a cute reply of no real substance, hoping to intimidate and distract from the issue—saying that he preferred to fight the Yankees at Franklin where "they have had only eighteen hours to fortify, than to strike them at Nashville where they have been strengthening themselves for three years."[44] Historian Stanley Horn's blunt evaluation of Hood's response was quite appropriate. The Confederate general, wrote Horn, "was neither accurate nor logical."[45] There was no decree in stone that a frontal assault must be attempted at either place. The issue was the strength of the Union defenses at Franklin. The time spent in construction and the alleged greater strength at Nashville were totally irrelevant. Cheatham, as his biographer said: "silently swallowed Hood's rebuke."[46]

By this time it must have been clear that all arguments against an assault were of no consequence. Hood had decided to attack and, stubborn man that he was, would persist in seeing the thing through no matter how foolish it might be. It would be Hood's battle, for better or worse, for he and only he forced the fight. "Gambling contrary to reasonable calculations," observed Sir Basil Liddell-Hart, one of the foremost twentieth-century military historians, "is a military vice which, as the pages of history reveal, has ruined more armies than any other cause."[47] A Southern veteran remembered that he heard Cheatham say, when the soldiers soon started forward toward the enemy line, that the attack "is a mistake," and there is "no comfort to me to say we are not responsible."[48]

General Alexander Stewart, in an 1897 letter to General French, said that Hood, early in the afternoon, "inquired if I thought it practicable to cross the Harpeth River with my command above Franklin. I replied that there were fords above the town, and I had no doubt of being able to cross." Stewart recalled that "Hood sent for me after the battle," and explained that he did not make the flanking move because "a courier from Schofield to Thomas had been intercepted" and the message "was such" that, Hood claimed, "I thought my time to fight had come." Hence the frontal assault. If Hood told Stewart the substance of the captured dispatch which allegedly so enlightened him, the corps commander did not mention it in his letter to French.[49] The possibility of crossing the river above the town is yet another conceivable explanation for moving Stewart's lead corps off to the right flank, rather than simply to insure that the enemy abandoned the Winstead-Breezy Hills, or to bring up Cheatham's corps (and particularly Cleburne's division?) and place it in the forefront of the fight, attacking straight up the pike.

Whether or not General Cleburne expressed his opinion to Hood, there is no question that he considered the attack unwise—to say the least. A recent biographer wrote that Cleburne "listened impassively" as Hood outlined his assault plan, saying that the Confederates must "go over the main works [of the enemy] at all hazards." A witness claimed Cleburne, as he left Hood to lead his command, matter-of-factly stated: "I will take the enemy's works or fall in the attempt."[50] Many years later Captain Joe Clark, a full-blooded Cherokee Indian who was said to have served as a scout for General Forrest, claimed in his memoirs that "General Pat Cleburne objected to [Hood's assault] order, and said it was foolhardy."[51] L. H. Mangum, one of Cleburne's aides, later said that

Cleburne opposed the assault, but that the general "was too blunt and frank" to influence Hood.[52] Whether Clark and Mangum meant to imply that Cleburne expressed his opposition to Hood is not clear.

As for Hood's own account, he claimed Cleburne evidenced "an enthusiasm which he had never before" shown, and said: "General, I am ready, and have more hope in the final success of our cause than I have had at any time since the first gun was fired."[53] Captain Buck placed Hood's story in proper perspective, writing that it was "incredible" that Cleburne could have made such a remark "at a time when any one above the degree of idiocy" had to know "that chances for final success of the Confederacy were desperate."[54] General Daniel C. Govan, Cleburne's good friend from Arkansas, later told Captain Buck that Cleburne "and the other generals" consulting with Hood, were all "opposed to attacking along the main pike, . . . as the enemy could have been flanked and compelled to abandon his strongly fortified position."[55] But Govan's words do not necessarily imply that Cleburne expressed his opposition to Hood.

The Irishman is known to have ridden forward to a knoll from which he could get a better view of the Union entrenchments. This "high, rocky hill," a half-mile or more to the Confederate front, slightly west of the Columbia-Franklin Pike, was known as Merrill's Hill and was occupied by some Southern sharpshooters. Explaining that he had left his field glasses behind, the general borrowed a telescope from a sharpshooter's Whitworth rifle and examined the enemy position. Sweeping the glass from end to end of the fortifications, he observed that they were "all completed." When finished, he simply remarked, "They are very formidable." After thanking the lieutenant from whom he had borrowed the scope and returning it, Captain Buck said Cleburne then seated himself "upon a stump [and] wrote rapidly for a few minutes in a small blank book, which he returned to his pocket." (The book has never been found.)[56]

General Govan added the interesting observation that he thought Cleburne "seemed to be more despondent than I ever saw him." Govan recalled that all the officers realized the desperate nature of what they were about to do. He said he paused and remarked to Cleburne that "there will not be many of us that get back to Arkansas." Cleburne's reply was one of resignation: "Well, Govan, if we are to die, let us die like men."[57]

Doubtless Cleburne's immediate responsibilities weighed heavily on his mind. But there was something more. When the thought of Susan Tarleton crossed his mind, as surely it did, he must have reflected that quite likely he would never see her again. "Thoughts of unrequited love must have torn at his very being," said one writer.[58]

Those in the ranks knew too the desperate nature of what Hood had asked of them. No better example can be cited than Sam R. Watkins of Columbia. A private in the First Tennessee Infantry who had been with the army all through the war, Watkins later wrote that as the audacious undertaking began to unfold: "I had made up my mind to die."[59] It is likely that many Southerners, from privates to generals, shared Watkins's resignation. A number of soldiers in General William A. Quarles's brigade went to chaplain James M'Neilly with "watches, jewelry, letters and photographs," requesting him to "take charge of them and send them to their families if they were killed." M'Neilly said: "I had to decline, as I was going with them and would be exposed to the same danger." The chaplain survived, and remarked that the next morning, nearly all who had come to him lay dead on the battlefield.[60]

By three o'clock General Hood, ignoring all opposition to the attack, had issued his orders and the troops were forming for the assault. Those who lived through the ordeal retained a graphic memory of the scene. Many soldiers were gaunt, their gray uniforms worn and dirty, perhaps a fourth of them without shoes. Still, as attested by both sides, the impression they made was unforgettable. Even General Cheatham, despite his staunch objections to the attack, afterward said that "as they wheeled into line of battle in full view of the enemy, their precision and military bearing was as beautiful a sight as was ever seen in war." Another witness recalled General Otto Strahl (who would die in the assault), "standing in front of his ragged, dingy-looking men, . . . exhorting them to make a valiant fight. . . ." It was said that he told the men, "Boys, this will be short but desperate." Still another remembered General Cleburne admonishing his troops to "use the bayonet." Weapons were to be loaded, but the men must not stop to fire, advancing in quick-time and assaulting with the bayonet. Likewise Brigadier General F. M. Cockrell was ordering his men "to march straight for the [enemy's] position in quick-time and not to fire a shot until . . . the top of the works" had been gained.[61]

Cheatham's corps would attack on the left, directly up the Columbia-Franklin Pike, with Brown's division to the left of the road and Cleburne's to the right. Bate's division would move toward the Carter's Creek Pike, behind Merrill's Hill, planning to turn and join up with Brown's left flank for the assault. Stewart's corps would attack on the right, up the Nashville & Decatur Railroad and the Lewisburg-Franklin Pike. Edward Walthall's division would be in the center, with French on the left and William Loring on the right. Edward Johnson's division, the one division present from Lee's corps, remained in reserve position. Forrest's cavalry would be divided, part on each flank of the attacking force.

Once the men were in line of battle, there was mostly an eerie silence, upon which several remarked. "It was perfectly still," remembered a surgeon of the Twenty-second Mississippi, with "no sound jarring upon the ear." He considered it an "ominous" sign, saying he feared "our men are going to be annihilated."[62] Of course not everyone was silent. And while some had no shoes, a few had no firearms. In Loring's division, a Private W. P. Peacock of the Fifteenth Mississippi, having just returned to duty and anxious to join his comrades for the battle, came up with a weapon and said: "Men, I have no gun; but I am going into this fight, and will carry an axe!"[63] Over in French's division, a soldier animated by the scene, suddenly offered a famous quote which no doubt he intended as inspirational. It was Nelson's message at Trafalgar: "England expects every man to do his duty!" The problem was that most of his company, and much of the regiment for that matter, were Irishmen, or descendents of Irishmen. Sergeant Denny Callahan responded instantly: "It's damned little duty England would get out of this Irish crowd!" Callahan's comment raised a laugh "long and hearty."[64] But even if some could laugh in the face of it, the attack would be "a fearful ordeal," as a veteran in the Twenty-seventh Alabama afterward characterized it, "advancing through the open fields under the most destructive fire we ever witnessed."[65]

General Govan later described the Confederate attack, as conceived by Hood, as a thing mad and haphazard. Besides attacking before the remainder of the army arrived to help, Hood did not deploy the strength of his forces to achieve his objective of penetrating the center of the Yankee line at the Columbia-Franklin Pike. His hope to break the Union center rested with only two divisions, General Brown's, advancing on the west side of the pike, and General Cleburne's, moving to the attack east of the pike. Their combined force consisted of only seven brigades out of a total assaulting force of eighteen brigades.

Somewhere in Franklin the hands of a town clock were approaching four o'clock in the afternoon. Atop the Winstead-Breezy Hills a crowd of men, women, and even children had gathered, watching the enthralling scene as the Graycoats deployed, and anticipating the assault to follow. "I'll bet they'll go right over them works," a bystander was heard to say. "I hope so," responded another.[66] And then the waiting was over.

Near the crest of Winstead Hill the flag went down—the prearranged signal for the attack to begin. Officers called out "Forward!" and in near perfect alignment the Confederate array advanced. Over one hundred regiments strong they came, perhaps eighteen thousand men, several bands playing, bayonets flashing, and tattered battle flags flying. General and staff officers and couriers were riding in front of and between the lines. The infantry marched at a quick-step. The artillery (one battery accompanying each corps) were being brought forward to fire when within range. "The sight inspired every man with the sentiment of duty," said Colonel Ellison Capers of the Twenty-fourth South Carolina Infantry, as he described the "magnificent battlefield spectacle."[67] An extraordinary, panoramic, never-to-be-forgotten martial display became a prelude to the engagement, as the last great Confederate assault of the whole bloody war got underway. When Brigadier General Francis Marion Cockrell's First Missouri Brigade of French's division, Stewart's corps, moved forward to the attack, its eleven-man brass band, recognized as among "the finest in the army," stepped out with the unit and struck up one of the most stirring Southern songs of the era, "The Bonnie Blue Flag." Several bands, in fact, apparently played the tune.[68]

Hardly any piece, in historical retrospect, could have been more symbolically appropriate. When one recalls the first lines, "We are a band of brothers, And native to the soil," and reflects upon the heavily populated and ever-more-rapidly industrializing North taking the measure of the rural, agrarian South—and perhaps never more heart-rendingly than on that late fall day in Middle Tennessee—the song seems to possess a haunting sadness, as if heralding that a way of life was ending. While the passing of a major part of that culture is surely not to be mourned—for who that believes in the inalienable rights of humankind would contend that one person should be permitted to own another—the slavery of the Old South has often obscured the inherent virtues of an agrarian civilization which, sans slavery, is arguably more wholesome than the life experienced by the urban masses.

"The Bonnie Blue Flag" has other memorable lines: "Then here's to our Confederacy, For strong we are and brave." The Grayclads were about to prove their strength and courage again (if anyone needed more proof), but élan and the bayonet could not carry a nation "native to the soil," not even Thomas Jefferson's "sacred" soil, to victory over such an opponent as the Southerners faced. Tragically for them, but fortunately for the United States, that fact was about to be demonstrated yet again.

Although Confederate manpower, as previously noted, was poorly deployed and probably numerically insufficient, under any circumstances, to overcome such strong enemy defenses, nevertheless, it is an intriguing fact that the Southerners were attacking in greater numbers than in the most famous charge of the war, the assault on the last day at Gettysburg. The Confederates also had greater numbers than in the well-known attacks against the "Hornets' Nest" at Shiloh. These Southern veterans of Shiloh, the Kentucky campaign, Stones River, Chickamauga, Chattanooga, and Atlanta presented what one Union soldier considered "the most imposing martial display that occurred during the war."[69]

"Spell-bound with admiration," a Federal officer looked southward, and reflected that "in a few brief moments . . . all that orderly grandeur [of the advancing Grayclads] would be changed to bleeding, writhing confusion, and . . . thousands of those valorous men of the South, with their chivalric officers, would pour out their life's blood. . . ."[70] Lieutenant Isaac Shannon, a sharpshooter of the Ninth Tennessee, was on Merrill Hill, from where he had shot down four Yankee gunners of Company A, Second Missouri Artillery. Shannon enjoyed a rather unique view of the Southern advance, watching from his perch atop that hill, as Cheatham's men swept around it, moving "as a great wave" against the enemy position.[71]

On came the Confederates. With weapons loaded and bayonets fixed, they grimly marched toward the Blueclad line. The Federals waited and tension mounted. Anxiety neared the panic level in the two advanced brigades of Wagner's division, astride the Columbia Pike on a slight rise of ground, a quarter of a mile or more in front of the main Union works.

"We had all supposed," explained Captain John K. Shellenberger, a Union company commander in Conrad's brigade east of the pike, that the advanced position "would be only temporary," but an orderly came with instructions from General Wagner saying, according to Shellenberger, that the position must be held "to the last man," and that the sergeants should "fix bayonets and . . . any man, not wounded, who should . . . leave the line without orders, would be shot or bayoneted by the sergeants."[72]

Such a thing was never the intention of Schofield, Stanley, Cox, or, presumably, anyone else in his right mind. In the event of a Confederate assault, the brigades were supposed to fall back within the main works. The near Federal disaster that resulted cost General Wagner his command within a week and became the subject of much controversy, as all the generals named above disavowed responsibility for the blunder. The most likely explanation is that Wagner was inebriated that afternoon. General Stanley testified that "Wagner was, to say the least, 'full of whiskey,' if not drunk. . . . He was in a vainglorious condition, though it was not known at the time by General Schofield or myself."[73]

Shellenberger continued his account of the fiasco, writing that "The opinion was universal that a big blunder was being committed in compelling us to fight with our flank fully exposed in the midst of a wide field. . . ." Shellenberger said the indignation of the men "grew almost into a mutiny and the swearing of those gifted in profanity exceeded all their previous efforts. . . ." There is a saying that timing is everything. Some men, their enlistments expired, were due to be mustered out of the service as soon as the army returned to Nashville. A first sergeant by the last name of Libey was among the group. As the advancing

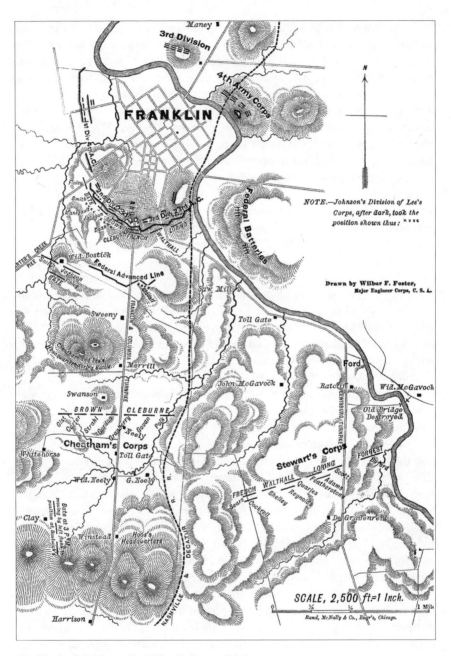

Franklin battlefield map. By Wilbur F. Foster, C.S.A.

Confederates drew nearer, Libey twice got up and started back toward the main line, vehemently stating that he "would not submit to having his life thrown away, after his time was out, by such a stupid blunder," only to return upon the blunt order of his captain, "God damn you, come back here!" Just as he feared, Libey had only a few minutes to live.[74]

Brown's and Cleburne's divisions quickly overran the advanced Union brigades. The Yankees, seeing their foe in great numbers on both their front and flank, turned and fled, Confederates running after them; toward the Federal line. Fearful of hitting their own men, the Union artillery stationed at the pike did not fire. It was a footrace with the Southerners to the Federal works, the pursuing attackers clubbing and shooting the terrified Bluecoats as they ran. One of Cleburne's command, Captain Samuel T. Foster, Twenty-fourth Texas Cavalry (dismounted) recorded the action in his diary: "As soon as they break to run our men break after them. They have nearly one half mile to run to get back to their next line—so here we go right after them and yelling like fury and shooting at them at the same time." Foster said the Graycoats killed some of them before they could reach their works (First Sergeant Libey being one of the number), "and [the Federals] that are in the [main] line of works are not able to shoot us because their own men are in front of us—and between us and them."[75]

In all the confusion, some of the Union infantry in the main breastworks on each side of the pike gave ground, and the animated Confederates, buoyed up by the enemy's unexpected bungling, charged toward the works with total abandon. One of the most graphic Southern accounts of the grand assault on the Federal center was penned by General George Washington Gordon, leading a brigade in Brown's division west of the pike. He captured something of the energy, noise, fervor, and awful slaughter of the spectacular episode. As the Yankees of Wagner's division raced toward their main line, Gordon said "the shout was raised, 'Go into the works with them!' This cry was taken up and vociferated from a thousand throats," the general wrote, "as we rushed on after the flying forces we had routed—killing some in our running fire, and capturing others. . . ." Gordon said that the Federals at the main line had "reserved their fire for the safety of their routed comrades who . . . were just in front of and mingled with the pursuing Confederates." But when the Yankees realized it was no longer safe for themselves to reserve their fire, Gordon testified that "they opened upon us (regardless of their own men . . .) such a hailstorm of shot and shell, musketry and canister, that the very atmosphere was hideous with the shrieks of . . . death."[76]

From the viewpoint of a Union officer, "The triumphant Confederates, now more like a wild, howling mob than an organized army, swept on to the very works, with hardly a check from any quarter."[77] However, even as the right and center of Cheatham's inspired corps bore down rapidly and furiously upon the enemy at the Columbia Pike—victory seemingly at hand if the Yankee blunder with their advanced brigades could be adequately capitalized on—major coordination problems had developed with the overall attack which likely already doomed to failure the desperate Southern effort. The energized ranks of Brown's and Cleburne's divisions charging into the Federal entrenchments could not have known, and probably many of their general officers did not realize, that Cheatham's left wing under Bate, as well as part of Stewart's corps to their right, were not converging on the Union line in a simultaneous assault.

With Blue and Gray strength closely matched, the Confederates could not afford such a disjointed attack. Yet that was exactly what happened as Cleburne's and Brown's men rushed through the gap on the pike near the Carter house, outdistancing any support on their left flank—and, of course, with no reserves to follow up a breakthrough. Nevertheless, at the dire moment when the animated Confederates surged into the enemy breastworks on both sides of the Columbia Pike, with a reckless élan, as if to defeat the Yankees at any cost, their chances of triumph must have seemed good.

Confusion prevailed among many of the Bluecoats at the point of penetration, as the Southerners not only broke through along the pike but also widened the gap by knocking a regiment loose from the breastworks on each side of the road. General Cox reported that "most of Strickland's brigade broke from the first line." Soldiers in the trenches, disconcerted by the fleeing infantrymen trampling over them, were confused by Wagner's officers calling upon their men to "get to the rear and reform," and supposing the order applied to them too, were carried away by the surging mass of sweaty, bloody humanity. Adding to the disorder were frightened horses galloping to the rear, taking away the ammunition chests for the batteries near the pike. The Confederates appeared on the breastworks, seemingly numbering in the hundreds, taking possession of the main Federal line on both sides of the road, the break extending from near the cotton gin on the east across Strickland's entire front on the west.[78]

The crucial moment was at hand with the battle only a few minutes old. With their foothold at the Columbia Pike, the Graycoats seemed to threaten the whole U.S. position. At that very moment, General Stanley was riding south from the river. "I arrived at the scene of disorder, coming from the town on the Columbia pike," he wrote.

> The moment was critical beyond any I have known in any
> battle—could the enemy hold that part of our line, he was
> nearer to our two bridges than the extremities of our line.
> Colonel Opdycke's brigade was . . . about 100 yards in rear

of the works. I rode quickly to the left regiment and called
to them to charge; at the same time I saw Colonel Opdycke
near the center of his line urging his men forward. I gave
the colonel no order, as I saw him engaged in doing the
very thing to save us, viz, to get possession of our line again.[79]

Cleburne's and Brown's spearheading penetration of the Union line did
not spread. Charging straight through the routed federals to plug the gap at the
pike came the brigade of Colonel Emerson Opdycke. His men, many needing
no orders, rushed into the break, fighting hand to hand with the Confederates,
some of whom were nearly spent after chasing Wagner's fleeing troops for a
quarter of a mile. Opdycke himself set a conspicuous example, first, according
to one account, "exhausting all the shots in his revolver," he then "employed it
as a club to drive up stragglers to the help of his heroic brigade; and when he
had broken the pistol, he dismounted and borrowed a musket, which he found
even more efficient in the work of persuasion. . . ."[80]

In the midst of the melee was nineteen-year-old Arthur MacArthur Jr., who
eventually received the Medal of Honor for his exploits the previous year at
Missionary Ridge. At Franklin he was commanding the Twenty-fourth Wisconsin Regiment of Opdycke's brigade. Shouting "Up Wisconsin!" the young major
mounted his horse, rode toward the foremost enemy ranks at the breakthrough
point, brandishing his saber and leading his men by example. One of his staff
officers said that MacArthur's horse was shot down, and the major was struck
in the shoulder. MacArthur nevertheless led the way on foot, came face to face
with a Confederate who shot him in the chest, but MacArthur managed to
stab his enemy in the stomach. Then the Southerner, as he went down, shot
MacArthur in the knee. MacArthur would survive the wounds and later became
the father of the twentieth century's General Douglas MacArthur.[81]

The ensuing struggle at the pike combined some of the grisliest features of
a frontal assault penetration and bayonet fighting in a general hand-to-hand
brawl. "The men fought like demons," a Southerner later wrote, as they used
"clubbed muskets and the bayonet." An Illinois colonel reported that "it would
be impossible to picture that scene in all its horrors. I saw a Confederate soldier, close to me, thrust one of our men through with a bayonet, and before he
could withdraw his weapon from the ghastly wound, his brains were scattered
on all of us that stood near, by the butt of a musket swung with terrific force by
some big fellow whom I could not recognize in the grim dirt and smoke that
enveloped us."[82]

And Opdycke himself, in a sometimes dramatic report, said "the battle
raged with indescribable fury" and credited his men "when the . . . masses of
the enemy had stormed and carried our main works at the key point of our

whole position," with rushing "grandly and defiantly forward, your bayonets gleaming . . . ," to assail "the victorious foe . . . , and saved the army from disastrous overthrow."[83] For his part in this action Opdycke would be promoted to brigadier general.

For all their fervent fighting, Opdycke's brigade had a great deal of help in sealing the breach at the pike. Colonel John E. White's Sixteenth Kentucky Infantry, in the second line of Reilly's brigade immediately east of the pike, played a major role in stemming the high tide of the Rebels. General Cox reported that "neither Colonel White . . . nor colonel Opdycke waited for the word to charge, but were in motion before the order could reach them. White was nearest the parapet and reached it soonest. . . ." In a brief, apparently accurate report, White said: "Observing a portion of the line in my front give way, I ordered my regiment to charge the enemy, who were occupying the works . . . abandoned, which it did, engaging them in a hand-to-hand conflict, which lasted about forty minutes. I succeeded in driving them beyond the works, inflicting a heavy loss." Colonel White received a severe wound in the face but refused to leave the line while the struggle was so fierce.[84]

The Federals who had fallen back from their line were being rallied by officers. Many returned to their posts and joined in the fight. General Cox reported that in some places there was "a wall three or four deep, those in the rear loading the muskets for those who were firing." General Stanley was assisting in rallying the men when his horse was killed, "and no sooner had I regained my feet," remembered the general, "than I received a musket-ball through the back of my neck. . . ." Stanley was only "reluctantly persuaded to return to his quarters for surgical help," said General Cox.[85]

Fighting raged all about the Carter house and the Carter gin house, as the Rebel onslaught was brought to a halt. In the face of the Union counterattack, the Confederates were slowly forced back, either to the main line of Federal works or beyond. Cleburne's men east of the pike and in front of the cotton gin found themselves in an awful position. Driven back from the Bluecoat line and pinned down, they were decimated by a cross fire made possible by the diagonal enemy line across the pike. "I never saw men put in such a terrible position as Cleburne's division was in . . . ," remembered James Barr of the Sixty-fifth Illinois. "The wonder is that any of them escaped death or capture."[86] The Confederate situation was especially deadly because some of the U.S. troops in Casement's brigade possessed repeating weapons, as in the Sixty-fifth Indiana and some companies·of the Twelfth Kentucky, and others had breech-loading rifles, weapons that could be fired much faster than the muzzleloaders carried by most of the Graycoats.

Part of Brown's division west of the pike rushed wildly past the Carter house. Their gallant effort was to no avail. Gradually they were pushed back, though grudgingly giving up the ground gained. General Cox wrote that "all the circumstances show that the gap west of the Carter house was longest open, and that bodies of the enemy got fartherest within our lines there." The focus of the fight, Cox believed, "was around the position of the Forty-fourth Missouri, just in the rear of the Carter house. . . ." He said the Forty-fourth "had more men killed than all the other regiments of the brigade." Cox also reported that "the condition of the atmosphere was such that the smoke [from the guns] settled upon the field without drifting off, and after the first half hour's fighting it became almost impossible to discern any object along the line at a few yards' distance."[87]

The soldiers of Brown's division were finally thrown back to the breast-works over which they had charged, and there they held firm, but only at a terrible cost. Brown himself was seriously wounded, and his division lost all four of its brigade commanders: Gist and Strahl killed outright, Carter mortally wounded, and Gordon taken prisoner. On Brown's right flank, the Federals leveled a terrible enfilade fire on the Confederates from their regained works. On the left flank, where Bate's division had not made connection with Brown's division, the Northerners also raked Brown's men with a flanking fire.

While the battle raged along the Federal line both east and west of the Carter house, General Schofield chose to remain at Fort Granger, fearing that the Rebels would attempt to cross the Harpeth and gain control of the pike and railroad to Nashville. It was to meet just such a flanking attack that Schofield had placed Wood's division on the north bank of the river and posted guns for their support. The Union general took some harsh criticism for staying at the fort instead of assuming command at the front. John Shellenberger spoke of Schofield as being "well beyond the range of every rebel bullet that was fired," and added that "when Stanley started for the front, Schofield started for the rear. . . ."[88] James Steedman caustically declared: "We do not say that General Schofield is a rank coward, but we can, from personal knowledge, safely state that he possesses the 'rascally virtue called caution' in an eminent degree. . . . We never knew him to be reckless enough to expose his carcass to the fire of the rebels."[89]

But if Hood were attempting to flank him, Fort Granger was a reasonable location for the Northern commander. And such a maneuver, as previously discussed, loomed as a distinct possibility, even a probability. Hood, however, never attempted to cross his infantry—no doubt both to Schofield's surprise and relief—and although parts of two brigades of Forrest's divided cavalry command did force a crossing of the river on the east, they were hard pressed by the Bluecoat troopers and eventually pulled back.[90]

Meanwhile nothing—after the Confederates were thrown back at the pike—went well for the attackers. The assault by Stewart's corps on the right saw French's division strike the Federal line slightly east of the cotton gin, some men charging to the enemy breastworks, only to be immediately killed or wounded. The advance of the other divisions of Stewart's corps—Edward Walthall in the center and William Loring on the right—was slowed by the curve of the river, which flowed northwestward until it reached the flank of the Union works near the railway cut at the Lewisburg Pike. Because of the course of the stream, the width of the ground contracted rapidly as Stewart advanced, necessitating readjusting and changing the direction of his lines on the center and right. More time was consumed when Walthall and Loring struck the railroad cut, which also forced a change of front toward the left.

Here the Southerners were struck by a galling fire from a battery of guns masked on the other side of the Harpeth. As Stewart's soldiers swung to the left, their flank was exposed to this enfilading fire. A severe bombardment from the three-inch rifled guns in Fort Granger punished them too, as did the fire of a battery positioned near the Lewisburg Pike. Then, as the men struggled through the massive abatis in front of the parapets, they were met by a murderous small-arms fire. Walthall's division especially suffered from the rapid fire of Blueclads armed with repeating rifles.[91]

Vividly conveying the savagery of the fighting and the heavy loss of life in Stewart's corps, General Walthall wrote: "There was an extensive, open, and almost unbroken plain . . . across which we must pass. . . . This was done under far the most deadly fire of both small-arms and artillery that I have ever seen troops subjected to." Bearing up under the dreadful punishment, the advance continued, reported Walthall, "terribly torn at every step by an oblique fire from a battery advantageously posted at the enemy's left, no less than by the destructive fire in front. . . ." Still, continued the general, "the line moved on and did not falter till, just to the right of the pike, it reached the abatis fronting the works. Over this," declared the division commander, "no organized force could go, and here the main body of my command . . . was repulsed in confusion; but over this obstacle, impassable for a solid line, many officers and men . . . made their way, and some, crossing the ditch in its rear, were captured and others killed or wounded in the effort to mount the embankment." Walthall said that a number of men from every brigade "gained the ditch and there continued the struggle. . . ."[92]

Farther to the right, over in Loring's division, Adams's brigade, one of the Confederates rushing toward the Yankee line was Captain William C. Thompson, Sixth Mississippi Infantry. A survivor of numerous campaigns,

Thompson had been among those who charged up the hillside just south of Shiloh Church against Sherman's division early on Sunday morning, April 6, 1862. As in that awful struggle, Thompson's men were again being raked by enemy fire from the front and the right flank. "During our division attack," the captain wrote, "the Federals had a battery planted on the right of the . . . river that we could not reach. This battery damaged us severely, using canister. The Confederate troops were being mowed down. . . . At the same time the whole division was suffering from galling musketry fire by the enemy entrenched in our immediate front." Concluding his account, Thompson said that immediately "after the three brigades combined, and in the midst of the enemy artillery fire, I was shot through the right leg. The ground about me was covered with the fallen. I managed with the assistance of the litter men to get to a point where the bullets were not flying so thick. I remained there for the remainder of the night, suffering great pain. . . ."[93]

Such primary accounts, all conveying the horrors of Franklin, may be heaped one upon another until literally they compose a huge stack. As black powder smoke obscured the view and daylight faded into twilight and darkness, the determined but by then desperate Southerners, all along the front, poured out their life's blood, creating scenes never to be forgotten by those who witnessed the butchery. Lieutenant Colonel Fountain E. P. Stafford assumed command of his brigade after three immediate superior officers were killed or wounded. Within minutes a fusillade of bullets ripped through the colonel. Because of the mass of corpses piled around, Stafford's dead body could not fall to the ground. The next morning it could be seen half-standing in the parapet, as if, some thought, he were still directing his men.[94]

One of the last attacks was made by Edward Johnson's division of Lee's corps. Johnson was instructed, despite total darkness engulfing the field, to find the Yankee line and assault it. Groping through the blackness of the night, his men did what they could, but their attack, as might be anticipated, was delivered in a piecemeal manner with some men never getting into the action. After nine o'clock the fighting finally ceased, tapering off as soldiers fired at the flashes of their enemy's guns. General Hood apparently remained unconvinced that he was beaten. When the artillery came up later that night, the general ordered that every gun should open fire early in the morning, each pounding the Federal works with one hundred rounds of ammunition. Then the Graycoats would charge once more. Fortunately for the Rebels, Schofield pulled out during the night and marched for Nashville, thus concluding the slaughter at Franklin.[95]

The Army of Tennessee had suffered approximately 7,250 casualties; the Union about 2,325. Actually, even these figures, which are more than three-to-one in favor of the U.S. army, do not represent accurately the one-sidedness of the battle. The loss in Confederate leadership was appalling. Killed on the field were Generals Cleburne, Gist, Granbury, Adams, and Strahl, while John C. Carter was mortally wounded. Five other generals were put out of action by their wounds and yet another was captured: George W. Gordon. The loss of leaders continued down the chain of command, with fifty-three regimental commanders included among the casualties. If one compares the total number of men killed in each army, using the commonly accepted figures, the Bluecoats had more than a nine-to-one edge: 189 U.S. dead to 1,750 Confederate dead.[96] The chances are, considering that many of those numbered among the Southern wounded were severely injured and eventually died, that the figure of 1,750 Graycoats dead is conservative. Among the mortally wounded Confederates was Captain Tod Carter, son of the owner of the house where General Cox made his headquarters. The captain, who had not seen his home for more than two years, was struck down within a short distance of the house. When the fighting ceased, his father and other family members carried him home to die in the house where he had spent most of his young life.

Many Americans, even many of those who know something of the Civil War, have never realized the enormity of what occurred at Franklin. When William R. Hartpence, a Federal veteran, wrote a history of the Fifty-first Indiana, he unabashedly declared that Franklin "stands without an equal in the history of the world." Hartpence said that the battle was "a succession of ferocious assaults, bloody hand-to-hand struggles and horrid scenes of carnage and destruction that beggar description."[97] A Southerner who conveyed a vivid image of that awful day wrote that "wounded Confederates who moved a leg or an arm were instantly selected as targets and were literally shot to pieces." He said "many of the dead" were actually "in shreds," and that all night long wounded men "crawled off of the field," some with "one leg trailing on the earth behind them, others with shattered shoulders or torn entrails, or ghastly flesh-wounds, or with smashed jaws, or with eyes shot out. . . ." They would "sink beside us and murmur [that] 'it was hell itself, boys.' And they would sink into sleep or death." This Mississippian, referring to "the specter of Franklin," declared that "I never before or after saw such a frightful battleground." The scene "stalked among us," he wrote, "livid with distorted features, with blood-streaming wounds, with ghastly, horror-stricken eyes. . . ."[98]

Every veteran who wrote of Franklin spoke of it as a battle in a class by itself. General Govan described the struggle where he was involved as "the most desperate fight I ever witnessed," and of the engagement as a whole, he said Franklin was "the bloodiest by far for the time it lasted, of all the battles in which [I have been] engaged."[99] An Alabama colonel spoke of the raging fury, "intensified by national hatred," in which "the annals of chivalry never exhibited more desperate valor, heroic courage, distinguished gallantry or . . . non challance to death." He asserted the position where he fought and somehow survived, was "worse than death."[100]

An Ohio soldier declared that "Franklin . . . will haunt me for the rest of my days."[101] Another Confederate spoke of the morning after the battle, saying that "such a scene presented itself to our view that I can not undertake to describe and was so appalling that the very thought of it makes me shudder, even to this day, and when we consider how it happened [a critical reference to Hood] makes it worse than ever."[102] Still another Southerner wrote to his wife: "I was detailed at Franklin, the . . . day after the battle, to carry in wounded. O what a sight it was to behold; our dead were laying in piles. I never want to see such a sight while I live."[103]

These men were not raw recruits, like so many at Shiloh for instance, who had never "seen the elephant." They were, for the most part, combat-hardened veterans; not easily impressed, at this stage of the conflict, by bloodshed or, one would guess, by much of anything. Yet most would recall Franklin as, in several ways, the ultimate, the climax of the ordeals they experienced.

On December 1, Captain Samuel T. Foster, Twenty-fourth Texas Cavalry (dismounted), commented in his diary on the awful losses at the Battle of Franklin: "At daylight this morning we can see the terrible results of the fight on yesterday and last night. . . . There is great destruction of human life here—I have seen places where the blood ran off in a stream, and also to stand in pools in places. . . ." Then the captain directed his pent-up wrath at the army's commander. "General Hood has betrayed us (The Army of Tennessee). This is not the kind of fighting he promised us at Tuscumbia and Florence, Alabama, when we started into Tennessee. This was not," the captain continued as he reiterated Hood's earlier words, "a 'fight with equal numbers and choice of the ground.' . . ." Foster concluded with a bitter condemnation: "And the wails and cries of widows and orphans made at Franklin, Tennessee, November 30, 1864, will heat up the fires of the bottomless pit to burn the soul of General J. B. Hood for murdering their husbands and fathers at that place that day." Foster finally charged that "It can't be called anything else but cold blooded murder."[104]

On the same day that Captain Foster wrote those words, General Hood issued General Field Order No. 38, to be read at the head of each regiment: "The Commanding general congratulates the army upon the success achieved yesterday over the enemy. . . . The enemy have been sent in disorder and confusion to Nashville, and while we lament the fall of many gallant officers and brave men, we have shown . . . that we can carry any position occupied by our enemy."[105]

Near nine o'clock in the evening of November 30, General George H. Thomas was at the Saint Cloud Hotel in Nashville when he received Schofield's victory telegram. The Rebels had struck and their assault had been thrown back with heavy losses. The news was a great relief to Thomas. Through much of November, the general had seemed "reticent and gloomy" and habitually wore his hat pulled down over his eyes. Worrying over Schofield and the arrival of Andrew Jackson Smith's command, he had been especially troubled on November's last day. Now, wrote Colonel James F. Rusling, his assistant quartermaster, "his hat [was] up and [his] face all aglow."[106] And soon after Schofield sent Thomas news of the battle, he began withdrawing his forces to Nashville.

5

Fortress on the Cumberland

Nashville is not as old as some Southern cities. New Orleans, St. Augustine, Charleston, Savannah, and a few others are more ancient. But the history of the city does go back to the 1700s, making it older than many, for example, Chattanooga, Atlanta, Memphis, Birmingham— the last not even of antebellum vintage. Regardless of age, Nashville's rich past is arguably the equal of any Southern city, and Nashville certainly had a storied beginning.

For centuries various Indians, particularly Shawnees, Cherokees, and Chickasaws, lived or hunted the Nashville region. Attractive game, such as buffalo, bear, deer, and turkey roamed the area in large numbers. Only in the late 1600s and early 1700s did a few white men occasionally appear on "The Bluffs" of the Cumberland River where downtown Nashville now stands. They were French traders from Canada or Louisiana.[1]

Later came the "long hunters" from east of the Appalachian Mountains, so called because they lived in the wilderness for months and even years at a time. The long hunter Thomas "Big Foot" Spencer stayed the winter of 1778–79 a few miles northeast of Nashville, reportedly making his "home" in a hollow tree. Timothy

Demonbreun, a trader from Quebec, has sometimes been hailed as the first white inhabitant of Nashville, because for a time in the 1770s he made his home in a cave in the bluff along the Cumberland River, about three miles upstream from downtown Nashville, and was present when the first party of settlers arrived. (Today the cave, enclosed by metal bars, is listed on the National Register of Historic Places, and is best viewed when boat riding on the river.) It is highly doubtful, however, if the activities of the long hunters or Demonbreun, in any direct way, would ever have brought about the planting of a community along the banks of the Cumberland.[2]

The true beginning of Nashville dates from late 1779—and a daring endeavor it was, entailing two expeditions traversing hundreds of miles via different routes through the wilderness before uniting on the west bank of the Cumberland River near the salt springs known as French Lick, the present site of Nashville. The intrepid James Robertson, a thirty-seven-year-old, blue-eyed, dark-haired, resourceful and decisive person, who has been called the "Father of Middle Tennessee," set out from Fort Patrick Henry, near present-day Kingsport, in October 1779, leading a group of some 250, most of whom were men. These settlers, who had grown increasingly restless and dissatisfied with their situation, were intrigued by reports of natural resources and abundant game to the west. Through the Cumberland Gap they trudged, hiked over much of what later would be southern Kentucky, traveling altogether perhaps four hundred miles to arrive at their destination, according to popular tradition, on Christmas day. The Cumberland River being solidly frozen, the party drove their wagons and stock across the ice to the future site of Nashville.[3]

Reaching the bluffs, about eighty feet above the Cumberland, the men began constructing rough housing to shelter them from the ravages of winter. They also began building a fort for protection against Indian attack. Christened Fort Nashborough, in honor of Francis Nash from North Carolina, a friend of Robertson's who had been killed at the Battle of Germantown, the fortress on the high bluffs of the Cumberland soon proved indispensable. A replica of the fort stands today on the river's west bank, not far from where Broadway dead ends at First Avenue. Within a few years the name Nashborough was changed to Nashville, probably as a consequence of the Revolution when France had allied with the United States against the British.[4]

John Donelson, Robertson's partner in the westward venture, led the other expedition on a journey by water of a thousand miles or more. Most of Donelson's party consisted of women (including Robertson's wife, Charlotte) and children. Departure was delayed as construction of the boats fell behind schedule. Then cold weather stopped them for a time. Various problems continued to plague the trip: Indian attacks, a smallpox epidemic on one of the vessels, insufficient food stores, and others. Finally, having traveled down the Holston River, down the Tennessee, up the Ohio, and up the Cumberland, Donelson's group joined forces with Robertson and the others at Fort Nashborough on April 24, 1780.[5]

A happy day it must have been as a number of families were reunited. Donelson wrote in his journal of Robertson and his party: "It is a source of satisfaction to us to be enabled to restore to him and others their families and friends, who were entrusted to our care, and who sometime since, perhaps despaired of ever meeting again."[6] Quickly the settlers acted to establish a civil government. In mid-May some 250 men signed the Cumberland Compact, "creating a voluntary association to provide law in the wilderness" and to guard their claims to the land.[7]

More importantly, they had to be constantly on guard for their lives. Native Americans, infuriated by the ever-advancing, "land-hungry" white man and incited by British agents as the American Revolution dragged on, made repeated raids on Nashborough. The single worst day came on April 2, 1781, when a band of Indians attacked the fort in an engagement that came to be known as "the Battle of the Bluffs." Hand-to-hand fighting raged all along what is today lower Broadway, with the Indians cutting off a number of the men from access to the safety of the fort. At that critical moment, Charlotte Robertson, credited with being the heroine of the battle, is said to have unleashed a pack of hounds. The dogs ferociously attacked and chased the Indians, and in the ensuing confusion the surviving settlers were able to regain the sanctuary of the fort. Clearly the hounds also deserve some recognition, as well as Charlotte, for the saving of Fort Nashborough.[8]

When the Battle of the Bluffs was over only about seventy of the people who came with Robertson and Donelson still survived. The toll of those killed, maimed, and kidnapped by Native Americans—Robertson, for example, had two brothers killed, two sons killed, and another son scalped, who fortunately survived the ordeal, while Robertson himself twice narrowly escaped death— was of course depressing and discouraging. Some settlers simply gave up and left the struggling settlement.[9]

If not for the strong, even-tempered leadership of Robertson, Nashborough likely would not have survived its early, difficult years. Serving as colonel of the militia, he instilled confidence that the Indians at last would be overcome. And at one point, as one historian has expressed it, "Robertson's strongest argument in maintaining the settlement was that it was more dangerous to go than to stay."[10] Eventually additional settlers made the westward trek to join the community and the population increased while Indian attacks became less frequent. The fortress on the Cumberland had survived.

As for Robertson, he lived until 1814. Then acting as an Indian agent for the United States government, he journeyed west to treat with the Chickasaws. The trip was made during heavy rains and Robertson had to swim several cold, rushing streams. Then in his seventies, he became exhausted, contracted pneumonia, and died. Eventually his body was returned to Nashville and, fittingly for the single most important figure in the early years of the city, his remains buried in the City Cemetery.[11]

By the turn of the century Nashville's population had grown impressively, especially considering the town's trials during the early years, and was approaching one thousand inhabitants. Among the newcomers was the man who would become the most notable of all Nashvillians—in fact, to this day the most famous of all Tennesseans. When Andrew Jackson rode into town on October 26, 1788, he was twenty-one years old. For the remainder of his life he would call Nashville home. With little or no formal education, the tall, slender young man had read law with two North Carolina attorneys, receiving his license to practice the year before he arrived in Nashville.

Jackson's temper became legendary, involving him in quarrels, brawls, and duels. Fortunately, he survived more than one situation where he was nearly killed. Fortunately also, he was intelligent, ambitious, forceful, and liked by a great many people. "Almost from the moment he arrived in 1788 until he died in 1845," wrote historians George R. Adams and Ralph J. Christian, "Jackson . . . strode center stage while [Nashville] matured." Marrying a daughter of John Donelson, acquiring land and financial stability, Jackson was increasingly well connected, both socially and politically.[12]

When Tennessee became a state in 1796, Jackson became Tennessee's first representative to Congress. But it was the military which provided the most important avenue for Jackson's advancement. Having risen to be major general of the Tennessee militia, the War of 1812 thrust him into the national limelight, first with victories over the Creek Indians in the territory which is now Alabama, and then most significantly, with his decisive triumph over the British at the Battle of New Orleans. Jackson emerged from the New Orleans battle with a military reputation second to no living American, enhancing that standing further by his subsequent foray into Spanish-held Florida. More than any single factor, military glory catapulted "Old Hickory," as friends affectionately called him in recognition of his toughness, into the presidency of the United States.

Serving for two terms, Jackson's presidency was certainly controversial. More significantly, he was one of the strongest presidents the nation has known, defining and demonstrating the strength of the executive branch of government as no one before had even come close to doing. People came to speak of

Jacksonian democracy and the Age of Jackson. And with it all, first as a military hero and then as chief executive of the country, Jackson made the name of Nashville known and brought the city great influence in national politics.

In 1844, James Knox Polk, Middle Tennessean and sometimes Nashvillian, became president of the United States. Although markedly different from Andrew Jackson in appearance and demeanor, the former governor of Tennessee and speaker of the House of Representatives was hailed as "Young Hickory," both because of Jackson's support of a fellow Democrat and Tennessean, and the hope that "Old Hickory's" popularity might prove decisive in electing Polk. Interestingly, while winning the presidency and despite the backing of the influential Jackson, Polk did not carry Tennessee[13]—a fact that might be of some ever-so-slight consolation to Tennessean and Democrat Albert Gore Jr., who also failed to win the Volunteer State in his 2000 bid for the presidency.

All the while that Jackson and Polk occupied the national stage, Nashville continued to grow in size, in prosperity, and in state politics. In October 1843, after Knoxville, Kingston (for a day), Murfreesboro, and Nashville had all hosted the state legislature for a time, the Tennessee General Assembly selected Nashville as the state's permanent capital.[14] Obviously this further guaranteed the continued development of Middle Tennessee's centrally-located city on the banks of the Cumberland.

That river proved indispensable to the growth of Nashville, especially from the 1820s onward. With the docking of the first steamboat in 1819 the city became increasingly connected with various important settlements, above all the metropolis of New Orleans. By the late 1840s steamboating enjoyed a "golden age" as forty to fifty vessels docked annually at the Nashville wharf. Transporting cotton, tobacco, corn, and other products to the Crescent City, ships returned to Nashville laden with sugar, coffee, clothing, furniture, and various other items, both necessities and luxuries. The city on the Cumberland soon became the main dispensary for numerous items delivered all over the mid-South.[15]

Already an extensive turnpike system, extending from Nashville in every direction of the compass, was well underway, construction dating from the twenties and continuing well into the fifties. To further solidify and exploit Nashville's burgeoning status as a center for trade, the city's ever-prospering merchants began calling for the iron horse. Primary among the backers of railroad construction was Vernon K. Stevenson. Relinquishing his successful merchandising career, Stevenson became "president, organizer, chief stockholder and promoter" of the Nashville & Chattanooga Railroad. By the time the Nashville & Chattanooga was finished in 1854, Stevenson had started the

Nashville & Northwestern, building from Nashville toward Hickman, Kentucky. Before that road was completed, Nashville would be involved in the Civil War.[16]

Ultimately, the most important of all rail construction for Nashville was the Louisville & Nashville road. In 1850 the Kentucky and Tennessee legislatures granted charters for building a railroad between their cities located, respectively, on the Ohio and Cumberland Rivers. Territorial squabbles, financial problems, and construction difficulties complicated the endeavor for a number of years. At last on October 27, 1859, the first train, a flag-bedecked special loaded with significant personages, black smoke billowing from the stack as the engine pounded southward from Louisville, made the trip to Nashville, where its arrival was greeted with remarkable fanfare. The excursionists were welcomed by the mayor and the city council, wined and dined, and most notably, entertained at the State Capitol.[17] The Louisville & Nashville would enjoy a long stand— more than a century before "progress" signaled its death knell—and now, as Kate Campbell sings in her hauntingly sad lyrics, "Trains [passenger] Don't Run from Nashville Anymore." (Sad indeed for one who grew up with the Pan American and the Humming Bird, and a stark reminder of that disconcerting truth about change—truth well expressed by one of Charles Frazier's characters in his novel *Cold Mountain,* that "as often as not the thing lost was preferable to the thing gained, so that over time we'd be lucky if we just broke even.")[18]

By the time the Civil War began Nashville also had rail connections directly south into Decatur, Alabama, on the Memphis & Charleston line, as well as farther to the east at Stevenson, Alabama, where Vernon Stevenson's Nashville & Chattanooga line joined the Memphis & Charleston road. Because of Nashville's location on the Cumberland River, its extensive network of turnpikes, and the newly completed railroads linking the city with Louisville, north Alabama, Chattanooga, and on to the young, thriving town of Atlanta, Nashville became one of the South's most important cities.[19]

In the last two decades before the Civil War, Nashville experienced rapid growth—in fact, its population more than doubled between 1840 and 1860—as well as an increase in the endowments of civilization. New businesses, such as banking, printing, publishing, iron manufacturing, and others, opened or expanded. Hotels welcomed travelers; impressive and elaborate homes—a few truly beautiful mansions—peppered the landscape; and educational institutions thrived. Middle Tennessee's growing metropolis was making its presence felt ever more broadly, both as a trade and manufacturing center and as a cultural influence.

A great city and the capital of a state requires a fitting state house. In 1845 Philadelphia architect William Strickland, who had already designed a number of nationally known buildings, such as the Second Bank of the United States,

Tennessee State Capitol, nineteenth century. Courtesy of the Tennessee State Library and Archives.

and was considered the nation's foremost authority on the Greek revival style, was engaged as architect of the Tennessee State Capitol. With the cornerstone laid under the sweltering sun on July 4 the same year, Strickland proceeded to turn Cedar Knob Hill into Capitol Hill. The architect's projection of a $250,000 building to be completed in three years eventually grew into a fourteen-year endeavor and a cost approaching one million dollars.[20] Unfortunately, Strickland died in 1854 before the structure was completed. But Nashville and the state of Tennessee finally enjoyed a truly magnificent Capitol, "the crowning jewel on the Nashville skyline," as James A. Hoobler wrote—at least for anyone who appreciates Greek revival architecture. As impressive in the twenty-first century as it was in the nineteenth, when a Union soldier wrote that it was "the finest building that I ever saw," the structure yet serves as the Tennessee State Capitol and a source of satisfaction to most Tennesseans.[21]

Strickland, who liked Nashville, is said to have designed several other structures in the city. Most notable, and definitely the work of the gifted artist, was the twin-towered, Egyptian revival style First Presbyterian Church, at the corner of today's Church Street and Fifth Avenue, and known since 1955 as the Downtown Presbyterian Church. The impressive St. Mary's Catholic Church has sometimes been attributed to Strickland, but is also said to have been designed by Adolphus Heiman, who came to the United States from Prussia in 1834, soon settling in Nashville. However this may have been, Strickland's single greatest contribution to Nashville was, of course, the Tennessee State Capitol. Appropriately, he was buried in a niche in the north portico.[22]

Among Nashville's most elegant antebellum, private mansions—complemented by beautiful gardens and extensive acreage—perhaps three were imminently impressive and, as this narrative is written, all three yet survive. The earliest was Andrew Jackson's Hermitage. Begun in 1819, the brick structure was remodeled and considerably expanded more than a decade later, only to burn in 1834 while Jackson was president. "Old Hickory" soon rebuilt it with additional touches of splendor. Standing today a few miles from Nashville on the north side of the Lebanon Road, the large home's magnificence is accentuated by its tasteful simplicity.[23]

By the 1840s John Harding and his son William Giles Harding had accumulated extensive land holdings (eventually thousands of acres) southwest of Nashville, along the road bearing their name. Christening the plantation Belle Meade (Beautiful Meadow), the Hardings erected a superb, stately, Greek revival mansion, which the son brought to its full magnificence in 1854. Today it is maintained by the Association of Tennessee Antiquities.[24]

In 1849 Adelicia Hayes Franklin, young widow of slave trader and land owner Isaac Franklin, was acclaimed by some as the wealthiest woman in America, with extensive land ownership in Tennessee, Louisiana, and Texas. When Adelicia, in the above year, married Colonel Joseph Acklen, the couple built on land owned by Adelicia an illustrious plantation house, showcasing one of Tennessee's most elaborate private interiors constructed before the war. The design is said to have been contributed to by both William Strickland and Adolphus Heiman. A Union soldier who visited the home said he "found it the best improved place I have ever seen. A million of dollars is said to have been

Tennessee State Capitol and equestrian statue of Andrew Jackson, twenty-first century. Photograph by John Hursh.

expended in improving it." Known as Belmont (Beautiful Mountain), the mansion today serves as a cherished hall on the campus of Belmont University.[25] By 1860 Nashville had a number of magnificent homes and no doubt some people would contend that they—at least several of the homes—are as deserving of remembrance as those selected above.

With each passing year Nashville's manufacturing and commerce became more diversified. By the time of the war, the city was home to several foundries and millwork and furniture plants. All manner of businesses, from building ships to brewing beer, were thriving. For example, Nashville had "a steamboat yard, a carriage factory, a boot and shoe manufactory, a brickyard, three patent medicine firms, a facility for producing artificial limbs, four insurance companies, two tobacco factories, three breweries, and several banks and hotels."[26] Of Nashville's hotels, none would be more notable than the Maxwell House, begun in 1859 by John Overton Jr., descendent of Judge John Overton, built at the corner of Church Street and Fourth Avenue. During the war, the still-unfinished

121

structure served as a barracks, hospital, and prison. Later lending its name to a Nashville-blended coffee, the hotel's fame was enhanced when Theodore Roosevelt pronounced Maxwell House Coffee "good to the last drop."[27] On Christmas night, 1961, the Maxwell House succumbed to fire.

The city had grown affluent by the mid-1800s. Time for cultural advancement became available and Nashville strongly supported two large theaters. The Adelphi, fronting on today's Fourth Avenue, just north of Charlotte Avenue, was designed by Adolphus Heiman in 1850. Praised for having the second largest stage in the United States, the theater hosted some of America's finest stage performers, such as Edwin Booth, John Drew, and Jenny Lind. The New Theatre was located at the corner of today's Fifth Avenue and Union Street, and also hosted excellent theatrical productions.[28]

Long before Nashville would be saluted in the second half of the twentieth century as "Music City USA," its citizens had proudly boasted that the city was "the Athens of the South." The foundation for such a claim was laid by 1860. Most indicative of the city's cultural advancement was the variety of educational institutions. The first school established was Davidson Academy, which grew into the University of Nashville and became a source of great satisfaction to Nashvillians by the 1850s. The medical department of the university particularly enjoyed an enviable reputation. In the mid-1850s the Western Military Institute became a part of the University of Nashville. (All of its cadets chose the Confederacy when the war began.) Also of significance was the Nashville Female Academy, founded in 1816, which by the 1850s became the largest school for women in the South and was renowned for its superb teaching. Too, St. Cecilia Academy for girls dates from the pre-war era. Free public schools opened in 1854, the earliest of any southern city. At the beginning of the war Nashville had five public high schools and numerous private grammar schools. The city also had a School for the Blind, established in the 1840s.[29]

In attempting to keep up with political events and other news, Nashvillians at times could read as many as five daily newspapers, although these tended to "come and go." If citizens were religiously inclined, and a great number were, they could choose from several Protestant denominations (the McKendree Methodist sanctuary, still facing Church Street between Fifth and Sixth avenues, hosted the famous Nashville Convention of Southern delegates during the national crisis of 1850). There were eight Methodist churches, apparently the most numerous Protestant institutions. Roman Catholicism was represented by two churches. Also there were two Jewish synagogues.[30]

In spite of all the religious trappings, there was no blinking at the fact that Nashville had a pronounced seamy side, particularly in the area known as Smokey Row, which is said to have encompassed "eight full blocks of prostitution." Bordering on the river, this red-light district took in a long stretch of Front, Market, and College (today's First, Second, and Third) streets. Most of the houses were ordinary, some hardly more than shacks, while a few were quite expensive. "The flagship of the Nashville bordello trade," wrote Thomas P. Lowry, was a luxurious house located at 101–103 North Front Street, and "valued at $24,000." That was an impressive amount of money in 1860. "Prostitutes, drunkards, and brawlers—black and white—gave Smokey Row its unsavory reputation," said one historian of Nashville's early period. The 1860 census, unlike any before or since in the city, listed the number of women willing to acknowledge themselves as prostitutes. The total was 207, a surprisingly large number for a city no bigger than Nashville. But the city then, as now, was affluent, and the river traffic was heavy. Actually, the number of prostitutes was probably greater than 207, as some Cyprians likely preferred to call themselves waitresses, seamstresses, or something other than what they were. Considering Nashville's religious interests, this side of the city's life must have been especially distasteful to many of the inhabitants.[31]

Nashville's total population in 1860, according to the United States Census, was about 17,000. Of that total, 13,043 were white and 3,945 were black, most of whom were slaves. Still, Nashville's free black population numbered a surprisingly large 719. With approximately 13,000 more people in its suburbs, the greater Nashville area was home to approximately 30,000 inhabitants.[32] With its well-diversified economy, wide-ranging transportation network, broadly based trade, cultural advancement, and political importance, Nashville was clearly Tennessee's leading city, even if Memphis, not yet half a century old, did claim a slightly larger population.

And then came the war. "It is one of the ironies of the Southern experience," observed Stephen Ash, "that in the very hour of the region's greatest public optimism and self-assurance, external and internal forces were conspiring to overturn the Southern world."[33] Certainly this general statement about the South applies to Nashville. In 1860, years of intense sectionalism at last reached a climax. Nashvillians must have sensed the danger. The emotionally charged, monumental issue of the expansion of slavery had swept aside all other considerations, resulting in a disastrous split of the Democratic Party, the only remaining national political institution. The election of Abraham Lincoln, candidate of the free state–based Republican Party, was all but guaranteed. Nashville's John Bell, former Whig, Speaker of the House of Representatives, United States Senator, and long an advocate of compromise on the issue of slavery expansion, ran for the presidency as the candidate of a hastily formed Constitutional-Union Party. Most of the nation was in no mood for such compromise. Bell won only three states, although one of those was Tennessee, Nash-villians supporting him by better than a two-to-one margin.[34]

When the war began in 1861, Nashville occupied a very significant strategic position. Stanley Horn wrote that "Nashville was the . . . most important city south of the Ohio River, with the exception of New Orleans. . . ."[35] Thomas Connelly went a step further, stating of Nashville: "No other western metropolis—not even New Orleans—was so vital to the Southern war effort."[36] Without question, Nashville emerged as the center of warfare in the Confederacy's western theater.

The city's strategic importance stemmed from several factors, location being one of the most consequential. Lying on a major, navigable river and centrally positioned on an east-west axis near the northern boundary of the western Confederacy, Nashville's strategic location was further defined by its extensive railroad connections: north to Louisville; south to Decatur, Alabama; southeast to Chattanooga and the Deep South; and west via the Nashville & Northwestern Railroad to the Tennessee River.

Nashville was rapidly turned into a major arsenal and supply depot. Existing manufacturing establishments were soon converted to war production. Construction of new war-oriented plants began. Nashville's warehouses, within a short time, "were bursting with food and clothing accumulated by the Commissary and Quartermaster Departments." One plant was "manufacturing 100,000 percussion caps a day." Others were producing sabers and muskets. Two foundries "were . . . casting cannon, and one of them was turning out rifled guns. The . . . rifling machine [was] made from plans obtained by a spy sent to a northern arsenal after the beginning of the war."[37]

Nashville was also the center of a very fertile agricultural region, including the surrounding counties of Montgomery, Robertson, Sumner, Wilson, Rutherford, Williamson, and Cheatham. Furthermore, the Confederacy's greatest iron ore–producing area lay west of Nashville, stretching to the Tennessee River. The most important gunpowder mills in the Confederacy were located along the Cumberland River just west of Nashville. The upshot of it all was that Nashville became the most important city of the western Confederacy for the manufacture and storage of all manner of war supplies, from heavy ordnance to shoes, flour, and bacon.[38]

Ironically, in spite of Nashville's unquestionable strategic significance as the major hub of warfare on the Confederacy's western front, almost nothing was done to prepare the city for repelling an attack should it become necessary. The idea of defensive works for Nashville "was laughed at" and General Albert

Sidney Johnston's chief engineer, Jeremy Gilmer, who advocated a defensive "line of the Cumberland," was mocked. "Johnston's dirt digger," he was called.[39] Tennessee's capital, thought its citizens, would be defended at Bowling Green, Kentucky, where General Johnston maintained his headquarters; or perhaps just south of the Kentucky state line, at Forts Henry and Donelson, under construction, respectively, on the Tennessee and Cumberland Rivers—or somewhere; somewhere other than the bluffs along the Cumberland where Nashville stood.

Like most Confederates, Nashvillians tended to be overconfident, some rash and frankly arrogant. No doubt some believed, as was the popular saying, that one Southerner could lick five Yankees. Or was it ten? (That, of course, was assuming the Northerners would fight at all, which many doubted.) Nashvillians reveled in the early Confederate triumphs. At Big Bethel, Virginia, two Union columns attempting to join forces fired at each other by mistake, inflicting a number of casualties, after which they were beaten by a Southern command only one-third their strength. At Wilson's Creek in southwest Missouri, the Union army retreated after a fierce fight, and in Virginia, at Ball's Bluff, the Federals were whipped again.[40]

Above all, Nashvillians thought of Manassas (Bull Run, the Federals called it). It was the war's first engagement that could properly be designated a battle and the only "big" battle of 1861. Fighting in Virginia, just a few miles from Washington, D.C., the Southern army, using gunpowder from the Cumberland River mills,[41] drove the Union army back to the capital, first in panic and at last in rout. Compared to this victory, inconsequential Rebel setbacks that occurred in West Virginia were soon dismissed from memory.

But for those Nashvillians who contemplated the future course of the war in late 1861, such thoughts of the past were woefully misleading as to the coming Federal campaigns. Nothing had yet occurred that even began to compare with what was about to happen. Nashvillians, most of them anyway, seem to have been taken totally by surprise.

The war was not yet a year old when it came to Tennessee in full force. The Union military struck suddenly and dramatically during the dead of winter in 1862, and the results were disastrous for the western Confederacy and for Nashville. In early February, a combined land and water invasion force led by U. S. Grant and Andrew H. Foote broke through the Confederate defensive perimeter across southern Kentucky. Driving south up the Tennessee River and then the Cumberland River, the Federals quickly captured Fort Henry and Fort Donelson, vital to the defense of those strategic riverways, and thus laid open to Union invasion the heart of Tennessee.

Fort Henry fell to the Bluecoats first. Their victory was incredibly easy. The Southern fort was "miserably located" on low ground, "poorly armed,"[42] and threatened "almost as much by the rising river as by the . . . Yankees."[43] With one-third of their fortifications under water, and their two big guns that had sufficient range to duel the Federal gunboats out of commission, the Confederate defenders, commanded by Lloyd Tilghman, surrendered. Already most of the garrison had pulled out, making their escape eastward to Fort Donelson. Thus the Tennessee River lay open as an avenue of enemy advance all the way to Alabama and Mississippi. The entire Kentucky-Tennessee defensive position of the Confederates was in imminent danger of collapsing.

A Southern soldier wrote to his wife that the fall of Fort Henry would "wake up" the South. "Before they would not believe that a Southern army however weak could be driven back, and would do nothing, in spite of General Johnston's remonstances."[44] But suddenly it was a different war. There was no longer time for the preparations that should have been made earlier. Fort Henry was like the first falling domino, setting in motion the rapid collapse of an entire row.

When Fort Henry fell, General Johnston abandoned Bowling Green, retreating through Nashville, eventually to northern Alabama, where he planned to concentrate his forces for a counter-offensive. However, the general ordered half of his troops to Fort Donelson, vainly hoping to maintain control of the Cumberland River and protect Nashville from the Northern advance. The effort was to no avail. In fact, it was a mistake resulting in the capture of a great many Confederate soldiers. Only ten days after the loss of Fort Henry, Fort Donelson also succumbed, following some hard fighting, amply mingled with Rebel bungling, disunity of command, and vacillation—in a battle transpiring in cold weather accentuated with snow and sleet.

The fall of Fort Henry and Fort Donelson was the turning point of the war in the western theater. A series of U.S. triumphs followed, several directly or indirectly attributable to the victories at the forts. Collectively, they left the western Confederacy struggling to survive, and it would never be able to recover. The situation was so shocking that some Southern newspapers, attempting to boost Confederate morale, boldly proclaimed that recent defeats actually foreshadowed positive results. The *Richmond Enquirer* said the defeats "were for our own good!" The *New Orleans Daily Picayune* consoled: "In the economy of Providence apparent evil sometimes becomes the prolific source of good. . . . So in every just cause, true faith . . . will make disaster itself the means of making a way to victory." A few days later a paradoxical editorial in the same paper startlingly proclaimed a "sincere belief" that "the fall of Fort Donelson secures the independence of the Confederate States."[45] Presumably divine providence, angered by Southern arrogance, was somehow teaching the Confederates an indispensable lesson through their defeats, though in the end their cause would surely triumph.

Actually, the fall of Fort Donelson led directly to the loss of Nashville. Unfortified and indefensible, Nashville had no way of contesting the Union gunboats soon expected to steam up the Cumberland. Grant's army rested only miles away downstream on the Cumberland, and Don Carlos Buell's army was advancing south from Louisville, while the Grayclad army of Johnston— removing all the military stores possible and attempting to burn both the suspension and railroad bridges over the Cumberland (succeeding only with the former)—retreated toward Alabama. Confederate Nashville was doomed.

The city's fate carried with it an added touch of cruelty. Early news reports from Fort Donelson proclaimed that a great Southern triumph had been achieved.[46] On Sunday, February 16 (the day Fort Donelson was surrendered), the people of Nashville were still celebrating the supposed victory. Completely unprepared for the sudden—and true—news of defeat which swept the city later that day, "there was," in the words of one historian, "a sickening revulsion of feeling, the pendulum swinging the full arc from elation to gloom."[47] Nashville simply gave way to panic.

All manner of rumors circulated. It was said that Union gunboats, expected momentarily, would blast the city to pieces. General Buell's army, alleged to be thirty-five thousand strong or more, was said to be only miles away and would be overrunning the city within hours. Women and children, so it was claimed, had been ordered to leave the city before the enemy arrived. These and other unverified reports flew through the city on that Sunday. Some people fled—by carriage, by rail, or on foot. Some simply wandered aimlessly through the streets. Others engaged in rioting and looting. On Monday, with stores and businesses closed, the panic began to subside. By the following Sunday, February 23, Buell's Federal troops appeared across the river in Edgefield. The next day Nashville's mayor, Richard B. Cheatham, surrendered the city to General Buell.[48] For the remainder of the war—more than three years—Nashville would be occupied by the Union army.

Nashville was both the first large Southern city captured by the Federals and the first Confederate state capital to fall. It was a great triumph for the Bluecoat forces, who came up from the river with bands blaring as they marched to the Capitol and hoisted the American flag atop it. The city would soon become for the Federal army what it had been for the Confederates: a center of transportation and communication, and their principal supply base in the West.

As for Nashville's citizens who did not flee—and the vast majority did not—a few were truly loyal Unionists, highly pleased by the unexpected turn of events and openly welcoming the Federal soldiers. There were others welcoming the Bluecoats, but their concern involved being on the winning side. Just as they supported the Confederates earlier, in the hope of personal gain, now their future rested with the Federals. Certainly most Nashvillians sympathized with the Confederacy and hoped that in time a Southern counter-offensive might succeed in reclaiming the city. Many made little effort to hide their hostility to the Union regime. Others, attempting to place themselves in position to aid the Confederacy in a secret manner, pretended to accept and cooperate fully with the new military government.[49]

The person appointed by President Lincoln to head that government hailed from East Tennessee. Andrew Johnson, former governor of the state from 1853 to 1857, and the only United States Senator from a seceded state to remain loyal to the Union, arrived in Nashville on March 12, 1862, soon claiming the chair left vacant at the Capitol by Governor Isham G. Harris, who moved out shortly before the Yankees arrived. Johnson unfortunately had a terrible temper. Plagued sometimes by poor judgment as well, made worse because he disliked any- one questioning his decisions, Johnson quickly proceeded to make a bad situa- tion worse.

To begin with, he had never liked Nashville's leaders, political, financial, or otherwise.[50] Requiring that city officials take an oath of allegiance to the United States, Johnson not only removed them from office when they refused, and replaced them with Union men; but he proceeded to have them arrested for treason. In fact, almost any criticism of Johnson or the United States was likely to be interpreted by the governor as "treasonable and seditious." Consequently, a number of prominent Nashvillians found themselves incarcerated in the state penitentiary. Johnson, in his peculiar wisdom, even decided to take on the clergy, summoning a half-dozen men of the cloth to appear before him and demanding that they swear allegiance to the United States. Upon their refusal, Johnson had them thrown into prison and eventually kicked out of town.[51] To a great many citizens it seemed that Johnson, one of the most well-hated figures in Nashville's history, a man bitterly referred to as "the King of Devils" by one young woman, went around much of the time looking for a fight.[52]

Although Nashvillians found themselves under a rigidly enforced martial law, a determined resistance movement, small though it was, operated day and night, helping secure supplies for the Confederacy. A Union observer described Nashville as "the great center to which thronged all the . . . smugglers, spies and secret plotters of treason, whom a love of treachery or gain had drawn to the rebel cause. . . . Lines of communication were kept open to every part of the South, and the rebel army supplied with valuable goods and still more valu- able information. Their shrewdness and secrecy seemed to defy every effort at detection. . . ."[53]

The man in charge of the efforts to detect these underground operatives— the head of the Union army's secret service in Nashville—was an unsavory character named William Truesdail. A person who insisted on being addressed by his self-conferred title of "Colonel," and whose tactics at times would have done the Nazi Gestapo proud, Truesdail boasted that his agents had infiltrated every hotel, railroad car, and steamer, and gained access to "the proudest and wealthiest . . . families. . . ." But the "colonel" so frequently suffered defeat in his efforts to control the Southern Ladies Aid Society, which was smuggling quinine and other drugs to Southern soldiers, that he officially adopted for his service the cynical slogan: "Don't Trust Women!"[54]

If anything, Nashvillians hated him more than they did Governor Johnson. Johnson himself, in fact, despised Truesdail, once describing him as a man "wholly incompetent, if not corrupt, in the grossest sense of the term."[55] After almost a year of misusing his power to arrest and incarcerate, Truesdail finally went too far: presuming to issue orders under the authority of General Rosecrans when "Old Rosy" had given him no such prerogative; also enriching himself while selling confiscated cotton, allegedly on behalf of the United States Army. Widespread and hearty approval greeted his removal, a Nashville paper describing Truesdail as "universally odious" in the judgment of "soldiers, officers and citizens."[56]

During the period while the Union army occupied Nashville, the city experienced a tremendous population surge. Easily offsetting both the loss of Nashvillians who had enlisted in the Confederate army, as well as citizens who went into exile, was the influx of refugees, black and white, plus the northern employees, who came by the thousands to work in various army establishments. By the spring of 1864 an estimated eighteen thousand civilians were working for the Federals in Nashville. And the city's total population was thought to be fifty thousand.[57] By the time of the Battle of Nashville, it may have been one hundred thousand.[58]

Increasingly common on the streets of Nashville, at least by late 1863, was the sight of black men in the uniform of the Federal forces. Yet the majority of African Americans in the city remained employed as workers for the army, rather than wearing the blue uniform. Many military authorities questioned the value of blacks as fighting men—particularly if deployed in the open field and on the offensive. Nevertheless, the great pool of willing black manpower was difficult to ignore and the recruitment of African Americans for the army steadily increased, justified on the basis of performing garrison duty, fighting from behind fortifications, etc.

Brevet Major Henry Romeyn, United States Army, recalled some of his experiences in enlisting blacks for the Army of the Cumberland, writing that the examination of prospective recruits "was provocative of much hilarity." He said considerable trouble ensued regarding names. For example, a man who had passed the medical exam was asked his name. When he replied "Dick," he was informed that every soldier, white or black, had two names. "Don't want none—one name enough for me," the man said. When told that he must have two names, and asked if he wanted to be called by his old master's name, the former slave emphatically replied: "No, sah, I don't. I'se had 'nuff o' ole mass'r." Another recruit, "one of the most athletic men I ever saw," said Major Romeyn, "when notified that he had passed the examination," was so enthusiastic that he "electrified everyone in the room by suddenly placing his hands on the shoulders of the next candidate and leaping clear over his head."[59]

Because Nashville was one of the largest Union army bases in the country, all the problems that accompany any army were present in the city. There were so many prostitutes that an Ohio soldier declared that Nashville was "the city of harlots"; another thought the army's very existence was threatened thereby; while a Nashville newspaper feared the city was becoming "a second Gomorrah."[60] If some Nashvillians thought the city's large number of prostitutes before the war was an embarrassment, they must have turned away in disbelief at the influx of "women of pleasure" after the Federal occupation of the city. Prostitution became so outrageously common and venereal disease so widespread that military authorities rounded up a large number of the women, and sent some north by rail, many more by steamboat, bound for Louisville. One of the steamboats, the *Idahoe,* was said to be carrying five or six hundred women. Some estimates of the total number expelled from the city ran as high as fifteen hundred.[61]

What the city of Louisville thought of this program evidently did not concern the army authorities in Nashville. Predictably, Louisville soon sent the women back—some of them at least. The *Idahoe,* for its part, failed to locate any port receptive to its unusual passengers and eventually returned the women to Nashville. (Even as this chapter is written, spring 2002, it is an interesting aside that Nashville, as periodically reported by the news media, is once more engaged in a major effort, the most extensive in decades, to control prostitution.) Obviously, since the women could not be successfully removed from the city on a permanent basis, and others kept coming, another approach to the problem was necessary. Thus the army began a program of legalized prostitution, making Nashville "America's first experiment with legalized, regulated prostitution."[62]

Medical examinations were required. Charging a fee of one dollar, a license was granted for those free of venereal disease "to practice their profession," returning every two weeks for another exam and, of course, paying another fee. Infected Cyprians were referred for treatment to Hospital Number Eleven, one of the twenty-three hospitals operated by the U.S. army in Nashville. (Incidentally, the remedy for syphilis in the latter part of the war was salts of mercury, leading to a soldiers' pun, "A night with Venus, a lifetime with Mercury.")[63] While hundreds of women complied with the army's regulations, many did not, risking the penalty of a thirty-day jail sentence if caught without a license. To some degree the military program brought in a better class of prostitutes, as a number of women were drawn to Nashville "by the comparative protection from venereal disease which its license system afforded."[64]

Nevertheless, Smokey Row continued to be thought of by many as, in the words of one outraged writer, "a foul breathing hole of hell." And the *maisons de plaisir* were never totally confined to that unsavory section of the city.[65] Nor were some practitioners of "the world's oldest profession." Although expected to remain at the brothels, the women occasionally paraded themselves on the streets. Also, the *Nashville Daily Press* observed that military officers were "frequently" seen in open carriages with known "ladies of the evening." In the fall of 1864, a woman rode into downtown, accompanied by an officer, and presented herself "entirely nude from her waist heavenward," as one Nashville paper described the sight. This zaftig Cyprian created quite a stir, especially when passing the Maxwell House Hotel, where scores of soldiers enthusiastically expressed their hearty and lusty admiration. The editor of the *Daily Press,* however, declared the lewd spectacle "loathsome, abominable and insufferably disgusting."[66]

Smokey Row seemed always to be presenting some kind of problem. One of the worst came on the night of November 25, 1864, only days before the Battle of Franklin. A group of regular army soldiers from the Thirteenth United States Infantry entered the district in quest of female company. Volunteers from the Ninth Pennsylvania and the Fourth Michigan appeared in the area about the same time and for the same purpose. Somehow (and the details are not clear) the men lost interest in the women and became involved in a heated discussion about whether the volunteers or the regulars were the better fighting stock. The result, hardly surprising, was a big brawl that resulted in some gunplay in addition to the use of fists.[67]

Whatever else may have demanded the attention of the Federals occupying Tennessee's capital, first and foremost, as the Union presence continued to swell in numbers and significance, was the defense of the city. The protection of Nashville from possible capture by the Rebels was an issue of major importance, both to the military forces and to Governor Andrew Johnson—the latter seeming almost paranoid in his insistence upon the construction of fortifications around the capital—particularly around the Capitol building. The Union military required no prodding from the governor. Soon after the Yankee occupation of Nashville began, General Don Carlos Buell ordered Captain James St. Clair Morton, Corps of Engineers, United States Army, to proceed to Nashville and choose sites for redoubts to defend the city.[68] Once again, Nashville was to become a fortress on the Cumberland.

And this time, as is the saying, it would be with a vengeance. During the next two and one-half years, Union troops built nearly twenty miles of earthworks. They constructed forts, barricades, and trenches, until at last Nashville could have competed with Washington, D.C., and Richmond, Virginia, for the distinction of being the most heavily fortified city on the continent. William Strickland's Capitol even received a great deal of attention—due to the efforts of the new military governor. Andrew Johnson, although awarded the rank of brigadier general by President Lincoln, actually knew very little about military affairs. However, his vivid imagination had him convinced that a Southern attack on the city was not only likely, but imminent.

Firing off telegrams to the War Department, Johnson repeatedly called for more soldiers to defend the city, while promising that he himself, if necessary, would defend the Capitol with his own blood. Governor Johnson may not have gotten everything that he wanted, but his histrionics clearly had quite an impact. Soon Johnson must have felt a bit more safe in the building after "a stockade of cedar logs and a barricade of cotton bales" were constructed around the Capitol, which was also protected by a battery of artillery (one source claims more than a battery, alleging fifteen heavy guns were in place) and a garrison of infantry, several companies strong, which was stationed inside the building.[69]

Meanwhile, such semi-comic distractions aside, the serious work of protecting Nashville went forward. From the city's beginning the Cumberland River played a significant role in Nashville's history. As the Federals prepared to fortify the capital, the river once again made its presence felt, the waterway's configuration generally dictating where Nashville's defensive lines should be constructed. Flowing east to west, the Cumberland makes a large loop around Nashville, encircling the city on the east, north, and to a degree, the west sides.

However, Nashville is not centered in the river's bend, instead lying snugly against the eastern side of the stream's big loop around it. From the heart of Nashville at the State Capitol, the distance eastward to the river is less than one-half mile. But the river west of the Capitol is fully three miles away. The Cumberland, with Union gunboats ranging up and down it, was somewhat like a giant moat protecting the city to the east and north. Thus Nashville's fortifications needed to be erected on a line to the south and west of the city, running from the river on the east to the river on the west.

Captain Morton envisioned three large forts to anchor the city's defensive system. On St. Cloud Hill the most famous of the forts would be raised: Fort

Negley. The hill is slightly over a mile directly south of downtown Nashville, measuring from the point where Broad Street dead ends at the river. St. Cloud Hill, much of it covered with oak trees, served as a picnic area before the war. The grove of oaks, some quite ancient, was soon leveled, most of the work done by slaves who were impressed by the Federal army for construction purposes. Captain Morton designed the fort with several angles and sides, the general structure measuring about one hundred yards wide by two hundred yards long. It was built of timber, stone, and earth. To open up a clear field of fire for the fort's guns, the School for the Blind was also destroyed. The fort took its name from Brigadier General James Scott Negley, who was left in command at Nashville when General Buell took most of the Army of the Ohio to Kentucky in the early fall of 1862, attempting to thwart the Southern invasion led by General Braxton Bragg.[70]

The two other major forts devised by Captain Morton were Fort Morton (named for the captain of course) and Fort Houston. The latter was named for Russell Houston, a staunch Union man whose house was razed to provide the site for the fortification. Before the war was over, Fort Houston would be renamed Fort McCook, in honor of a sixty-five–year-old Ohioan, Brigadier General Dan McCook, mortally wounded in 1863 while pursuing Confederate raider John Hunt Morgan. Fort Morton was built on a high hill approximately a half-mile west and slightly south of Fort Negley, west of the Franklin Pike and just to the south of the present South Street. Fort Houston lay about three-quarters of a mile northwest of Fort Morton, on yet another rise of ground, where today's Sixteenth Avenue South intersects with Division Street. Smaller fortifications were planned at other strategic places.[71]

Construction of a strong line of breastworks also got underway, both to connect the forts and provide an unbroken defensive chain around the city on the south and west sides. Month after month the work continued. And the cost mounted. Nashville's defenses were requiring such a large financial expenditure that the War Department, fearing waste (or worse), decided to investigate the project. Brigadier General Zealous B. Tower, superintendent of West Point, was dispatched to Nashville with instructions to delve into the matter fully. Not only did Tower find nothing askew, he concluded and recommended that the defenses be strengthened further. Nashville's strategic importance as a Union base for western operations demanded that its defenses be impregnable.[72]

By the time that General George H. Thomas established his headquarters at Nashville in the fall of 1864 and began concentrating troops to halt the advance of the Confederates led by Hood, the city had several more fortifications complementing Forts Negley, Morton, and McCook (as Houston had then come to be known). Fort Casino was one of the more notable and lay immediately west of the Franklin Pike just a few hundred yards south of Fort Morton. It was on the hill which has long since been used as a city reservoir. Also notable was Fort Gillem, situated about a mile and a quarter northwest of Fort McCook, on a hill that later became a part of the Fisk University campus.

Yet another mile to the northwest stood Fort Garesché, named for Colonel Julius P. Garesché, the assistant adjutant general (chief of staff) to General William S. Rosecrans at the Battle of Stones River. Serving in his first battle, Garesché was decapitated by a cannon ball while riding beside Rosecrans. Fort Garesché was a formidable work, mounting fourteen guns, with a good field of fire in every direction, and situated roughly three-quarters of a mile directly east of the river. Several other strong points, less impressive perhaps but significant, further enhanced the Nashville defenses.[73]

The line of breastworks south and west of the city was still not fully constructed when the Confederates moved into southern Tennessee. With hundreds of slaves, as well as many citizens who were conscripted, work on these entrenchments was pushed forward at a rapid pace. On the east, the line began at the Cumberland River where the City Hospital has long stood. It ran southwest to Fort Negley and on to Fort Casino. From that point two lines were developed. The inner line bent back to Fort Morton, before extending directly west through what eventually became the Vanderbilt University campus. From there the line passed north and east of today's Centennial Park (adorned by its magnificent, full-size replica of Greece's Parthenon, complete with a forty-foot-tall statue of Athena) continuing northwest to Forts Gillem and Garesché and finally to the river.

The outer line of breastworks was developed southwest from Fort Casino for almost a mile and a half to a formidable salient, located shortly east of the Hillsboro Pike on the present Linden Avenue. From there the line turned west and then northwest across a high hill (today's Love Circle) just to the east of the Harding Pike, before running basically north to the Cumberland. The upshot of it all, after two and one-half years of work and the expenditure of $365,000 (an immense sum in that day), was that Tennessee's capital, under Union occupation, had indeed become a fortress on the Cumberland.[74] And yet General Hood came on, despite the bloody disaster at Franklin, hoping to place the Federals at Nashville under siege.

6

"Siege" at Nashville, Folly at Murfreesboro

Once more strapped to his saddle, the one-legged commander of the Army of Tennessee rode toward Nashville. Soon dispatching a misleading communiqué to the Secretary of War in Richmond, Hood conveyed the impression that he had triumphed at Franklin, while neglecting to accurately inform the government of the extent of the army's losses.[1] (Richmond would not learn the full truth until February 1865, when Hood filed his final report of the campaign, a document packed with blame for other officers.) With his left arm dangling useless at his side, and some seven thousand of his soldiers dead and wounded on the bloodstained fields north of the Winstead–Breezy Hill range at Franklin, John Bell Hood was symbolic of the shattered force he led. The strength of the Rebel army, considering casualties in earlier skirmishes, disease, and straggling, numbered at the most 25,000 men. Hood himself claimed only 23,053 effective troops when he arrived at Nashville.[2]

Although the general knew, or at least should have known, that the enemy's strength was much greater (actually the Yankees had well over a two-to-one advantage), still Hood came to place the capital city under "siege." And then, as if the Confederates were not already badly weakened, Hood would detach the greater part of Forrest's cavalry, and portions of two brigades of infantry, to Murfreesboro. Probably, when the hardships of cold weather on the poorly equipped troops are factored in, Southern strength on December 15, when the Battle of Nashville began, numbered less than 20,000 effectives; possibly little more than 15,000 or 16,000.

The Confederate commander's plan was to entrench on the city's southern outskirts, wait for the Federals to attack, and hope for reinforcements from Texas—or so he claimed in his memoirs. He would, in his own words, "accept the chances of reinforcements from Texas, and even at the risk of an attack in the meantime by overwhelming numbers," the general declared that he was adopting "the only feasible means of defeating the enemy with my reduced numbers, viz., to await his attack and, if favored by success, to follow him into his works."[3]

By early afternoon of December 1, General Stephen Dill Lee's corps had moved past those who were busy digging graves, and was en route to Nashville. Stewart's and Cheatham's corps followed the next day. On the morning of December 2, the Rebel line of battle began to form and the siege of Nashville got underway. Forrest's cavalry deployed with Chalmers's division on the left and Buford's and Jackson's commands on the right. The vanguard of the infantry soon followed. Hood was far too weak to attack the city and his hope for reinforcements was forlorn. Probably reinforcement was a later thought attempting to justify his decision to push on to Nashville, for there is no evidence that he had any realistic expectation of additional troops. General Beauregard twice wrote Kirby Smith in the Trans-Mississippi Department, the only conceivable place that the Napoleon in Gray could think of where Hood might get reinforcements, but Kirby Smith did not received the messages until the battle at Nashville had been fought. When at last he replied to Beauregard on January 6, 1865, he explained in detail why he could send no troops to Hood.[4] General French later claimed, in a touch of irony, that written in big letters on the wall of Hood's tent was the statement, "An army that can obtain no recruits must eventually surrender."[5]

In fairness to Hood, acceptable alternatives did not exist. To swing around the U.S. forces at Nashville and march for the Ohio River invited an attack in flank and rear by superior enemy numbers. The Butternut invasion of Kentucky in 1862 testified that no significant number of Rebel recruits could be acquired in the Bluegrass State. To head for Virginia to join Robert E. Lee in his effort to deal with Grant seemed even more unrealistic. To retreat, of course, would be an admission of defeat—probably unthinkable for Hood.

And the U.S. commander at Nashville was certainly no incompetent who might be expected to play into Hood's hands with a reckless assault; the type of thing, for example, that enabled Lee to severely punish Ambrose Burnside's forces at Fredericksburg. (Or, for that matter, that Hood himself had just done at Franklin.) Thus having determined to come to Nashville, Hood's greatest mistake for the unfortunates in his army—although he later said he believed the troops would be "better satisfied, even after defeat if, . . . a brave and vigorous effort had been made to save the country"—the Confederate commander did the only thing he could: wait for the Union to attack and drive him back.[6]

Of course the dead body of many a Confederate who had made "a brave and vigorous effort" at Franklin, afterward blended into a bloody canvas of battlefield horror. December 1 dawned bright and crisp, revealing a large expanse of ground on both sides of the Columbia-Franklin Pike that, in the words of John Johnston, "was literally strewn with the dead." Many of the badly wounded were still on the field as well. James Cooper also walked over the ground that morning and declared that the scene "baffles description." Some of the dead "were shot all to pieces. One man I saw had forty-seven bullet holes through him. The place looked like one vast slaughter pen. . . . I felt sick at heart for days afterward." Cooper believed the survivors were demoralized, "so disheartened by gazing on that scene of slaughter that they had not the nerve for the work before them."[7]

Chaplain James M'Neilly had labored all night at a field hospital, assisting the surgeons as best he could. Informed that his brother had been killed, M'Neilly at dawn tramped across the battleground from the railroad cut near the Lewisburg Pike to the vicinity of the F. B. Carter cotton gin. "I could have trodden on a dead man at every step," he said. "The dead were piled up in the trenches almost to the top of the earthworks." Many dead horses were also on the field and M'Neilly remembered walking past the dead mount of General John Adams, which remained atop the earthworks. Then the chaplain's sad mission came to an end. He found his brother's body, lying close to where General Cleburne lay.[8]

The day would be long remembered, the day when the Franklin dead were buried. Soldiers labored for hours as they dug graves. Some burial details worked all day; some toiled for two days. There were units in which the slaughter had been so great that the survivors called upon other commands for help. The dead were in such great numbers that sometimes long trenches were dug and the bodies laid side by side; sometimes more than one layer of bodies, occasionally even Blue and Gray buried together if found near each other.[9] Crudely devised wooden head boards marked the site of some graves, recording bits of information about the bodies resting beneath the soil. Others remained unmarked—and forever lost.

The winter of 1864–65 proved to be extremely cold and gradually the wood markers disappeared, as people appropriated them for firewood. Colonel John

The Carnton (John and Randall McGavock) House. Photograph by John Hursh.

McGavock, owner of the Carnton mansion, believed the Franklin dead deserved a more fitting and commemorative burial ground. He later designated two acres of land next to his family cemetery, and only a short distance from the Carnton house, as the final resting place for as many of the Confederate dead as could be located. All were not found, but the remains of nearly fifteen hundred soldiers were placed in the cedar-lined cemetery. Buried by states, the identities of some, however, were unknown.

The generals killed at Franklin were interred elsewhere. For a time the bodies of four of them—John Adams, Patrick Cleburne, Hiram Granbury, and Otto Strahl—lay on the lower back porch at Carnton. The mortally wounded States Rights Gist died during the night at the residence of William White, located on the far western side of the battlefield. John C. Carter survived until December 10, when he died at the Harrison house.[10] At the Carnton mansion various Franklin ladies ministered to the wounded, doing whatever they could to help, as they did at many places in the town where temporary hospitals were established. A wounded Georgian, James A McCord, wrote his brother that he was "well cared for. . . . The people are the kindest in the world, *especially the ladies* [McCord's emphasis]."[11] Carnton's two stories were packed with wounded men. Puddles of blood stained the hardwood floors a deep red in some places. Casualties were so numerous, running into the hundreds, that the outbuildings of the mansion also served as crude hospitals. And many wounded soldiers lay on the ground in the yard. Mrs. John McGavock supervised the makeshift nursing, a service for which she would be long remembered.

Colonel William Dudley Gale provided details, as wounded men continued to be brought to Carnton all through the night: "Every room was filled, every bed had two poor, bleeding fellows, every spare space, niche, and corner under the stairs, in the hall, everywhere. . . ." Observing that the wounded and dead filled the yard, as well as the outbuildings, Gale said that "our doctors were deficient in bandages," and Mrs. McGavock "began by giving her old linen, then her towels and napkins, then her sheets and tablecloths, then her husband's shirts and her own undergarments." During all the night, as the surgeons labored, "amid the sighs, and moans and death rattles," Mrs. McGavock constantly worked, also furnishing "tea and coffee and such stimulants as she had, and that, too, with her own hands."[12]

Private Joseph N. Thompson of the Thirty-fifth Alabama Infantry, whose Company B suffered seventeen of twenty-three members killed or wounded at Franklin, was among the wounded carried to the McGavock home, where he spent an agonizing night on the ground awaiting medical attention. Later Thompson recorded the following: "Twenty four hours after the Battle of Franklin and while the writer was being carried to the operating table under the trees, he noticed a pile of arms and legs as high as the table; when he was removed from the table following an operation, his leg topped the pile."[13]

During the morning of December 1, a number of General Cleburne's men appeared at Carnton for one last view of their dead commander. Then the bodies of Cleburne, Granbury, Strahl, and three other officers were transported to Columbia for burial. On a cold December 2—"a day of darkness and distress" for Charles Quintard—the Episcopal chaplain at noon officiated at the funeral of General Strahl, Captain James Johnson, and "a dear friend," Lieutenant John H. Marsh. At 3 P.M. the chaplain conducted another service, that time for Cleburne, Granbury, and Colonel R. B. Young, with interment following in Columbia's Rose Hill Cemetery.[14]

The choice of burial sites disturbed Quintard. "I could not content my mind with the resting place which had been chosen by the sexton for our gallant dead—in close proximity to the graves of soldiers . . . of the Federal army." The prominent chaplain soon arranged for the bodies to be disinterred and removed to Ashwood Cemetery, behind St. John's Episcopal Church, a beautiful red-brick structure of Gothic architecture that still stands, in the midst of magnolias, oaks and hickories, about halfway between Columbia and Mount Pleasant.[15] The site was especially fitting for General Cleburne. Only a few days before, when advancing from Mount Pleasant, Cleburne had been drawn to the church. It likely reminded him of the Athnowen Churchyard in Ireland, his father's place of burial. Walking in the rain, and touched by the graceful surroundings, the general remarked to a staff officer that it was "almost worth dying for, to be buried in such a beautiful spot."[16] Cleburne's body would remain at Ashwood for more than five years, eventually removed to Evergreen Cemetery, overlooking the Mississippi River from a height near Helena, Arkansas. One wonders if the Irish general would have preferred that his body remain at Ashwood.

Despite the horrors of the Battle of Franklin, as the armies moved on to Nashville the beauty of Middle Tennessee continued to impress. General Lee wrote his wife that he was in "the most beautiful country in the world," and declared that it was "too beautiful [for] infernal Yankees. . . ."[17] Both armies certainly had their share of disreputable men, examples of which have been referenced in previous chapters. But as the Federals fell back to Tennessee's capital following the Franklin engagement, a group of truly "infernal Yankees," tramping along the Del Rio Pike, happened upon an impressive Georgian-Federal home known as Meeting of the Waters. The name came from the nearby confluence of the West Harpeth and Big Harpeth Rivers. What then transpired would be considered by some as too improbable to be believable, had some novelist presented the story as fiction.

The band of soldiers set about plundering and stealing, boasting that after taking whatever they wished, they would torch the house. The fine house, which dates back to the early 1800s, was then owned by Nicholas Edwin Perkins, who was in no position to resist. Not only was Perkins badly outnumbered; his right hand was hopelessly crippled from a dueling wound inflicted by a fellow student when both were attending Centre College at Danville, Kentucky.

Perkins proceeded to lock his wife and daughter in an upstairs room, which he intended to guard as best he could if necessary, while sending his son running to seek a Union officer in the hope of gaining help. Fortunately, the son soon returned with an officer who, with drawn sword, chased the marauding soldiers from the house. One can only speculate as to what Perkins must have thought when, extending his left arm in gratitude to his Good Samaritan, he realized the Union officer was the same man who years before had wounded him in the duel at Centre. It was a happening that Margaret Mitchell, had she known of it, well might have worked into *Gone with the Wind.*[18]

By December 2, at the latest, virtually all the Yankees, "infernal" or otherwise, were united at Nashville. John Schofield, with Thomas J. Wood, who had replaced the injured David Stanley, rode in some time before midnight on November 30. General Thomas greeted him, as Schofield later wrote in his memoirs, in his "usual cordial but undemonstrative way," and congratulating him, said that he "had done well." Schofield replied that he hoped "never again to be placed in such a position," and afterward told General Jacob Cox that he did not feel very grateful to Thomas. While Thomas and Schofield were conversing, Colonel James F. Rusling came in with news that Andrew Jackson Smith was finally arriving. Rusling had heard the steamboat whistles down on the Cumberland, as they signaled Smith's coming. Within a short time Smith walked in and, according to Rusling's account, General Thomas "literally took him in his arms and hugged him. . . ." Perhaps the touchy Schofield was impressed by the difference in the greeting that Thomas gave the two. Soon, however, all were discussing the battle at Franklin, after which the conversation turned to the situation at Nashville. Early in the morning of December 1, Colonel Rusling said that Thomas, Smith, Schofield, and Wood had maps spread on the floor and were down on their knees examining the positions for the troops around Nashville. The mood was one of optimism. With the arrival of Smith and Schofield, the Union force at Nashville had been increased by more then thirty thousand, bringing the total U.S. strength to well over fifty thousand.[19]

Meanwhile, as the Confederates came up in front of Nashville, General Lee's forces took position astride the Franklin Pike. Deploying to Lee's right was Cheatham's corps, while Stewart took position on the army's left. "The entire line of the army will curve forward from General Lee's center," instructed Hood, in order "that General Cheatham's right may come as near the Cumberland as possible above Nashville, and General Stewart's left as near the Cumberland as possible below Nashville."[20] Soon the Graycoats were laboring to throw up entrenchments confronting the Union works. General Cheatham, incidentally, was fortunate not to have been killed on one of the days. The corps commander and his staff rode up on an open spot to observe the enemy, making themselves a conspicuous target. One of the Confederate gunners thought it "a foolish thing to do," because Fort Negley "had our range exactly." In less than five minutes an enemy shell burst in their midst, "killing and wounding a number of men and horses, and knocking down Cheatham," who immediately scrambled for cover along with the other survivors.[21]

Extending the Rebel line "as near the Cumberland as possible" proved to be, on both flanks, not very near at all. The Southern line, which covered a distance of approximately four miles, actually was too long to be adequately covered by some twenty thousand men. (Even thirty thousand, had they been available, would have been none too strong.) And still Cheatham's right flank lay two miles from the river on the east, while Stewart's left flank was nearly four miles from the Cumberland on the west. Thus the Confederate line covered only four of the eight roads into Nashville: the Nolensville, Franklin, Granny White, and Hillsboro Pikes. The Lebanon and Murfreesboro Pikes were open into the city from the east and the Charlotte and Harding Pikes from the west.

Hood's cavalry patrols, especially after he sent well over half of Forrest's command to Murfreesboro, were much too weak to satisfactorily cover such an expanse of territory. Consequently Hood's position was highly vulnerable to an enemy envelopment on either flank. Cheatham's flank could be turned by the Murfreesboro Pike and Stewart's by the Harding Pike. The entire position was weak because the whole line was stretched dangerously thin. "Had he tried," charged historian Tom Connelly, "Hood could not have aligned his troops on a worse position." Historian Steven Woodworth characterized the deployment as "an atrocious defensive position."[22]

Some seventy-five years ago, Thomas Hay pointedly contended that Hood's line "should have bent southwards on the east side of the Franklin Pike in the direction of Overton Hill. . . ." Hay observed that "the general trace of the line of works was concave, thus necessitating movement from one part of the line . . . to another on the outside of a circumference."[23] Simply put, the Confederates were dealing with exterior lines of communication. While never good, this was especially bad when confronting an enemy with markedly superior numbers. This is why Hay said the line should have bent southward east of Franklin Pike, instead of continuing in a northeastward direction to a point beyond the Nolensville Pike. Then the exterior line problem, to a great degree, would have been corrected, making much easier the shifting of troops from points experiencing minimal pressure from the enemy to those under the greatest stress.

Connelly rightly argued that Hood could have found "a far better line" a mile or so to the south. He referred to the impressive Overton Hill range, extending from the Franklin Pike westward toward the Hillsboro Pike, and merging into the equally rugged Harpeth Hills.[24] Certainly the Overton Hill range, just south of present-day Tyne Boulevard, would have put Hood on higher, more formidable ground, making it also tougher for General Thomas to flank the Confederates, and easier for them to protect their line of retreat. It is noteworthy that both Hay and Connelly, who were fine historians, believed this would have been a better position for the Southern army. Hay wrote that when General Thomas's concentrations and intentions against Hood's left flank became evident, the Rebel commander should have drawn back his army to the higher ground, "without allowing his troops to become seriously engaged."[25] The arguments of both historians are sound. General Hood needed far greater strength than he possessed if he were going to defend successfully the position he had staked out.

Worse still, valuable time had been wasted when General Hood decided that the Southern line, which crossed the Franklin and Granny White Pikes slightly north of today's east-west running, I-440 highway, and just where Gale

Lane and Granny White presently intersect, had been located too close to the Union fortifications and, in fact, was untenable. Much of the line was then hastily relocated, under terrible weather conditions, a short distance to the rear. Portions of the abandoned entrenchments were afterward manned by a skeleton-like skirmish line. By this time Hood's "masterpiece of suicidal folly,"[26] —Stanley Horn's memorable phrase in description of the Murfreesboro sideshow—was proving, perhaps, the single worst of all Hood's Nashville blunders.

On December 2, by order of Hood, General Bate's division was sent eastward for the purpose of destroying "the railroad from Murfreesboro to Nashville, burning all the bridges and taking the block-houses and then burning them."[27] Soon General Forrest, with two of his cavalry divisions, was also ordered eastward to join in the railroad destruction, proceeding in the direction of Murfreesboro. Under orders from Hood, Forrest and Bate joined forces, with Forrest assuming command of the combined infantry and cavalry. Still more infantry appeared, also orchestrated by Hood—the brigades of Claudius Sears and Joseph B. Palmer, giving Forrest a total command of approximately sixty-five hundred men. Most historians have viewed the mission's objective, in addition to wrecking the railroads, as intended both to prevent the Murfreesboro garrison, about eight thousand strong, from joining Thomas at Nashville, and possibly gain an easy triumph by forcing the garrison to surrender.[28]

Wiley Sword, however, suggested a different thesis, one in which Murfreesboro became the main focus of Hood's dreams of victory at Nashville. "Murfreesboro," wrote Sword, "became an increasingly central element in Hood's calculations, reflecting his growing conviction that it was the key to taking Nashville." Sword thought, like most students of the campaign, that Hood's initial concept was to keep the Federals at Nashville and Murfreesboro "separated by destroying the railroad between the two sites." However, by December 11, according to Sword, Hood "had modified his plans to 'force the enemy to take the initiative.'"

Hood would apply continuous pressure, contended Sword, "on what he understood was Murfreesboro's six thousand (actually eight thousand) man Federal garrison," believing that General Thomas "might be forced to march to their relief." Much of Sword's argument seems dependent on Hood's December 11 statement in which the Confederate commander wrote: "Should this force attempt to leave Murfreesboro, or should the enemy attempt to reinforce it, I hope to be able to defeat them."[29] Sword presented a thought-provoking view. But if forcing Thomas to "take the initiative," with the hope of a Rebel strike against the Yankees in flank, was Hood's objective, the plan obviously did not work. In fact, the expedition in general, whatever the objective, left much to be desired.

Back on the morning of Sunday, July 31, 1862, then Brigadier General Nathan Bedford Forrest moved against the little town of Murfreesboro from the east, heading a cavalry column fourteen hundred strong. The day was his forty-first birthday and Forrest had told the troopers that he wanted to celebrate the occasion in a special way. Striking at dawn, the vigorous cavalryman demonstrated his genius for battle. Combining brilliant tactics with a talent for bluffing, Forrest captured about twelve hundred Federal officers and men, destroyed the depot containing government supplies that could not be carried with him and wrecked the Nashville & Chattanooga Railroad bridges in the vicinity. By late afternoon the general and his command, having suffered only a handful of casualties, left Murfreesboro by the same road on which they had come. Proud citizens of the town were soon referring to the episode as "the Battle of Murfreesboro."[30]

More than two years later, in early December 1864, Lieutenant General Forrest was again approaching Murfreesboro, this time from the west. He and General William Bate experienced some initial success in destroying sections of the Nashville & Chattanooga Railroad; also capturing and burning several blockhouses. When Forrest took command of the combined infantry and cavalry forces on December 5, the aggressive cavalryman envisioned a strike against Fortress Rosecrans at Murfreesboro. The largest U.S. fortress constructed during the war, it was named in honor of General William Starke Rosecrans, who commanded the Union army at the Battle of Stones River. Built soon after that engagement, and lying slightly west and north of the town, Fortress Rosecrans encompassed about two hundred acres, and included "nine lunettes, four redoubts, two batteries, two demi-lunettes, and a redan. . . ."[31] On December 6, Forrest conducted a "careful reconnaissance" of the fortress, then garrisoned by approximately eight thousand men, under the command of General Lovell H. Rousseau, and concluded the fortification was too formidable to carry by assault.[32]

Thus the Confederates took up a position west of the fortress, along the Wilkinson Pike, and beyond the range of the fifty-some-odd guns in the fortification. While General Rousseau was aware of the Rebel presence, he knew nothing of their numbers, precise location, or intentions. Troubled by the unknown, Rousseau decided to send out a reconnaissance in force. Major General Robert H. Milroy was chosen to lead the troops, over three thousand strong. He would march south and west along the Salem Pike, then turning north toward the Graycoats and hopefully learning something of their numbers and position, before finally swinging eastward and back to the safety of the Union fortress.

Milroy was a man on a mission, desperately seeking, as he expressed it, to wipe out "the foul stigma of my arrest by the infamous scoundrel Halleck"; and that before the conclusion of the war forever eliminated any opportunity "of military fame and renown," which from "earliest boyhood," confided the general to his wife, had been "the dream of my life. . . ."[33] Milroy referred to an embarrassing defeat at the hands of Richard S. Ewell's corps, as the Rebels moved northward in mid-June 1863, on a march that ultimately led to Gettysburg. Ewell's forces surprised Milroy with an attack at Winchester, Virginia. The Bluecoat general and his men fled in the night, abandoning guns and ammunition and suffering about forty-five hundred casualties. (Approximately one thousand Union soldiers died in the melee.) Milroy and some twelve hundred Federals managed to escape, but the debacle led to the general's arrest.

Although exonerated by a court of inquiry, Milroy's reputation had suffered grave damage and the Indianan found himself dispatched to the western theater. "I have been so badly treated that I sometimes wish that Jeff Davis and the Devil would take the country," he wrote his wife Mary in late October of 1864.[34] Besides General Halleck, "the infamous scoundrel," a favorite phrase that Milroy delighted in employing, he also blamed "the West Pointers," who allegedly had gotten him "out of the ring of all honorable service and are determined to keep me out. . . ." Milroy directed his wrath at the president as well, calling him "the weak Lincoln," who though acknowledging Milroy's "merits and the injustice done [him] . . . is too cowardly to order [a redress] of my great wrongs."[35]

Thus on December 7, excited and emboldened by reports that the legendary Forrest commanded the Confederate forces, General Milroy envisioned the possibility at long last of a redemptive triumph in the field against one of the enemy's most illustrious generals. Moving out the Salem Pike at midmorning and marching for three and one-half miles, Milroy then swung northward at Gresham Lane heading in double column toward the Butternuts, located a mile and a half to his front. When General Forrest first sighted the Federals on the Salem Pike he was "fully satisfied that [the enemy's objective] was to make battle."[36] Understandably he assumed that the Union force was advancing to attack him in flank. Pulling back to the west along the Wilkinson Pike until he was near Overall Creek, the Southern "Wizard of the Saddle," as some came to call Forrest, hoped first to draw the Yankees farther from their base, and then fall upon their flanks with his cavalry while Bate's infantry held the enemy's attention in his front.

The ensuing fight, as so often in war, did not develop as either commander hoped. When the U.S. forces drew near the Confederates, "a magnificent artillery duel [raged] for about an hour," reported General Milroy. "I was in hopes that the Rebs would come across the field and attack me," continued Milroy.[37] But it was not to be. Perhaps it was well for Milroy that the enemy did not attack. As the general surveyed the scene, he realized that the Confederate left flank was as near Fortress Rosecrans as his own right flank. If the Southerners should attack and overpower him, his forces might well be cut off from the fort. Besides, the Federal artillery was nearly out of ammunition. Suddenly alert to potential peril, Milroy pulled his lines back for several hundred yards into an expanse of cedar trees (and the ensuing engagement, fought on the old Stones River battleground, would come to be known as the Battle of the Cedars), where they were lost to Confederate view. Many Rebels assumed the Yankees were retreating to Fortress Rosecrans, but the ambitious Milroy had no such intention.[38]

Instead he led his men east and north, screened by a ridge as well as the cedars. When positioned with Fortress Rosecrans to his back, the general rapidly formed his troops facing westward astride the Wilkinson Pike. Although still uncertain of the Graycoats' strength, Milroy immediately moved forward to attack. The moment proved opportune. Surprised Rebels were compelled to retreat from the fortifications they had recently thrown up, or be taken in their left flank. Hurriedly redeploying across the Wilkinson Pike to oppose the on-coming Yankees, a comedy of Confederate errors unfolded. Some Southerners moved too far to the left, others formed their line at an improper angle, and a gap, perhaps one hundred yards in length, existed in the new line. General Bate summarized the situation in his report: "The time of the reappearance of the enemy emerging from the woods, when he was thought to have retired to Murfreesborough (no information being received by me from the cavalry in my front), did not admit of sufficient time to adjust the line before [the enemy] was upon us."[39]

General Forrest, despite the confusion, hoped to counter the Yankee assault and gain the tactical initiative with a cavalry charge against the rear of the Federals. Riding up to the First Florida Infantry Regiment, he pleaded with them to hold their ground: "Men, all I ask of you is to hold the enemy back for fifteen minutes, which will give me . . . time to gain their rear with my cavalry, and I will capture the last one of them."[40] But the Federal attack had surprised the Graycoats and the Union troops had the upper hand. They were not about to relinquish their advantage. The U.S. attack struck hard at the Confederate center and right wing. Fortuitously for General Milroy, as explained by General Bate, the Federal assault "came diagonally from the left and struck [Jesse] Finley's and [Joseph] Palmer's brigades, crumbling and driving them from their temporary works."[41] A terrible blunder may also have been a factor. One historian concluded that "friendly fire," to employ today's terminology, contributed to the Confederate collapse. Some troops of Jackson's brigade, coming up behind the Floridians, the latter wearing blue Yankee jackets acquired at Franklin, may have mistakenly opened fire on their comrades.[42] Such a disheartening occurrence would help explain the sudden collapse of the Florida line. However this may be, the Southerners gave ground on both their left and right, as more and more men headed for the rear, some in panic.

Seeing that the Butternuts' line was going to pieces, General Forrest rode in among the infantry, trying to halt the fleeing men and restore order. "He rode up and down the line, shouting, Rally, men—for God's sake, rally!" according to a Southern artilleryman. But the panic-stricken soldiers ignored the general. Forrest called out to a color-bearer "who was running for dear life," and ordered him to halt. When the frightened soldier paid no heed, Forrest, claimed the artilleryman, "drew his pistol and shot the retreating soldier down." Then seizing the colors, the general vigorously waved them in front of the men racing to the rear, as he screamed at them, his shouts punctuated with threats and profanity, to halt and fight. Forrest's chief of artillery, Captain John Morton, called Milroy's attack "the hardest blow" that Forrest took during the whole war.[43]

One wonders how long the battle might have continued, and with what ultimate results, if General Milroy had not been recalled to the fort. General Rousseau, acting on reports of a significant force of Confederate infantry to the north (a false report, as Forrest makes plain, generated from the presence of Buford's cavalry demonstrating against Murfreesboro), urgently directed Milroy to return to Fortress Rosecrans. Obeying orders, the general pulled back, reformed, and started for the fort.[44] The battle was over. That Milroy was pleased with his performance on December 7 is an understatement. He was near ecstatic. Writing to Mary on the day after Christmas, Milroy said: "I have been out and examined my battleground of the 7th instant and I am very much surprised at the greatness of my victory. . . . I drove [the enemy] in 32 minutes from three strong lines of breastworks. . . . It is in many respects the best fight of the war."[45]

On New Year's Day, Milroy wrote a long letter to his wife and went into detail about the December 7 battle. Claiming he could have "whipped two or three times" as many Butternuts as he did, the general said "my good genius" prevented him from charging the enemy in their first position and "led me to fall back and pass around to take them in flank. . . ." He wrote that his officers and men could not understand what he was doing and supposed he was going back to the fort until he faced them about and attacked. "This flank movement and its splendid results sealed my reputation among the officers and soldiers," proudly declared Milroy. "They all swear I am the best general living. . . ." Mary replied, actually responding to her husband's earlier rendition of the battle: "You no doubt are in your element again."[46]

While Milroy's crowing provides an amusing read, the general had indeed bested the great Forrest in the December 7 fight on the old Murfreesboro battlefield. As a Union soldier, W. S. Carson, expressed the event in a letter to his wife Elvira, General Milroy and his men "went in to [Forrest] like killer snakes. We whipped him like a turkey and captured two hundred of his men," claimed Carson.[47] Contrary to Milroy's hopes, however, the triumph did little to restore his reputation. When Milroy is remembered today, if he is remembered at all, it is usually for the Virginia failure at the hands of Richard Ewell's command. As for Forrest, his legacy was solidly based on many campaigns throughout the war. One untoward incident was not about to change that.

After the Battle of the Cedars, Forrest continued to wreck the railroad, making it increasingly difficult for supplies to reach the Yankees at Fortress Rosecrans. The fortress garrison was effectively cut off from Nashville. But General Thomas would send no rescuing troops. Nevertheless, the Yankee Murfreesboro garrison contributed to the overall Union effort by keeping Forrest and the bulk of the Grayclad cavalry occupied. General Forrest and most of his troopers would play no part in the fighting at Nashville—a great loss for the Rebels; much greater than the loss to Thomas of the use of eight thousand garrison troops at Fortress Rosecrans.

Meanwhile in Nashville, there seemed to be only one significant problem for the U.S. forces. General Wilson's cavalry needed better mounts and equipment. Back on December 1 Thomas had wired Halleck at Washington: "If Hood attacks me here he will be more seriously damaged than he was yesterday [at Franklin]; if he remains until Wilson gets equipped, I can whip him and will move against him at once."[48] But the administration in Washington demanded action immediately. Thomas's telegram inaugurated a series of proddings from the capital. Halleck turned the general's message over to Secretary of War Stanton who soon conferred with the president. Lincoln was not pleased. The idea of Thomas remaining behind the Nashville fortifications until Wilson got equipped reminded the president of "the McClellan and Rosecrans strategy of do nothing and let the enemy raid the country." Stanton wired General Grant at once, conveying what the president had said and requesting him to "consider the matter."[49]

Grant quickly applied himself with characteristic intensity of focus, dispatching Thomas two telegrams that same day, advising him to attack before Hood could fortify his position. Continuing to write, he instructed Thomas about details and warned that Hood would attack the railroads or cross the river and march into Kentucky. On December 6 Grant ordered Thomas, "Attack Hood at once," and on the eighth the hero of Vicksburg told Halleck that Thomas was too cautious to ever take the initiative, and if he "has not struck yet, he ought to be ordered to hand over his command to Schofield."[50] Like others in Washington, General Grant did not appreciate the difficulties of Hood's situation, and exaggerated what the Rebel commander might be able to accomplish.

While admitting to Thomas on December 2 that "at this distance . . . I might err as to the best method of dealing with the enemy," Grant nevertheless continued to instruct as if fully convinced that his Nashville general was the one in error. Actually Grant never really understood the situation at the Tennessee capital. Even years later in his memoirs he wrote: "The country was alarmed, the administration was alarmed, and I was alarmed lest . . . Hood would get north." Apparently he had never realized, or at least never acknowledged, the difficulties faced by Hood if he attempted to move farther north.[51]

Secretary Stanton, also far removed from the military forces at Nashville, sarcastically weighed in, favoring immediate action regardless of the problems for the Union cavalry, as he told Grant: "Thomas seems unwilling to attack because it is hazardous, as if all war was anything but hazardous. If he waits for Wilson to get ready, Gabriel will be blowing his last horn."[52] Then, on December 9, General Halleck added his voice, again conveying the urgency of attack, as he said to Thomas: "General Grant expresses much dissatisfaction at your delay in attacking the enemy. If you wait till General Wilson mounts all his cavalry, you will wait till doomsday, for the waste equals the supply. Moreover," claimed the general, "you will soon be in the same condition that Rosecrans was last year—with so many animals that you can not feed them."[53] By this time, however, General Thomas was indeed prepared to launch into the enemy's forces.

And then came the cold weather—again; and worse than before. Much worse in fact, and the bitter cold seemed accentuated by the relatively mild days preceding. On December 8 the mercury plummeted and a cold rain set in, later changing to sleet and snow, as the temperature hovered around ten degrees. The frozen ground, covered with ice, proved hazardous to man and beast, with soldiers and horses slipping, sliding, and falling. The entire country around Nashville was paralyzed. Five days later the morning temperature was still only thirteen degrees.[54]

Many soldiers from northern states wrote home about the miserably cold weather. Some Confederates from the deep South said it was the worst weather they had ever experienced. The author was in Nashville on Sunday, December 10, 1995, armed with binoculars and revisiting many of the significant battle sites—Peach Orchard Hill, Shy's Hill, several of the redoubt locations, etc. The car's outside temperature gauge fluctuated between fourteen and seventeen degrees throughout that morning and a cold, damp wind blew briskly much of the time; a truly "cutting wind," as people sometimes describe it. After being away from Nashville for several years, first in southern California and then in southeastern Alabama, the author was pleased, uncomfortable though that day certainly was, to have his memory refreshed as to just how miserable Nashville weather can sometimes be, and to reflect on how harshly the weather treated the Civil War soldiers.

Intense suffering was endured by many Confederates who were inadequately clothed, housed, and fed. "The weather was bitter cold," said the Eighteenth Alabama's Edgar Jones. "Many men were still bare-footed, and more becoming so every day. There were no blankets except the ones we carried all summer." Observing that "no man got a new blanket," Jones wrote that he "had but one, and that had eighteen bullet holes in it." Georgian Hezekiah McCorkle thought that Sunday, December 11, brought the "coldest weather I ever felt." Alabaman J. P. Cannon agreed, writing in his diary on December 11: "This is the coldest day I ever saw." Cannon continued, saying "Our position in the open fields, with [nothing] to break the force of the wind, which is blowing a perfect gale from the north, no wood to make fires and most of us thinly clad, our suffering is intense. It seems like we are bound to freeze unless a change occurs very soon."[55]

Some men dug into the frozen ground to escape the cold, biting wind. Another Alabama soldier described how the men tried to cope with their awful circumstances. George E. Brewer reported that "the men dug holes in the ground, constructing fire-places in the earth on one side, with barrel chimneys. The holes were several feet deep, dug lower toward the fire place, thus leaving on three sides an elevated flat for seats and beds. Covers were improvised by piecing blankets, dog-flies, or anything that would shelter." Edgar Jones also talked about the soldiers' quarters dug in the ground. He said the holes were two or three feet deep and large enough for three men to lie down. "We got twigs of rushes or weeds or anything of the sort and laid them in the bottom of our pits, put our blankets down, reserving the larger part [for] cover. . . . It was astounding how much warmer it was in the holes than on the top of the ground." Jones believed that "many more men would have died from exposure if it had not been for . . . getting under cover of the soil." The thought did occur to him that it was "very much like laying down in a soldier's grave."[56]

The Fourteenth Mississippi's William Barry, again writing to his sister, was clearly miserable. "I am too cold and the fire is smoking too bad," he began in explanation of a very brief letter. Noting that he was well, and "we are gradually working ourselves around Nashville," Barry quickly returned, and concluded, with the subject on which he had begun: "It is so cold and smoking you must really excuse me for not writing, as it is all most impossible under the circumstances to see the paper. My love to all, Your affectionate brother, William."[57]

While the U.S. forces on the whole were undoubtedly better equipped to face the elements than were the Confederates, the weather made life very uncomfortable for them as well. A Federal from Missouri wrote to his wife on December 12. His words about the weather could just as well have been penned by a Johnny Reb. "I received your last letter last Friday and should have written sooner, but the weather got so very cold that I had no chance to write," said F. A. Cline of the Fortieth Missouri. Declaring that "it was all we could do to keep from freezing to death," Cline added that "we have nothing to lay in but those small dog tents. We are laying at the out most rifle pits in front of Nashville." Cline also noted, evidencing the superiority of Union equipment, "we all have new guns and we mean to make them tell when we are called upon to use them."[58] Another Federal soldier, an officer on the staff of Colonel Sylvester G. Hill, reported that the ninth of December "was severely cold," and because "the men had but one blanket each, they were allowed to go to the city for tents which had been stored there. . . ."[59] A soldier of the Eighty-ninth Indiana wrote in his diary on December 9 that snow was coming down "briskly" and also used the phrase "severely cold" to describe the weather. Saying that winter "with all its horror" was upon the army, he declared the men could "hardly keep warm by our fires," and claimed he was doing nothing except "hauling wood and building fires, then shivering around them. . . ." On December 10 he said it was "too bad for any humans to be out [of] doors," and noted that "some of the boys . . . were robbed of their clothes. . . ."[60] Clearly the soldiers of both armies, in the words of Nathaniel Cheairs Hughes, were waging "this terrible war with nature."[61]

On December 14 the weather, at last, moderated. Among the top-ranking U.S. officers perhaps no one was more pleased than the embattled General Thomas, who knew that General Grant was "very much dissatisfied with my delay in attacking,"[62] and may have suspected that Grant was on the verge of relieving him from command if he did not attack soon. Very possibly too, Thomas may have suspected that he had a general in his camp who was intriguing against him.[63] General Schofield's role in the days preceding the Battle of Nashville became a matter of controversy after the war. On the cold and icy evening of December 10, General Thomas summoned his corps commanders to a council of war. Schofield, Wood, Smith, Steedman, and Wilson listened as Thomas informed them of Grant's orders to attack at once and expressed his belief that obedience was impracticable.[64] General Wilson later penned an account of the conference, declaring that as he was the junior corps commander present, in years as well as in rank, he spoke first and conveyed his full approval of Thomas's decision to withhold battle. The other corps commanders were equally outspoken, according to Wilson, except for Schofield, who "sat silent and by that means alone, if at all, concurred in the judgment of those present. . . ."[65]

Schofield always told a different story. Stating that Thomas had been ordered to surrender his command (though he did not say to whom) unless he attacked Hood at once, Schofield wrote that one of the corps commanders asked Thomas to show them the order. Thomas declined, claimed Schofield, which confirmed his belief that the successor could be none other than himself. Thus, to spare Thomas the humiliation of being removed from command, and without waiting for an opinion from the junior members of the council, Schofield immediately replied that he would sustain Thomas in his determination not to fight until he was fully ready. Then, declared Schofield, all the other commanders expressed their concurrence.[66]

Yet another account, that of General Steedman, contradicts Schofield's and confirms, with only minor variations, the record of General Wilson. Steedman charged Schofield with "deliberate falsehood when he [claimed] that, as the ranking officer next to the commanding general, he waived his right to speak last and promptly sustained General Thomas." Steedman declared that Schofield spoke last and then only laconically said that he "would obey orders." Steedman went on to charge that Schofield was intriguing to replace Thomas and had been telegraphing Grant, complaining that Thomas was too slow in his movements.[67] Schofield always denied the allegations of "the viper," as he afterwards referred to Steedman. No dispatches to Grant were ever found, although Sanford C. Kellogg, aide-de-camp to General Thomas, believed the evidence was removed from the War Department files while Schofield was Secretary of War in the late 1860s.[68]

Whether Schofield sent such messages or not—and it seems likely that he did[69]—and whether at the council of war he spoke first, last, or at all, and regardless of whose account is accepted as accurate, the evidence is conclusive on one matter: Schofield was never willing to acknowledge any necessity for Thomas's delay before the storm. Besides the testimony of Wilson and Steedman, there is a pertinent statement in one of Schofield's letters to Jacob Cox. Addressing Cox from Rome, December 5, 1881, Schofield clearly was disturbed that his own words were being interpreted as condoning Thomas's delay at Nashville. He wrote:

> I have been quoted as claiming priority in the support given by
> subordinates to General Thomas at Nashville in respect to his delay.

I never meant to claim anything of the kind. On the contrary, I
presume all the corps commanders deserve more credit than I do
in that regard. What I do claim is very different, viz: that when the
crisis came in which I alone could give him the effective support he
needed to save him from impending humiliation, I promptly and
emphatically gave him that support without waiting for the advice
or opinion of anyone.[70]

And in his autobiography Schofield wrote: "Indeed, Thomas could have given
battle the second or third day after Franklin with more than a fair prospect for
success."[71]

Perhaps Schofield was correct. Whatever the truth of that issue, on the
morning of December 14, 1864, there was a welcome rise in the temperature at
Nashville. A warm sun began to melt the ice and frozen ground. Thomas
planned to attack the next day and straightforwardly wired Halleck: "The ice
having melted away, the enemy will be attacked tomorrow morning."[72] That
evening he held another council of war with his corps commanders to discuss
battle plans. Basically these were the same as for the previously postponed
assault. As finally modified, apparently at Schofield's suggestion, they called
for a feint against the Confederate right flank, while a grand wheeling movement by the entire Union right wing overwhelmed the Rebel left. Wood's corps
would form the hub for this wheel, Smith's corps the spoke, and Wilson's cavalry the rim. Schofield's command would be in reserve near Smith's left flank
to become engaged wherever needed. A demonstration would be conducted
all along the line for the purpose of pinning the enemy in position. Altogether,
General Thomas would be sending more than fifty thousand men against possibly twenty thousand Confederates—at the most.[73]

7

A Perfect
Slaughter Pen

Dawn on Thursday, December 15, 1864, was warm in Nashville. Patches of snow and sleet were still visible from the recent storm, but these were rapidly disappearing and much of the earth had become soft and muddy. The day would be short, for the winter solstice was at hand. As it turned out, the day was even shorter than anticipated, because Nashville was enshrouded by a heavy morning fog. The Union advance, scheduled for 6:00 A.M., was delayed quite some time. The fog did not clear away until nearly 9:00. Eventually, the warm morning turned out to be sunny.

Nevertheless, reveille had sounded at 4:00 A.M. All along the Federal lines the blare of bugles jolted men awake. Minds quickened from the realm of dreams began to focus upon the deadly work scheduled for the day. Perhaps the eerie gray veil that had descended upon the camps, clouding one's vision even at a very short distance, seemed appropriate on a day that would be devoted to war. Whatever their thoughts—and General Wood said the morning was "dark and somber"—soldiers were soon eating breakfast, gathering their fifty or sixty or one hundred rounds of ammunition, two or three days worth of rations, blankets and overcoats (the amount varied from unit to unit). It was so foggy that, according to one soldier, "men got lost while groping about their own camps." Yet the troops were ready on time. It simply was not possible, however, to conduct the movement of large bodies of soldiers until the dense fog lifted. And so they waited.[1]

The army's commander had also arisen early, like his troops. General Thomas was staying at the St. Cloud Hotel, just a few blocks up from the river. The hotel stood on the northwest corner of present-day Church Street and Fifth Avenue, diagonally across the intersection from the impressive and thankfully still surviving, Downtown Presbyterian Church, whose twin towers were then prominent on the Nashville skyline. As General Thomas left the St. Cloud, the gaslights of the city shone dimly through the fog. He mounted his horse, and accompanied by his staff officers, prepared to ride to the front for the opening of the battle. He had gone but a short distance through the foggy street when he spotted a quartermaster officer in charge of fuel, standing on the sidewalk. Thomas pulled up his horse at once and conferred with the man, the incident revealing something of the general's character. Asking the officer if he, Thomas, had drawn all of his allowance of coal for the month and being informed that he had not, General Thomas then told the major to send fourteen bushels to a neighbor named Harris, from whom he had borrowed coal some days earlier when his own supply was out.[2]

Satisfied that the officer would see to the matter, Thomas and his staff rode off into the fog, heading for the high ground where he expected, eventually, to view the development of the battle. Thomas likely selected Lawrence Hill for the purpose, a high salient in the Union's outer line of defensive works; a site that would provide, once the fog lifted, a sweeping view over much of the field, especially to the south and east, as the action unfolded. The elevation was located between Granny White Pike and the present-day Belmont Boulevard, immediately north of Ashwood Avenue, where the Metro Police Tower currently stands. The eminence lay northeast of the Confederate salient on Montgomery Hill, a slightly lower elevation which was only about one-third of a mile distant.

Probably General Thomas would have alternated between Lawrence Hill and the high ground to the west, where present-day Linden Avenue and Eighteenth Avenue South intersect. The ride from one site to the other is short, and this defensive salient, approximately 1,500 feet east of Hillsboro Pike, is almost directly north of Montgomery Hill. Alternating between such commanding ground, General Thomas could view much of the battle area (although there is no one site, or even two sites, from which all the fight might satisfactorily be observed) and hoped to see his attack evolve successfully, beginning with the intended demonstration against the enemy's right flank on the Nolensville Pike.[3]

But war rarely develops according to plan—not precisely anyway. The Battle of Nashville was no exception. Actually, the battle began on the Cumberland River; at least that was where the first firing took place. Early in the morning, Naval Lieutenant Commander Le Roy Fitch set forth to engage the Southern batteries of Lieutenant Colonel David Kelley, located on or near the bluff across from Bell's Mill, eighteen miles, as the river flows, below Nashville. Fitch steamed down the Cumberland with seven boats: the *Brilliant, Carondelet, Fairplay, Neosho, Reindeer, Silver Lake,* and the *Moose,* the last serving as Fitch's flagship. (Fitch and *Moose,* incidentally, had a key role in the defeat of the famous John Hunt Morgan at Buffington, Ohio, back in 1863.) A division of cavalry, commanded by Brigadier General Richard W. Johnson, was to cooperate with the navy, so as to place the Confederates under fire from both the water and the land; that is to say, from both front and rear.[4]

Arriving on the scene long before the cavalry, Fitch sent one of his vessels, the *Neosho,* commanded by Acting Volunteer Lieutenant Samuel Howard, on down the river below the enemy batteries, to "feel their strength," and then return with his report. Soon the distinctive booming sounds of the heavy guns reverberated up and down the banks of the river as the *Neosho* carried out her mission, steaming past Kelley's guns and drawing their fire. The *Neosho,* of course, was only engaging to attract the attention of the Rebels and soon returned upstream—unscathed as it turned out—with a report for Fitch that only four enemy guns were in position. "These I could easily have silenced and driven off," claimed Fitch, but realizing that Federal ground forces were not yet at hand and fearing that a general bombardment might inflict casualties on the friendly forces as they came up, he decided to withdraw a short distance upriver. There he would "maneuver around" until the Yankee cavalry "reached the desired position in the rear." Fitch had to wait for quite a while. General Johnson did not get into position until nearly noon.[5]

Meanwhile, the fog having at last cleared, the advance of the Union army began. George R. Lee, an artilleryman from Illinois, vividly recalled his battery waiting anxiously for the order to move forward. "Our time (of enlistment) was out in four days," he wrote. "Just as the bugler began to sound . . . the advance," a courier arrived with an order that the battery "was relieved from active duty" and would only "hold itself in . . . reserve." Experiencing an overwhelming sense of relief, Lee said "the joy was so sudden that many of the men cried like boys. They saw wife and children and home for sure now, whereas a moment before the future . . . was very dark." Thus for a few Federal soldiers a reprieve from the agony of battle had come at the last possible moment. No such luck was experienced by the vast majority of men on both sides.[6]

The Northern strike against the Southern right flank got underway soon after the fog lifted. By the time it did, the Federal cannon around the city had begun to fire, the opening salvo coming from Fort Negley. The belching guns generated so much noise that at times the sounds were heard in neighboring towns: Gallatin, Lebanon, and others. A former slave later remembered: "When the Yankees on Capitol Hill gave the signal—God bless your soul—it sounded like the cannons would tear the world to pieces. I could hear the big shells humming as they came. They cut off trees like a man cutting weeds with a scythe."[7] No doubt the heavy and fierce firing from the Federal forts and other vantage points terrified some people and inflicted a few horrible casualties. But the actual effect of the booming guns, as usual throughout the Civil War, proved more noisy than destructive. The action developing on the eastern flank of the Confederate line would soon result in a great many more killed and wounded than the fire of the heavy guns.

In command of an intended strong demonstration against the right flank of the Grayclads was Major General James Blair Steedman. The forty-seven-year-old Steedman was one of the more interesting and significant characters who rose to high rank in the Northern army. Orphaned at an early age, and with little formal schooling, he grew up to become a successful Ohio printer, editor, and Democratic politician, who supported Stephen Douglas for the presidency in 1860. Commissioned as colonel of the Fourteenth Ohio Infantry in 1861, he had made brigadier general a year later. A big, strong man, he first became known as "Old Steady" to his troops, but later the veterans would call him "Old Chickamauga," honoring his greatest service of the war—perhaps second only to General Thomas—in that bloody battle. Steedman had headed the lead unit of Gordon Granger's reserve force, coming up barely in time to reinforce Thomas's corps at Snodgrass Hill at the climax of the Battle of Chickamauga. Shouting to a staff officer to see that his name was spelled correctly in the obituary column (Steedman rather than Steadman)—a matter that was always of great concern to the general, even to the extent of making a major point about it in his will—he turned and directed his men to the attack. In less than thirty minutes, between one-third and one-half of his force became casualties on that September afternoon in 1863. When his horse was shot from under him, Steedman led an attack personally, taking up the colors of an Illinois regiment and shouting encouragement to his wavering men.

To soldiers beginning to fall back, Steedman yelled above the din of the battle, as he waved the colors high: "Go back, boys, go back; but the flag can't go with you!" He had struck the right note. The men cheered, turned, and followed him toward the enemy. When again they wavered, Steedman picked up rocks from the ground and hurled them at his troops, roaring that they must stand and fight. Glenn Tucker, in his excellent account of that battle, wrote that "the suddenness and initial ferocity of Steedman's attack startled the Confederates . . . and his personal exertions as much as any other factor prevented the

repulse of his division, the loss of Snodgrass Hill and perhaps the rout or capture of the army."[8]

Certainly Steedman had proven that he was not the least bit afraid of a
fight. But since Chickamauga his lifestyle had become the subject of considerable attention. For the greater part of 1864 Steedman had commanded the post
of Chattanooga. While there he had become "dead in love" with a woman
whom he frequently entertained. If Brigadier General David S. Stanley is to be
believed, Steedman was "so taken up with making love . . . and drinking cham-
pagne, that it was difficult to see the great potentate of Chattanooga."
Regardless of what anyone might say about Steedman's style of living, General
Thomas, after the war, once stated that Steedman was the best division commander he ever had—high praise indeed, and from an impressive source.[9]

When Steedman rode up to General Thomas at the crisis of Chickamauga,
Thomas remarked, "I have always been glad to see you, but never so glad
as now. How many muskets have you got?" Steedman replied that he had
"seventy-five hundred muskets, General."[10] On the morning of December 15,
1864, at Nashville, Steedman again had approximately seventy-five hundred
men, but the makeup of his force at Nashville was quite different from that at
Chickamauga. The single most noticeable difference in his Nashville command
was that many of the troops were black.

The recruitment of black soldiers for the Union army began in 1863. The
majority of those recruited were fugitive slaves, along with some free blacks.
Middle Tennessee proved to be a fruitful recruiting ground, with three full regiments raised at Nashville as early as the winter of 1863. Many more blacks
were recruited in the Tennessee capital in the following months. Black regiments were also organized in Gallatin, Clarksville, and Murfreesboro. In general, the black troops were put to work as laborers or to guard the military railroads against Rebel attackers. They were not assigned to military campaigning
because the predominant white opinion was that black soldiers were not capable of combat roles.[11] This had been the opinion of General George H. Thomas.
Colonel Thomas Jefferson Morgan, commander of the Fourteenth United
States Colored Troops (USCT), and one of the strongest advocates of giving
blacks combat responsibilities, later wrote of Thomas's viewpoint before the
Battle of Nashville. Morgan said Thomas asked him if he thought his men
would fight. The colonel replied that they would, to which Thomas responded
that he thought they might if behind breastworks. Morgan said "they would
fight in the open field," but Thomas thought not. As a result of the impending
battle Thomas would change his mind.[12]

The commanding general was experiencing some change of attitude about
the black troops even before the battle. Otherwise he would have simply
left them manning fortifications around the city. Their assignment against the

*James B. Steedman.
Massachusetts Commandery
Military Order of the Loyal
Legion and the U.S. Army
Military History Institute.*

enemy right flank would provide a test case of their combat prowess. General Steedman also seemed heartily ready to put the African Americans into the battle. A Union officer wrote that Steedman had sworn to Colonel Morgan that "if opportunity offered, the niggers should have all the fighting they wanted."[13]

The task would not be solely theirs, however, for General Steedman, in his force that was known as the Provisional Detachment (District of Etowah), had a white brigade in addition to two black brigades. Steedman's command left something to be desired—quite a lot, in fact, according to Thomas biographer Francis McKinney, who described it as "a hybrid . . . made up of fragments from . . . ill-provided regiments. A large portion were unfit for duty. . . . Some of these troops were not armed until the evening of the fourteenth. Some of the recruits were untrained. Many were unable to speak or understand English."[14] Whatever their shortcomings, Steedman's brigades would not be lacking in numbers, for each brigade was about the size of a Confederate division.

As the Union attack would develop, the African American brigades would shoulder a major part of the work. In leading the black troops, no one was more important than Colonel Thomas Morgan. His long and loud protestations

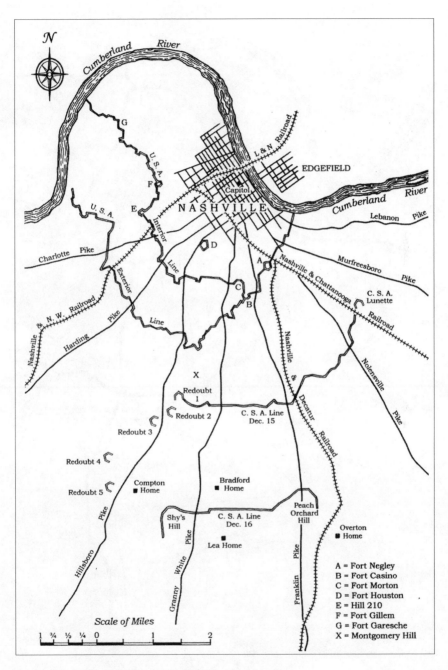

N

Cumberland River

G

U.S.A.

F

E

U.S.A.

L & N. Railroad

EDGEFIELD

Capitol

NASHVILLE

Cumberland River

Lebanon Pike

Charlotte Pike

Interior Line

D

A

Nashville & Chattanooga

Murfreesboro Pike

C

C. S. A. Lunette

Exterior Pike

B

Nashville & N. W. Railroad

Harding Pike

Line

Railroad

Nashville & Decatur Railroad

Nolensville Pike

X

Redoubt 1

Redoubt 2

C. S. A. Line Dec. 15

Redoubt 3

Redoubt 4

Redoubt 5

Compton Home

Bradford Home

Peach Orchard Hill

Overton Home

Hillsboro Pike

Shy's Hill

C. S. A. Line Dec. 16

Lea Home

Granny White Pike

Franklin Pike

A = Fort Negley
B = Fort Casino
C = Fort Morton
D = Fort Houston
E = Hill 210
F = Fort Gillem
G = Fort Garesche
X = Montgomery Hill

Scale of Miles

1 ¾ ½ ¼ 0   1   2

Battle of Nashville, December 15–16, 1864. By Jim Moon Jr.

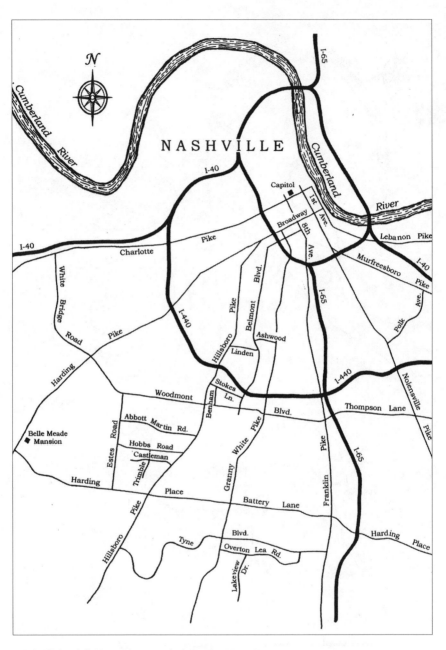

Nashville battlefield area (present day). By Jim Moon Jr.

against being merely "an overseer for black laborers" was a major reason—perhaps the primary one—that his troops were now cast in a real combat role.[15] Morgan had organized the Fourteenth Regiment USCT at Gallatin in late 1863, and despite non-combat roles, continually drilled his men, looking to the day when a more meaningful assignment would come, for he believed that "the ultimate status of the Negro was to be determined by his conduct on the battlefield."[16]

Morgan was a very religious man (after the war he became a Baptist minister) and also, some would say, perhaps a trifle strange. There was the manner, for example, that he organized his regimental companies according to the height of the men. The four center companies were all composed of tall men, the companies on the flanks of medium height, while the shortest men were stuck in between. Too, a recent episode at Decatur, Alabama, convinced some that Morgan was irresponsible with his religious practices. Although in a position exposed to enemy fire, Morgan ordered the regiment to "parade rest" for the purpose of engaging in prayer. During the time at prayer, if (and it is a big "if") Colonel Henry C. Corbin is to be believed, some men were actually killed and wounded, prompting Corbin to remind Morgan, in the strongest terms, that the men were there for activities other than prayer. The relationship that developed between Morgan and Corbin was not ideal, but for the most part, Morgan seems to have been respected by the black troops.[17]

On the morning of December 15, Morgan led the First Colored Brigade, composed of the Fourteenth, Fifteenth, Sixteenth, Seventeenth, and Eighteenth USCT Regiments, with most of the Fifteenth and Sixteenth held in reserve. Morgan's brigade was assisted by the Twentieth Indiana Artillery. Colonel Charles R. Thompson led the Second Colored Brigade, made up of the Twelfth, Thirteenth, and One Hundredth USCT Regiments, with the First Battery of Kansas Light Artillery assisting. A third brigade composed of white troops was headed by Lieutenant Colonel Charles H. Grosvenor. This unit consisted of the Sixty-eighth Indiana Regiment, the Eighteenth and Twenty-first Ohio, and the Second Battalion of the Fourteenth Army Corps.

The Union plan of attack envisioned the two brigades of Morgan and Grosvenor advancing east along the Murfreesboro Pike until their march carried them beyond the right flank of the Rebels. They would then turn sharply to the south, and move against the enemy's right rear, hoping to catch the Graycoats by surprise. As they made the attack, the sound of their guns would be the signal for Thompson's Second Colored Brigade, meanwhile advancing along the line of the Nashville & Chattanooga Railroad toward the Confederate front, to launch its supporting assault. All of this, as previously noted, was

A portion of the Confederate lunette positioned on the army's right flank. Photograph by John Hursh.

intended to be a diversion, albeit a strong one, for the purpose of confusing the Rebel commander about where the Yankees were making their main attack.[18]

By mid-morning Morgan's and Grosvenor's brigades, with Morgan in the lead, had reached a point on the Murfreesboro Pike beyond the Confederate flank, probably in the general area where present-day Fesslers Lane, Polk and Foster Avenues intersect the Murfreesboro Road. There they turned right, formed in battle lines, and moved quickly toward the rear of the Southern position. The Federals were advancing with confidence and Colonel Morgan believed the attack was developing according to plan. The colonel personally had conducted a night reconnaissance. He thought that he was moving against, as he described it, simply a "curtain" of logs and a line of rifle pits on the enemy's eastern flank.[19]

Actually, Morgan had no idea what he faced. First, there would be no surprising the Southerners. They had been closely observing the Bluecoat advance for some time. On the contrary, the Federals were about to experience the surprises. In the light of day Morgan soon discovered, although too late for an effective response, that what appeared in the dark to be logs really was a lunette; that is, a projecting field fortification having two faces, with a protective ditch in

Nashville and Chattanooga Railroad cut, looking south from Polk Avenue Bridge. Photograph by John Hursh.

front for infantry support. Mounting four guns, it would shortly open fire on the U.S. troops at close range.[20]

The lunette was not the worst surprise. Neither Morgan nor anyone else among the Union soldiers seemed to know of the railroad cut through which ran the Nashville & Chattanooga tracks. The cut was a good twenty feet deep and several hundred feet long. It blocked the Federal march only a short distance ahead. Thanks to the work of the General Joseph E. Johnston Camp of the Sons of Confederate Veterans, a portion of the lunette, as well as part of the ditch in its front, may be seen today, located a few hundred yards east of Nolensville Road, where Polk Avenue crosses two parallel railroad cuts, which are less than two hundred yards apart. The lunette, lying immediately south of Polk Avenue, is beside the railroad cut farthest to the east, a cut constructed in the twentieth century that destroyed much of the fortification. Approximately four hundred feet west of the lunette is the railroad cut of Civil War days, through which the Nashville & Chattanooga tracks passed.

The Confederates defending their army's eastern flank, as earlier noted, belonged to the corps of Major General Benjamin Franklin Cheatham, who, incidentally, was in the lunette as the Blueclad attackers advanced. Posted on

Rains Hill, close to the Nolensville Pike, and extending on to the railroad cut, the Southerners occupied good defensive ground and were dug in. True, they had been staggered by the loss of many comrades, as well as Generals Cleburne and Granbury, in Hood's ill-advised and badly orchestrated assault at Franklin. (Granbury's brigade, for instance, which had mustered eleven hundred men going into the Franklin attack, now numbered less than four hundred effectives and was commanded by Captain Edward Broughton.) But on this day it would be the U.S. troops attacking and the Grayclads defending a strong position.

Furthermore, the impending fight took on a new perspective; one giving added incentive to the Rebels: they saw that many of the men marching against them were African Americans; or, as one Southerner expressed it, "white negroes and black negroes."[21] Many Confederates were enraged to see blacks, whether former slaves or not—and certainly many had been slaves—wearing the blue uniform. One Confederate, describing the recent episode at Dalton, Georgia, conveyed the intensity of feeling characterizing large numbers of Southern troops. "Reaching Dalton . . . we found it garrisoned by negroes," he wrote. "They surrendered. . . . I think there were about 700. . . . The officers had a hard time to keep the men from falling on them. . . ."[22]

Now, dug in on the right flank at Nashville, the Southerners prepared to "fall on" the black troops with a vengeance. "Everyman was on the alert," remembered Charles Martin of the First Georgia Volunteers, because "this was the first time our corps had come in contact with negro soldiers" on the battlefield.[23] Or, as Private Philip Stephenson from Arkansas expressed the racial prejudice, it was the first time that the Army of Tennessee "had ever met our former slaves in battle," an occasion that "excited in our men the intensest indignation." That indignation manifested itself, said Stephenson, "in a way peculiarly ominous and yet quite natural for the 'masters.'"[24] Charles Martin added that "every step [the African Americans] took . . . was watched by angry eyes and [men] with twitching fingers on gun triggers" who only "awaited the signal to exterminate" the black troops.[25]

Silently observing the approach of Morgan's black brigade, Granbury's Rebels held their fire until the lead elements of the Federal force were only a hundred feet or so distant and trapped from farther advance by the railroad cut. When the Confederates opened on them, it was as if a wall of musketry and artillery fire had smashed into the flesh and bone of those Bluecoats. "Up rose the line of gray and crash went that deadly volley of lead full into the poor fellows' faces," wrote Private Stephenson. "The carnage was awful," continued Stephenson. "It is doubtful if a single bullet missed."[26]

Samuel Alonzo Cook of the Seventeenth Texas Cavalry (dismounted) remembered that when the Rebels began firing they "had a perfect slaughter pen with the Negro soldiers."[27] The fire was so devastating that some of the African Americans, as they attempted to find cover, jumped into the railroad cut. The twenty-foot drop resulted in broken arms and legs. Then the Confederates closed off the mouth of the cut and shot them down. Still other blacks, according to one source, rushed "into a small pond made from the embankment of the railroad," only to be killed "until the pond was black."[28] Samuel Cook wrote in his diary: "We did not give them any quarter." Charles Martin concurred. "We took no prisoners," he said. "We had the negroes in our trap," Martin wrote, "and when we commenced firing on them . . . all that remained on the ground were good niggers." Another disparaging remark was recorded in the diary of Confederate Thomas J. Key, who, noting that the blacks "suffered severe loss," referred to their "leaving quite a number of the fuliginous skins lifeless and vimless on the cold ground."[29]

According to a Union account, there had been such little confidence in the fighting prowess of the black troops that a line of Yankees, with bayonets fixed, had been formed behind the blacks, with the plain intention of "holding them to their work." To the credit of those doomed African Americans, this measure proved unnecessary. The historian of the Thirty-sixth Illinois recorded that the "gallantry and steadiness" of the negroes could not have been surpassed by "any body of regulars."[30] Another source told of a black soldier who was "standing in the open, firing as rapidly as possible, until his superior ordered him" to take cover.[31] Still another witness recalled that "the colored troops," though under a heavy fire, "rushed to the fray . . . and did not falter for a moment."[32] And Colonel Morgan later would write: "Colored soldiers had fought side by side with white troops. They had mingled together in the charge. They had supported each other. They had assisted each other from the field when they were wounded, and they lay side by side in death. . . . The day [had seen] . . . a record of coolness, bravery, and manliness, never to be unmade."[33]

Unfortunately for the black troops of Morgan's brigade, fate had dealt with them in a cruel manner. When the Rebels opened fire, the African Americans were caught in a situation where they had no chance of winning the fight. They were quickly cut down—killed and wounded by the score. Survivors could only fall back, hoping for luck to get out of range before they too became casualties. Morgan had lost over three hundred men.[34] One Rebel remembered that the butchery in front of "Granbury's Texans . . . was particularly sickening."[35]

Not all of the Union dead at the railroad cut were blacks. Captain Gideon Ayers, a white officer, was mortally wounded, lying in agony for some time before his sufferings were relieved in death. Instantly killed was Captain Job Aldrich, the brother-in-law of Colonel William R. Shafter, who commanded the

Seventeenth USCT. Based on Aldrich's earlier actions, Shafter was convinced the captain had a premonition he would die in the coming battle. Shortly after midnight, Aldrich had written a touching letter to his wife, the sister of Colonel Shafter. His closing words were: "At 5 the dance of death begins around Nashville. Who shall be partner in the dance? God only knows. Echo alone answers who? Farewell."[36]

Colonel Morgan's command was already whipped when Charles Grosvenor's supporting brigade got up. Confederate preoccupation with the slaughter of Morgan's men had enabled Grosvenor's soldiers to tramp across open ground and through a muddy cornfield with very light casualties. As they drew near to the Graycoat lunette, however, their luck ran out. Suddenly they were confronting a formidable ditch and heavy log defenses. Just at this instant, the Southerners, having devastated Morgan's brigade, turned their fire on these new targets. Grosvenor's Second Battalion panicked; "behaving in the most cowardly and disgraceful manner"; the white troops, with only a few exceptions, broke formation and streamed toward the rear. The quality of these troops left much to be desired, being composed, according to Grosvenor, mainly of "new conscripts, convalescents and bounty jumpers."[37]

In a short time the rest of Grosvenor's brigade began falling back. When his Second Battalion collapsed and fled, the Rebels, in Grosvenor's words, were "free to converge [their] whole fire upon the Eighteenth Ohio," at last forcing it to retreat. The Eighteenth had made a valiant effort, directed by their captain, Ebenezer Grosvenor (a relative of the brigade commander), whom Lieutenant Colonel Grosvenor described as leading "the head of his regiment full upon the work of the enemy," then firing his pistol "in the very face of the enemy and while springing over the embankment he fell forward dead, shot by two balls."[38]

Farther to the Federal right, Colonel Thompson's black brigade skirmished with the Grayclads for some time. These Union troops crossed the railroad just north of the cut, and occupied some works between the railroad and the Nolensville Road. Their advance ultimately was to no avail, and they found themselves under artillery fire at times for the remainder of the day.[39] The Union efforts under Morgan, Grosvenor, and Thompson accomplished nothing beyond providing many names for the list of Federal casualties. General Steedman maintained that he had placed strong pressure on the Confederate right flank. Actually, his diversion was a total failure. Despite some Northern claims to the contrary, General Hood was not deceived as to where the main Federal assault would come, and did not send any troops from other parts of the line to shore up his right flank. From noon onward, Steedman merely kept up a long-range skirmish fire with the Rebels.

A Confederate private thought the afternoon hours "dragged painfully . . . and men began to sink back to a . . . state of philosophical indifference." The soldier also would long remember vividly a lull in the firing when "the smoke drifted away, and to my astonishment I saw two females between the lines!" The women were bareheaded and without any wrap, he wrote, walking in the open toward the Southern line, off to the left from the private's position. They moved calmly, appearing unconcerned about their safety, "showing no sign of fear," he said. Then smoke once more obscured the area as the volume of firing increased. "I think these women escaped injury," wrote the soldier, "but I do not know." It was a strange and puzzling scene.[40]

Meanwhile, a mile or so farther to the Union right, General Thomas J. Wood, West Point class of 1845, had been waiting through the late morning, his Fourth Corps, nearly fourteen thousand strong, standing in line and poised for action. They were facing the Graycoats' Montgomery Hill, an imposing height whose elevation was only slightly less than the Federals' Lawrence Hill, where General Thomas maintained his headquarters. Today the eminence is just north of I-440, between Hillsboro Road and Belmont Boulevard, at Cedar Lane, so named because the eastern approach to the Montgomery house (which had burned earlier) was once lined on both sides with cedar trees. For some time Wood's Bluecoats had witnessed an awesome display of fire power as they waited. The guns of Forts Casino, Gillem, Houston, and Morton had joined with those of Fort Negley, whose pieces had opened the action, in sending a continuous barrage of shells screaming over the Federal troops and bursting above the Confederate lines.

General Wood anxiously awaited the opportunity to attack with his big corps. One of two Civil War generals from the little town of Munfordville, Kentucky (the other being Simon Bolivar Buckner, with whom Wood had played along the banks of the Green River when they were boys, and who cast his fortunes with the Confederacy), Wood still chafed under the ignominy of having pulled his division out of the line at Chickamauga—even if he was obeying orders as he understood them—and created a gap through which the Rebels charged, cutting off a major segment of the Yankees, along with the army's commander and two of the three corps commanders, ultimately bringing a Southern victory. If Thomas and Steedman were considered heroes of that sanguinary struggle along the banks of the "river of death," as some have claimed to be the meaning of the term Chickamauga, then Wood was seen, however unfairly, as the man who got the army into the mess from which Thomas and Steedman had to extricate it. Now, at Nashville, Wood was still seeking to prove himself militarily, and with the largest command he had ever exercised—indeed the largest corps in the army—the moment seemed opportune.[41]

The time was somewhere between noon and one o'clock when Thomas's headquarters ordered the great movement to begin that would send nearly fifty thousand troops—a good two times as many as the Graycoats had in their entire army—wheeling to envelop and crush the enemy's left flank. Wood's command constituted the hub of the wheel, basically moving south, with the infantry of Smith and Schofield forming the spoke and swinging wide to strike from the west, while Wilson's cavalry was the rim, riding for the rear of the Confederate left flank.

Three divisions made up Wood's Fourth Corps. On his right General Wood had placed the Second Division, commanded by Brigadier General Washington L. Elliott, with instructions to move out by his right, forming and advancing in echelon with the left of Smith's corps. The First Division, occupying the central position in the corps' movement, and advancing to the left of Elliott, was led by Brigadier General Nathan Kimball. To Kimball's left would be the Third Division, under Brigadier General Samuel Beatty—the division that was in the best position to deal with Montgomery Hill.

General Wood was elated as he gave the order to move to the attack. "When the grand array of troops began to move forward . . . the pageant was magnificently grand and imposing," he wrote. The corps moved forward "in such perfect order that the heart of the patriot might easily draw from it the happy presage of the coming glorious victory."[42] Wood had a tendency to wax eloquent, a tendency which he frequently indulged. The "patriots" who watched, however, were mostly of the Confederate persuasion, several thousand of whom were lining hills and ridges on the city's southern side, peering to see anything of the battle not obscured by the heavy pall of gun smoke, which was not much, of course. A Bluecoat officer remarked that "citizens of Nashville, nearly all of whom were in sympathy with the Confederacy, came out of the city in droves. All the hills in our rear were black with human beings watching the battle, but silent."[43]

Evidently some of the more bold among the civilian onlookers made a nuisance of themselves. The *Nashville Dispatch* reported that the military authorities were "much annoyed by the large numbers . . . who went out on Thursday to witness the fighting," and determined to put a stop to it. Orders were issued "to put all to work who showed themselves at the front." According to the paper, "several sightseers were thus caught, but . . . allowed to retire on promise of returning to town immediately."[44]

Montgomery Hill appeared to be a tough objective, very possibly the most formidable portion of Hood's line. Besides defending high ground, the Southerners, according to Wood's report, "had encircled the hill just below its crest with a strong line of entrenchments"; also, an abatis was complemented by

Thomas J. Wood.
Courtesy of the Hart County
(Kentucky) Historical Society.

"rows of sharpened stakes firmly planted in the ground" to impale men attempting to charge over them. Observing that the ascent on the east of the hill
was not as pronounced as on the front (north), the Yankees quickly concluded
to make their main effort against the former.[45]

At 1 P.M. General Wood gave the order for the assault. Swinging to the left
and coming into position for the attack from the east was Beatty's Third Division, formerly led by General Wood. Beatty chose his Second Brigade, Colonel
Philip Sidney Post commanding, to lead. Post was a thirty-one-year-old native
of New York State, educated at Union College, Schenectady, and practicing law
when the war began.[46] Beatty's First Brigade, under Colonel Abel D. Streight,
would support Post, moving on his left and advancing "a little in echelon to
him." Streight was the man who, in the spring of 1863, had led the so-called
"mule brigade," a contingent of nearly two thousand men mounted on mules,
in a raid across northern Alabama toward Georgia with the objective of striking
the Western & Atlantic Railroad south of Chattanooga. Streight proved to be a
resourceful commander and capable opponent of his pursuer, the formidable
Nathan Bedford Forrest. Aided a bit by luck and considerably by bluff, Forrest
overtook Streight's column near the Alabama-Georgia border and convinced
Streight to surrender—a move the colonel clearly regretted when he realized he

had been tricked by Forrest into thinking the Grayclads had overwhelming manpower. Now Streight was back, still full of fight, readying his men along the Granny White Pike for the assault on Montgomery Hill.[47]

Surely it looked like a demanding assignment as the Blueclads moved out and began ascending the hill. But if the men were initially filled with trepidation, their mood quickly changed. Montgomery Hill was all but abandoned! The formidable-appearing line of entrenchments near the crest of the eminence was manned by nothing more than a handful of pickets who fired a couple of volleys as the sea of Federals came on and then scurried like startled rabbits to the rear. Only a few days before, as previously recounted, General Hood had decided to reform his main line approximately nine hundred yards to the rear, stretching along, and just to the south of, present-day Woodmont Boulevard. The withdrawal, although skillfully done under cover of bad weather, had become known to a few Federals via reconnaissance, but somehow escaped the attention of several key officers, including General Wood. As Wood watched in astonishment on the afternoon of December 15, his soldiers bounding to the top of a supposedly heavily defended hill, Wood again wielded an eloquent pen: "As sweeps the stiff gale over the ocean, driving every object before it, so swept the brigade up the wooded slope, over the enemy's entrenchments; and the hill was won."[48]

General Beatty said that Streight's intended supporting brigade, "was fired with the spirit of the charge, rushed forward, and the charge almost became a race [with Post's brigade] to the summit of the hill."[49] The effervescent Federal soldiers tramped about at the top of Montgomery Hill, catching their breath, some looking for souvenirs; others marveling at their good luck. As for the Fourth Corps commander, General Wood obviously tried to paint in his report the picture of a dazzling triumph. It seems likely, however, that the bitter truth must have weighed upon his mind: the general's big corps had just overwhelmed an undefended hill. The attack was anything but the victory for which he had hoped. Furthermore, the time then being early afternoon, Wood's corps presumably would still have to assault the Graycoats' main line to the south.

At yet a third location, over on the extreme Federal right near the Cumberland River, the Bluecoats were achieving nothing of significance—just as with the efforts of Steedman and Wood. Here the key officer for the Union was Brigadier General Richard W. Johnson, commanding the Sixth Cavalry Division. Like General Wood, Johnson was a native Kentuckian and West Pointer, class of 1849. Also like General Wood (only perhaps more so), an embarrassing incident

Robert W. Johnson.
Courtesy of the
Tennessee State
Library and Archives.

tainted his Civil War career. Given a mission to seek the Rebel raider John Hunt Morgan, Johnson set forth from Nashville with seven hundred troopers, in August of 1862, boasting that he would bring Morgan back in a band box. Johnson caught up with Morgan near Gallatin, Tennessee, only to be defeated, compelled to retreat, and finally captured while attempting to cross the Cumberland River.[50]

On the morning when the Battle of Nashville began, two brigades composed Johnson's Sixth Division, one under command of Colonel James Biddle and the other led by Colonel Thomas Harrison, a total of over two thousand men. Johnson's mission was to move out the Charlotte Pike, driving any Graycoats before him, while operating as the right flank of Wilson's magnificent cavalry force, some twelve thousand troopers altogether. Johnson had his division ready to advance at six o'clock, only to find John McArthur's infantry division blocking the path. Johnson chafed under the delay and reported that it was about eleven o'clock before McArthur's men at last cleared his front, enabling him to move out.[51]

The Confederates had very meager numbers with which to resist the Union advance in that area. David Kelley, whose guns had briefly engaged the

Federal gunboat *Neosho* early in the morning, still manned his battery of four guns on the banks of the river across from Bell's Mill. Brigadier General James Chalmers had one brigade of his cavalry division, that of Colonel Edmund Rucker, positioned some distance to the right (east) of Kelley's battery, on high ground near the Charlotte Pike and behind Richland Creek. (This is approximately where today's White Bridge Road intersects Charlotte Pike.)

Last of all, and farther to the Southerners' right, was the small brigade of Matthew Ector's mostly Texas infantry. Though still known as Ector's brigade, the unit had been led by Colonel David Coleman of North Carolina since Ector lost a leg in the fighting around Atlanta. It consisted of three dismounted Texas regiments, the Ninth Texas Infantry, and two North Carolina infantry regiments. (The Texas cavalry had been dismounted for more than two years due to the need for infantry.) Coleman had the brigade situated on a ridge just north of Harding Pike and west of Richland Creek, where the men had thrown up breastworks. (The position was roughly parallel to the current White Bridge Road, slightly west of that road's intersection with Harding Pike.) Altogether, Coleman commanded about seven hundred men. Kelley and Rucker, under Chalmers, and Coleman's infantry: these were the forces—obviously little more than a nominal defense—with which the Graycoats, to the west and north of the main Confederate line, awaited their antagonists.[52]

What strength the Rebels possessed was soon weakened even more. When the Federals began moving forward in the late morning, Ector's brigade quickly retreated. Lieutenant J. T. Tunnel, who commanded the skirmish line of the brigade, later recalled the events for the *Confederate Veteran*. Spying "a vast body of cavalry," and a "large brigade of infantry" advancing rapidly and directly toward the Grayclads, Tunnel immediately notified Colonel Coleman. Sizing up the situation, Coleman concluded to fall back at once with his brigade, instructing his picket commander to "hold the line until forced to retire," and then make a run for the Hillsboro Pike, some two miles distant, where they were to rejoin the brigade. Thus early on, the Confederate "defense" had been reduced to Chalmers's cavalry and Kelley's artillery. Coleman, supposedly supporting Chalmers's right flank, apparently did not dispatch a courier to inform Chalmers that he was pulling out.[53]

Chalmers had no idea that his right flank lay wide open, via the Harding Pike, to a turning movement by the Bluecoats. "The First intelligence I had of [the enemy's] presence on that pike," Chalmers wrote in his report, was when "they were already two miles in my rear."[54] Thus General Richard W. Johnson, with superior numbers, had a wonderful opportunity to deal a hard blow to the Rebels in his front by getting on their flank. Unfortunately for Johnson, he failed to take advantage of the chance. Once the road cleared for his advance Johnson moved out slowly. Not only that, Johnson placed his dismounted brigade, under Colonel James Biddle, in the lead. Approaching Richland Creek, where Rucker's Grayclad troopers, with General Chalmers at hand, were drawn up along the ridge on the far side, Johnson ordered Biddle to cross the creek and assault the Rebels. Colonel Thomas Harrison, with his mounted brigade, received orders to "hold himself in readiness to follow up Biddle's attack."[55]

Within a few minutes Biddle's "assault" became a fiasco. Difficulty in crossing the creek was compounded by the cavalry's unfamiliarity with maneuvering as foot soldiers. Possibly their greatest difficulty came from their sabers. With scabbards swinging wildly, sometimes tripping them up, Biddle's men were making such little progress that a frustrated Johnson ordered Colonel Harrison's mounted brigade to move to the front. Johnson criticized in his report "the commanding officer of the Fourteenth Illinois Cavalry [(Biddle) who], with a singular shortsightedness, permitted his men to bring [their sabers] with them. . . ."[56] One would think, in all fairness, that at least a portion of the blame for such bungling should rest upon Johnson himself, who, through the morning hours, would seem to have had ample opportunity to observe and correct the problem—particularly if he intended to have the dismounted troopers leading his advance.

Regardless of who deserved blame for the encumbrance of the sabers, the success or failure of the Federals depended upon Harrison's men. Crossing Richland Creek to the left of Biddle's floundering brigade, Harrison's troopers formed and charged mounted up the ridge. "I never saw a charge more gallantly made or more persistently pressed," claimed General Johnson. However, the Bluecoat troopers were brought to an abrupt halt by a stone wall. Unable to leap their horses over the obstacle, the men were forced to dismount and tear down a part of the wall before they could get beyond it. By the time they did, the Confederates had pulled back to another position on the Charlotte Pike, along another ridge, closer to Kelley's artillery.[57]

Johnson reformed his command and pursued, only to find the Rebels, if anything, in a stronger position than before. Harrison was spearheading the pursuit. Earlier Johnson had instructed him, when moving around Biddle's men, to attack "with all possible energy." Perhaps that order was still fresh in Harrison's mind as he approached the Confederates a second time. Apparently overly zealous and "not appreciating the advantage of the enemy's position," to quote Johnson, Harrison rushed to the attack, only to have the Seventh Ohio suffer a bloody repulse.[58]

In the midst of the fight at this point a passionate, seventy-five-year-old Confederate sympathizer by the name of Mark Cockrill, rode up on his horse, making a conspicuous target of himself, while cheering on the Rebels and

The Belle Meade Mansion. Photographs by John Hursh.

shouting curses at the Yankees. As fate would have it, he survived the afternoon unscathed.[59]

General Johnson next called upon the navy for help. After waiting around since early morning, the *Neosho* and *Carondelet* came up and lobbed shells toward the Graycoats for a while, the horrendous explosions rending the air, sounding as if great damage were surely being inflicted. Actually, the only noticeable destruction was dealt to some civilian property in the area, not to Chalmers's cavalry. As for General Johnson, he had become convinced, from testimony of prisoners captured, that all of General Chalmers's cavalry division was in his front. Calling for reinforcements he did nothing more of note as the afternoon waned.[60]

General Chalmers, though, at last learned the Yankees were on the Harding Pike and in rear of his position. Fearing, of course, that if he stayed longer at his present location his command would be cut off, Chalmers pulled his men back for some distance until, at last, he could ride cross country and join up with the main body of the Southern army. Colonel Kelley, with his artillery, also retreated from the banks of the river.[61]

While Chalmers was working to safely extricate Rucker's brigade from its precarious position, he sent Lieutenant James Dinkins, commanding a company, riding straight for the Belle Meade mansion (which fortunately still stands), to bring off the wagon train parked at William G. Harding's race track. Arriving at Belle Meade slightly before dark, Dinkins found that the train had been captured and burned, and Federal soldiers were milling about the mansion grounds. Dinkins proceeded to form up his cavalry and charge, scattering the surprised Bluecoats; only to immediately encounter more of the enemy coming up. Thus the Rebels, now outnumbered, were forced to fall back. As the fire fight raged, "bullets were clipping the shrubbery and striking the house," and several men were killed or wounded. In the midst of the melee, one of the Harding daughters, who bore the name of the Greek goddess Selene (Captain Dinkins observed that "she looked like a goddess") was standing on the front steps of the house waving her handkerchief as she cheered the Confederate cavalry. Fearing for her safety, Dinkins rode up and urged her to go in the house. She refused, continuing to stand in harm's way until the Rebels had retreated out of sight, behind the barn.[62] Bullet scars on the columns of the mansion may still be seen today.

In the meantime, General Richard Johnson had not realized that the Confederates were gone from his front; only when Colonel Harrison moved forward the next morning would Johnson discover they had left.[63] Whether the various Union problems of the day are attributed to bad luck, incompetence, "the fog of war," or a tough enemy—and it seems all the above were factors in varying degree—General Thomas nevertheless commanded too many men and too much fire power not to eventually deliver a blow which the Southerners could not withstand. Over on the Hillsboro Pike, in the general area of the present-day Green Hills shopping center, that blow was being struck against the left flank of the Confederate line.

8

Situation Perilous in the Extreme

The view from atop the hill where Confederate redoubt number four once stood reveals today a typical scene of urban American civilization. The site is approximately one-half mile west of Hillsboro Road, extending both north and south of present-day Hobbs Road. From slightly south of Hobbs, about where Castleman Drive, paralleling Hobbs, intersects with Trimble Road, the redoubt evidently, considering the fortification remnants in the rear of the Abbottsford complex, stretched northward across Hobbs Road for a short distance. The hill is one of the half-dozen or more highest points in that section of the city. From its vantage point, when the trees are depleted of their leaves, as they are in mid-December, a person can see even to downtown Nashville. One's attention, however, tends to gravitate to the center of the Green Hills community, strung out along five-lane Hillsboro Road for a distance of approximately two miles.

There one of Nashville's major shopping centers, the Green Hills Mall, meshes with restaurants, movie theaters, fuel stations, grocery stores, banks, Hillsboro High School, a public library, condominiums, apartments, private homes, office buildings, and several churches. Standing atop the hill in the daytime and looking eastward toward Hillsboro Road, the sounds of accelerating motors, the droning of jet engines above, perhaps a wailing siren—the many noise pollutions of present-day urban culture—force themselves upon one's psyche, in spite of the beauty of a blue, sunny sky. The Green Hills complex covers about the same area where the refused flank of the Confederate left wing, dependent primarily upon its five redoubts to hold off the Yankees, rested during the Battle of Nashville.

How different from today the view must have been on December 15, 1864. This is not to say that the scene was better; only different, dramatically different. During the late morning of December 15, General John Bell Hood—according to some accounts, though others dispute it— rode up on the high ground where redoubt number four was still under construction. If indeed General Hood visited the site and gazed westward down the slope and across the valley, in the direction from which the enemy was expected soon to appear, he saw a great expanse of open ground, with a few patches of snow and sleet still visible. The area could not have looked very attractive, as only trunks of trees dotted the landscape. Much of the timber had been cut away, used for fuel, construction of redoubts and breastworks, and, of course, to clear a field of fire, the better to dispatch the advancing U.S. troops when the time for battle would be at hand.[1]

On that mid-December morning the time was at hand. It had come sooner than General Hood had expected, or desired. During the early morning the general had been at his headquarters in the Overton home, Traveler's Rest. There he was still refighting the Battle of Franklin—in his mind and on paper. Perhaps the general feared his announcement of "victory" at Franklin was wearing thin at the capital in Virginia. Word of the appalling number of Confederate lives sacrificed at Franklin continued to spread; and with it the critical implications about Hood's judgment in formulating an assault so disastrous. The general had just been stung anew by newspaper accounts of Yankee claims that thirty Southern flags had been captured in the battle. Concerned about what Richmond must be thinking and attempting to defend himself, Hood fired off a dispatch addressed to James A. Seddon, the secretary of war. "The enemy claim that we lost thirty colors in the fight at Franklin. We lost thirteen," he stated, hedging the truth, "capturing nearly the same number. The men who bore ours were killed on and within the enemy's interior line of works." One wonders what the secretary thought of Hood's message, particularly the last sentence.[2]

Hood also again called upon General Beauregard, asking for help in strengthening his forces. And even as the Union troops, then unbeknownst to Hood, were moving in great strength toward the Southern left flank, his assistant adjutant general was preparing instructions, absurdly in retrospect, for the completion and defense of the redoubts along that refused line: "The party for each [redoubt] will be selected at once, and as far as practicable camped near the work which they are to defend. . . ." Furthermore, directed Major A. P. Mason, the men must hold the redoubts "at all hazard, and not . . . surrender under any circumstances."[3]

While Hood worked through the early morning, the sounds of guns could be heard at Traveler's Rest. At first the noise was believed to be nothing more than another Union "demonstration," several of which had been staged since the Grayclads arrived in front of Nashville. Yet the firing seemed to grow more intense as the time passed. Reports were received that the Yankees were advancing against both Southern flanks. Finally, sometime after ten o'clock, with precious minutes ticking away, the general became so concerned that he mounted up and rode to Stewart's corps at the Hillsboro Pike, where the sounds of the guns seemed to be reaching the greatest volume and the reports were the most troubling; like the 10 A.M. message from Brigadier General Claudius Sears that "the demonstration of the enemy on the left is increasing."[4] There, spying the heavy blue columns in the distance and watching them maneuver, he saw that much more than a demonstration was underway.

Apprised that the Confederate right flank was holding strongly, Hood correctly surmised that the main effort of the Federals was developing on his left, where General Stewart informed him that although his "line was stretched to its utmost tension," it could not reach "far enough toward [redoubts] 4 and 5" without creating a significant gap for the enemy to penetrate. Reinforcements for the left flank were needed at once and Hood issued orders for both Stephen Lee (whose troops in the center did not appear to be threatened) and Frank Cheatham to send soldiers from their corps: Edward Johnson's division would come from Lee, and William B. Bate's division from Cheatham.[5]

Surely General Hood knew that redoubt number four, together with number five, positioned a third of a mile farther south, constituted the most vulnerable area of his left flank. Well might Hood be concerned because, like the attack at Franklin, the redoubt concept originated with him. Only a few days before, the general had set forth his plan to defend the rear of his left flank with "strong self-supporting detached works." These fortifications, in Hood's judgment, would secure the flank "against any attempt the enemy might make to turn it." General Stewart, commanding the corps on the left flank, received orders to "superintend in person as much as possible [the construction] of these works," while urging upon all officers and men the importance of pressing forward the construction that "we may be fully prepared to meet any movement of the enemy."[6]

Thus began the erection of five redoubts: small, enclosed fortifications, constructed on high ground of timber and earth, intended to house four artillery

pieces manned by fifty cannoneers, with about one hundred infantry supporting the guns in trenches dug nearby. Redoubt number one was located at the
extreme left of the main Confederate line, a few hundred feet from the northeast
corner of today's intersection of Hillsboro Road and Woodmont Boulevard.
Situated on the highest point of a hill, immediately west of present-day Benham
Avenue, which parallels Hillsboro, the site is owned, fortunately, by the Battle
of Nashville Preservation Society, and some of the Confederate earthworks still
exist. From redoubt number one to redoubt number five, which lay farthest to
the south, and near the northwest corner of the current intersection of Hillsboro
Road and Harding Place, was a distance of one and three-quarters miles.

Redoubt number two lay only a short distance from number one, situated
south of Woodmont and just east of the Hillsboro Road. Redoubt number three
was placed southwest across the Hillsboro Pike. It was a few hundred yards
from number two, and located on the hill where Calvary United Methodist Church now stands. Thus the first three redoubts were reasonably close
together; but a distance of nearly a mile separated numbers three and four, with
number four, as previously noted, located a half-mile west of the Hillsboro Pike.
Numbers four and five were clearly the most isolated.

The summary picture was that redoubts three, four, and five were located
too far apart to support one another and there was no plan for an entrenched
line to connect them. (No infantry support was available to man such a line anyway, without stripping the defenders from some other section of the Southern
position.) Of course the concept was, again in Hood's words, that the fortifications would be "self-supporting detached works." The fact that Hood thought
these far-spaced redoubts could be self-supporting and together protect the
entire left flank, is likely more evidence (along with sending troops to Murfreesboro as previously discussed) that the general, regardless of claims to the
contrary in his autobiography, underestimated the strength of the Union forces
at Nashville. This would seem to be the most charitable interpretation of his
redoubt plan. One writer suggested that Hood simply did not know how to use
artillery.[7]

Whatever the verdict on the redoubts, by mid to late morning of December 15, General Hood concluded that the U.S. forces were massing for an attack
on the Southern left flank. Later the Confederate commander would reestablish
his headquarters just east of the Granny White Pike, and a short distance south
of present-day Battery Lane, at the home of Judge John M. Lea. While closer to
the left flank than Traveler's Rest, Lealand, as the property was known, lay still
approximately a mile and a half south of the Confederate line.

For a brief time during the late morning, General Hood conferred with Captain Charles Lumsden, commander of Lumsden's Alabama Battery, stationed at

redoubt number four. Lumsden was a graduate of the Virginia Military Institute who had served as commandant of cadets in Tuscaloosa at the University of Alabama.[8] He seemed to know his business, which is to say that he could not have been optimistic about the situation in which he found himself. Construction on the fortification he manned had not been completed. Worse was the knowledge that only one hundred infantry of the Twenty-ninth Alabama supported his cannoneers. These facts, coupled with his isolated position, were not promising of success. Already Lumsden had told General Stewart that an enemy attack would overrun his guns rapidly. Stewart replied that he must hold on as long as possible.[9]

At least Lumsden did possess four guns, two more than redoubt number five, off to the south. The guns faced westward toward a ridge, perhaps six hundred yards away, where the Bluecoats were expected to appear momentarily. General Hood ordered Captain Lumsden to "hold the work at all hazard," as Major Mason had instructed in his circular, penned a short time earlier. Probably Hood told him that reinforcements had been ordered to the left flank. Regardless of what else their conversation entailed, Lumsden and his men would acquit themselves well, maintaining their ground longer than Hood had any reason to expect.[10]

Sometime before noon, when the men of Ector's brigade, retreating from the Harding Pike, came rushing past redoubt four, Captain Lumsden pleaded with them to stop and help him hold the position. "You *must hold* this ground," he told Colonel David Coleman. "Orders are that it must be held to the last limit." James Maxwell, sergeant in charge of the redoubt's fourth gun, remembered Coleman's reply: "Captain, we can't do it. Their skirmishers alone outnumber us two or three to one." One of the brigade's veterans called out that a whole army was advancing behind them. On went the brigade, not stopping until the Hillsboro Pike, where they took position on the left of Walthall's division. Soon, however, a report reached General Stewart that a U.S. force farther to the south was advancing northward on the Hillsboro Pike. Ector's brigade was ordered to move toward it immediately, to defend the pike and protect the refused Confederate left flank.[11]

Meanwhile, "Old Straight" Stewart contemplated the coming Union attack, the brunt of which he realized soon would fall upon his corps. Although the line of his command was not exposed and isolated like the two southernmost redoubts, the general knew the ground he needed to hold was much too great an expanse for the number of defenders under his command. On the right of the corps was the division of William Wing "Old Blizzards" Loring. Occupying an entrenched line, approximately a mile in length, the division stretched, right to left, from just east of the Granny White Pike to the site of redoubt number one, near the Hillsboro Pike. For most of that distance the line ran parallel to and slightly south of today's Woodmont Boulevard. The division consisted of three brigades: Brigadier General Winfield S. Featherston's on the right; Brigadier General Thomas M. Scott's in the center, commanded by Colonel John Snodgrass after Scott was wounded in the Franklin battle; and Brigadier General John Adams's unit on the left, that brigade led by Colonel Robert Lowry since the death of Adams.[12]

At the Hillsboro Pike, the line of Stewart's corps angled about ninety degrees to the south, thus running at a right angle to the main line of the Confederate army. By this time Stewart had only two divisions in his corps, having attached the division of Major General Samuel G. French, which was small, to the command of Major General Edward C. Walthall. A brigade of French's command (although French himself was not present due to a severe eye infection) occupied the refused line immediately south of redoubt number one, on the east side of Hillsboro Pike. Stretching south to a point more or less in rear of redoubt number three, these infantry were commanded by Brigadier General Claudius Sears.[13]

Extending the line from Sears's left flank was Walthall's division proper, strung out behind the protection of a stone wall east of the pike. From right to left, three brigades were in position under Brigadier Generals Daniel H. Reynolds, George D. Johnston (who replaced the wounded William Quarles after Franklin), and Charles M. Shelley. This line stretched a mile or more along the pike, ending almost directly in the rear of redoubt number four. Walthall's command was missing about two hundred men, sent forward at Hood's order to support the cannoneers in redoubts four and five. Also Walthall reported that he had no artillery whatsoever along the pike. Some of his guns had been ordered into the redoubts and the rest of his pieces "it had been found necessary to post at other points where guns were needed on the main line."[14]

Bleak indeed was the situation as the Grayclads of Stewart's left flank alone prepared to face an assault by Union forces twice as numerous as the Confederates had in the whole of the Army of Tennessee. For whatever their ignorance may have been worth to their peace of mind, the Southerners probably had little concept of what they were about to confront. When the Bluecoats at last swept forward, their striking force was far more powerful than any of the Confederates had supposed.

The Union assault had been slow to get into gear. Coordinating the movement of so many men, in so many units, and of all arms—infantry, cavalry, and artillery—in a difficult wheeling maneuver across several miles of hills, valleys, and plains, was a demanding, time-consuming exercise. No one showed more concern for the complexities of the advance than the cavalry commander, Brevet Major General James Harrison Wilson. Only three months beyond his twenty-seventh birthday, and called "the boy general" by some when speaking behind his back, General Wilson—although inferior in the field to the Rebel veteran Forrest, as previously discussed, and as were many Federal cavalry leaders—was an intelligent, highly confident, and hard-driving officer.[15]

Since arriving in Nashville, Wilson had developed an impressive cavalry arm of some nine thousand mounted troopers, well trained and equipped, and armed with the Spencer seven-shot repeating carbine. He had another three thousand unmounted men, the whole of his corps constituting a very formidable force and organized into three divisions. Wilson's troopers would be advancing on the right flank of the Bluecoat infantry and the general wanted every detail of the movement fully understood by his division and brigade commanders. He provided them with both oral and written instructions, pointing out the ground over which they were to advance, with the objective clearly defined and emphasized: envelop the enemy's refused flank.[16]

Undoubtedly some Nashvillians were pleased when they learned the Yankee cavalry at last were going into action. "General Wilson will do a good thing," the *Nashville Daily Union* editorialized on December 14, "if he will place in the van [when the battle comes] the dashing fellows on fine horses, who constantly gallop through our streets to the peril of footmen."[17]

Moving forward on the cavalry's left flank would be the division of Brigadier General Edward Hatch. A major responsibility for Hatch was to keep his left flank in touch with the right flank of the advancing infantry, conforming to the movements of the infantry. Brigadier General John T. Croxton led the cavalry brigade on Hatch's right (the other two brigades of Edward M. McCook's division having been detached to pursue Rebel raiders in Kentucky) and Richard W. Johnson's division was on the right of Croxton. Finally came the division of Brigadier General Joseph F. Knipe, "in readiness to reinforce any portion of the general advance" which might meet with difficulty.[18]

General Wilson also initiated a conference with General Andrew Jackson Smith, whose infantry corps would move in cooperation with the cavalry, the better to coordinate the advance and eliminate any possible blundering when cavalry and infantry surged forth. According to Wilson, he and Smith had an understanding concerning the movement of Brigadier General John McArthur's infantry division. McArthur, then positioned to the right of the cavalry, needed to relocate on the left of the troopers for the advance. Smith agreed with Wilson that McArthur should march his division behind the cavalry on the morning of the fifteenth, rather than in front of them. Because Wilson, moving on the outer arc of the wheeling movement, would have to cover a greater distance than the infantry, and many of his men were dismounted, the general wanted to ensure that his initial movement would not be hindered in any way.[19]

The forces of nature of course, in the form of a heavy morning fog, initially hindered anyone from moving. When the fog at last lifted, Wilson was disgusted to find McArthur's infantry, in spite of all his planning, marching across the front of his troopers and delaying them still more. Wilson always had a tendency to be hypercritical, viewing himself as a perfectionist surrounded by, in the words of his biographer, "the sloppiness and incompetence of others."[20] It was nearing eleven o'clock, according to Richard Johnson, before the enraged Wilson could get under way. After this early bungling, however, the Union advance proceeded rapidly.

Andrew Jackson Smith, commanding three infantry divisions, had Brigadier General Kenner Garrard's division on the left flank of his advance. Garrard hailed from Bourbon County, Kentucky; had attended Harvard before graduating from West Point in 1851. Like many another future Civil War officer, he served in Texas with the Second Cavalry. Most recently, Garrard had commanded first a cavalry division, and then the entire cavalry arm, in Sherman's Atlanta campaign. Sherman was never one with any faith in the cavalry, frequently indulging, and sometimes loudly, in cynical remarks about the mounted arm. One wonders if Uncle Billy's rough growling—"Whar's Garrard? Whar in hell's Garrard?"—still rang in the Kentuckian's ears. Probably, even if Garrard never actually heard such bellowing from Cump, others had relayed the words to him. It seems likely that Garrard was pleased both to be away from Sherman and commanding infantry.[21]

Advancing on Garrard's right was John McArthur's division. McArthur was a Scotsman, born in Erskine, who immigrated to the United States in 1849. Gaining a partnership in a Chicago iron works, he also became involved with the local militia and helped raise a regiment when the war began. McArthur had seen a lot of action, at Fort Donelson, Shiloh (where he was wounded), and most notably in the Vicksburg campaign, leading a division in the corps of James McPherson and earning the respect of both Grant and Sherman.[22]

Marching behind Garrard and McArthur, and attempting to maintain a central position, was Smith's third division, led by Colonel Jonathan B. Moore, acting as the corps' reserve. By afternoon the plan of attack at last seemed to be coming together for the Union. As previously noted, the U.S. forces were using Thomas J. Wood's corps as their hub for the grand wheel. Wood's command, having taken the all but abandoned Montgomery Hill, next approached Stewart's entrenched line between the Granny White and Hillsboro Pikes. The greater bulk of Federal manpower, however, was swinging to the west of

John McArthur.
Library of Congress.

Wood's soldiers, advancing south and east between the Harding and Hillsboro turnpikes, aiming to envelop the Rebel left flank.

Smith's infantry corps was pivoting on Wood's corps, while Wilson's cavalry command moved on the right of Smith and on the rim of the advance. Initially, John McAllister Schofield's corps resided in rear of Smith's command, functioning as a reserve. In the early afternoon, when General Thomas realized how far the Confederate left was refused along the Hillsboro Pike, he ordered Schofield to bring up his corps, and go into position on the right of Smith and left of Wilson, thereby allowing Wilson to sweep farther south, "striking the Hillsboro Pike," according to Thomas, "six or seven miles from the city, [and turning] the enemy's left completely. . . ." If the Hillsboro Pike could be opened, continued the Federal commander in a bit of understatement, "we can strike the enemy a severe blow."[23]

The advance of Smith's corps was then halted, allowing time for Schofield to move up. (Possibly, this just might have been the time when Brevet Major George H. Heafford, one of General Smith's staff officers, did his "thing," later described with entertaining and refreshing honesty: "Wearing the largest shoulder straps I could purchase . . . , and being otherwise in full uniform, . . . I rode up and down the line . . . for the purpose of inspiring the men with confidence and enthusiasm. Not until I had returned to my proper station did I discover that . . . their backs being toward me all the time, they had not seen me, and consequently failed to 'enthuse' to any appreciable extent.")[24]

The advance of Smith's corps was then halted, allowing time for Schofield to move up. Once Schofield would come into line, the total Yankee forces committed against the Confederate flank, from Wood's corps through Wilson's, would number nearly fifty thousand. Stopping Smith's march for a bit was not unwelcome to the dismounted cavalry who, having farther to travel than the infantry, sometimes were moving at the double-quick. They continued to advance while Smith waited on Schofield. General Wilson, in order for his troopers better to conform to the infantry's movement, had instructed the cavalry to move out dismounted, with the led horses in rear of their respective regiments, but keeping one regiment in each brigade mounted for a charge should the occasion present itself.

Such an opportunity occurred as Hatch's Second Brigade was crossing the Harding Pike near the Belle Meade mansion. Sighting a wagon train moving south (General Chalmers's, as noted in the previous chapter), Colonel Datus E. Coon, brigade commander, at once sent Colonel George Spalding's Twelfth Tennessee Cavalry in pursuit. Overtaking and driving the enemy in confusion, the Twelfth Tennessee captured more than twenty wagons and forty-three prisoners.[25]

Meanwhile, the great mass of Bluecoat troopers—minus Johnson's division which, as earlier recounted, became embroiled for the rest of the day with a single brigade of Chalmers's division near the Charlotte Pike—was swinging rapidly toward the Hillsboro Pike, "much of the time at a double-quick" pace, reported Colonel Coon. The time perhaps was nearing two o'clock when Coon's brigade of veterans, many of whom had wreaked havoc across Mississippi on Benjamin Grierson's 1863 raid, topped a rise and sighted a Rebel fortification crowning a hill only a few hundred yards distant. It was redoubt number four.[26]

General Hatch, as well as Colonel Coon, were close at hand. They soon had Battery I, First Illinois Light Artillery, positioned on Coon's right flank. The Federal cannoneers began putting enfilade fire on the Confederate fortification while the cavalrymen deployed for action. Coon had the Seventh Illinois on his right flank, the Second Iowa and Ninth Illinois in the center, and the Sixth Illinois on his left. U.S. infantry were arriving as well, coming up on the left flank of the cavalry, with Colonel William McMillen's brigade of General McArthur's division in the lead. (Schofield's corps was still some distance to the rear, needing more time to reach its assigned position.) McMillen said he placed a battery within four hundred yards of the redoubt "and opened on [the enemy] with a rapid and telling fire." The infantry colonel was also forming his men in anticipation of making a charge, with the Seventy-second Ohio deployed as skirmishers, while the Ninety-fifth Ohio and Tenth Minnesota composed the brigade's front line, with the One Hundred Fourteenth Illinois joining the Ninety-third Indiana in a second line. Men threw off their knapsacks, blankets, and overcoats, and fixed bayonets for the charge.[27]

Within a short time two more Union batteries came up, unlimbered, and began placing fire on the Confederate fortification. The Southern gunners were returning fire, but clearly they were overmatched. Artillery fire horribly mangles its victims, seldom killing or wounding in a simple, "clean" manner. And occasionally those it mauls are not even the intended targets; rather they are unfortunate sufferers from a disheartening accident. Thus it was with the Second Iowa Light Battery. A gunner lost both of his arms, "torn off above the elbows," because of "a premature discharge" from one of the cannon. A fellow cannoneer, Lewis F. Phillips, blamed the tragic occurrence on "the gun not being properly swabbed," and noted that it was the second accident of that kind experienced by the Second Iowa. Phillips also said that, only moments later, he "came near being killed by concussion" from a gun fired early, while he was still between the hub and the muzzle of the piece.[28]

The artillery duel went on for some time, generating immense noise in addition to its destructive powers. Spectacularly, according to one Yankee report, a Rebel caisson was blown up, flames and smoke leaping and billowing skyward. According to Colonel Coon's report, "a lively [artillery] fire was kept up on both sides for an hour."[29] All things considered, it was probably less than an hour. The afternoon was fast waning. Sunset would be about four thirty, with darkness soon following. Already the shadows cast by the trees were lengthening across the landscape. General Hatch, aggressive as usual, decided the artillery bombardment had gone on long enough; the time to close with the Graycoats was at hand. He ordered Colonel Coon to charge the redoubt, holding his fire until within a short distance of the Rebels, when the repeating carbines of the troopers would give them a deadly advantage.[30]

Sometime around two thirty—maybe slightly later—the strains of the bugler's charge rent the air, the cry "Forward!" was given, and the cavalry moved to the attack. The brigade's right wing charged across an open field, impeded by two stone fences, while the left wing had a heavy thicket to pass through. These proved to be "very slight impediments in the way of this veteran brigade." The Confederate cannoneers, when they saw the Yankees coming, began firing canister. Their infantry supports were also loading and firing as fast as possible. Much of the Confederate fire, however, was too high, passing above the heads of the Federals. Nothing the Graycoats did had any noticeable effect; hardly even slowing the Union assault. In fact, Colonel Coon said that "each regiment was competing with the others to reach the redoubt first." Apparently there was also competition with the infantry of McMillen's brigade, simultaneously charging on the left of the cavalry, as to who would be first to reach the parapet of the redoubt.[31]

A frantic, bloody, hellish scene engulfed number four. "We gave [the Yankees] a few charges of canister as they crossed the last 100 yards in our front," said James Maxwell, and then "they were upon us, entering our redoubt right at my gun where the . . . infantry of our support were supposed to be, but were not." Already Maxwell's gunner had been disabled, another cannoneer shot in the groin (a wound from which he died that night), and Maxwell was serving at the gun when U.S. cavalry and infantry simultaneously swarmed over the redoubt walls. Lieutenant Cole Hargrove shouted for the men to "run towards our right," which Maxwell reported they "quickly did, after firing the last charge of canister in the faces of the charging enemy."[32]

Maxwell said he heard someone shout a warning, "Lookout, Jim!" He dropped down on hands and knees as another gun "belched a double charge of canister right over my head," aimed at the enemy already at his gun that had just been abandoned. "I sprang to the side of that second piece," continued the sergeant, and "helped to load and fire it twice." Again the gun was loaded, but the man with the friction primers had already made for the rear. Captain Lumsden shouted, as Maxwell recalled it, "Take care of yourselves, boys," and everybody fled, of necessity abandoning all four guns to the enemy.[33]

Down the eastern slope ran the Confederates, heading for the pike and the safety of their line behind the stone wall. Some of the Union troops were chasing after them, a few of the pursuers on horseback, firing their pistols at the runners. Maxwell said he ran across an infantryman's abandoned rifle, and noticing it was ready to fire, grabbed it up, turned and shot at "a Yankee at our guns waving his hat and hurrahing." Having fired, the sergeant instantly, as if in one motion, turned and dropped the weapon, continuing his flight without knowing whether or not the missile found the target.[34]

Maxwell at last reached the relative safety of the Confederate line, joining up with the "remnants of our cannoneers who had gathered around Captain Lumsden and Lieutenant Hargrove near a red brick farm-house, . . . east of the Hillsboro Pike." One of the cannoneers who did not survive was a young fellow named Hylan Rosser, part of whose head was blown off during the battle. Later, as Captain Lumsden was attempting to wash his hands and clean up a bit, he kept picking something from his beard. Finally, he said to Sergeant Maxwell, "Maxwell, those are part of Rosser's brains." As for Lumsden, he would survive the war only to die three years later in a lumber manufacturing accident.[35]

The Southerners had been quickly overwhelmed; no more than 150 men defending their position in the face of four Yankee cavalry regiments and nine regiments of infantry (altogether perhaps six to seven thousand Federals), who swarmed about them on every side. And the Graycoats knew there was no possibility of reinforcements coming to their assistance. Credited with being the first U.S. soldiers to scale the Confederate works were Second Lieutenant George W. Budd, Second Iowa Cavalry, and his company, only a second behind. All the rest, cavalry and infantry, had closed fast. Fierce and gory, the fight was waged with bayonets, rifle butts, pistols, and sabers. Then as the surviving Grayclads fled to the rear, the Union troopers were claiming the four guns of redoubt four as their capture. Somewhat reluctantly, the Federal infantry would acknowledge the claim, General McArthur saying in his report that he "conceded" the capture of the guns to the cavalry, "their gallantry on that occasion being conspicuous," although he added the contention that "the fort had been rendered untenable by the fire from my batteries."[36]

Elated by their triumph, the Yankees yelled and screamed, fired at the retreating Rebels or, filled with enthusiasm and impetuosity, a few raced down the eastern slope of the redoubt chasing the fleeing enemy. Others simply milled about trying to catch their breath after the tiring charge. But there was little time for either rest or argument about whether cavalry or infantry deserved credit for taking the four guns.

No sooner had the Bluecoats overrun redoubt number four than their attention was resoundingly demanded by number five. A salvo from Confederate guns in that fortification suddenly whistled toward the celebrating Federals in the redoubt they had just captured. The Grayclads' infantry supports soon added their rifled-musket fire to the artillery shots. Within seconds the Union troops in redoubt number four were jolted back to reality. This was not the time for celebration. Quickly they turned the captured guns on the Rebels to the south, who soon faced the fire of at least three Bluecoat batteries. The triumphant Yankees in number four stood to gain nothing by staying put (and could surely expect casualties if they did so); and certainly they were not about to retreat. The only acceptable choice was once again to attack. Without hesitation General Hatch ordered his bugler to blow the charge. Lieutenant O. A. Abbott of the Ninth Illinois Cavalry remembered Captain Joseph W. Harper pointing at redoubt number five, "to the right and south of us," and shouting: "That's the one we want now, boys!"[37]

The Federals were all mixed together, regiments intermingled; even infantry and cavalry all mixed together. "We started for the fort," said Lieutenant Abbott, "more like the wild rush of a mob than an orderly charge."[38] To regroup would have consumed precious time. Together they moved down the slope from their captured hill, across the narrow valley between the fortifications, and started up the rise toward redoubt number five.

The cavalry were really "blown." Their long march earlier in the day (much of it at double-quick time), then the charge in taking the first redoubt, and only a brief interval before the second charge, rendered it difficult for many of the cavalrymen to manage much more than a walk. They were not as accustomed to marching as the infantry anyway. Many of the troopers fell to the ground exhausted. Some, realizing they could not go farther without catching their breath, stopped to fire their carbines at the enemy's infantry supports. Lieutenant Colonel John Lynch, commanding the Sixth Illinois Cavalry, while at the head of his regiment leading his men, collapsed and was carried from the field. Other troopers were felled by enemy fire. The redoubt "was not far away," recalled Lieutenant Abbott, "yet I never reached it," brought down by "a bullet through my left lung."[39]

Some men, too tired to walk, were seen actually crawling toward the objective. When within twenty yards or so of the Confederate work, Colonel Coon, who was on horseback, said he found Sergeant John F. Hartman, color-bearer of the Second Iowa Cavalry, "completely exhausted and halted in advance of the line." The Colonel asked him: "Sergeant, can you put those colors upon the works?" His reply—"I can, if supported"—was followed by Coon yelling for the Second Iowa to support their colors. Coon then roared for all to hear: "Second Brigade, take those guns before the infantry can get up!" Coon's officers immediately were echoing the Colonel's words, and once more the charge became a race between the cavalry and McMillen's infantry.[40]

The Second Iowa's color-bearer proved as good as his word. John Hartman indeed planted the regiment's colors on the Rebel works only instantly to be mortally wounded by rifle fire through the abdomen.[41] But the Confederate situation at redoubt five was hopeless. When the Yankees drew near, the Rebel cannoneers loaded their two howitzers from Edward Tarrant's battery with double charges of canister and succeeded in mangling a number of their antagonists. The Bluecoats were coming by the thousands, however. General McArthur, seeing the cavalry and his infantry of the First Brigade charging, ordered Colonel Lucius F. Hubbard, commanding the Second Brigade, to charge from his position northwest of the Confederate fortification. A battery attached to the Second Brigade worked its way up the hill of redoubt number four and opened fire on number five—as if the Northerners did not already have sufficient artillery striking that work. Like a replay of the attack on number four, the fight for number five was soon over, the surviving Confederates making for the rear and the Federals, some of them, racing after their enemy, while others rounded up prisoners and celebrated the capture of two more guns.[42]

The fall of redoubts four and five left the Confederate flank in a perilous situation. There might have been a slim chance of saving it, if strong reinforcements, fully prepared to sacrifice themselves, had arrived earlier in the afternoon. However, General Lee said it was noon before he even received orders to send assistance to Stewart. The division of Ed Johnson was selected for the work, with the brigades of Arthur Manigault and Zachariah Deas to lead off, followed by those of Jacob Sharp and William Brantley. Although the brigades would be moving on an interior line of march, considerable time elapsed before any of the men reached the Hillsboro Pike. For one thing, disengaging the brigades from their northward facing works was not a rapid process. Then the men moved out in piecemeal fashion, "each brigade starting as it was disengaged from the works," wrote Lee—and predictably arrived in the same fashion.[43]

The reinforcements ordered from Cheatham's corps were even later getting underway than Lee's, and faced a longer route of march. This was the division commanded by William B. Bate, positioned at the Nolensville Pike. Not only was Bate shifting from one end of the army to the other; he also had to march on an exterior line in order to accomplish the movement. This was necessitated by the Confederate line angling sharply southwestward from the Nolensville Pike to the Franklin Pike, before turning due west. Bate reported that it was "the evening of the 15th when I was ordered by General Cheatham to move to the left," which statement leaves the reader with no idea of a specific time. However, Bate said that when he crossed the Franklin Pike the signs of retreat were everywhere as "streams of stragglers, and artillerists, and horses without guns or caissons . . . came hurriedly from the left." Bate also said "it was [then] nearly dark." Whatever, precisely, the time may have been, and whatever the reason, or reasons, Bate did not begin his march until the day was too far gone to render assistance in defending the left flank.[44]

Thus the Confederate hopes for reinforcements rested solely upon the division of Ed Johnson; and as events developed, only half of that division: the brigades of Manigault and Deas. Both brigades, like all of Johnson's division, had seen heavy fighting at Franklin. General Lee had high praise for the division's performance in that battle. "Their dead . . . mostly . . . fell in a desperate hand-to-hand conflict on the works of the enemy," he wrote. Then he added: "I have never seen greater evidences of gallantry than was displayed by [Johnson's] division."[45] Both Manigault and Deas were wounded at Franklin, resulting in Manigault being unable to command his brigade at Nashville when their men approached the Hillsboro Pike on the afternoon of December 15.

Orders were to form on the left flank of Walthall's division, behind the stone wall, with Manigault's brigade almost directly east of redoubt number four, and Deas to his right. Walthall's line, even more thinly stretched than earlier, direly needed help. Walthall had pulled Reynolds's brigade out of the line on his right flank, sending those men a few hundred yards farther south. There, in anticipation of a Federal assault following the fall of redoubts four and five (and a few Yankees were already across Hillsboro Pike), Reynolds was forming diagonally to the enemy, on a northwest to southeast line. The position was just north of the Felix Compton house, long a landmark of the battle, which ultimately succumbed to "progress" in the latter years of the twentieth century. To fill the gap created along the pike by the departure of Reynolds's infantry, Walthall's two remaining brigades shifted some of their strength farther to the right, resulting in a dangerously thin line until reinforcements arrived. This was the situation as the brigades of Manigault and Deas came up, approaching Walthall's left flank.

As these two brigades from Johnson's division were going into position, they could see the Yankees advancing in force. In fact, by then Schofield's corps was coming up on the right of Smith, enabling Wilson to remount much of his cavalry and begin wheeling farther to the south. Clearly the Federal infantry, en masse, would soon be upon Johnson's men. Already a Union battery had opened fire. Suddenly shells were exploding right on top of the Graycoats. The whole scene must have conveyed a sense of helplessness and a large number of Johnson's men, veterans of many a fight though they were, turned and ran.[46]

All soldiers, however well trained and experienced, have a breaking point. In *The Face of Battle*, John Keegan approvingly quotes from the American report on "Combat Effectiveness" in World War II: "There is no such thing as 'getting used to combat.' . . . Each moment of combat imposes a strain so great that men will break down in direct relation to the intensity and duration of their exposure."[47] One is tempted to speculate that the awful fight at Franklin was climactic in bringing many of Johnson's veterans to the point where they proved useless at Nashville. Fear, when it strikes deeply, is both destructive and contagious.

To the rear of Johnson's men was an open field. Before they could cross it, however, the Federal gunners were putting shot and shell all over the ground. The ricochet of solid shot pummeled the field, while shell bursts promised an indiscriminate array of horrifying wounds. A host of panic-stricken men, as if in some bizarre nightmare, as if running away had come to seem more hazardous than staying put, turned and rushed back to the stone wall from which they had just fled, seeking some semblance of protection from the artillery fire. Captain Joseph R. Reed, commanding the Second Battery Iowa Light Artillery, described the strange scene in his report of the battle. He said "a confused mass of the enemy broke from the stone wall at the pike and started to the rear across an open field." On this ground, Reed reported that he "opened all my guns with shot and shell, plowing through and exploding amongst them; a large number . . . ran back to the wall and, as I afterward learned, surrendered."[48]

No sooner had the Southerners gotten back to the stone wall than the Yankee infantry were upon them; men of McArthur's Second Brigade, Colonel Hubbard commanding, who had advanced on redoubt number five from the northwest. Many of these soldiers, realizing that McMillen's First Brigade, together with the cavalry, were overrunning the Rebel fortification before they could reach it in strength, rushed on past the work toward the Hillsboro Pike. "Our troops, flushed with victory, swept forward, with bayonets fixed, at a double-quick, breaking the enemy's lines," wrote one of Hubbard's regimental commanders. The result, he said, was the killing and wounding of large numbers, and the capture of hundreds of prisoners.[49] Colonel Hubbard, in his more matter-of-fact style, gave credit to the artillery fire as well as his infantry, led by two companies, one each from the Eighth Wisconsin and the Eleventh Missouri. Charging at a run, Hubbard said they "had a very demoralizing effect upon the enemy, who surrendered in large numbers, or retreated in utter disorder." The number of prisoners he placed at about 450.[50]

By this time the Graycoats clearly had no chance of maintaining their position on Hillsboro Pike. Two redoubts were gone and the enemy was rapidly approaching number three. The left of the Southern line behind the stone wall had been overwhelmed, more and more Yankees already were appearing east of the Hillsboro Pike, and literally thousands of Blueclads were fast approaching the pike. Confederate reinforcements proved proverbial: too little and too late.

General Stewart himself, aided by some of his officers, tried to rally the remnants of Manigault's and Deas's brigades, who were rushing eastward without any semblance of organization. Desperate for some means to halt the crumbling of the Confederate flank, Stewart earlier had ordered a battery withdrawn from William Loring's portion of the main line, which Stewart said was "not being yet pressed."[51] He positioned it farther south, on an elevation the general described as "a commanding hill" east of the Hillsboro Pike. To support this battery, Stewart somehow succeeded in stopping the pell mell retreat of survivors from Johnson's two brigades.[52]

But approaching across an open field, advancing straight toward the high hill just occupied by the Confederates, was another Blueclad, combined cavalry-infantry force, with the dismounted troopers in the lead while the infantry came on close behind and to the cavalry's left. These troopers, like those who had engaged in the assaults on the southernmost redoubts, were from General Hatch's division. That earlier action, as already recounted, primarily involved Colonel Coon's Second Brigade. Now the First Brigade, commanded by Colonel Robert R. Stewart, was moving rapidly forward in search of the enemy, seeking their own share of the combat. Very likely they sensed the desperate circumstances of the Graycoats, a realization surely contributing to the enthusiasm with which they advanced.[53]

195

The Union infantry following shortly behind were from General Schofield's Twenty-third Corps, Major General Darius N. Couch's Second Division, which like Stewart's cavalry, was late in getting a chance to close with the enemy. Couch had placed his First Brigade, led by Brigadier General Joseph A. Cooper, on the left of his advance, which had positioned them slightly behind the cavalry. An eagerness for action characterized the brigade, and may have contributed to the death of James H. Cohron, Company B, Twenty-sixth Kentucky Infantry, who, while forming in line, was instantly killed by the accidental discharge of his own gun.[54]

As the Yankees advanced across the open field, the Rebel battery atop the eminence ahead opened fire, the Confederate infantry joining in with their rifled musketry. Instantly the Federals, as if they had found precisely the challenge they sought, "without waiting for orders, commenced cheering and rushed forward," reported General Cooper, "charging up the hill at double-quick [time]." Several officers tried to stop them, knowing that such a rapid charge over difficult terrain would result in their lines being "much broken." Officers wanted a more disciplined, methodical approach.[55]

Once started, however, there was no halting the men, carried forward both by a contagious confidence that they would succeed, and an instinct that the best hope of survival was escaping the open field, storming the hill, and meeting with the enemy as fast as possible—killing the Rebels before the Rebels killed them. Probably also, as earlier in the day, there was a sense of competition between cavalry and infantry. Although General Cooper acknowledged "the extreme difficulty of climbing the hill," nevertheless he said his men scrambled up the height very quickly and, together with the cavalry, some of whom went around the base to cut off the retreat of the enemy, overwhelmed the Grayclads. With minimal casualties the hill was gained and three pieces of artillery captured, together with a number of prisoners. As the Federals seized the hill, Confederates behind a stone wall to the Union left opened an enfilading musketry fire. This challenge was met by the Sixth Tennessee Volunteer Infantry changing front to the left, charging the wall, and capturing a reported 150 prisoners.[56]

Reading the report penned by U.S. General Couch, the distinct impression gained is of infantry overwhelming the Confederates on the high hill, "assisted by a few hundred dismounted cavalry." Strikingly different, however, is the report of cavalry General Hatch; almost like another engagement is being described. It is a story of the cavalry, with infantry support that "was in its rear," charging the hill, "sweeping over it rapidly," capturing "four pieces of artillery," and turning them "on the [fleeing] enemy with good effect."[57]

Besides providing a touch of amusement, the two reports serve to remind one of the difficulties an historian often faces when attempting to determine what really occurred in battle. Regardless of whether Union cavalry or infantry are deserving of primary credit, another Confederate position, hastily conceived as it was, had quickly disintegrated. "On the approach of the enemy," as reported from the Confederate perspective by corps commander Stewart, the men he had rallied from Manigault's and Deas's brigades, "again fled," abandoning the battery, which was shortly captured. Soon after this debacle, the other two brigades of Johnson's division finally came up, although much too late for their presence to be of any value. They arrived only in time to fall back before the Federal advance. General Stewart said some of the enemy were already a half-mile beyond the Hillsboro Pike, "completely turning our flank." Even if the general's estimate of a half-mile was exaggerated, the condition of the Rebel flank was indeed dire. It was at this point that General Stewart pronounced the Confederate situation "perilous in the extreme."[58]

9

The Final
Gamble

Meanwhile, the Federal assault on redoubt number three developed very quickly, thanks in no small degree to the aggressiveness of Colonel Sylvester Hill, Thirty-fifth Iowa Infantry, then commanding the Third Brigade of McArthur's division. Sylvester Gardner Hill was a forty-four-year-old native of Rhode Island. A man of average size, weighing about 160 pounds, Hill had spent most of his life engaged in the lumber business, residing in Cincinnati and California before settling in Muscatine, Iowa. Participating in the Vicksburg and Red River campaigns, he also saw service in operations against Forrest in Tennessee and Sterling Price in Missouri. Now, at Nashville, General A. J. Smith looked upon Hill as a brave and capable subordinate.[1] Hill's brigade, wheeling to its left, was advancing across open farmland almost due west of redoubt number three, its men eager for battle, as was their commander. General Smith conferred with Hill, pointing out that the Confederate redoubt had begun placing fire on the flank of McArthur's other units advancing on Hill's right. Obviously the corps commander wanted to reduce that enemy fortification as soon as possible.

Immediately Hill volunteered the Third Brigade for the task, promising that his men would take the redoubt "without a bit of trouble," alleging that "nothing can stop them." But General Smith thought an assault with a single brigade was too risky. Smith ordered Colonel Hill to wait until he got the Second Brigade positioned to join in the effort. "Hold . . . where [you] are until you hear my bugle," instructed the general. Then Smith rode off to the south to locate Colonel Hubbard and bring his brigade, or at least some of it, into the advance on redoubt number three.[2]

But Colonel Sylvester G. Hill did not wait. Perhaps with the deafening noise of battle resounding in his ears, Hill did not fully understand General Smith's instruction. Perhaps that beguiling enchantress called glory beckoned to Colonel Hill and he was powerless to resist. Whatever the reason, despite Smith's instruction to wait, Hill immediately proceeded to attack. Lieutenant Colonel John H. Stibbs, commanding the Twelfth Iowa Infantry, said that within a minute after the corps commander rode away to the right, Colonel Hill instructed his bugler to "sound the charge!"[3]

The colonel's decision matched the mood of the men in his brigade, who only a short time before had been shouting when General Smith rode by that they too wanted a fort to capture; almost as if, or so it might have seemed to a detached onlooker, they were engaged in some great sporting event. The brigade was formed with the Twelfth Iowa and the Thirty-fifth Iowa in front, and the Seventh Minnesota and Thirty-third Missouri following. Colonel Hill directed that the colors of the Twelfth Iowa should be carried directly to the center of the redoubt. Charged with the responsibility of seeing that the Twelfth's colors were borne inside of the works was Major David W. Reed, a veteran of the "Hornets' Nest" at Shiloh, then acting as adjutant for the commander of the regiment.[4]

At once the men surged forward, some in silent determination; many yelling fiercely, bellowing loudly, cursing incessantly, crying out in agony when wounded—emitting all the horrendous sounds that have swept across innumerable battlefields through the centuries—and advancing in spite of a "fierce artillery and musketry fire" from the Rebel defenders. Colonel Stibbs said the brigade was halfway to the redoubt before "I heard General Smith's bugle sounding the charge on our right." Thus the Third Brigade easily reached the objective before the Second could do so. Fortunately for the Federals of Hill's brigade, many of the Confederate infantry, just as when redoubts four and five had been under attack, were shooting too high, and the cannoneers were unable to depress their pieces enough to strike the oncoming enemy, particularly as they charged up the rather steep hillside. Nearly all of the Southern fire, as the Yankees drew closer and closer, was passing harmlessly over their heads. Hold-

Sylvester G. Hill. Massachusetts Commandery Military Order of the Loyal Legion and the U.S. Army Military History Institute.

ing their fire as they moved toward the redoubt, the Federals only discharged their weapons as they swarmed into the fortification.[5]

By then many of the Graycoats were gone. Once the cannoneers realized there was no chance of defending their position against the sea of blue sweeping toward them, they tried to save the two-gun section from Joseph Selden's Alabama battery, but were forced to abandon the pieces. Probably the majority of Southerners were racing away to the east when the Yankees overran the fort. As soon as the Federals possessed it, however, they found themselves under fire from the artillery of redoubt number two, a few hundred yards away, on the other side of the Hillsboro Pike. The Confederate fire was on target. Captain Theodore G. Carter of the Seventh Minnesota Regiment claimed (possibly with a bit of exaggeration?) that "the [Rebel] gunners cut their fuses so that every shell burst inside of [the redoubt], and there did not seem to be ten seconds' interval between the discharges."[6] The fortification just won had quickly become a death trap for the Federals. Clearly the men could not stay long, enduring the intense fire, without taking heavy casualties.

Colonel Hill was on the scene, leading by example and buoyed up with a sense of triumph, perhaps even a sense of invincibility. Indicating redoubt number two, he roared out an order, directing his men to take that fort also! Instantly, Hill "was shot through the head, and died in a few minutes, without speaking," wrote Colonel William R. Marshall, Seventh Minnesota. A Federal surgeon with Hill's brigade said that the colonel's son, while acting as an orderly for his father, had been killed only a few months before by a bullet to the head, and that the colonel was riding the very same horse his son had been astride when shot and killed. Because of the noise of battle, some men had not heard Hill's last order. Most had not been reorganized for further action anyway, although several officers were soon working toward that end.[7]

It is impossible to know if Major Reed, who had been in front of the charging men of the Twelfth Iowa, heard Colonel Hill's order. Possibly Reed's leadership sprang simply from the instinct of a war-wise combat veteran, immediately sensing the position captured was untenable unless the enemy's guns playing upon it were seized. Reed's actions, whether or not he heard Colonel Hill, seem to have been instantaneous. His regimental commander, Colonel Stibbs, who was close at hand, left the following account: "Major Reed, who was in front of our charging column, did not stop on reaching the enemy's works, but calling on the men to follow him, he pushed forward with the left wing of my regiment. . . ." Joined by Colonel Marshall of the Seventh Minnesota, "who had about one third of his regiment with him," according to Stibbs, the two officers led their men in a charge diagonally across the Hillsboro Pike, hell bent on taking redoubt number two.[8]

Once again many of the Confederates fled as the Bluecoats drew near. The Federals' prize consisted of one artillery piece, several ammunition wagons and horses, and a large number of small arms, besides the prisoners taken, of which Colonel Marshall claimed about two hundred were captured in the two works.[9]

For some minutes after the death of Hill, command of the brigade rested with Colonel Stibbs. His immediate task, following the capture of the two redoubts, was to reform the brigade, readying it for the possibility of further action as quickly as possible. The colonel, however, was without his horse. Regimental commanders had charged on foot, and the orderlies had been slow to bring up the mounts. "Where is the Colonel's horse?" shouted a soldier, recognizing the colonel's disadvantage in trying to handle the brigade without a mount. Others took up the cry: "Where is the Colonel's horse? He ought to have a horse."[10]

Then someone spotted an artillery horse hitched to a tree. Thinking it better than nothing, the huge animal—"eighteen feet high" claimed Stibbs—was brought up, "harness and all, and I was helped aboard." With the iron trace chains dangling about the horse's legs, Colonel Stibbs proceeded to yank the animal around over the rough ground as best he could, while trying to reform the brigade, inadvertently presenting an entertaining, comical spectacle.[11]

Actually, the senior officer of the brigade after Colonel Hill's death was the Seventh Minnesota's Colonel Marshall, and Stibbs sent an orderly to notify him of the death of Hill. Within a short time Colonel Marshall took command of the brigade, Colonel Stibbs got his own horse back, and the Third Brigade was reformed.[12] The unfortunate Colonel Hill, the highest ranking Federal officer to lose his life in the Battle of Nashville, who would be breveted brigadier general "for gallant and distinguished service" on December 15,[13] had been correct; his brigade alone was capable of taking both redoubts number three and number two "without a bit of trouble." The Rebel left flank was going to pieces.

The sun was fast sinking; that magnificent, fiery disc already having slipped below the higher hills to the west. Even on a short December day it was evident that the sun god had favored the Union. Any hope earlier held by the Southerners that darkness might save the Confederate position before the Federals swept over it was forlorn. The sun was symbolically fitting on that mid-December day. Seventy-seven years had come and gone since the Constitutional Convention drew to a close in Philadelphia. That grand old man among the delegates, eighty-one-year-old Benjamin Franklin, often had gazed upon the chair of the convention president, at the back of which the sun upon the horizon was depicted, and wondered—the symbolism implicit for the fledgling nation—whether it was a rising or a setting sun. At last Franklin said he had come to believe that it was a rising sun.[14]

After three years and eight months of a Civil War far longer and more bloody than anyone had imagined at the beginning; a war constituting the greatest ever testing of the nation's strength to endure; the Battle of Nashville was abundantly dramatizing what was already clearly manifest to those with unfettered eyes: that Benjamin Franklin's sun indeed had been rising, while the Confederate sun was rapidly setting.

Now the fight came to redoubt number one. Located a few hundred feet east of the Hillsboro Pike, at the point where the Rebel left flank was refused to the south, this Confederate fortification stood alone after the fall of redoubt two. If number one went, everything went—the entire left flank, and with it the position of the whole army. Situated on high ground, the defenders of redoubt number one had a good view of downtown Nashville, only a few miles to the north, where William Strickland's State Capitol then dominated the skyline.

The Grayclads had an even better vantage point from which to observe the approach of the enemy, which undoubtedly was the focus of their attention. To say that the outlook was not good is an understatement. Large numbers, in fact overwhelming numbers of Bluecoats were close at hand, converging from both north and west. And after the loss of the nearest redoubt to the south, the enemy well might appear from the rear.

As events evolved, however, the immediate threat to the Confederates seemed to be coming from the north. Approaching from that direction was General Wood's Fourth Corps. Having easily overrun Montgomery Hill in the early afternoon, the corps' half-mile advance to the Grayclads main line proved to be a time-consuming affair.[15] The loss of time, in part, resulted from General Thomas's instruction to Wood that his reserve troops be shifted, in Wood's words, "as much to the right as could be done compatible with the safety of my own front."[16] The commanding general, having sent Schofield's corps to move up on the right of General Smith's advance, wanted more reserves shifted into the general vicinity vacated by Schofield, thus preventing a gap developing between Smith's left and Wood's right. Wood further reported that the Confederate artillery of redoubt number one "had been annoying us seriously all day"; that annoyance presumably constituting another factor in delaying the advance of the Fourth Corps.[17]

In response to the smoothbore Rebel guns, two Federal six-gun batteries were brought forward and located to place a converging fire upon the redoubt—rifled batteries, at a range of less than half a mile. The result was "a galling and continuous fire," according to General Kimball; a fire which sometimes penetrated the Confederate embrasures, killing or wounding several men at once. The advance of Wood's corps also resulted in some "severe skirmishing," as recorded in the journal of the Fourth Corps kept by Lieutenant Colonel Joseph H. Fullerton—yet another time-devouring factor.[18]

The time was approximately four o'clock when Wood's command at last was in position to attack. The corps was still aligned as earlier in the day, with the Second Division, commanded by General Elliott, on the right; the First Division, led by General Kimball, in the center; with General Beatty's Third Division to the left. Their line of advance, swinging up toward the enemy's works, generally brought Elliott's and Kimball's divisions toward the Confederate redoubt, with the front of Elliott's command noticeably contracted as it approached from northwest of Hillsboro Pike, while the left portion of Kimball's command extended eastward well beyond the site of the redoubt. General Beatty's division was moving up still farther to the east.[19]

General Wood selected Elliott's division to make the assault against the Confederate fortification. But Elliott did not move. He said that he was waiting on "General Smith to come up and connect with his right flank." Clearly General Wood was irritated. Thirty minutes later Elliott was "again ordered to move forward." By that time General Kimball, having requested and received Wood's permission to assault the enemy's position, was rapidly moving up the formidable hill, across ground heavy with mud, and cluttered by brush and fallen timber, the brigades of Isaac Kirby and William Grose leading the way. Charging "with loud cheers" and the "most exalted enthusiasm," to quote General Wood, Kimball's men "rushed forward up the steep ascent." Elliott's division was soon following.[20]

But a small band of men from the Thirty-sixth Illinois, making up a part of the skirmish line in front of Elliott's division, was also on the move. They were led by Lieutenant William Hall, who realized a general movement of the whole Federal line had begun. Hall and twenty-two soldiers broke from their cover in a stand of trees not far north of the redoubt, raced across the Hillsboro Pike and scrambled for shelter behind a stone wall paralleling the pike on the right (west) side. Protected by the wall from the fire of the Graycoat infantry, Hall and his men advanced several hundred feet until they were beyond the redoubt. From such an angle Hall could see that the enemy was in confusion. Panic-stricken Confederates—watching huge numbers of Blueclad troops rapidly climbing the hill in their front, relentlessly drawing closer and closer—began filtering to the rear, both individually and in small clusters.

Lieutenant Hall instantly sensed that the time to get the job done was at hand. Exhorting his men with a few well-chosen words, Hall led them in a charge to the rear of the fortification. There they quickly ascended the wall of the redoubt, confronted the enemy and demanded his surrender. "Without the firing of a gun or the slightest manifestation of resistance," wrote the historians of the Thirty-sixth Illinois, "the Rebels threw down their arms and surrendered." The quick action of Hall's small band of skirmishers bagged 120 prisoners and three field pieces with their caissons and ammunition—if one accepts the Thirty-sixth Illinois regimental history.[21]

Hall and his men had little more than taken possession of the fortification from the rear when Federal infantry came storming in from the west and north; troops from the corps of both Smith and Wood. Among them was a second lieutenant who brusquely demanded that the captured guns be turned over to him. "Not by a damned sight!" growled Hall; to which replied the second lieutenant: "I am a staff officer, sir . . . and you men had better be careful what you do." Hall had been on the picket line all night and throughout the day, tramping through thickets and briar patches, crawling through mud, his clothes torn, hair disheveled, face unshaven and smeared with powder and dirt. Lieutenant Hall was a rough-looking character and his mood was not one with which to be trifled. He responded: "I am a Lieutenant, sir, and bossing this job, and if you lay your hands upon these guns to take possession, I will cleave you to the earth. To the Second Division belongs the honor of their capture, and to General Elliott alone will I deliver them."[22]

This arresting account of courageous action by Lieutenant Hall and his band of skirmishers, as recorded in the history of the Thirty-sixth Illinois, without question constitutes the most dramatic story of the fall of redoubt number one. It should be noted, however, that other versions exist. Particularly interesting and straightforward is the report of Hall's brigade commander, Colonel Emerson Opdycke. "Volunteers had been called for from the skirmish line to go to the rear of the position and carry it," according to the colonel. "They carried the position gallantly," Opdycke wrote, "aided greatly by the charge in front. A number of my men had a hand-to-hand contest in the work." He said the Southern cannoneers "used their revolvers until overcome by our bayonets," after which a Federal lieutenant "seized one of the [artillery pieces], turned it on the [fleeing] enemy, and . . . fired it a number of times." Opdycke also credited a captain with placing a guard over two guns "until a written receipt was obtained for them. That receipt is now in my possession."[23]

Although casting Hall's role somewhat differently, Colonel Opdycke's report leaves an unmistakable impression that his (Opdycke's) brigade, a part of Elliott's division, overran the Rebel fortification. Yet the journal of the Fourth Corps credits General Kimball's division with capturing the redoubt and its battery, while stating that "General Elliott's division arrived upon the hill just as it was captured."[24] In fact, Lieutenant Colonel S. N. Yeoman, commanding the Ninetieth Ohio Regiment, in Kirby's brigade, Kimball's division, claimed that "my regimental flag [was] first on the enemy works."[25] Also asserting first arrival at the fortification were men from Smith's corps, McArthur's division, Hill's brigade—soldiers who had just taken redoubts three and two.[26] With so many attackers arriving at the redoubt from different directions and within seconds, or at most, minutes of one another—plus the many contradictory and/or self-serving accounts afterward penned—it is impossible today to determine precisely who did what and when. Conquest and confusion reigned simultaneously; that, perhaps, is the only given.

While some of the Yankees zealously claimed the spoils of victory, a few men rushed on after the fleeing enemy; but many of the exultant Federals were nearly as disorganized by their triumph as were the Confederates by defeat. Although General Thomas wanted the enemy pursued, and so ordered, some thirty minutes was consumed before the troops of Wood's corps could be reformed and started in lines of battle eastward toward the Franklin Pike. Darkness overtook the slow advance, which was halted about six o'clock, having carried only to the

Granny White Pike. "Rude works" were thrown up, said Colonel Opdycke, "and we bivouacked for the night." Much of Smith's corps, also disorganized after the successful attack, became absorbed with collecting prisoners and guns and conveying them to Nashville, under the charge of the Seventy-second Ohio Regiment. Consequently, most of the corps never got far beyond the Hillsboro Pike before darkness was upon them and they went into camp.[27]

Fortunate indeed for the Graycoats was the Federal confusion. As redoubt number one fell, and Union troops both to the south and east of that fortification surged upon the Confederate lines, Stewart's corps everywhere was falling back. Even a few minutes gained from the disarray of Yankee units could determine whether or not some Confederates extricated themselves from impending death, wounding, or capture.

No Confederate general was under greater pressure from the advancing Union troops than Brigadier General Claudius Wistar Sears. Commanding the small, 210-man brigade split between redoubts number two and three, Sears said the enemy broke his line, "just to my left." With some of his men the forty-seven-year-old West Pointer managed to retreat, although acknowledging that the pull back was "not in good order." A short distance to the rear, Sears found his horse "Billy," which he had left in charge of an orderly. The animal had been with Sears all through the war. The General remembered that Billy was "very uneasy," but once Sears had mounted, the horse "soon became quiet." Riding to the rear, "through a corn stubble," General Sears suddenly pulled up on a rise of ground and, for a moment, turned to observe the Federals with his field glasses.

At that instant he felt something strike his leg, and looking down, "saw my leg swinging helpless. The ball (solid) ricocheted, passed through my poor dear old horse and crushed my left leg." The horse died within seconds and Sears's mangled leg was amputated that night. Years later, a Confederate soldier by the name of R. N. Rea claimed to have witnessed the wounding of Sears, and wrote in the *Confederate Veteran* that when Sears realized his horse had been killed, the general seemed more upset by the loss of his animal than by his own misfortune. Rea said that Sears, with tears on his cheeks, exclaimed, "Poor Billy! Poor Billy!" Many thought Sears too would not survive, but he recovered to spend nearly a quarter of a century as a professor of mathematics at the University of Mississippi.[28]

As the Grayclads of Sears's brigade, in fact the whole of Stewart's corps, poured east and south in retreat after the collapse of the army's left wing, the immediate and imperative task of General Hood and his staff was to rally the men along another defensive line. The high hill chosen to anchor the left flank of the new position lay approximately a mile east of the Hillsboro Pike and just short of the Granny White Pike. Hood had used it as an observation post during the afternoon. Located southeast of Felix Compton's house, the eminence was called Compton's Hill, soon to become known as Shy's Hill, renamed in honor of the twenty-six-year-old Confederate Colonel William Shy, who was killed there the following day. Looming higher than any of the nearby knolls, Union General Schofield described it as a summit "without possession of which [the Confederate] position north of Brentwood was untenable."[29]

Late in the afternoon of December 15, General Hood sighted Ector's small brigade falling back from the Hillsboro Pike, at once choosing the Texans as a nucleus with which to defend the new flank. Positioning the men at the zenith of the hill, he cried out to them: "Texans, I want you to hold this hill regardless of what transpires around you." They told him: "We'll do it, General!"[30] Fortunately for the Confederates, darkness was at hand and only Schofield's men, coming up late and having seen little action, continued to press eastward after the retreating Graycoats. For a brief time, probably less than half an hour, some of these Federals engaged Ector's brigade, exchanging fire until it became fully dark.

This appears to have been the last action of the day. By this time Bate's division had been directed to support Ector, as would eventually the whole of General Cheatham's corps, digging in to hold the flank on and around Shy's Hill. An Arkansas soldier critically remarked: "General Bate, with his usual dashing presumption, demanded the 'post of honor.' At least that was camp talk," said the private, "so his infantry found themselves . . . perched upon this rocky knoll [Shy's Hill] comparatively isolated from the rest of the army."[31] Elsewhere General Hood and his staff worked to establish the army's new line farther to the east.

Along the Granny White Pike, as soldiers retreated in large numbers, one of the battle's oft-told, famous, and dramatic moments occurred—and involved a young Nashville lady. Not surprisingly, more than one version of the story has come down through the years. Slightly east of the Granny White Pike and just north of where the new Confederate position was being established, resided a Mr. Edward Bradford, who had a daughter named Mary. Colonel William Gale, assistant adjutant general of Stewart's corps, wrote to his wife soon after the battle, saying: "As our men fell back before the advancing Yankees, Mary Bradford ran out under heavy fire and did all she could to induce the men to stop and fight; appealing to them and begging them, but in vain—Deas' brigade was here."[32]

The other version, passed down by descendents of the Bradford family, is that Mary "observed a Confederate officer striking some of the members of his company with the flat side of his sword, trying to rally them." Outraged by such a sight, "Mary raced out of the house and denounced him." The retiring Grayclads halted, watching and listening as "their commanding officer was addressed in strong terms," and, of all things for that age, by a woman.[33] Whatever role, precisely, that Mary Bradford played on that evening, as Colonel Gale observed the retreating Confederates, he was deeply disturbed by what he saw. "I never witnessed such want of enthusiasm," he wrote. The men seemed "utterly lethargic and without interest" in the fray. Gale said he "began to fear for [the fight] tomorrow," and hoped that "General Hood would retreat during the night. . . ."[34]

Indeed it was decision time for the thirty-three-year-old general who headed the Army of Tennessee. Should he accept battle on the morrow, or pull out before dawn and head south? Some would have said, to express the matter in current slang, that the decision was "a no-brainer." Stewart's corps on the left flank had been severely dealt with in the afternoon and compelled to retire in rapid, sometimes pell mell fashion. With Stewart's position overwhelmed, the entire Confederate line had to be abandoned and the army retreated nearly a mile and a half. No fall back position had been prepared. The new location was assumed in the dark, with all the problems attendant thereto, while the overpowering numbers of the U.S. army gathered on the Rebel flanks and front, preparatory to resuming their onslaught the next day.

If such pessimistic considerations troubled the cerebrum of John Bell Hood, they were soon shunted aside. General Hood had been an ambitious young man whose courage and secretive scheming had combined to propel him to a high rank and responsible position that called for abilities beyond his capacities. Now a series of bad decisions had left the army drastically weakened in numbers; inadequately, even woefully equipped; with many soldiers suffering both physically and from low morale. The general faced a desperate situation. He knew that retreat meant acknowledging his campaign was a failure. After the loss of Atlanta, the blundering at Spring Hill, and the debacle at Franklin, a retreat from Nashville probably would mean Hood's removal from command. The thought of losing his position had to weigh heavily upon his mind.

On the other hand, if he stayed and fought again—and if his lines somehow held against the massive Federal onslaught (After all, had not the center and right fallen back only when the Rebel left flank was overpowered?)—Hood might yet succeed. He might still turn impending defeat into triumph; proving that he, John Bell Hood, made a wise decision when he led the army into Tennessee. He might emerge from the campaign with his military reputation not only intact, but greatly embellished. And one wonders if the thought of Sally ("Buck") Preston, far away in Richmond, did not cross Hood's mind as he weighed his decision. Would success or failure before Nashville possibly determine the outcome of his campaign to marry the young, socially well-connected beauty?[35]

Hood by nature was a gambler. There were the army tales of how he once put a thousand dollars on one card in a faro game and won. Of late he had given ample evidence that he was nothing if not a gambler, moving into Tennessee with no more than half the supply wagons he needed for the army; counting on reinforcements and conscripts that realistically could not be expected to materialize (a mere 164 men had been conscripted since the army entered Tennessee[36]); ordering the disastrous frontal assault at Franklin against the advice of major subordinates; afterward moving on to Nashville despite the appalling losses of men and officers in that battle, to face far greater numbers of the enemy at the capital of Tennessee; and that with winter coming on. Now, on the night of December 15–16, Hood would gamble again—this time venturing the army's total ruin. It was the final gamble.

By eight o'clock, at the latest, Hood had made the decision to dig in and fight again. A major repositioning of the army took place. Stephen Lee's corps, which occupied the center of the original line, had been only lightly engaged throughout the day's action, except for the portion of Johnson's division sent to reinforce the left flank. Lee merely withdrew his men down the Franklin Pike for nearly two miles. There his corps anchored the army's new right flank, positioned across the pike and occupying high, rocky ground on its east side. Approximately two miles away to the west, as the crow flies, lay Shy's Hill, where Cheatham's corps was placed on the left flank, having shifted from one end of the army to the other. Both flanks bent southward.[37]

Positioned between Lee and Cheatham, of course, was the roughly handled and weakened corps of General Stewart, which had been rallied to occupy the center of the line. Running parallel with and slightly south of today's Battery Lane, the battle line included a stone wall, then signifying the northern boundary of Judge Lea's property. The stone fence would be substantial protection against Yankee rifle fire. Along Stewart's line east of the Granny White Pike, picks and shovels bit into the ground as breastworks were hurriedly thrown up during the night by men haggard and worn. The line between the flanks meandered somewhat, making the length considerably more than two miles altogether.[38]

Thomas Hay, one of the earlier historians of the campaign, said the position "was none too favorable, but was forced on [Hood] because of the fewness of his numbers and the necessity, if possible, of keeping open a line of retreat for Cheatham on the Granny White Pike."[39] Whatever the verdict on the inherent strength of Hood's new position, its hurried overnight development could not possibly provide defensive works equal to those of the original line, which had been improved over a period of several days. When coupled with the casualties just suffered, especially in Stewart's corps, General Hood must have sensed, if he was even marginally realistic, that the odds of the army holding the line on the morrow were not good. Consequently, he ordered all the army's supply wagons south to Franklin at dawn. Further anticipating the possibility of defeat, Hood sent instructions to his corps commanders regarding their line of retreat in the event of "disaster," as the general expressed it. Stewart's corps was to fall back on the Franklin Pike while Lee's corps, because it suffered only light casualties during the first day's engagement, would hold position until Stewart was safely away. Cheatham was told to withdraw via the Granny White Pike, with Chalmers's cavalry covering his retreat.[40]

As for the Confederate cavalry's position on the night of December 15, General Chalmers fortunately escaped being trapped by Wilson's troopers, and stationed Colonel Edmund Rucker's brigade on the Hillsboro Pike, except for the Seventh Alabama. Those troopers remained on the Charlotte Pike to bluff Richard Johnson into thinking the entire Rebel brigade still confronted him. (Chalmers's other brigade, under Jacob Biffle, was off on the far right flank.) Meanwhile, General Forrest, with two cavalry divisions, was completely out of the battle, some thirty miles away to the east. General Hood's continuing fascination with the Yankees at Murfreesboro had led to the incredible folly of keeping most of the Rebel cavalry, commanded by one of the best generals in the history of mounted warfare, from participating in the engagement at Nashville. Forrest reported that on the evening of December 15 "I received notice from General Hood that a general engagement was then going on at Nashville, and to hold myself in readiness to move at any moment." Pulling his then widely scattered troopers together, Forrest prepared to ride for Nashville, awaiting only the order from Hood. That order never came. Forrest heard nothing more from the army's commander until the next night, thus missing altogether the fighting at Nashville.[41]

The long arm of the Southern army was also hurting. Stewart probably had no more than seven artillery pieces in line. About nineteen had been captured and some eight or ten more had been sent off to Murfreesboro and Columbia. Additionally, two pieces (Parrotts) were with Colonel Kelley. Lee had twenty-eight pieces, and Cheatham thirty-four. Some batteries, due to a combination of darkness and mud, could not be maneuvered into position on the line.[42] The Union had far more guns and more rifled guns than the Southerners. Perhaps the Army of Tennessee's artillery was in better shape for the battle on the morrow than its cavalry, but by any objective standard, that was not much consolation. The Confederate situation was dire. Maybe some Rebels subscribed to the old adage: "It is always darkest before the dawn." Others well might have thought a variation on that saying was more appropriate: "It is always darkest before total blackness."

Caught in the midst of the tumultuous Confederate retreat on the night of December 15 were the wounded, many of them spending an agonizing night—the last night some would ever know—"on the damp, cold ground." It was a night of blackness in which even healthy men "shivered the long night through."[43] At Glen Leven, a fine home still standing on the east side of Franklin Pike, just south of Caldwell Lane, the surgeons labored under adverse conditions in their makeshift hospital, reportedly even being forced to use the piano as an operating table.[44]

Located a few hundred yards northwest of Glen Leven, across the Franklin Pike, was the four-room brick cottage of Laura Sevier, granddaughter of early Nashville leader John Sevier, who had given Laura the land on which she and her husband Henry Norvell lived. Confederate soldiers had camped on the grounds, cut trees, dug trenches, and generally abused the property. Then when the fighting started, the house was turned into a field hospital, where similar scenes to those at Glen Leven were being enacted. Today, the Longview Mansion, constructed by Mr. and Mrs. James E. Caldwell in the late 1880s, is built around the original four-room cottage of the Norvells' Civil War residence.[45] A number of other notable homes were also serving as makeshift hospitals.

The wounded who remained upon the ground presented a hideous panorama south of Nashville; a grim testimony to the horror and misery that the savagery of war produces. All night long wounded soldiers, Union and Confederate, called out for help, for a fire, for water, for a stretcher, for death—and some were unable to call. A Union officer yielded to an urge to revisit one of the captured redoubts. With two other officers, he made his way in the darkness back to redoubt number three, where Colonel Sylvester Hill had lost his life, and there came upon a mortally wounded Confederate. "Our stretcher bearers and ambulance corps had been over the field caring for friends and foe alike," said the Federal colonel, "but here was a hopeless case, a man shot through the head, unconscious and in a dying condition. . . ." What intrigued the Union officer was that someone had straightened the wounded man's legs, "wrapped a chunk of wood in a piece of horse blanket, and placed it under his head for a pillow," and then pulled an empty ammunition box beside him. On the box, wrote the colonel, lay "a hard cracker, a small piece of fat bacon, and a tin cup half filled with water. . . ." The officer pronounced it "a gruesome sight," and said that "it filled us with sympathy for the dying man." The Union officers could do nothing for the soldier, of course, and "so we turned and left him there to die alone. . . . Such is war."[46]

The Federal army was much better prepared to take care of their wounded than were the Confederates. Anticipating a large number of wounded soldiers, the superintendent and director of United States General Hospitals at Nashville had taken possession of "every building that could be made use of for hospital purposes and had them fitted up" with all necessary equipment. The sites included churches, public buildings, and private homes. Consequently, some four thousand vacant beds were available. Also, the assistant surgeon-general had ordered to Nashville a large number of medical officers, many of whom arrived before the battle began. Division field hospitals were established as near to the battle area as practicable, with strict orders for the surgeons to "operate on the field upon all requiring it, previous to transferring the men to the general hospitals in the city."[47]

As the Union corps had advanced to the fight, numbers of ambulances had also moved forward, keeping close in the rear of the troops. Other ambulances were parked behind the defensive lines, ready to move up if required. Stretchermen too were assigned to each regiment. A veteran Union artilleryman remarked that the care of the wounded at Nashville was much improved from earlier days of the war. As soon as the army moved forward, he said male nurses "were following in the wake . . . , caring for the wounded. Only a sup of water, or coffee, or perhaps a stimulant, but it was the immediate care that counted. . . ." Others followed with the ambulance corps, transporting the wounded to the hospitals. "And women were there," he wrote, ". . . to sooth the dying, and alleviate suffering as only a good woman can!"[48] Another Federal soldier who had served at Nashville revealed a more cynical attitude, offering his opinion that most of the women present were primarily searching for husbands, rather than having come "to act as nurses and attendants in the hospitals." He added that "The boys (poor fellows) see so fue of the fair sex that they think every woman they see is an angel if she is in any ways pretty. For my part these Army *followers* make no impression on me."[49]

Generally speaking, the Army of the Cumberland was well prepared to minister to its wounded. An exception was Major General Steedman's extemporized corps, which had no organized medical staff. All unattached surgeons, who might have been on leave of absences, etc., were thereto assigned. The medical officers of the United States Colored Troops joined in as well. There being no ambulance corps for Steedman's command, ambulances and other makeshift vehicles found throughout the city, were impressed and sent into the field. "But the want of system and organization [in treating the wounded of Steedman's corps] was most apparent," reported Surgeon George E. Cooper, U.S. Army Medical Director.[50]

Surgeon J. Theodore Heard, who was with the Fourth Corps, made the observation that most wounds treated "were caused by conoidal balls," much as might be expected. Wounds from exploding shells and solid shot were much more rare than pistol and rifled-musket fire. Another Federal surgeon, Stephen

C. Ayres, remarked: "My two wards were completely filled, and I had my hands full. Johnnies and Yanks were lying side by side now, but there seemed to be no enmity between them." He said that some were shot through the chest and several through the legs and arms, while "one man had a bullet in the sole of his foot, and I did not leave him until I had extracted it." Ayers explained that a similar case had been brought into the hospital from the battlefield of Franklin, "but the surgeon into whose care he fell did not detect it, and the result was, the poor fellow had lock-jaw and died in consequence." Ayres concluded that he and his fellow medics worked "all night long . . . until nearly morning, when we laid down for a short rest." During and after the battle, "our hospital admitted 597 wounded men, of whom fifty-seven were Confederates."[51]

There is no way of knowing, in most cases, who treated whom, or where, specifically, the treatment took place. Among the wounded Union soldiers was Lieutenant Abbott of the Ninth Illinois Cavalry. Hastily examined on the battlefield during the afternoon, Abbott's injury was pronounced "a spent ball on the ribs," and the young trooper found himself transported to "an abandoned building on the outskirts of the city." Abbott said he knew "it was not a spent ball on the ribs. We were much too near the enemy to gather spent balls; we gathered only hot ones that day. But who argues with his doctor? And besides, I was not in fit condition for argument." All night the lieutenant lay on his back, in a row with others suffering from all manner of wounds, still in his bloody clothing, unable to turn over or speak except in a whisper, "or draw a full breath without feeling the ends of those broken ribs grind upon each other." When dawn came at last Abbott still was not moved, listening in silence as a surgeon instructed the attendants, "Leave him; he will die anyway," and watched as others were selected for treatment who were thought to have a better chance of living.[52]

While soldiers of both armies suffered, bled, and died, many people, according to the *Nashville Daily Union,* "went about as if nothing unusual was occurring." The Howes and Norton Circus entertained a sizeable audience, much as it had for some time, not missing a performance during the Battle of Nashville. The theaters also continued with their performances, the New Theater featuring the "Nalad Queen," while "Aladdin" continued to be the ticket at "the old temple," playing to an overflow crowd, reported the *Daily Union;* there appearing to be "no end to the enjoyment afforded by this beautiful spectacle."[53] On the seamy side, along the dingy streets of Smokey Row and in the slums of Black Bottom, prostitutes proffered their services in a "business as usual" manner, although minus to be sure the customary soldier traffic, most of it at least. Apparently, a considerable portion of the populace, regardless of class lines, financial status, or race, refused to let the battle interrupt life's customary activities.

General George H. Thomas, on the night of December 15, was flushed with victory. In the words of Shelby Foote, the general "watched his army's campfires blossom where Rebel fires had burned the night before."[54] Then riding back to his quarters in downtown Nashville, Thomas got off a telegram to Washington: "I attacked the enemy's left this morning and drove it from the river, below the city, very nearly to the Franklin Pike, . . . about eight miles," he said. "The troops behaved splendidly, all taking their share in assaulting and carrying the enemy's breast-works." Promising that he would attack the enemy "again tomorrow, if he stands to fight," the Virginian concluded that if the Graycoats retreated during the night, he would pursue, "throwing a heavy cavalry force" in their rear, "to destroy [their] trains, if possible."[55]

Soon the secretary of war responded with a wire hailing "the brilliant achievements of this day," which he hoped would be "the harbinger of a decisive victory," crowning both Thomas and his army "with honor," while contributing "much toward closing the war." General Grant also sent congratulations to the Union commander. Admitting to Thomas that he himself had just started for Nashville, Grant promised that, having received the good news of Thomas's attack, he would "go no farther." The hero of Vicksburg nevertheless was moved to admonish Thomas: "Push the enemy now, and give him no rest until he is entirely destroyed. . . . Much is now expected." President Lincoln's congratulations came in the next morning.[56]

General Thomas well may have thought that Hood would retreat. There were certainly good reasons, as previously noted, for the Confederate commander to have done so. But Hood was preparing to make the final gamble; to fight it out to the death of his army if such be his fate. Sometime after dark General John Schofield received his orders from Thomas. He claimed that he found them puzzling. In substance, he was instructed to "pursue the retreating enemy early the next morning," taking the advance on the Granny White Pike, while at the same time the cavalry would start by a road to the right.[57] Schofield, however, believed that Hood would not retreat. Mounting his horse, Schofield rode at once into Nashville to find Thomas and discuss the matter.

Later Schofield wrote that General Thomas "seemed surprised at my suggestion that we would find Hood in line of battle . . . in the morning."[58] Schofield thought it likely that the Rebel commander might even launch a counterattack against the Northern right flank. Consequently, Thomas then ordered that Wilson's cavalry remain in position until Hood's intentions to fight or retreat might be clarified. Thomas also sent some troops from Smith's command to reinforce Schofield. These were used to fill a gap existing between Cox's and

Couch's lines.[59] No new orders were issued anticipating the next day's battle. Evidently the same general plan would be followed, that is holding down Hood's right and center while hammering his left; at least that was the situation according to Schofield's later account.[60] General Thomas, in his report of the engagement, said: "The whole command bivouacked in line of battle during the night . . . whilst preparations were made to renew the battle at an early hour on the morrow."[61]

10

They Came
Only to Die

Like the first day of battle, dawn on Friday, December 16, 1864, was warm in Nashville. By mid-morning the temperature was into the sixties. The early morning also was foggy, although not generally as dense as on the previous day. Again there would be fighting on the eastern flank of the armies, only not as early as the day before. Once more the Bluecoats would attack. Once again they would suffer greater casualties than the Southerners. In fact, the result of the Yankee assault on the Confederate right flank would be the bloodiest fighting of the Battle of Nashville.

The Confederate flank was well positioned on high, rocky ground known as Peach Orchard Hill, sometimes referred to as Overton Hill because it was located on property belonging to the John Overton family. The hill was slightly to the east of the Franklin Pike—at the point where present-day Battery Lane–Harding Place crosses the pike to form one of the busiest traffic intersections in the city—and a short distance west of the Nashville & Decatur Railroad track. On a clear day one can stand at the top of that hill and look westward, along Battery Lane, and see all the way to Shy's Hill

217

rising in the distance. Not only did the Graycoats here possess the high ground; they also had the strongest corps in their army with which to defend it, that of Stephen D. Lee. His corps had two divisions which had not been bloodied in the Battle of Franklin, because they had still been on the march from Columbia when Hood made his ill-starred attack on the last day of November. Furthermore, they had hardly been involved in the first day's encounter at Nashville. The only negative was that Lee was marginally short on artillery, his corps starting the day with twenty-eight pieces. While the twenty-eight guns arguably might have been enough, orders had been given "not to fire except on lines of battle," which indicated a shortage of ammunition.[1]

Lee's division that had the key ground where the Yankees would concentrate their assault was commanded by Major General Henry Clayton. At the center of the division, Clayton posted the brigade of Brigadier General James T. Holtzclaw, located right across the Franklin Pike, with "the road being my center," Holtzclaw wrote, and "my left behind a stone wall." To Holtzclaw's left was the brigade of Brigadier General Randall L. Gibson, whose men were also behind the stone wall, which offered protection for several hundred yards. To Holtzclaw's right, extending the line along Peach Orchard Hill, and composing both the right flank of the division and the army, was Brigadier General Marcellus A. Stovall's brigade. The right half of Stovall's line was refused toward the south. For artillery support, eight guns were also placed on the hill. Positioned to the left of Clayton's division lay the division of Major General Carter L. Stevenson, whose right wing brigade under Brigadier General Edmund W. Pettus would also see action when the Federals attacked, Pettus's right flank resting adjacent to Randall Gibson's left.[2]

These Confederate brigades had taken up their new positions around midnight or shortly thereafter. There was "no time for rest," reported General Stovall. Despite the darkness, the Southerners were soon throwing up entrenchments as best they could and, continued General Stovall, they would be "engaged upon [constructing] the fortifications when the action [of December 16] commenced."[3] The advantage of the Rebel position, however, was as much the natural defensive strength of the site as the man-made obstacles confronting an attacker. The hill was high, the approaches the Yankees must take on the north and east sides were steep, and except for a thicket of trees and underbrush at one point, the ground was generally clear, providing an excellent field of fire for the defenders. Even the thicket lay several hundred feet down the slope from the Graycoat lines, leaving an attacker, once he cleared the clump of trees, fully exposed. "About the middle of the day mist and rain arose," wrote General Stevenson, making it difficult to see very far in any direction.[4]

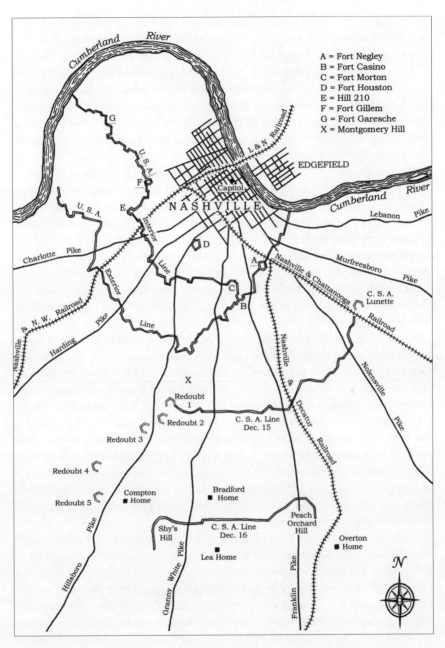

A = Fort Negley
B = Fort Casino
C = Fort Morton
D = Fort Houston
E = Hill 210
F = Fort Gillem
G = Fort Garesche
X = Montgomery Hill

Battle of Nashville, December 15–16, 1864. By Jim Moon Jr.

Of course the resulting soft ground and mud, with men slipping, sliding, and falling, would make the Federal approach more time-consuming and thus more hazardous. One Union soldier described the approach to Peach Orchard Hill as "a gentle slope; a distance of four hundred yards through scattering trees in one of those beautiful woods pastures so common in Middle Tennessee, until very near the enemy's works, where the ascent became much steeper."[5] The soldier's observations, punctuated by the last phrase—"where the ascent became much steeper"—seem to strike an ominous note, as if a forecast of the "beautiful" pastoral setting transformed into a bloody, hellish scene of war.

Coming up to confront the Graycoats at Peach Orchard Hill was the Union division with which Frank Cheatham's corps had dealt so roughly on the previous morning, that of James Steedman. The division moved forward about seven o'clock in the morning, across the battlefield of the previous day, with Charles Grosvenor noting the horrible sights of wasted humanity as "we . . . found our dead all stripped of their clothing and left exposed upon the open field."[6] William Shafter soon came upon the lifeless body of his brother-in-law, Captain Job Aldrich. Aldrich was lying face down. Like so many others, the Rebels had taken "all his clothes, *everything*."[7] Steedman's division passed over the gory spectacle, but the men were long delayed in their advance by Confederate skirmishers retiring slowly before them. Eventually, about noon, the division joined up, on its right flank, with the corps of General Wood, whose men had also moved into position confronting the eastern flank of the Rebels.

The Union had much the superior artillery (not necessarily better cannoneers, but certainly more guns, and rifled guns, and more ammunition) and soon began to use it. All the batteries in General Wood's corps were brought to the front, "placed in . . . position in short range of the enemy's works," and ordered to "keep up a measured but steady fire on [the Confederate] artillery." Wood pronounced their fire "uncommonly fine." The general said that the ranges were "accurately obtained, the elevations correctly given, and the ammunition . . . unusually good." Thus he reported the artillery fire was "most effective" and "really entertaining to witness."[8]

Surely the Grayclads who found themselves targeted by the Federal artillerists would have been hard pressed to recognize entertainment in such hellish tribulation. Unanimous agreement prevailed among the Southerners that enduring the Union fire was an awful ordeal. For a long time the firing continued. General Carter Stevenson reported that he had never seen an atillery fire that surpassed it "for heaviness, continuance, and accuracy." General Holtzclaw reported being under "a most furious shelling" from three six-gun batteries, with the firing being concentrated mainly against his right flank. A battery of "unusually heavy guns" was brought up the pike to within six hundred yards

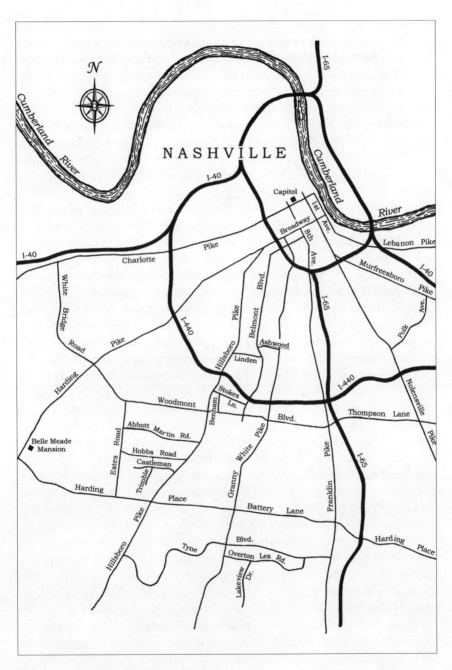

Nashville battlefield area (present day). By Jim Moon Jr.

of Holtzclaw's line. Confederate sharpshooters were used in an effort to pick off the Union gunners, but Holtzclaw said the conformation of the ground made it difficult for them to be effective. "During the whole day," according to Lieutenant Colonel Llewellyn Hoxton, chief of artillery in Lee's corps, the Yankees kept up "a terrible artillery fire" which, in addition to the human casualties, "destroyed a large number of horses in the best cover I could obtain."[9]

Probably Marcellus Stovall's brigade suffered the most punishment of any Butternut unit. General Clayton reported there was "considerable damage" to Stovall's command from "a concentrated fire" upon the hill. General Stovall's own words convey a strong sense of the destruction his brigade endured. "The Federals had guns which completely enfiladed my entire front," he wrote. "I was therefore subjected to a fire of artillery, both direct and on my left, quite as severe as any to which I have ever been exposed." The Confederate horses were scenting danger from the first, and their awful neighs of fright and pain rent the air, adding still more disconcerting noise to the ear-splitting reports of the artillery pieces. Besides the killing of horses, limber chests were exploded, some guns disabled and, of course, men were killed and wounded.[10]

A soldier in the ranks, situated off to the left of Stovall, wrote in his diary: "The cannonading was terrific and continued almost without intermission during the day. Shells and solid shot passed through the stone fence behind which we were sheltered, scattering stones in every direction and mangling men in a shocking manner." In conclusion, he pertinently observed that "to lie under such a destructive artillery fire produces a feeling of dread that cannot be described. This is more demoralizing than to be actively engaged in battle."[11] To describe the experience as terrifying would seem a bit of understatement; yet most of the men, hunkered down as best they could, survived the ordeal.

The Rebel artillery responded only occasionally and briefly, conserving ammunition, which was very scarce, anticipating a possible Yankee assault when the gunners would be able to inflict much greater damage to the Federals at close range. Nevertheless, the mangling of so many horses bode ill if the Graycoats should need to pull back again. To take off their guns would be very difficult.

As midday approached, General Thomas rode up to confer with General Wood, meeting him on the Franklin Pike near the most advanced position of the Union line along that front. Thomas told his corps commander that "the general plan of battle for the preceding day—namely to outflank and turn [the Confederate] left—was still to be acted upon." His specific instructions for Wood's corps, according to Wood's report, were to "vigorously" press the enemy in his front and "unceasingly harass" him by artillery fire. Then Thomas added something intriguing that surely stimulated Wood's thinking. The army commander directed General Wood (again according to Wood) to be "constantly on the alert for any opening for a more decisive effort, but for the time to bide events."[12]

Philip Sidney Post. Massachusetts Commandery Military Order of the Loyal Legion and the U.S. Army Military History Institute.

Here were discretionary orders, as Wood interpreted Thomas's words, to take the offensive if "any opening for a more decisive effort" presented itself. As Thomas moved away, riding toward the army's right flank where his greatest troop strength was being marshaled, General Wood was inspired to action. Possibly he had an opportunity to make the decisive attack of the battle. After "a close examination of the [Confederate] position," Wood concluded that if Peach Orchard Hill could be carried, "the enemy's right would be turned, his line from the Franklin Pike westward would be taken in reverse, and his line of retreat . . . commanded effectually. The capture of half of the rebel army would almost certainly" be the result.[13]

Soon General Wood was conferring with Sidney Post, perhaps his most aggressive brigade commander: a colonel of the Fifty-ninth Illinois Infantry, who had been encouraging him to attack. Some of the soldiers under Post thought the former Illinois lawyer was both hungry for glory and determined to wear a star on his shoulder, cost whatever it might in the loss of men. Wood instructed Post to "reconnoiter the [Rebel] position closely," seeking to learn if an assault was advisable. If so, Wood also wanted Post's opinion as to the best point of attack. Post spent the better part of an hour studying the situation—"a thorough and close reconnaissance," avowed Wood. Pronouncing the Graycoat position "truly formidable" and predicting it would be "very difficult to carry," Post neverthe-less proceeded at once to recommend the assault and volunteer his brigade for the work. The attack should go in, he thought, on the northern slope of the hill.[14]

This was all that General Wood needed to hear in confirmation of his own desire to make the assault. He ordered Post to prepare his brigade for an imme-diate attack and instructed Colonel Abel Streight, he of the "mule brigade," to form his unit for the support of Post's advance. Wood also conferred with Gen-eral Steedman, informing him of the impending assault, and requesting his sup-port for Post's left flank. Steedman readily agreed. Finally, General Wood ordered the corps artillery to open a concentrated fire on the Rebel batteries and defenses, continuing the fire "as long as it could be done with safety to our ad-vancing troops."[15]

General Wood surely knew that his men faced a brutal, Herculean task. He himself spoke of the Confederate line of entrenchments, "strengthened with an abatis and other embarrassments to an assault."[16] There was no hope whatso-ever of a surprise attack. Because of the openness of the country, the Federal preparations could not be concealed from the eyes of the Southerners. The as-sault must take place over several hundred yards of largely open and ascending ground, part of it a cornfield, while the rain then falling made the turf increas-ingly heavy and slick. Upon the enemy breastworks a large number of flags were visible from the Union lines, a strong indication that the Confederate posi-tion was heavily defended. All signs were ominous.

The general was gambling against the odds—long odds which decidedly favored the men in gray. What was General Wood thinking? Was he remem-bering the ease with which Montgomery Hill had been taken the previous day? Did he seek another chance to remove the stain of Chickamauga? One wonders if the general might have thought of Chattanooga. Had not Missionary Ridge appeared impregnable? Few if any in the Northern army had believed that an assault on the center of so forbidding a height could possibly be successful. Yet Thomas Wood had watched as his division, along with three others, success-fully executed the seemingly mad surge up the ridge. It was a magnificent charge—colorful, courageous, incredible—and it broke the center of the Rebel line. A good case can be made that men of Wood's division were the first to break through the enemy's defenses atop Missionary Ridge. In Federal memo-ries the charge came to seem almost invincible. No one who witnessed it ever forgot it. Only in recent years have students of that battle realized how badly the Graycoats botched their defense of Missionary Ridge.[17]

Whatever Wood may have been thinking at Nashville on December 16, the facts were that the Rebels atop Peach Orchard Hill had sufficient manpower to defend their position successfully. They also had it deployed efficiently and had made good defensive use of the terrain. The fight shaping up on the Southern right flank at Nashville would be nothing akin to Missionary Ridge.

And so it was about to happen—on a misty, gloomy, and increasingly cool Friday afternoon in December. An awful, yet spectacular and breathtaking episode of the battle was at hand. Nervous Yankees, perhaps ten thousand strong, anxiously awaited the signal, a battery of artillery pieces fired in quick succession, to move out across the open, ploughed ground toward the formidable Confederate line atop Peach Orchard Hill.

Philip Sidney Post's brigade was in the center of the Federal assaulting force. He had the Forty-first Ohio Regiment deployed as skirmishers. To the rear of the skirmishers, the brigade's first line consisted of the Ninety-third Ohio on the right and the One Hundred Twenty-fourth Ohio on the left. Composing a second line were the Fifty-ninth Illinois and the Seventy-first Ohio.[18]

In support of Post, and forming in rear of his command, would be the brigade of Abel D. Streight, arrayed in three battle lines. The Fifteenth and Forty-ninth Ohio regiments were in the first line, while the second line consisted of the Eighth Kansas and Eighty-ninth Illinois, with the Fifty-first Indiana composing the third line.[19]

To the left flank of Post's brigade was James Steedman's division. Steedman, for the primary work, placed the black brigade of Colonel Charles R. Thompson on his right flank, adjacent to Post's command. (Of Steedman's three brigades, Thompson's had seen the least fighting on the previous day.) Thompson's first line consisted of the One Hundredth Regiment USCT on the right and the Twelfth USCT on the left, while the Thirteenth USCT made up a second line.[20] The left side of Steedman's division consisted of Lieutenant Colonel Charles Grosvenor's brigade, with the Eighteenth USCT and the Second Battalion in the front line; the Eighteenth Ohio and the Sixty-eighth Indiana in the second line.[21]

The enthralling scene as the Federals deployed for attack was viewed by many Butternuts. It seemed like a grand prelude, perhaps a kind of macabre death dance. Minutes passed, but to some it was as if time briefly stood still. And then the preparations were complete and the signal to advance was given.

The time probably was near three o'clock.[22] Tense Confederates on the high ground of Peach Orchard Hill, their weapons tightly clutched in readiness for brutish, bloody work, watched silently and intently as the impressively aligned Federals marched against them. "On they came in splendid order," remembered a Southern artilleryman. Banners were waving as officers with drawn swords rode in front of the advancing lines.[23] The forward sweep of the U.S. troops was accompanied by a fierce cannonade, further darkening the rainy sky with smoke, and striking into the lines of the Confederates. The screaming missiles passing over the heads of the Bluecoats seemed to promise the killing or disabling of a few more Rebel defenders, during the minutes while the Federal regiments marched together, black and white, into the breach.

But for all its crashing fury, the Yankee artillery had only a brief period of clear firing time before it must cease or inflict casualties indiscriminately on both sides when the Union soldiers drew near the enemy line. Many Confederates, after enduring the shelling from the big Yankee guns for hours, welcomed the opportunity to inflict destruction and death on their enemy at close quarters. Peering down their gun sights as the Bluecoats came on, the Confederates realized that black troops were among the attackers. Some Southerners were furious. "To our disgust," wrote a member of the Eighteenth Alabama, "they were all negroes." That discovery, he declared, "seemed to remove all doubt as to what the result [of the Yankee assault] would be."[24]

The Union troops had not advanced very far when the Rebels opened fire. Volleys of musketry, shell, and canister ripped through the Bluecoat lines. A Federal said the advance had not gone fifty feet before the men were "smitten by the storm," as the Grayclads began firing. Their shots were effective in finding their mark. One shell even took out a whole file of men from a company in the Twelfth USCT.[25] Confederate General James Holtzclaw particularly complimented the right side of his brigade for their calm demeanor and efficient work, carried out, he reported, "with a coolness unexampled."[26]

Bravely the Yankees moved forward with flags flying, advancing across the muddy ground and closing up their ranks as the Graycoat fire steadily dropped men in their tracks. Sidney Post's brigade, just as the colonel desired, led the way. Post's front was heavily covered with skirmishers, the whole of the Forty-first Ohio Regiment so deployed, with orders to "advance rapidly," as far as possible "for the purpose of drawing the fire of the enemy."[27] The intention was to get Post's battle lines close to the Rebel position while suffering minimum casualties. Possibly then a massed charge could succeed in overwhelming the Confederates at that point.

The skirmishers indeed moved quickly, and to within a short distance of the enemy's entrenchments. But there, maybe a hundred feet from the Southerners, a formidable abatis brought them to a halt. They could not get through the obstacle. Going to ground, seeking any semblance of cover available, the skirmishers opened fire at their adversaries atop the hill. Post's battle lines were not far behind; however, intense Confederate fire stopped both lines on the side of the hill before they reached the abatis.

The barrage from the Butternut line was devastating. Among the victims claimed was Sidney Post himself. The colonel's horse was killed while, almost at the same moment, Post was seriously wounded by canister tearing through his side—a wound at first thought mortal.[28] He survived to receive the Congressional Medal of Honor, as well as being breveted brigadier general "for gallant and distinguished service" in the Battle of Nashville.[29] (If indeed the colonel, as some critics charged, primarily sought military glory, he must have been pleased.) Command of the brigade devolved upon Lieutenant Colonel Robert L. Kimberly, leader of the Forty-first Ohio. Kimberly was especially impressed by the determination of the brigade's second battle line, which he reported "made a desperate effort to push on over the works" of the enemy. Kimberly thought a handful of men "actually accomplished the feat," only to be quickly killed or captured.[30]

Soon it was evident—as the brigade held the hillside ground for some minutes, during which time many soldiers were killed and wounded—that Post's attack had failed. Reluctant to give up the effort that had cost so much in blood and lives, a few men rose and struggled up the hill, attempting to rekindle the assault, but to no avail. Most recognized that defeat stared them in the face and began falling back.[31]

Meanwhile, Abel Streight's supporting brigade was also in serious difficulty. When Streight's brigade advanced toward the Graycoats, orders had been that each line commander should "keep within 150 yards of the preceding line," reported Colonel Streight, "and every effort was made to retain . . . formation, but as the several preceding lines approached the enemy's works each seemed to waste away, until all became intermingled in one mass. . . ." Colonel Frank Askew, who commanded the Fifteenth Ohio, recorded his perspective of the brigade's attack from his first line position: "When Colonel Post's brigade started, we moved forward and kept within a short distance of his second line, and in good order, but when we reached the depression directly in front of the enemy's works it was evident," declared the colonel, that "Colonel Post's attack had failed, and the fire of the enemy was so severe that the line was thrown into confusion. . . ."[32]

The Forty-ninth Ohio, also in Streight's front line, charged almost to the enemy works. A few of the men, incredibly, "succeeded in gaining them under a very heavy fire," reported Captain Joseph R. Bartlett, who took command when Major L. M. Strong was severely wounded in the attack. The gallant effort of those few who reached the Rebel works was quickly snuffed out. The second battle line did no better, withering under the galling Southern fire and throwing themselves upon the ground.[33]

Then the third line came on. They could see that the effort of the first two lines had failed. Nevertheless, "supposing they were to charge the works," said Captain W. W. Scearce of the Fifty-first Indiana, these Bluecoats swept right through and over the Federal lines in front of them, "regardless of orders, until they reached . . . some thirty feet from the [enemy] works." A Federal by the name of Fred Tellsman was said to have here scaled the Rebel parapet, confronting a Confederate lieutenant who profanely demanded his surrender. Replying with somewhat similar language, Tellsman shot the Southerner in the stomach, then had the presence of mind to leap back among his comrades rather than continuing to make himself a conspicuous target. Tellsman managed to survive.[34]

The fire fight was desperate. As if the Yankee situation were not bad enough, their left flank was exposed to the fire of a Rebel battery—"a most galling fire of grape and canister," reported Captain Scearce. Another member of the Fifty-first Indiana, William Hartpence, said "the rebels . . . slashed the canister and solid shot into us with a prodigality that was appalling." Some of the war's most horrible wounds resulted, of course, from artillery fire, and here Hartpence witnessed a particularly gruesome one, as a cannon ball struck First Lieutenant Peter G. Tait, of the Eighty-ninth Illinois, "near the center of his body, tearing a great hole in the left side. As he fell, he threw his right arm around to his side, and his heart and left lung dropped onto it." Hartpence estimated that Tait's heart continued to throb for twenty minutes, "its pulsations being distinctly seen by his agonized comrades" who watched "the noble life fade out. . . ." For some long minutes these Northerners endured the punishment meted out by the Confederates; then they gave way, rushing to the rear. Lines became intermingled in the commands of Post and Streight; confusion reigned in a number of regiments and men retreated as best they could, some streaming to the rear. "Fall back! Fall back!" some were yelling. Many needed no encouragement, having already headed back to the Union line.[35]

The attack went no better for the black troops on the left of Post's brigade. If anything was different, their experience was more deadly, as distressing, frustrating blunders plagued their advance. These men knew the assault would be perilous. Silently preparing for the awful undertaking only a few minutes earlier, some of the blacks requested their officers to safeguard their money or valuables. Captain D. E. Straight of the One Hundredth USCT thought they "showed a settled resolution to unflinchingly face death in the cause of freedom and nationality." The African Americans of Thompson's brigade only had minimal combat experience. The Twelfth and Thirteenth USCT had been at Johnsonville during Forrest's recent attack. And there was the brigade's supporting role on December 15. Neither compared with the events at Peach Orchard Hill. "Here for the first time," Thompson said, "these troops were . . . under such a fire as veterans dread." Their inexperience made the situation even worse.[36]

Thompson's brigade began moving out when Post's brigade had advanced about forty yards. On the left of Thompson's first line was the

Twelfth USCT Regiment, with the One Hundredth USCT to their right and the Thirteenth USCT composing a second line. Directly in front of the Twelfth USCT was a clump of trees and heavy underbrush ("a dense briar thicket," according to Thompson) that could not be penetrated. The Twelfth had to move some eighty yards in column to get around it and then deploy for the continuation of the advance.[37]

Once past the thicket, Thompson intended to halt the entire command and see how the brigade under Post, advancing ahead and to his right, was progressing. Then he would decide "how . . . best to charge the [enemy] works." At once, however, his plan went awry. The Twelfth Regiment, having passed the thicket, was deploying at double-quick time. This sight confused men in the One Hundredth USCT on their right. Many troops concluded that a charge had been ordered and they immediately surged forward at a double-quick pace. The whole thing was contagious. Numerous men were soon charging toward the enemy line. Thompson believed trying to stop them, especially under heavy fire, would be futile, causing more harm than good. Thus he ordered a charge, simply recognizing and authorizing what was already developing.[38]

This initial blunder rapidly escalated into a tragic comedy of errors and the U.S. casualties mounted proportionately. Post's advance and Thompson's advance soon converged, both moving toward the very same section of the Southern defenses. To avoid running directly through the left side of Post's line (and a few of Thompson's soldiers did just that) Thompson's front line regiments veered to their left. The movement at once subjected their right flank to a terrible enfilading fire, likely emanating from Marcellus A. Stovall's brigade of Georgians and the Eufaula (Alabama) battery. The Rebels raked them with musketry and double-shotted canister, firing into the flank with devastating effect.

Some of the black troops raced for whatever cover they could find, particularly seeking the trees, with their large branches, that had been cut down in front and below the enemy works. Many of the blacks continued struggling forward, their path taking them diagonally across the line of march of Grosvenor's advancing troops—"throwing a portion of those troops into confusion," reported Grosvenor—and finally coming up on the left flank and front of Grosvenor's soldiers.[39]

To the confusion caused by Thompson's men charging across their front was added the galling fire poured into Grosvenor's ranks from the Rebels above. And again, as on the previous day, the inexperienced white conscripts of the Second Battalion began falling back. Soon large numbers were heading for the rear. "They could not be rallied," reported Grosvenor, who also said that he "saw [them] no more during the campaign. . . ." The remainder of his brigade, unable to withstand the withering Confederate fire, could advance no farther than "the base of the hill under the enemy's works."[40]

The fighting at Peach Orchard Hill raged all along the line, with the U.S. troops sometimes rising in desperation from their scant, pitiful cover below the Rebel works and charging the enemy; some in determined silence while others were screaming and cursing. Without exception they were thrown back, killed, or wounded. Among the wounded was Henry Dodson, a black private of Company B, Twelfth USCT, who survived the battle despite being thrice wounded: a gunshot in the right ankle, a bayonet wound in the chest and a saber slash on the left arm. Clearly he was involved in the thick of the fight. A friend in the One Hundredth USCT testified that Dodson recovered, living into the 1890s before he succumbed to consumption while in destitute circumstances and entirely dependent on public charity.[41]

Also surviving the melee on Peach Orchard Hill was another African American whose name was Edward Polk. A thirty-year-old native of Robertson County, Tennessee, Polk was a member of Company H, Twelfth USCT, who suffered bayonet wounds in the right shoulder and hip. While Polk lived into the twentieth century, the combination of the wounds at Nashville and exposure to bad weather left him partially disabled and often in pain.[42]

The black troops attacking Peach Orchard Hill seem to have been the most aggressive, judging from the reports of officers, as well as other primary sources—and the casualties they suffered. Private Benjamin T. Smith, a Federal soldier from Illinois, recorded in his journal that the black troops charged "with a yell that sounded above the rattle of musketry." He thought the Confederates were "awesomely" aroused when they "saw the black faces of their foe." Going into "a frenzy," the Rebels fought "like demons, slaughtering the poor blacks fearfully," wrote Smith. Also, he said some of the Graycoats were "yelling no quarter . . . to niggers," as they fiercely cut them down.[43]

The last of Colonel Thompson's units to get into the fight was the Thirteenth USCT, composing his second line of attack. No Yankee unit, black or white, charged with greater determination. Assaulting with absolute abandonment of any concern for their lives, the Thirteenth drove beyond most of those who had gone before. Past all obstacles, even the abatis, some of the strongest charged. A few of the men even mounted the parapet. A color-bearer took the flag almost to the works before the Rebel fire dropped him. Another and still another took up the flag, only to be shot down: five color-bearers shot down in all, as the black troops rushed the Confederate works several times. "There were very few negroes who retreated in our front," said a Confederate defender, "and none were at their post when the firing ceased; for we fired as long as there was anything to shoot at."[44]

Some casualties of the Thirteenth USCT were from the ranks of their white officers. Among the wounded whites was a thirty-three-year-old, six-foot, blue-eyed lieutenant from New York State whose wrist was badly mangled by a gunshot. Never fully healing, the ever painful wound, complicated by pieces of dead bone, rendered manual labor on his farm impossible for the remainder of James Babbitt's life—a life eventually terminated by cancer of the prostate.[45] But most of the Thirteenth USCT's casualties were black soldiers, of course. One of them was a nineteen-year-old Tennessee native of Company A named Hays Moore. Private Moore simply recorded that he "was seriously wounded" in the fight, being "shot through and through" and carried to "Number 16 Hospital on College Street" where he spent "the remainder of [his] service."[46] Also transported to Hospital Number 16 was another African American private by the name of Thomas Cross, suffering from gunshot wounds in the left knee and hip. The wounded knee was particularly bad, resulting in Cross, for the rest of his life, experiencing difficulty when walking. He had survived the battle, however, and for that feat should have considered himself fortunate.[47]

The magnificent attempt of the black troops seemed to deserve a better ending. But there was no hope of success. Without support on either side, the African Americans found themselves under fire from both flanks as well as the front. General Stephen Lee reported that the Confederates "reserved their fire until [the enemy troops] were within easy range, and then delivered it with terrible effect."[48] Once more it was proven that strength and courage, though great their manifestation, can never match a well-placed bullet as it rips through the flesh and bone. The Thirteenth USCT took more casualties than any regiment on either side in the course of the battle, losing nearly 40 percent of its strength.

"They fell like wheat before a mowing machine," said a Confederate corporal. A man whose words convey contempt for the African American soldiers, he wrote that "the ground was literally blue and black with dead and wounded niggers. We certainly laid them out." Soon a mass of the black troops charged again. "Let's put an end to them this time," yelled some of the Rebels, as reported by the Alabama corporal. Once more a withering fire from the Grayclads stopped the assault, inflicting horrible casualties upon the men of the USCT.[49]

Then a Confederate ran forward to grab up a Federal flag that had fallen to the ground and brought it back within his line. Written on the flag in large letters was the inscription: "Thirteenth Regiment U.S. Colored Infantry. Presented by the colored ladies of Murfreesboro." A Southerner who glanced at the flag while continuing to load and fire his weapon, said that he at first "overlooked the word 'colored,' and . . . for a moment thought that white women had done what seemed to me to be an outrageously low-down thing, and my indignation burned, but only for a moment." When the Butternut realized what the regimental flag actually said, he reported that his indignation "turned to wrath at the idea of Negro . . . [women] being called ladies."[50]

Not all Confederates were consumed with such disdain for their black enemy. In fact, Brigadier General James T. Holtzclaw, commanding the brigade whose fire devastated the Thirteenth USCT, was deeply impressed by their furious and desperate assault. He reported how the blacks "gallantly" assaulted, as they attempted to overwhelm his line. Again and again they charged to the abatis, "but they came only to die," wrote Holtzclaw, as he acknowledged the tragic scene of wasted humanity in front of his brigade. They were "killed by the hundreds," he said. "I have seen most of the battlefields of the west," the general continued, "but never saw dead men thicker than in front of my two right regiments. . . ."[51]

Further detailing the slaughter, Holtzclaw reported that "the great masses and disorder of the enemy" enabled his left regiment "to rake them in flank," while the regiment on his right, "with a coolness unexampled, scarcely threw away a shot at their front." His account lends credence to the local tradition that bodies of dead and wounded Federals were so numerous along the north side of Peach Orchard Hill that a bluish hue covered the ground and a person could have walked down the hill without touching the earth, simply stepping from body to body. General Lee provided additional testimony, reporting the Federal loss was "very severe," while General Clayton recorded that the enemy "suffered great slaughter, their loss being estimated at 1,500 or 2,000 killed and wounded."[52]

At last the Yankees gave up the attempt to overrun Peach Orchard Hill. Holtzclaw reported that "the enemy seemed now to be satisfied that he could not carry my position, and contented himself by shelling and sharpshooting everything in sight."[53] When the failure of the Northern assault became obvious to the Southerners, many of the excited troops were so elated with a sense of victory that they wanted to pursue the enemy, convinced that a counterattack would overwhelm the disorganized Union ranks. Only with considerable difficulty could the Grayclad officers prevent their charges from pursuing.

Certainly the Bluecoats anticipated a possible counterattack. General Wood, although keenly disappointed at the failure of the assault, immediately sent an order for all the batteries bearing on the hill "to open the heaviest possible fire so soon as their fronts were sufficiently cleared by the retiring troops to permit it." Colonel Frederick Knefler, commanding the Third Brigade, Third Division, of Wood's corps, was ordered to "hold his command well in hand," ready to charge the enemy should the Rebels attempt to pursue the retreating Federals.[54]

Meanwhile, Union officers were struggling to reorganize the ranks of those men who had made the charge and were still healthy. The Federal leaders need not have worried, for the officers of Lee's corps had no intention of risking a replay, with sides reversed, of the bloodletting just witnessed. What the charge manifested to the Union, at least those whose minds were not closed to the matter—was that black soldiers would fight. All they needed was better leadership and combat experience.

One Union officer said he "never saw more heroic conduct shown on the field of battle" than was demonstrated by the black troops.[55] General Steedman—a lifelong Democrat who remarked that he wondered what his Democratic friends on the other side would think of him "if they knew I was fighting them with 'nigger' troops?"—undoubtedly learned the lesson of the black soldiers' martial prowess.[56] Reporting the heavy losses of his division, he noted that the larger portion "fell upon the colored troops." With a memorable turn of phrase he then concluded: "I was unable to discover that color made any difference in the fighting of my troops. All, white and black, nobly did their duty as soldiers, . . . such as I have never seen excelled in any campaign of the war in which I have borne a part."[57] (Evidently Steedman chose to ignore the actions of some white troops in Grosvenor's brigade who hardly "did their duty" when they fled from the field.)

As General Thomas later rode over the ground and saw the bodies of black soldiers "on the very works of the enemy," it was reported that he turned to his staff and said: "Gentlemen, the question is settled; negroes will fight."[58] And on the morning of December 17, as Thompson's brigade pulled out on the Franklin Pike, moving to pursue Hood's retreating army, Henry Norton of the Twelfth USCT said the brigade was met by General Thomas and his staff. "Reining out to one side," wrote Norton, the famed "Rock of Chickamauga" stood with "uncovered head until the whole brigade passed by."[59]

The *Nashville Daily Union* also extolled the valor of the African Americans: "Negro stock has gone up wonderfully within the past few days. The late battles have satisfied every sceptic with an ounce of brains, that negroes make good fighting soldiers."[60] The Eighty-first Indiana's William D. Evritt told his wife: "You will see some praise to the colored troops in the papers which will trouble the Butternuts considerably, but let me assure you they fight with great bravery and I believe the almighty intended that this cruel war should give them their freedom and I say Amen!"[61] Perhaps the single greatest tribute came from Confederate James Holtzclaw when he formally cited the bravery of the African Americans in his official report, "an almost unheard of circumstance involving a Southern general and black troops."[62]

Of all the witnesses who penned accounts of the blacks attacking at Peach Orchard Hill, none was of more interest to the author than the reminiscence of twenty-two-year-old Ambrose Bierce, later recognized as a brilliant writer.

Known for his wit and satire, Bierce's short stories, rooted in his war experiences, have come to be considered classics. A veteran of such bloody engagements as Shiloh, Stones River, and Chickamauga, at Nashville Bierce was "just sitting in the saddle and looking on," still disabled by a serious wound suffered when struck in the head by a bullet during the Atlanta campaign.

"Seeing the darkies going in on our left," wrote Bierce, "I was naturally interested and observed them closely." Bierce testified that "better fighting was never done." Describing the front of the Confederate earthworks, he said "it was protected by an intricate abatis of felled trees denuded of their foliage and twigs. Through this obstacle a cat would have made slow progress; its passage by troops under fire was hopeless from the first—even the inexperienced black chaps must have known that." Nevertheless, Bierce reported that the blacks "did not hesitate a moment: their . . . lines swept into that fatal obstruction in perfect order and remained there as long as those of the white veterans on their right."

He claimed the assault by the black troops "was as pretty an example of courage and discipline as one could wish to see. . . . I was told afterwards that one of their field officers succeeded in forcing his horse through a break in the abatis and was shot to rags on the slope of the parapet." Then, revealing something of his sardonic and enigmatic personality, Bierce concluded: "But for my abjuration of faith in the Negroes' fighting qualities [Bierce earlier applied for rank as a field officer of African American troops, only to "back out"] I might perhaps have been so fortunate as to be that man!"[63] Nevertheless, the numerous accolades for the black troops could not change the outcome of the assault at Peach Orchard Hill. The Union troops had not carried the hill; had not even come close.

Not that the facts hindered General Wood from trying to formulate a different conclusion when he wrote his report of the day's action. According to the general's version of the fight, the impression conveyed (or "spin" to use today's buzz word) was that his troops were reformed, once more assaulted Peach Orchard Hill, and in the face of formidable resistance, overwhelmed the Southern defenders; his Blueclad corps rushing forward "like a mighty wave, driving everything before it."[64] As an example of "history" written by the victor, this is a fine rendition. Actually, when Wood's troops were carrying the hill, most of the Confederate defenders either had already evacuated the position or were in the process of so doing. Following the collapse of the left flank of the Rebel line late in the afternoon, and with the center of their line also giving way, it was manifest to the Southerners defending Peach Orchard Hill that their army was beaten. General Lee and his division commanders began pulling back their men as rapidly as possible. This was the situation when Wood's "mighty wave" of attackers drove "everything" before it.

The terse reports of several Federal regimental commanders clearly convey what actually happened. Captain Joseph R. Bartlett, commanding the Forty-ninth Ohio, wrote that the Confederates, "having been routed on our right, fell back rapidly from their works in our front, and we advanced pursuing them until dark." Lieutenant Colonel John Conover, commanding the Eighth Kansas, reported a Union advance "in pursuit of the enemy, who had been flanked from their works. . . ." And Lieutenant Colonel James Pickands, commanding the One Hundred Twenty-fourth Ohio, said that after hearing heavy firing to their right, the Federals of his command "soon after saw the enemy leaving their works on the hill" to the front, when "the First Brigade [Colonel Abel D. Streight's unit] was ordered forward, and our brigade [Colonel P. Sidney Post's unit] followed them. . . ."[65]

General Wood's attack on Peach Orchard Hill was a blunder. The assault had been a hastily conceived affair and had cost the U.S. troops dearly. Well over a thousand men were killed or wounded. Possibly General Clayton was not far wrong in his estimate of fifteen hundred or two thousand. Federal General Jacob Cox, in his account of the battle, said, "the [Union] casualties in this assault were probably half of all that occurred in the battle."[66] Once more, as so often in the Civil War, glory-hungry commanders and frontal assaults against strong defensive positions had proven to be a lethal combination.

Possibly, too, there just might have been a modicum of willingness on the part of some Bluecoat officers to employ blacks as cannon fodder, although the author has discovered no specific evidence of such. The Federals, in addition to proving that blacks would fight, did accomplish one more thing of significance, although it was not a part of their planning. Their attack pulled some Confederate troops away from the other end of the Southern line. General Hood became so concerned about the fighting on his right flank that he dispatched troops from Cheatham's corps for reinforcements. He sent the division commanded by General James A. Smith (Cleburne's division). General Lee put them in position, although he said they were not needed.[67] He spoke the truth for, as just recounted, the Bluecoats never seriously threatened to take Peach Orchard Hill.[68]

Unfortunately for the Southerners, within a short time the division from Cheatham's corps would be sorely needed on the left flank, where they were originally stationed. Quite possibly, considering the long odds against the Confederates on that end of the line, this relocation made no difference in the outcome of the battle. But surely the Graycoats faced even longer odds without the division under Smith on their western flank. And if the Yankees had not made a strong effort to take Peach Orchard Hill, all of Cheatham's troops would have remained on the opposite end of the line. Ironically then, the Union accomplished on the second day of the battle, and without so planning, what it had hoped and tried to do (and some Federals erroneously claimed to have done) on the first day: to alarm General Hood into stripping troops from his left flank in order to reinforce his right. If there was any consequence of Hood's action, it would seem to have been worth more to the Bluecoats on December 16 than it would have been the day before.

11

The United States Flag Is on the Hill

The value of "twenty/twenty hindsight," that oft-presumed invincible tool of historians for analyzing past events, sometimes proves to be exaggerated. The Confederate position on December 16 offers a case in point. Thomas Connelly asserted that the new Southern line was "even more precarious" than the previous day's position, but Shelby Foote called the line on the second day "much stronger than the line of the first day of battle" and wondered why Hood "had not occupied it at the outset . . . two weeks earlier. . . ." Obviously neither writer approved of the original position.[1]

Connelly contended that Hood "could have found a far better line" approximately one-half mile south of the Confederate location of December 16. This was "the massive, high Overton Hill range" which extended "from the Franklin Pike toward the Hillsboro Pike, where it blended into the equally rugged Harpeth Hills." A defensive line along these ridges, argued Connelly, "would have been of great strength and would have covered the direct approaches on Franklin via the Franklin, Granny White, and Hillsboro pikes."[2] Presumably, Connelly would also have favored the Overton Hill range for the Southern position on day two of the battle.

Clearly the Confederate line of December 16 was shorter than on the 15th, and certainly an improvement, in that respect, when Graycoat numbers were so scarce. Too, the second Southern position did not have the exterior line problem of the first location. When Connelly wrote of the "even more precarious" line of the second day, he likely was focusing on the problems of Shy's Hill— shortly to be addressed in detail. Perhaps Foote, in contrast, thought of the defensive potential of the whole line, which indeed seemed greater than the earlier location.

Whatever may be the explanation of Connelly's and Foote's differing analyses, a consensus prevails among most writers that Hood's position for December 16 "was none too favorable," as Thomas Hay expressed the matter. Hay observed, as previously noted, that Hood had the location "forced on him because of the fewness of his numbers and the necessity, if possible, of keeping open a line of retreat for Cheatham on the Granny White Pike." Actually Hay, like Connelly, believed a better position for the Grayclads could have been manned just south of present-day Tyne Boulevard, along the Overton Hill range. He wrote that "on the 15th as soon as Thomas' concentrations and intentions, on [Hood's] left, became evident and without allowing his troops to become seriously engaged," the Confederate commander should have "drawn back his army" to the Overton Hills.[3]

The author of a recent book-length account of the campaign, Anne Bailey, abstains from a consideration of alternative locations for the Confederate army on December 16, laconically stating that with the refused flanks at each end of the Southern position, "the distance they defended was over three miles. With only about fifteen thousand effective troops and eighty pieces of artillery, Hood manned a weak line."[4] Portions of the line were certainly weak, but war situations sometimes appear quite different from what they really are, particularly to soldiers who face an imminent clash, rather than later studying the battle at leisure through maps and after action reports.

To many eyes in the U.S. army the Confederate left flank anchored on Shy's Hill appeared very strong, perhaps even impregnable. If some had not thought of storming the height, others who had considered the prospect clearly did not believe that an assault on so forbidding an eminence could possibly be a success. Colonel William McMillen, commanding McArthur's First Brigade, described the position as "being so steep, it was supposed no assaulting party could live to reach the summit." Captain Jacob Miller of the Sixteenth Kentucky, reported that the hill "looked very formidable," and Lieutenant Colonel John H. Stibbs, commanding the Twelfth Iowa, said the front of the eminence was "so precipitous that it seemed foolhardy to attempt its capture by direct assault."[5]

Actually, unlike the Southern right flank at Peach Orchard Hill, the position was quite vulnerable. First, the Confederates lacked the numbers essential to defend Shy's Hill against an assault. General Stewart reported that the Bluecoats "confronted us everywhere with a force double or treble our own."[6] The Butternuts on Shy's Hill faced even greater odds, probably four to one, maybe more. Cheatham's corps, primary defenders of the hill, had Bate's division facing north and west, with Jackson's brigade on their right, Finley's Florida brigade in the center, and Tyler's brigade to the left.

Initially Ector's brigade of French's division, Stewart's corps, had been stationed to the left of Bate's men (posted on the hill about dark of the previous day), but Ector's command later was pulled out of the line and then placed on the east side of the hill in reserve. About noon on December 16, Ector's brigade was ordered due south, at a double-quick, in an attempt to check the Federals who were threatening the rear of the Confederate flank. Bate was upset, having been compelled to stretch his already thin line farther to the left. He complained to Cheatham and argued that he must have reinforcements from somewhere. Cheatham had no reinforcements to send him, informing Bate that he "had nothing that could possibly be spared."[7]

Positioned on the left of Bate's overstretched line was John C. Brown's division, then commanded by Brigadier General Mark P. Lowrey. These troops occupied the ground immediately south of Shy's Hill and extended onto the next hill south of Shy's. Also holding a portion of the high ground south of Shy's Hill was Cleburne's division, commanded, of course, by James A. Smith. That division's left flank was refused eastward, close to today's Tyne Boulevard. However, sometime around three o'clock General Hood became so concerned about the Yankee assault on the army's right flank at Peach Orchard Hill, that he withdrew two brigades from Smith's command (leaving only Govan's brigade on the eminence south of Shy's Hill, the fourth brigade under Charles Olmstead being on detached duty at Murfreesboro), and sent them to reinforce his eastern flank. This turned out to be a big mistake, as noted in the preceding chapter. Not only did Stephen Lee's corps need no assistance, but there was not sufficient time for the two brigades to return to the left flank before the Union attacked.[8]

Worse still, another brigade was pulled out from the Shy's Hill sector, making four in all that Hood withdrew that afternoon. This was Reynolds's brigade, from Walthall's division of Stewart's corps. Walthall was posted on the right of Bate, covering a bit of the northern, but mainly the eastern slope of Shy's Hill and extending to the Granny White Pike. About three o'clock,

Reynolds was withdrawn to reinforce Ector to the south. Obviously, Walthall's division had then to be stretched more thinly in an effort to cover the vacated ground.[9]

Furthermore, the Confederate commands were badly depleted in numbers. In some cases, a single Northern regiment mustered greater strength than a Southern brigade. After the Franklin butchery, Granbury's Texans numbered less than 350 soldiers. Suffering thirty more casualties on December 15, Granbury's brigade, commanded at Nashville by Captain E. T. Broughton, numbered barely over 300 men, less than one-third the size of a full-strength regiment. Confederate regiments at Nashville were sometimes little more than skeletons of their original manpower. The Forty-ninth Tennessee of Quarles's brigade in Walthall's division was down to only seventeen men after the losses at Franklin. Admittedly the Forty-ninth Tennessee is an extreme example, but many regiments were seriously under strength. General Bate wrote of Tyler's brigade, commanded at Nashville by Brigadier General Thomas Benton Smith, as consisting of the Thirty-seventh Georgia and, as Bate phrased it, "the consolidated *fragments* of the Second, Tenth, Fifteenth, Twentieth, Thirtieth, and Thirty-seventh Tennessee regiments [emphasis added]." Such a "brigade" would have been hard pressed to muster numbers equal to most Federal regiments, which at that period of the war typically numbered from 350 to 400 men.[10]

The Confederates holding the salient atop Shy's Hill looked down on heavily massed Union power. Schofield's corps was positioned north and west of the hill. Couch's division had thrown up entrenchments facing the height's northern slope. Lying on a generally east-west line, these Bluecoats were dug in across an eminence just north of Shy's Hill, with only a few hundred yards separating the blue and gray troops. Looking west from the top of Shy's Hill, one could see Cox's division below, posted on a north-south line. These Federals also rested behind breastworks prepared during the night. A gap initially existed between Couch and Cox, but two regiments of Colonel Orlando H. Moore's brigade soon deployed there to ensure a continuous line.[11]

Immediately east of Couch's men impatiently waited the Union division soon to play the key role in the battle: that of Brigadier General John McArthur. From west to east, McArthur deployed the brigades led by McMillen, Hubbard, and William Marshall—the latter commanding after the death, on the previous afternoon, of Colonel Sylvester G. Hill. Thus four strong Federal divisions of infantry were arrayed against Shy's Hill on the north and west, while General Wilson deployed two dismounted cavalry divisions that were approaching the hill from the southwest, threatening to command the Granny White Pike and cut it off as a possible avenue of escape. By noon Wilson reported he had "a continuous line of skirmishers stretching from the right of Schofield's Corps across the Granny White Pike."[12]

The Union forces were prepared to employ their long arm as well—and with pronounced superiority. Enjoying artillery advantage in both numbers and rifling, the Bluecoats also had superior positioning and angles of fire. To oppose nearly one hundred Federal guns, Cheatham's corps had thirty-four cannon at hand, but many of them were bogged down in mud and could not be maneuvered into acceptable locations. What was true of Cheatham's corps was true of the whole army. One Confederate gunner thought "possibly half the guns of the army were in the same fix"; that is, unable to find a satisfactory spot from which to fire, "and like us, did not fire a shot that shameful day."

Some of the problem resulted from taking up their new position at night. General Bate explained the difficulty of trying to position the artillery during the night. He said "the field intervening the turnpike and my position was impassable to artillery; the earth had thawed, and the cultivated low ground was an obstruction through which even the ambulances could not pass with success. . . ." As a result, Bate left all the guns in the rear for the night. At daylight he did find a rough road skirting the eastern slope of the hill, "over which artillery could pass," and managed to get a few guns into position, but only with considerable effort.[13]

One section of howitzers commanded by Captain René T. Beauregard, the son of General P. G. T. Beauregard, was placed on "a small plateau" on the eastern slope of Shy's Hill. Soon thereafter, Major Daniel Truehart joined Beauregard with four more guns. Eventually Lieutenant William Turner, after a great struggle, somehow got his Mississippi battery, attached to Brown's division, onto the hill south of Shy's. With these few smoothbore pieces, the Southerners attempted to answer the fire of several times as many Yankee guns, a number of which, of course, were rifled weapons.[14]

To say that the Union artillery had "the bulge" on the Confederates is a marked understatement. All through the morning Federal artillery played back and forth across the Southern position. Shy's Hill was pounded by a devastating barrage from every direction of the compass except the east, and even there, fire was incoming from the northeast. Confederate sharpshooters "annoyed [the Federals] considerably" and managed to pick off some Bluecoat cannoneers, but not enough to silence any of their batteries. The enemy shelling was so heavy that the Graycoats had much difficulty in reloading. Union General Cox claimed the superiority of the U.S. artillery was pronounced to such a degree that "the Confederate gunners were forced to reload their pieces by drawing them aside . . . to the protection of the parapet." The Twelfth Iowa's commander, John H. Stibbs, positioned slightly east of the Granny White Pike, said that Captain Joe Reed of the Second Iowa Battery afterward told him "that he had secured the range so accurately . . . that he could explode every shell squarely over the enemy's works." Indeed, a considerable portion of the Southern breastworks was totally knocked apart as the Union batteries blasted the hill with their cross fire. One of the Northern batteries west of the eminence fired 560 rounds into the hill.[15]

Overmatched though they were, Confederate gunners sometimes found their target. "A caisson in our front was exploded, and the picture was one that was indelibly fixed on my mind," recalled a Union officer. "We saw the explosion and the cloud of smoke, and before the sound of the explosion reached us," he said, "we saw a man thrown into the air fully twenty feet high, and with arms and legs extended he was spinning around after the fashion of a school boy doing the wagon wheel act."[16] While the Union did suffer some casualties, the damage meted out to the Confederates was far greater. In the early afternoon the Federals were laying down a constant, heavy artillery fire on the height.

General William Bate, somewhere atop Shy's Hill, was directly in harm's way. He penned perhaps the most vivid account of any Confederate who described the fierce cannonading. "The enemy opened a most terrific fire of artillery and kept it up" throughout the day, wrote Bate. In the afternoon the situation only became worse, as the Federals "planted a battery in the woods in the rear of Mrs. Bradford's house and fired directly across both lines composing the angle [on Shy's Hill]; threw shells directly in back of my left brigade"; also positioned a battery diagonally to Bate's left which, the general declared, "took my first [right] brigade in reverse." The rifled guns of the Bluecoats "were so close," said Bate, that "they razed the works on the left of the angle for fifty or sixty yards." Confederate General Walthall's report helps further to visualize the agonizing scene created by the federal artillery fire against Shy's Hill. The Southern soldiers, he noted, "were annoyed by a constant fire from the enemy's sharpshooters, but the concentrated artillery fire endured by the troops on the hill . . . was heavier, I observed, and seemed to be more effectual than . . . at any other point of the line within my view." In sum, the Confederates atop Shy's Hill continually faced a heavy artillery fire from the front, usually from the rear as well, and sometimes from the flank also.[17]

But perhaps none of the above factors—not Southern numerical weakness, not Union artillery superiority, nor Federal cavalry threatening the rear—is the worst aspect of the Shy's Hill position. That ignoble distinction is the location of the Confederate defenses at the hill's physical crest rather than what is termed the military (tactical) crest; that is, the defenses were placed along the topmost geographic line of the hill rather than along the highest line from which the enemy could be seen and fired on. The Graycoat breastworks were constructed so far back from where they should have been that defenders could not see an attacking enemy until he was almost upon them, as close as fifteen or twenty feet in some places, and no more than fifty or sixty feet at any point.[18]

The Confederate line had been established after dark, which certainly contributed to its misplacement. General Bate, fortunately for the sake of history, wrote a detailed account of his occupation and development of the position. His report clearly reveals the difficulties and confusion associated with such a nighttime endeavor. Bate said that General Cheatham, about eight o'clock on December 15, "took me with him to find the line I was to occupy." Cheatham declared that he was acting on Hood's orders to "extend a line of battle from the apex of the hill (now known as Shy's Hill) occupied by Ector's brigade, in the direction of Mrs. [Edward] Bradford's house on the Granny White turnpike, so that a prolongation of the same would strike the [left of the] line then occupied by General Stewart."[19]

Bate and Cheatham tramped to the rear of Mrs. Bradford's house, where the left flank of Stewart's corps lay. Informed that Stewart's line extended eastward into a wooded area, General Cheatham then ordered that a fire be started on the Bradford property. This fire, visible from atop Shy's Hill, would indicate the direction in which Bate's line should be developed in order to connect with Stewart's. "I moved my command into the position" assigned, wrote Bate, "but with much delay, attributable to the darkness of the night and the marshy fields through which I had to pass." Thus Bate's line, from the apex of Shy's Hill, stretched northeastward, approaching the Granny White Pike diagonally. "I at once put the men to making defenses with such tools as I had," remembered Bate. He said they "worked with alacrity the balance of the night . . . and constructed works along my entire front impervious to ordinary shots."[20]

But as dawn ever so slowly grayed the east on Friday, December 16, the general began to realize that his men were occupying a very vulnerable position. Daylight revealed that his right flank no longer connected with Stewart's corps. Stewart's "two left divisions [had been] retired in echelon from my right," reported a startled Bate. They "had been moved back several hundred yards from the point toward which I was directed to extend my right." These were the divisions of Walthall and Loring, the former repositioned west of Granny White Pike, while Loring lay east of the pike, a few hundred feet south of present-day Battery Lane and behind the stone fence (part of which is still extant) that represented the northern boundary of the Lealand estate, on which Hood had earlier established his headquarters. Stewart's engineer believed this was a stronger defensive position for the two divisions. No doubt the stone wall was a formidable barrier, but when Stewart's men pulled back about two o'clock in the morning, no one notified General Bate that they had left their first location.[21]

Recognizing at daylight that his right flank was badly exposed, Bate retired it at once, bringing it into alignment with Walthall's left. This meant, however, that Shy's Hill became a dangerous salient, which the Union could fire on from three sides. It also meant that much of the energy expended by Bate's men in constructing breastworks during the night had gone for naught. Preparing new entrenchments during the daylight would put the troops at serious risk from Federal sharpshooters.

The single worst aspect of Bate's position did not present itself until after Ector's brigade was taken out of the line, compelling Bate to extend his already thin line to the left. At that time Bate discovered that Ector's line, "located in the darkness of the night," was both "too far back from the brow of the hill" and that "the works were flimsy, only intended to protect against small-arms. . . ." Furthermore, Bate noted that the entrenchments "had no abatis or other obstruction to impede the movements of an assaulting party." And nothing could be done about these weaknesses, which were not appreciated until daylight. The situation "was impossible to remedy" because of "the constant fire of sharpshooters from the neighboring hills. . . ." The sharpshooters, testified Bate, literally made it "fatal" for anyone attempting in daylight to construct a new breastworks to the front. Also, the devastating artillery fire that was kept up throughout the day further discouraged any effort by the Confederates to remedy the problems of their location.[22]

For the Southerners, Shy's Hill was the proverbial "disaster waiting to happen." The Confederate salient was punished by Federal cross fire from three directions. The thin defensive line, protected only by "flimsy" works, was precariously situated at the geographical rather than the military crest of the eminence. "The curvature of the hill," again to quote General Bate, "as well as the gradual recession of the lines from the angle," guaranteed that no flanking fire could be directed at an attacker.[23] Worse still, the salient assured that Confederate fire would be diverging, thus promising the existence of gaps where there would be no defensive fire whatsoever.

Most of these Confederate weaknesses were not readily apparent to the Federals as they gazed at Shy's Hill through the rain that sometimes descended during the afternoon. General Schofield, in fact, long before daylight on December 16, was worrying about the strength of the Rebels. "Apprehensive that the enemy . . . would mass and attack our right in the morning," Schofield said he "requested that a division of infantry be sent to reinforce his right flank." As a result, Colonel Jonathan B. Moore's Third Division of Smith's corps, with accompanying artillery, was ordered into reserve position to guard Schofield's exposed flank. Moore moved in as instructed before daylight.[24]

Schofield was still nervous, perhaps spooked by his recent experiences with Hood at Columbia, Spring Hill, and Franklin. He thought, incorrectly of course, that the Southerners were continuing "to mass troops [in his front] during the early part of the day." There were also troubling reports of mysterious Confederate troop movements. General Couch, commanding Schofield's division posted north of Shy's Hill, sent a 7:45 A.M. message to General Cox, with instructions to pass it on to Schofield, saying: "It is reliably reported that a rebel column has been moving to my right for nearly two hours." There were disturbing reports coming in from the cavalry as well. General Wilson sent Schofield and Thomas copies of two messages from Brigade Commander John H. Hammond. One reported that "numerous detachments" of the enemy were "moving toward our left generally." Again Hammond claimed that "heavy masses of infantry [were] constantly moving to our left, and have been for nearly an hour."[25]

Schofield was in a quandary. At 11 A.M. he sent a dispatch to General Thomas. "I am at a loss to understand the infantry movement which General Wilson reports," he said; then speculating "unless it be troops arriving from a distance. The enemy has not yet made any demonstration on my front. The ground masks his movements from the rear." Schofield was thinking only of defense. A few days later, in his official report, Schofield admitted that "during the morning [of the sixteenth] our operations were limited to preparations for defense."[26] Clearly General Schofield was worried. Were the Confederates being reinforced? Was an enemy column somehow moving in behind him? The terrifying specter of some Rebel ghost army suddenly falling upon his flank or rear, or both, haunted the Union general.

And making matters worse, Schofield received another message from Wilson, in which that general complained that the rugged country between the Hillsboro and Granny White Pikes was "too difficult for cavalry operations." Wilson proposed shifting his troopers to the "other flank of the army [where] I might do more to annoy the enemy. . . ." The thought of Wilson pulling out must have alarmed Schofield. He told the cavalry commander, "Until you receive other orders from General Thomas, you had better hold your forces in readiness to support the troops here, in case the enemy make a heavy attack."[27]

Fearing such "a heavy attack," General Schofield decided he needed more reinforcements and called upon both General Thomas and General Smith for another division. Thomas was ready to grant it and his order to Smith sheds more light on Schofield's mindset. The order reads: "The major-general commanding directs that you send a good division to support General Schofield's right against a threatened attack by the enemy. The force you have sent he reports inadequate." One wonders how many troops Schofield would have needed to feel secure against an attack. General Smith was not sympathetic with Schofield, objected to General Thomas, and after sending a staff officer to evaluate the situation on Schofield's front, refused to send another division. Offensive operations against the Southern left flank, if dependent on the initiative of Schofield, would not have happened on December 16. In mid-afternoon Thomas received another message from Schofield. Among other things, he told Thomas: "I have not attempted to advance my main line today, and do not think I am strong enough to do so."[28]

Fortunately for the Union, Brigadier General John McArthur was present, and observing Shy's Hill from a point slightly to the northeast of that Confederate-held height. McArthur was neither a career army man nor a West Pointer. But the Illinois general had a knack for command and an eye for terrain. He was a man accustomed to getting things done. As he studied Shy's Hill he was not impressed by the Rebel position. This apparent strongpoint, McArthur realized, was actually the enemy's weakness. He told Lieutenant Colonel John H. Stibbs after the battle that "he saw [the enemy] could not use their artillery against a charging column," because the muzzles of their guns could not be depressed enough. Discharges from the Southern cannon would go high over the heads of the assaulting Federals. Neither would Confederate infantry be effective, "except as they exposed themselves," due to their entrenchments being positioned too far back, at the very top of the hill, rather than on the tactical crest.[29]

Fully convinced that a successful charge could be launched against Shy's Hill, McArthur consulted, more than once, with General Couch, commanding the division on his right flank, attempting to enlist his support in the endeavor. Couch firmly refused, saying that he "had no orders to advance." The sky was dark and rain, in the form of a mist, was descending. Darkness was fast approaching. A good chance for a decisive assault, in McArthur's judgment, was about to be lost. McArthur feared that if action were "delayed until the next day the night would be employed by the enemy to our disadvantage."[30]

The time was about three o'clock, perhaps slightly later, when McArthur decided to wait no longer. His lead-off charge would be made with brigade strength. Having "determined to attack," the general alerted Colonel William McMillen to prepare his brigade to "take that hill." McMillen said he immediately moved his regiments "by the right flank to a point opposite the hill to be carried; forming in two lines outside of the works occupied by and in front of Couch's division. . . ." The front line, from right to left, consisted of three regiments: the One Hundred Fourteenth Illinois, the Ninety-third Indiana, and the Tenth Minnesota. Composing a second line were the Seventy-second Ohio and the Ninety-fifth Ohio. Colonel McMillen said he instructed his regimental commanders "to move out silently," when signaled to advance, "with fixed bayonets, and, if possible, gain the enemy's works before delivering their fire." McArthur sent orders to his Second and Third Brigades to "keep watch of McMillen's men, and when they were half way up the hill to charge en eche-

*William L. McMillen.
Massachusetts
Commandery
Military Order of
the Loyal Legion
and the U.S. Army
Military History
Institute.*

lon." Preparations completed, General McArthur sent a staff officer to his corps commander, General Smith, with a message saying that he could carry the hill by assault, had everything in readiness to do so, "and unless he received orders to the contrary within five minutes, he would order the charge."[31]

Smith was then in consultation with General Thomas, "some distance in the rear," when McArthur's staff officer rode up. Thomas, who had hoped for significant action against the Confederate left flank earlier in the day, was pleased by the prospect of an imminent attack. However, the army's commander wanted maximum force applied in a coordinated assault. "Don't let him start yet," he told Smith; "hold him where he is until I can ride over and see Schofield, and I will have him charge at the same time." At once General Thomas rode off in the direction of Schofield's headquarters, while McArthur's staff officer started back to the division commander. Before his horse could carry him there, the five minutes had expired and General McArthur proved to be a man of his word.[32]

McArthur's bugles sounded the charge. At once all three batteries of the division, eighteen guns in total, opened fire, striking along the crest of the Grayclad works. Federal cannoneers were instructed to maintain the punishing barrage until the Union infantry drew near the top of the hill, ceasing only when the danger from "friendly fire" became too great a risk. Colonel McMillen's First Brigade, with bayonets fixed, instantly led the way as ordered. Moving out quickly and steadily in two lines, the troops refrained from firing, cheering, or halting. Many who witnessed the spectacular event later characterized the charge as magnificent. Watching the men climb the hill in silence, some experienced an eerie sensation, a feeling rather indescribable. In the memories of Union veterans, the assault on Shy's Hill became one of the war's most courageous and glorious moments.[33]

The hill was so steep at places that the ascent required all the strength one could put forth, together with assistance from grasping bushes, vines, saplings and limbs, pulling one's self up by them. The charge soon lost much of its semblance of order, as men sought the least difficult path to climb. In many places, however, the very steepness of the ground protected the assaulting infantry from an effective enemy fire. The steeper the ground, the greater the difficulty experienced by Confederate artillerists attempting to depress their few guns and fire accurately down the height. The steeper the ground, the more likely were the Southern infantry to overshoot, even if they had a clear field of fire, which, in many cases, they did not. And damage inflicted by their frontal fire also proved minimal because, as previously noted, many Butternut defenders were stationed too far back from the tactical crest, while the curvature of the hill inherently lent itself to a diverging fire anyway.

Actually then, most of McMillen's brigade was only marginally exposed to frontal fire while the soldiers were scrambling up the hill. The brigade's losses, McMillen reported, "mainly fell upon the Tenth Minnesota," composing the left wing of the charge, "which was exposed to a flanking fire." The Tenth Minnesota suffered about seventy casualties in the assault.[34] But the Confederates had no position from which to lay down flanking fire on the remainder of McMillen's front, the Ninety-third Indiana and the One Hundred Fourteenth Illinois. This they desperately needed to do, for the U.S. soldiers were coming en masse.

Before Colonel McMillen's First Brigade was even halfway up the northern slope of Shy's Hill, the Second Brigade was ordered forward. Impatient soldiers of the Ninth Minnesota manned the brigade's right front. Considerably annoyed by Rebel sharpshooters through the morning and afternoon, they received the order to charge "with a shout that [could] be heard for miles away," declared their commander. Comrades of the Fifth Minnesota manned the left front of the

*Lucius F. Hubbard.
Massachusetts Commandery
Military Order of the Loyal
Legion and the U.S. Army
Military History Institute.*

Second Brigade, while the Eighth Wisconsin and the Eleventh Missouri composed a second line. With bayonets fixed, just as with McMillen's men, the brigade moved into the open at a double-quick pace, rushing forward, according to the Fifth Minnesota's commander, into "the most terrific and withering fire of musketry and artillery" that he ever "beheld or encountered." The Ninth Minnesota's Colonel Josiah F. Marsh called the fire "from the rebel works the most destructive and terrible we had ever met. . . ."[35]

Conspicuous out in front of the charge was Colonel Lucius F. Hubbard, commanding the Second Brigade. Animated by the danger and the challenge, Hubbard was waving his hat over his head and shouting encouragement to his men. Hubbard's horse was shot from under him. "I mounted another and he too was shot," wrote the colonel to his aunt, Mary Hubbard. "My staff was falling all about me," he continued, and "I was struck by a minnie ball on the neck and knocked headlong to the ground, but was soon on my feet again."[36]

Hubbard's line of advance lay across a muddy cornfield, softened by the recent rains, for a distance of about six hundred yards. Soldiers sometimes sank ankle deep in the mud. "Through every foot," Hubbard reported, "the men were exposed to a direct fire from the line of works in front. . . ." He also said "a battery on my left enfiladed my line . . . with fearful accuracy. . . ." This enfilading fire, striking from guns positioned on Stewart's front just east of Granny White Pike, was particularly deadly because Hubbard's brigade was angling southwestward in its advance on the lower, northeastern slope of Shy's Hill.[37]

Commencing canister fire at a range of about four hundred yards, the Confederate guns ripped the Federal ranks with twenty-foot swaths of death-dealing missiles, metal pieces both round and jagged. Hubbard's men suffered the greatest losses of McArthur's three brigades, a total of 315 killed and wounded in two days of action at Nashville, with the bulk of those coming in the assault on Shy's Hill. As always, men carrying the flag drew marked attention. The Fifth Minnesota had four color-bearers shot down (three of them killed), while taking a total of one hundred casualties. This was approximately a 25 percent loss, the greatest of any regiment in the brigade.[38]

Meanwhile, over on Schofield's front west of the hill, General Thomas had just arrived, and he and Schofield had little more than exchanged greetings when cavalry commander Wilson rode up. Wilson had intercepted a dispatch from Hood to Chalmers that said: "For God's sake, drive the Yankee cavalry from our left and rear, or all is lost." Wilson was seeking Thomas to personally show him the dispatch and urge an immediate attack. Wilson claimed that he pointed in the direction of his cavalry, then moving against the left and rear of the Rebels, and impatiently called upon Thomas to order the infantry forward at once. Scanning the field with what Wilson thought was "unnecessary deliberation," Thomas directed Schofield to attack. Wilson said nothing about McArthur's attack. Obviously intending for all possible credit to go to the cavalry (and its young commander), Wilson left the impression in his memoirs that if it had not been for him, perhaps neither Schofield nor Thomas would have ordered a charge. Despite Wilson's bias, his account does add further evidence that Schofield himself, so critical of Thomas for not attacking earlier, was not very aggressive on December 16.[39]

Events transpired rapidly as the afternoon's martial climax developed, and the exact role played by each general is difficult to determine. The official report of General Thomas is quite different from Wilson's much later account and actually is not very helpful since, as Stanley Horn observed, Thomas "seems to be making a studied effort to give credit and praise to all who participated, finding fault with nobody."[40] Thomas B. Van Horn's account of Thomas and Schofield is more detailed and seems to ring true—even if Van Horn did tend to glorify Thomas.

Riding to Schofield's position, General Thomas, according to Van Horn, directed Schofield to advance. But Schofield was reluctant, fearing to move because of the loss of men that an attack would entail. Thomas said: "The battle must be fought, if men are killed." Then, seeing McArthur's troops already attacking up the hill, Thomas added: "General Smith is attacking without waiting for you; please advance your entire line."[41] At a sign from Schofield, Cox's division started "on the run," charging up the western slope of the height. Schofield afterward remembered that "our whole line advanced and swept all before it." The exuberance of the moment was contagious. A member of General Thomas's staff, Colonel Henry Stone, commented that "everywhere, by a common impulse, they charged the works in front, and carried them in a twinkling."[42]

While the interactions of Thomas, Schofield, and Wilson on that gloomy December afternoon remain somewhat vague to this day, there is no doubt of the decisive role played by Brigadier General John McArthur as the overwhelming assault developed against Shy's Hill. His actions initiated the attack. His division led the way. His leadership was paramount in gaining the ultimate triumph—even if he did attack without orders.

McArthur's Third Brigade, in its turn, took up the charge. McArthur reported that, like his Second Brigade, the Third had orders "to charge as soon as the First had advanced half-way up the hill. . . ."[43] Colonel William R. Marshall (commanding only since the death of Sylvester Hill on the previous afternoon), however, left the clear impression that he initiated the advance of the Third Brigade on his own authority. "Seeing that Colonel Hubbard ought to be supported," wrote Marshall, "I ordered the brigade to follow and charge the works in our front. Most bravely did the lines rise," declared the colonel, "and with cheers . . . charge and carry the very strong works on the left of the [Granny] White Pike."[44]

The Twelfth Iowa's Lieutenant Colonel Stibbs later penned a much more detailed and helpful explanation of the Third Brigade's success in achieving an objective which initially appeared quite difficult. He said the men "moved quietly through the cornfield" in their front, and the Southerners, preoccupied with watching the two Union brigades charging the hill to their left, failed to discover the advancing Bluecoats until they had reached the opposite edge of the field.[45]

Upon emerging from the cornfield, however, Stibbs was shocked as he viewed "the nature and apparent strength" of the Rebel position. "I could see no weak spot in it," he wrote, and thought "it would be impossible for us to take it, and for a moment . . . believed our charge would be repulsed. . . ." In an instant though, Stibbs's perception of the situation changed dramatically and he realized that good fortune favored the Union. The Rebels, explained Stibbs, "had sent out an unusually large force of skirmishers, who had sheltered themselves in pits dug well up towards the cornfield, and they too had been watching the movement on Shy's Hill, and did not discover us until we were well on them, when they rose in a body and started for cover."

It seemed a godsend for the U.S. army, prompting Stibbs to declare that "the Lord was on our side that day." As the Confederate skirmishers then raced for the supposed safety of their main line behind the stone wall, they inadvertently served as a shield for the pursuing Yankees, who followed as fast as possible. Realizing the Southerners at the wall could not fire without hitting their own men, the Federals rushed after the skirmishers "with a wild shout," and like "a howling mob," as Stibbs described the scene. "Before the last of the skirmishers had traversed half the distance to their line," the fastest Union runners were among the Butternuts, "capturing them right and left," said Stibbs. Then, through a hole blown in the stone wall by the Northern artillery, the Yankee infantry of the Third Brigade charged. The Federals were upon the Confederates so quickly and in such numbers, that the Southerners immediately east of the pike were quickly overcome.[46]

And about the same time, probably slightly before, McArthur's First Brigade broke over the top of Shy's Hill with a rush, rapidly killing or capturing Confederates who did not flee. In fact, the entire Rebel position on the hill was fast crumbling, Yankees penetrating at several points, with a roar of triumph, and flanking and enveloping Confederate positions right and left. Sometimes the Federals turned captured artillery pieces on the fleeing Southerners. Long after the last gun of the war had been fired, Union veterans, particularly those of the four Minnesota regiments in the front lines of McArthur's brigades, argued about which regiment first gained the Rebel works.[47] Regardless of which Federal unit may have deserved recognition for initially penetrating the Confederate line, the Yankee assault, from beginning to end, consumed very little time. One Federal staff officer thought "the whole work . . . was accomplished in ten minutes' time."[48] Perhaps he exaggerated, but the evidence suggests that it would not have been by much. With Schofield's corps moving enthusiastically to the support of McArthur's animated division, the Union assault rapidly became overwhelming.

Fraught with apprehension, Confederates atop Shy's Hill watched the U.S. army's advance. Few if any Southerners could have empathized with General Hood's later account, contending he believed the Confederate position secure, and by late afternoon had "matured"—the general's own word choice—his plan for the next day. He claimed he would have taken the offensive! Withdrawing his "entire force during the night," Hood said in his memoirs that he intended to strike the Union army on their right, hitting them in flank and rear.[49] If this idea was anything more than years-after poppycock (possibly the most generous interpretation of Hood's claim), then the general would seem to have had no realistic concept of either U.S. strength on their right flank, or Southern weakness at Shy's Hill.

And perhaps he did not. Hood's report soon after the disaster, dated February 15, 1865, seems out of touch with reality. Stating that the Confederate position "occupied by Bate's division, suddenly gave way," the general then remarkably declared: "Up to this time no battle ever progressed more favorably. . . ." Next admitting the loss of fifty-four artillery pieces, Hood explained that the horses to pull the guns had been sent to the rear for safety, because, claimed the general, he "[thought] it impossible for the enemy to break our line. . . ." Nevertheless, the Southern position had been overrun "so suddenly that it was not possible to bring forward the horses to move the guns. . . ."[50]

The totally different perspective conveyed by many a Grayclad might cause an innocent reader to wonder if General Hood described some other battle than Nashville. Such is the memoir of twenty-year-old James L. Cooper of the Twentieth Tennessee. Consolidated with segments of several other Tennessee regiments, the unit was commanded by Lieutenant Colonel William L. Shy, brigaded under Brigadier General Thomas Benton Smith, and serving in Bate's division. Obviously, Cooper lay very much in harm's way. After falling back on the eve of December 15, he wrote: "With sad and heavy hearts, forewarning us of the day to come, we took our position and made preparations for the dreaded morrow." Occupying the top of "a very steep hill [Shy's Hill]," Cooper reported that "we had no entrenching tools and could make but little preparation." Some logs and trees provided a bit of shielding "from minie bullets, but were nothing against artillery."[51]

The young man said the U.S. army's artillery began a concentrated fire against the hill about noon of December 16. "At one time the fire of at least twenty guns were concentrated upon our position. . . . It was almost a miracle that anyone escaped." While this terrifying barrage continued, Cooper remembered that "rain was falling nearly all of the evening, and the ground was very soft and miry." Besides the artillery fire, Union sharpshooters watched for any opportunity to pick off a Southern soldier. "If a man raised his head over the slight works, he was very apt to lose it," remarked Cooper. He also recalled that General Smith "would occasionally send some reckless gallant soul (there were lots of them there covered by those old dirty rags) to creep to the edge of the hill and report the progress of the affair." Cooper said they "would bring back such cheerful items as 'Can't see down that hollow for the Yankees.' Or, 'They'll give us hell directly.'" Cooper thought "they had been giving us that all afternoon."

Shy's Hill seen from Peach Orchard Hill via zoom lens. Photograph by John Hursh.

Finally, "just before sun-down," Cooper said "the Yankees made a vigorous charge on our position, and the breastworks being leveled to the ground, and half of the men killed or disabled, of course they took it."[52]

But for a short time the Confederates put up quite a fight. A few Southern infantrymen engaged in fierce hand-to-hand encounters. Other Graycoats attempted to fight with bayonets, or shoot it out at close range, as the number of Yankees on the hill rapidly mounted. Some Confederate cannoneers fought with their swab sticks, only to be quickly overpowered and killed or captured. One of the Confederates facing the tenacious Federal onslaught was a veteran of the entire war, Private Sam R. Watkins of Columbia, Tennessee, a member of the First Tennessee Infantry. Deployed as a skirmisher with two veteran friends, J. E. Jones and Billy Carr, Watkins recalled that the Yankees were suddenly upon them and demanded that they surrender.

"We immediately threw down our guns and surrendered," said Watkins. Nevertheless, a Federal at once shot and killed Jones, while "another Yankee raised up and took deliberate aim at Billy Carr, and fired, the ball striking him below the eye and passing through his head." Watkins testified that Carr had been wounded "in every battle" in which they had fought, and finally, "in the very last battle of the war," he was killed. Instantly, Watkins said, "I picked up my gun, and as the Yankee turned I sent a minnie ball crushing through his head, and broke and ran." Watkins declared he was "certain that I killed the Yankee who killed Billy Carr. . . ." As Watkins fled, the Union soldiers sent "a hail storm of bullets" after him. The private somehow made his escape, and he claimed: "I had eight bullet holes in my coat, and two in my hand, besides . . . one in my thigh and finger."[53]

Watkins was fortunate. He fought in every major battle in which the Army of Tennessee was involved and survived to write about his experiences. Young

Lieutenant Thomas Shaw was not so lucky. Shaw was atop Shy's Hill as a member of the Cumberland Rifles, Company C, Second Tennessee Infantry. He bravely stood his ground in the face of the Blue onslaught until he was slammed down and pinned to the ground by a Yankee bayonet. Taken as a prisoner to a Nashville hospital, he soon died of the agonizing wound.[54]

Also mortally wounded, and dying instantly atop Shy's Hill, was the officer who became the most famous Confederate killed at the Battle of Nashville. Lieutenant Colonel William L. Shy and a few of his men, refusing to surrender, fought until they were almost surrounded by the U.S. troops. Shy was then shot through the head, the large-caliber killing weapon so close that the face of the twenty-six-year-old officer was powder-burned by the discharge. After the battle, Shy's body was removed to the home of Felix Compton and "Compton's Hill" has ever since been known as "Shy's Hill."[55]

Another Confederate fighting hard to hold Shy's Hill was Brigadier General Thomas Benton Smith. Soon realizing, however, that the enemy numbers were overpowering and the struggle hopeless, Smith surrendered, only to meet a tragic fate. Unlike Billy Carr, he was not shot down and killed after surrendering—although some might have considered immediate death a more kindly resolution of the general's life. Disarmed and sent to the rear of the Federal line under the company of guards, an incident there occurred with a Union officer (an incident never fully explained) in which the Bluecoat struck Smith over the head several times with his saber, beating him to the ground, laying his skull open with deep gashes.

The U.S. surgeon who attended the general expected him to die. Although Smith survived, he never recovered. The damage from the saber licks was compounded by infection, resulting in serious and permanent injury to his mind. As a result, Smith was admitted to Central State Hospital for the mentally ill in 1876. The institution was on Murfreesboro Road, directly across the road from today's Berry Field, the main Nashville airport. Dell Computers is presently located on the spot. There Smith spent the rest of his long life, dying in 1923 at the age of eighty-four. (For nearly fifty years a street that crosses the eastern slope of Shy's Hill has been known as Benton Smith Road.)[56]

Immense pressure on the Confederates atop Shy's Hill, intensifying as more and more U.S. troops charged onto the height, proved everywhere impossible to resist, as suddenly the entire position seemed to collapse, one historian remarking that it "shattered like a porcelain dinner plate." Sam Watkins said "it was one scene of confusion and rout." He thought Finley's "Florida brigade had broken [first, and] before a mere skirmish line," and soon everybody "had caught the infection, had broken and were running in every direction. Such a scene I never saw."[57]

Thomas Benton Smith.
Courtesy of the Tennessee
State Library and Archives.

James Cooper was not so specific. "It was said that Bate's division ran first," he wrote, "but I think all ran together. It seemed to me a simultaneous running. . . . All was confusion and disarray. . . ." Convinced that "the Confederacy was indeed gone up, and that we were a ruined people," Cooper believed only one course of action then made sense: "Mounting my horse," the young man quipped that he "made arrangements to go to Corinth." A host of Confederates were likewise "making arrangements to go to Corinth," while "the vile Yankees"—to again quote Cooper's choice words—"were right after them, shooting as fast as the Devil would let them. . . . In addition the varmints had turned our own cannon on us," and, declared Cooper, "were using it better than we ever could do."[58]

Close to Shy's Hill stood Confederate Colonel Luke W. Finlay, watching the debacle unfold, as more and more Southerners came plunging down from the eminence and made for the rear. Then a man next to the colonel pointed to the top of the hill. "Look there at the United States flag on the hill!" he exclaimed. "And sure enough," said Finlay, "the stars and stripes were planted . . . on the summit of [Shy's] Hill." Concluding that the situation was hopeless, Finlay directed his men to "Make for a gap in the hill on the opposite [east] side of Granny White Pike about two miles distant, and so we were soon in full retreat."[59]

12

It Is All
Over Now

Darkness was rapidly approaching and a cool, heavy mist hung in the air as the Confederate right wing savored its victory against the determined Yankee assaults at Peach Orchard Hill. "The troops of my entire line were in fine spirits and confident of success," remembered General Stephen Lee, "so much so that the men could scarcely be prevented from leaving their trenches to follow the [retreating] enemy on and near the Franklin Pike. . . ."[1] Clearly a sense of triumph permeated the ranks of Lee's Grayclad units. And then suddenly and unexpectedly, in the midst of the rejoicing of Lee's soldiers, disaster threatened the whole army.

The time was about four o'clock. General Lee reported that "all eyes were turned to . . . our line of battle near the Granny White Pike," where it was immediately obvious that the U.S. troops had broken through the Southern position. A formidable force of Union infantry advanced steadily, sweeping everything before it. "Our men were flying to the rear in the wildest confusion," said Lee, while "the enemy followed with enthusiastic cheers."[2] The hard-fought Confederate triumph on their right flank at Peach Orchard

Hill thus became of no consequence. The Northerners, from their right to left (west to east), were taking up the charge all along the line, and soon moving against Lee's left flank units. Lee knew at once that he must act fast to extricate his corps before they too would be consumed in the wake of the disaster that had engulfed the left and left center of the Rebel line.[3]

The general, then astride his horse east of the Franklin Pike and in the rear of Henry Clayton's division, rode rapidly west, across the pike, leaping two stone fences and coming up in the rear of Carter Stevenson's division, where Yankee troops could be seen approaching the flank of his corps. Some of the Butternuts were panicking as they spied the enemy moving against them from the flank and even the rear. Already Ed Johnson's division, the left flank of Lee's corps, had fallen away, its troops scrambling eastward toward the Franklin Pike in rear of Stevenson's position. Stevenson's line also had begun to crumble. At this moment General Lee, according to Louis F. Garrard of the general's escort, who witnessed the episode:

> rode right into the midst of the fugitives, . . . seized a stand of
> colors from a color-bearer and carried it on horseback, making
> himself a conspicuous [target] for the Federal infantry. His example
> was inspiring. He looked like a very god of war. I recall his words
> as if only yesterday. . . . One appeal was: 'Rally, men, rally! For God's
> sake, rally! This is the place for brave men to die!' To those who
> came in contact with him and under the spell of his presence and
> personal magnetism the effect was electrical.[4]

Garrard said that men instantly began to gather in groups of four or five, moved "by individual gallantry" and soon Lee "had around him other stands of colors, three besides himself carried on horseback." The rallying Confederates here brought the advancing Blueclads to an abrupt halt. Garrard remembered a mounted Yankee officer leading his men, and holding aloft a flag. "I think he was wounded and fell to the ground," wrote Garrard. "At any rate, if he was not killed, it was not because he was not shot at often enough. I think his falling aided in checking the [enemy's] advance."[5]

General Lee had succeeded in rallying some of the troops of his left flank and thereby saved the army from total ruin. His action enabled Henry Clayton, whose troops otherwise would have been cut off, to retire his division in good order and, joined by many others of Lee's corps, form a new line a mile or so to the rear at the Overton Hill range and crossing Franklin Pike. Louis Garrard thought that line "was a memorable one. It was certainly a brilliant array of colors, and struck me as a rally of color bearers."[6] From that point, General Lee, with darkness hindering the victorious but disorganized enemy, continued an

Stephen D. Lee.
Library of Congress.

orderly withdrawal, which ultimately sheltered many of the fleeing soldiers of Cheatham's and Stewart's corps; those who were able to make their way east-ward to the Franklin Pike.

Cheatham's orders, if a retreat became necessary, had instructed that his corps should withdraw along the Granny White Pike. But General Wilson's troopers, with their repeating carbines, were in the rear of the distraught Con-federates and forced the Southerners to flee eastward from Granny White. This many of them did, via a country road that more or less followed the path of today's Overton Lea Road and Lakeview Drive. The brigades of Daniel H. Reynolds and David Coleman (Ector's old command), positioned just east of Granny White, rendered yeoman service in courageously blunting some of the onrushing Yankees until their panic-stricken comrades could make their escape.[7]

By this time the mist was changing to rain and the soft ground was quite muddy. With mud caking on their shoes and slowing their progress, some of Cheatham's men quickly divested themselves of such encumbrances, as their obsession with escaping from the Union pursuers obliterated any consideration of future needs.[8] The men of Stewart's corps were also making for the rear as fast as possible. An Alabama soldier of that corps penned a vivid diary account. In line behind a stone fence, which today may be viewed stretching both east and west of Lealand Lane about two-tenths of a mile south of Lealand's intersection with Battery Lane, J. P. Cannon saw the Bluecoats "sweeping back our lines like chaff before the wind."

The Federals, coming by the thousands, said Cannon, were yelling for the Confederates to surrender. "Some of us, however, determined to escape if possible," he wrote. "A race of half a mile for life and liberty through open level fields to a range of hills [the Overton range] covered with timber was our only hope. . . . Some were killed immediately after leaving the stone fence and many others struck down within the first hundred yards. . . . We climbed about half way up the hill, which was very high and steep, to some large trees where we took cover long enough to recover breath and view the scene below.[9]

Cannon and his surviving companions, having left the stone fence with empty guns, there reloaded and fired on the Federals, some of whom had reached the foot of the hill. Continuing their ascent of the rugged eminence, the Butternuts periodically stopped, loaded, and fired at the enemy until they gained the top, when it seemed the Yankees had ceased their pursuit, so far at least as Cannon and his comrades were concerned. "From our elevated position we had a good view of all that was going on below," declared Cannon. "Lee's corps, which had been on our right, was making a gallant retreat," he observed. The young Confederate thought it all "a grand spectacle, but distressing to us, as we . . . thought of the dead and dying comrades in the valley below." Also, said Cannon, the thought of "the crushing defeat we had suffered" weighed upon his mind, "and the train of consequences which must inevitably follow." Then he and the others started down the southern slope, trudging through woods, "wandering over hills and hollows" in the darkness, trying always to angle southeastward until at last they came into the relative safety of the Franklin Pike about ten o'clock that night.[10]

Some officers in both Cheatham's and Stewart's corps made an attempt to rally the fleeing soldiers. Cheatham himself succeeded in temporarily halting one Grayclad by blocking the man's path with his horse, only to have the wily soldier slip underneath the general's steed and continue his flight when Cheatham tried to stop some other panicked troops.[11] Major Joseph B. Cumming of Hood's staff, astride a white horse, was among the officers vainly attempting to rally the fleeing troops around General Cheatham. Years later, Cumming said he was standing on a street corner in Augusta, Georgia, talking with a policeman whom he "knew fairly well," when the man said: "Major, I saw you on one occasion when I thought you were a perfect damn fool!" Cumming said he replied that "there were doubtless many occasions in my life when I was justly liable to that imputation," but wondered to what particular occasion the police sergeant referred. "It was at the battle of Nashville," the man responded. "You were dashing about on a white horse trying to stop the men" who were fleeing. "I said to myself," continued the sergeant, "What a damn fool! If I had that horse I would make better use of it!"[12] Even if he did not have a horse on which to flee, nevertheless the man managed to escape the Yankee pursuers.

Colonel William Dudley Gale, assistant adjutant general of Stewart's corps, was hoping to rally some troops in the area where Reynolds's brigade was holding on. "NOT A MAN WOULD STOP!" he exclaimed, writing in capital letters. Then riding to where he thought General Stewart would be found, only to discover the general was not there, while "the Yankees" instead were close at hand, Gale decided the time had come to save himself—if it were not already too late. "I turned my horse's head," he wrote, "and spurred away.... The first place that I struck the hill was too steep for my horse to climb, and I skirted along the hills hoping to find some place easier of ascent, but none seemed to exist." At last Gale reached a spot that seemed not quite so steep and turned his horse for the climb. "The bullets began to come thick and fast," he wrote.

> Now I found my saddle nearly off, and was forced to get down, but on I went on foot. All along the poor, frightened fellows were crying out to me, "Let me hold your stirrup, for God's sake!" "Give me your hand and help me...." Some were wounded and many exhausted from anxiety and over-exertion. On I struggled until I too became exhausted.... By this time the enemy had gotten to the foot of the hill and were firing at us freely. What was I to do? I twisted my hand in my horse's mane and was borne to the top of the hill by the noble animal.

At that point the realization struck the colonel that "I was safe," as he began to descend the southern slope of the rugged ridge. Observing that the darkening woods were filled with retreating men, Gale said "I joined the crowd and finally made my way to the Franklin Pike, where I found General Stewart who was much relieved, for I had been reported as certainly killed or captured."[13]

Still another Confederate who made his escape by climbing the rugged slope to the army's rear, paused at the summit to survey the scene below. "Like a panorama," he said,

> the whole of the plain was spread at my feet. A sickening scene, the closing act in the terrible tragedy of Nashville. Our army was pressed against the foot of the ridge on which I stood and was struggling desperately to make its way in a side-long manner to

the only avenue of escape, the Franklin Pike. . . . The blue masses
pressed closer and closer. . . . Their numbers seemed inexhaustible.
The plain seemed covered with them. . . . Here and there a squad of
our men would stop and fire a few rounds . . . , but that was all. . . .
On and on up to the very base of the hill came the enemy. . . . They
were close enough, the foremost of them, for me to see their faces,
and oh woeful humiliation, what did I see! The faces of Negroes!
Pushed on by white soldiers in their rear, but *there,* . . . in the front
rank of those our men were running from. Our cup was full to the
very brim. Such was the battle of Nashville.[14]

More than one Confederate account has stated or implied that the men of the
United States Colored Troops were being forced forward by white soldiers in
the rear. Apart from reports such as the above, that convey a racial bias, the
author has found no evidence that the African American soldiers required any
prodding; rather they advanced aggressively to the fight and the pursuit.

Meanwhile on the Granny White Pike about two and one-half miles south
of the broken Rebel line, a severe night fight in the rain, later called the Battle
of the Barricades, erupted when Wilson's troopers, pounding down the pike,
came up against James Chalmers's Graycoat cavalry. Wilson was moving southward, planning to turn east and hit the flank of the retreating Confederates on
the Franklin Pike. But Chalmers, reacting to Hood's order to "hold the Granny
White Pike at all hazards," had thrown up "a barricade of brush, logs, and fence-
rails" across the Yankee path. "Without pausing to ascertain who or what it
was," related General Wilson, "the gallant troopers formed front into line and
dashed headlong in the thick darkness against the layout which barred their
way. The blaze of the enemy's carbines plainly indicated its extent and," declared Wilson, "one of the fiercest conflicts occurred that ever took place in the
Civil War."[15]

The site of the barricade on the Granny White Pike was evidently "just
south of [today's] Norton Court, on a rise in the road," with much of the fight
taking place on the property of the present-day Richland Country Club.[16] It
was a peculiar engagement, as well as an intense struggle, in which Colonel
Edmund Rucker's brigade, made up largely of Tennesseans, bore the brunt of
the Confederate defense. Among the U.S. troops opposing the Graycoats was
the Twelfth Tennessee (Union) Cavalry, commanded by Colonel George
Spalding. As a chilling rain pelted the combatants, and a general hand-to-hand
fight raged, in which few could distinguish friend from foe in the darkness,
perhaps the strangest occurrence involved Rucker and Spalding, as Tennesseans fought Tennesseans. General Wilson left the following account:

In the midst of the clash a clear voice rang out: "Who are you, anyhow?" The answer came back in defiance: "I am Colonel George Spalding, commanding the Twelfth Tennessee Cavalry," whereupon Rucker rushed at Spalding, grabbing at his rein and calling out fiercely: "You are my prisoner, for I am Colonel Ed Rucker, commanding the Twelfth Tennessee Rebel Cavalry!" "Not by a damned sight," shouted the Union Colonel, and giving his horse the spur, with a front cut in the dark, he broke the grip of his antagonist and instantly freed himself.[17]

Suddenly another Union officer challenged Rucker, conspicuous on a white horse in the darkness, and as the two combatants fought, somehow in that nighttime melee, they exchanged sabers. Then as the contestants whacked at each other with the other's weapon, "a pistol shot from an unknown hand," to employ Wilson's words once more, "broke Rucker's sword arm," abruptly ending his fighting and resulting in his surrender. Later in the night, a U.S. surgeon amputated the badly mangled arm and Rucker spent the rest of the night in a bed at Wilson's headquarters.[18]

The game Confederates, perhaps a thousand or twelve hundred strong and significantly outnumbered, somehow managed to hold their ground for a remarkable time, then falling back to a fresh position and then still another—at least that was the way Wilson remembered it. Wilson characterized the scene as "pandemonium, in which flashing carbines, whistling bullets, bursting shells and the imprecations of struggling men filled the air. . . ." He declared that night was "one of the most exciting of the war." It was nearly midnight when the fight ended, Chalmers's men at last withdrawing to the Franklin Pike. Wilson did not pursue, ordering his men to bivouac, and take up the chase on the morrow. The story was told that Colonel Rucker, after his capture, convinced General Wilson that General Forrest was present and in command of the Confederates; and Wilson, regarding Forrest as too dangerous a foe to confront in the night, determined not to push any farther.[19]

The young Union major general later paid tribute to Chalmers and his Rebel troopers for doing their work "gallantly and well." Wilson said: "He [Chalmers] was overborne and driven back, it is true, but the delay which he forced upon the Federal cavalry by the stand he had made was sufficient to enable the fleeing Confederate infantry to sweep by the danger-point that night, to improvise a rear-guard, and to make good their retreat the next day."[20]

Among the Southerners who had opposed Wilson's cavalry on the Granny White Pike was a Private John Johnston of the Fourteenth Tennessee Cavalry. It is interesting to set his remembrance of the fight beside that of General Wilson:

Some [who left accounts of the battle] tell of running fights, hand
to hand conflict, the clashing of sabers and pistols, etc., when nothing
of the kind occurred. The only fighting we did that night was while
we were dismounted and the only clashing of sabers, if any, was that
which is said to have occurred between General [actually Colonel]
Rucker and Colonel Spalding at the time [Rucker] was captured.
Another writer gives color to the scene by stating that the ground
was covered with snow, which had frozen and become slick as glass
and that the fingers of the troopers were so frozen that they could
scarcely handle their sabers or guns. The fact is there was no snow
on the ground at all. It had been raining a good deal, and the rain
had been at times mingled with flakes of snow, but it had melted
as fast as it fell.[21]

Like Wilson, however, Johnston clearly considered the clash a fierce encounter, and also like Wilson, thought the Grayclads' "last stand on the Granny
White Pike" quite significant. Johnston wrote: "I have always felt a pride in the
conduct of our Cavalry . . . , especially . . . on the Granny White Pike. There seems
to be no question . . . that the single resistance we made at this place put a stop
to the movement of the Federal Cavalry, and saved the Confederate Army from
destruction that night." Indeed, as both Wilson and Johnston testify, General
Lee's corps, having continued its orderly fall back along the Franklin Pike,
reached the Hollow Tree Gap, south of Brentwood, where the general felt he
could safely give the men a little rest, and his soldiers went into bivouac. A final,
poignant note from John Johnston seems appropriate. Drawing near the Franklin
Pike after the Granny White clash, he could see the Confederates moving
steadily south. "Just then," he wrote, "the clouds broke and the moon shed a brilliant light over the scene. While I sat on my horse and saw this long line of
infantry passing, my heart sank within me, for . . . I felt that our cause was lost."[22]

As for Wilson, he also remembered General Thomas riding up to him on
the Granny White Pike. Earlier, when Thomas had been pressured by Washington to begin the battle in spite of the atrocious weather, the Nashville commander had confided to his cavalry general: "Wilson, they [meaning General
Grant and the War Department] treat me as if I were a boy and incapable of
planning a campaign or fighting a battle. If they will let me alone I will fight
this battle just as soon as it can be done, and will surely win it. . . ." On the night
of December 16, when it was so dark that men could recognize each other only
by their voices, an effervescent Thomas suddenly rode up on Wilson's right
and exclaimed in what Wilson said was "a tone of exultation never to be forgotten": "Dang it to hell, Wilson, didn't I tell you we could lick 'em?"[23]

❦

Back at Nashville, the United States forces had gathered a host of prisoners in the wake of the Confederate collapse. Southern sources are of little assistance in determining how many men were captured. Only a few of the brigade and division commanders made a report of the battle, as their defeated army was soon broken up in north Mississippi and sent by divisions to the Carolinas and the command once more of General Joseph E. Johnston, albeit much too late for any effective action against Sherman's marauding army. Those who did pen accounts of the Nashville battle, like William Bate, were severely handicapped by the lack of subordinate reports. Bate noted that all three of his brigade commanders were captured. He also indicated that many men of his division became prisoners, although making no attempt to provide a number.[24]

General Hood offered nothing specific on the subject, advising the secretary of war on December 17 that his loss in prisoners was "not yet ascertained," but claimed the number was "comparatively small."[25] What that meant was anybody's guess. Probably George H. Thomas is the best authority on the matter. Thomas reported that "during the two days' operation there were 4,462 prisoners captured, including 287 officers of all grades from that of major general, 53 pieces of artillery, and thousands of small-arms."[26]

As prisoners were rounded up all across the battlefield, a gifted painter well might have formulated an impressive martial collage of the apprehensions. Scenes ran the gamut from the ordinary to the amusing, from the pathetic to the tragic. When Brigadier General Henry R. Jackson was attempting to escape from the on-rushing Yankees, his boots became so caked and heavy with mud that he had difficulty in walking and became exhausted. Sitting down to pull off the encumbering boots, the general was overtaken by Union pursuers. As Jackson was about to be captured, one of the Southerners with him pulled the general's coat collar down, covering his general's insignia in order that his captors would not realize who had fallen into their hands. Unfortunately the collar, as Jackson struggled with his boots, slipped back into its natural position, immediately attracting the attention of a U.S. corporal who walked around Jackson, carefully observing the general. Then suddenly, obviously pleased with his prisoner, the soldier exclaimed something to the effect of "Captured a General, by God! I'll take you to Nashville myself." Proudly the corporal started back to the city with his prized prisoner.[27]

Some of the Rebels did not want to surrender to a black man. The historian of the One Hundred Twelfth Illinois told of a USCT sergeant calling upon a Confederate officer to surrender. The fiery Southerner replied that "he would never surrender to 'a ——— nigger,' but if they would send for a white man, he would surrender to him. Quick as lightning the sergeant's gun went to his shoulder," remembered B. F. Thompson of the One Hundred Twelfth, and covering the haughty Rebel, the black man replied: "Can't help it massa; no time to send for a white man now." And then he told the Confederate in blunt fashion that he better come down from his horse. "The ominous click of the sergeant's gun convinced the Confederate officer that the '———— nigger' would not be trifled with, and he came down, and was sent to the rear in charge of a colored guard."[28] The Graycoat should have considered himself fortunate. The chances are that not all black troops would have exercised such patience.

"The colored soldiers joined in the pursuit with as keen a zest as the most enthusiastic of the veterans," wrote the historians L. G. Bennett and William Haigh of the Thirty-sixth Illinois Infantry. In passing a house near the road on which the Federals were pursuing, "a not altogether subdued Rebel was observed still in possession of his Enfield rifle and military accoutrements." A member of the Thirty-sixth ordered him to "throw it down and surrender, which he reluctantly proceeded to do." Just at that moment a black soldier came up at a run, with a broad grin across his face, and said to the soldier of the Thirty-sixth, as reported by that man: "Dis am high ole fun. . . . Say, suh, has yer enny caterges? I'me plum out; spended dem in de complemens ob de season wid dem Rebbils." The white soldier then directed the black man to appropriate the contents of the cartridge box belonging to the surrendered Grayclad. "Johnnie was slow in complying with the demand . . . and looked daggers at the sable son of the South, muttering something that sounded like 'd——d niggers.'" Nevertheless the black man soon replenished his ammunition and dashed on in high spirits, concluded the Illinois soldier.[29]

It was inevitable that such intense hatred sometimes manifested itself in violent action. Private Benjamin T. Smith of the Fifty-first Illinois recorded in his journal that "the rebels who were captured by the colored troops gave up with a very bad grace, the officers especially, thinking it was a disgrace to be captured by niggers who perhaps were their former slaves," and upon whom they possibly "had laid the lash" before the war. Private Smith said he observed a "rebel captain who was marching to the rear, who seized the gun from the hands of one of his guards and shot the negro down," only to be "promptly run through the body by a sword in the hands of a white officer who was just behind him."[30]

Scenes of meanness, treachery, and violence in the battle's aftermath were all about. Two officers from the Twelfth USCT and another from the Forty-fourth USCT fell victim to Confederate cavalry. Captured, stripped of their clothing, and marched for the better part of two days—supposedly toward General Forrest's headquarters—they were then directed into a ravine three or four miles west of Lewisburg and shot in the head. One of the three was

Lieutenant George W. Fitch of the Twelfth USCT, who lived despite a revolver bullet lodged behind his ear, pretending to be dead until his would-be executioners moved on.[31]

The tragic fate of young Brigadier General Thomas Benton Smith, whose mind was permanently impaired by an attack after his surrender, has already been recounted. Neither Smith's assailant, nor the reason for the disabling assault, have ever been satisfactorily determined. Stanley Horn examined the matter in a detailed footnote, his study suggesting that possibly Colonel William L. McMillen, whose brigade captured Smith in the charge up Shy's Hill, was the person responsible.[32] But this has never been proven, and Lieutenant W. J. McMurray of the Twentieth Tennessee, later a physician and historian of the regiment, told a different story, one based on the testimony of two other members of his regiment who claimed to have been eyewitnesses of the affair. According to McMurray's account, "a cowardly Federal dressed in a major's uniform" rode up to Smith, and without provocation, "began to curse and abuse him," finally striking him over the head several times. Smith's only reply, as reported by McMurray's sources, was "I am a disarmed prisoner."[33] Whatever else may be said of war, it is a given that horrible events will occur in conflict, and sometimes victors are satisfied neither by simply killing, nor by merely capturing, their foe.

In fact the death of Colonel William Shy provides another case in point. According to one account, and seemingly from a creditable source, the young colonel, when found atop the hill ever since bearing his name, had been totally stripped of his clothing, shot through the forehead, and impaled on a tree with a bayonet. According to another source, the colonel's lifeless body was eventually transported to the home of Felix Compton, whose house was one of the nearest, if not the nearest, to Shy's Hill, and lay for a time upon the front gallery of the home. Reportedly some 150 dead and wounded, some from both armies, were also to be found at the Compton home.[34]

And all across Nashville, in private houses, in churches and public buildings, and in hospitals, a large number of wounded men were suffering and many dying. The newspaper reported that "all the churches in the city, with one exception [that exception was not named], have been taken for hospitals. They could not be put to better use at present." The paper also declared that due to a shortage of ambulances to bring in the wounded, "every hack in the city was pressed into service, to the annoyance of some and the amusement of others."[35]

The saga of Lieutenant O. A. Abbott continued to unfold. Shot in the attack on redoubt number five, but left unattended on the floor of a building in Nashville by a doctor who pronounced that the lieutenant soon would die anyway, Abbott was in constant pain and hardly able to move. Not until December

17 was he at last transported to a clean cot in one of the churches. Even so, Abbott said five days passed after his wounding before the exit hole of the bullet was discovered under his left side, proving that he had not been the victim, as first reported, of "a spent bullet." In the meantime, Abbott had been "coughing violently during those slowly passing days and nights from the fluids of the body that found their way into the lung cavities," or so Abbott explained his ordeal, whether or not he was medically correct. Later removed to a hospital in Louisville, where he remained until April, the lieutenant would survive, but said that when he left Louisville he was "the merest ghost" physically of what he had been when felled by a bullet on the first day of the Battle of Nashville. With him Abbott carried "my blood-stained diary . . . cut open by the bullet" that had almost taken his life; along with "two letters in it, one from my sister, also mutilated by the same bullet."[36]

Surgeon and Brevet Captain Stephen C. Ayres was still busy, of course, serving the wounded of both armies around the clock, hardly stopping except for a brief rest. He said that among the medically interesting cases, he treated a Kentucky captain who was astride his horse on December 16, when wounded during the afternoon near the Granny White Pike. "The shot entered his mouth, struck his tongue and passed backward, carrying with it two or three of his lower incisors," Ayres remembered. The Captain "fell insensible and was carried off the field, but soon rallied. When I saw him he could with difficulty speak above a whisper," continued the surgeon.

> I extracted one of his teeth from the interior of his tongue, and as
> he was not bleeding, I passed onto other more severe cases. The
> next day he was comfortable, and there was no evidence of the bullet
> in or around his tongue. I told him that it was possible it had passed
> through the base of his tongue, had entered the oesophagus, and that
> he had swallowed it. I told him to be on the lookout for it, and the
> next day he showed it to me in triumph, it having passed entirely
> through his alimentary canal.

Ayres also told of a "Confederate soldier . . . lying with a gunshot wound through his abdomen, perforating the bowels. In those days we could do nothing for him, but modern surgery would have enabled us . . . probably . . . to save his life." Next to the doomed Southerner

> were two more Confederates, both shot through the upper part of
> the thigh. One of them was a short, heavy-set man, belonging to the
> Thirty-third Mississippi, C.S.A. The ball entered the back part of the
> thigh and came out in front, a short distance below the hip joint. I
> did the amputation, and he got along very well for nearly two weeks,

when he had a secondary hemorrhage. But this was checked, and he was in a few weeks forwarded to Camp Chase, and later on to his old home. More than twenty years afterward a tall, lank fellow came into my office and asked if I was the Doctor Ayres who was in the army. Receiving an affirmative answer, he said: "Well, you treated my brother-in-law at Nashville after the battle, and he made me promise to call and see you and return his thanks to you for your kind and skillful treatment of him. He says he will never forget you."

Captain Ayres recounted also witnessing a novel parade at Nashville. He said that on a bright, sunny day, "the one-armed and one-legged fellows wearing both the blue and the gray concluded to have a dress parade. . . ." Sending word to the different wards, summoning all who were well enough to move about, they soon gathered "all those who had lost an arm or a leg, and all who were on crutches, formed in line and marched past the officers' quarters. They cheered us, and we returned the cheer with a tiger." This, of course, was several weeks after the battle.[37]

Another Federal surgeon remembered the case of a lieutenant wounded by "a grape shot, which after shattering [several] ribs, . . . lodged below the shoulder blade. . . ." The surgeon said he "removed it through an incision made near the spine," but from the first knew the wound would be fatal. The lieutenant "made an effort to appear jovial and insisted that he would recover." However, a day or two after his removal from a field hospital to a post hospital, and "having only a few moments before declared his belief that the terrible wound would not cause his death," the young man suffered a hemorrhage "and Lieutenant S. Ed Day was no more."[38]

Civil War medicine at this late stage of the conflict was still quite primitive, compared not only to the twenty-first century, but even to advancements by the opening of the twentieth century. However, one significant improvement had occurred a relatively short time before the war. The awful practice of bleeding patients, which had caused the death of many people who otherwise might have lived, had finally been rejected.

As the wounded of both armies suffered at Nashville—and Franklin as well—the Army of Tennessee, no more than a fragile shell of the once powerful force that had contested the U.S. army on equal terms at Stones River and thrown it back in defeat at Chickamauga, plodded steadily southward. Perhaps, judging from several accounts of both Rebels and Yankees, one-third of the survivors were either barefoot or their shoes on the verge of disintegrating. "The combined catastrophes at Franklin and Nashville wiped out a good portion of the army, and after the second battle," wrote Cheatham biographer Chris Losson in a well-crafted summation, "it must have been obvious to Cheatham and his men that the war was lost. This depressing reality was suppressed, at least temporarily, by the struggle to escape from the Union troops who hounded the Confederate retreat."[39]

Yet, strange as it may seem, some men seemed to believe the defeated Southern army could make a stand at Columbia. Chaplain Quintard and another officer urged Hood, in a long conversation with the general on Sunday, December 18, to establish a defensive line along the Duck River "if he could possibly do so." Quintard contended that "falling back across the Tennessee will dispirit the men [and] cause desertion among the Tennessee troops." (Some of them, convinced the cause was lost, as John Johnston had thought when he viewed the long gray line passing in retreat at Brentwood, were already gone from the army.) If the Duck River line could be held, Quintard believed "the campaign, even with our reverses, will be a splendid success." Quintard, judging from his diary, thought that Hood was giving serious consideration to the idea.[40]

Fortunately General Forrest arrived at Hood's headquarters before dawn of Monday, December 19. Doubtless he was surprised, perhaps amazed, to hear talk of trying to remain in Tennessee. Interjecting a healthy dose of realism into Hood's thinking, Forrest at once squelched the concept and told the general that he must withdraw without delay south of the Tennessee River. Forrest succeeded in bringing the army's commander to his senses. In fact Forrest was then placed in command of the rear guard, assisted by several badly depleted infantry brigades led by General Walthall—a tough assignment, but Forrest handled it well.

The retreat was an exhausting ordeal, physically, mentally, and emotionally, for most Southerners involved, as evidenced by many reminiscences of soldiers, both Confederate and Union. Federal J. C. Harwood said that "all along the road" the Rebels had abandoned "guns, cartridge boxes, blankets, meal, hay, wagons, ambulances and about everything you could think of and we met squad after squad of prisoners coming [toward Nashville] which the cavalry had captured."[41] In an unexpected twist, however, one of the Federal pursuers was almost captured by the Graycoats. Shot in the shoulder and seeking treatment, he had stumbled into the enemy, luckily realizing that several Rebels were close by before they became aware of his presence. He threw himself face down behind a log and pretended to be dead. The Confederates soon discovered him though, claimed his weapon, searched through his pockets, and were removing his boots, he said, when a band of U.S. troops appeared and frightened off the enemy. Thus Reuben Lumby was saved from capture or death, exclaiming to his comrades, "They thought they had me dead, but I am not by a damned sight!"[42]

Certainly the near capture of a pursuing Yankee was an aberration. Most Confederates were thinking only of escape, and they were, in the words of a

Columbia resident, "the worst looking and most broken down looking set I ever laid eyes on."[43] A soldier of the Sixteenth Tennessee Infantry remembered "the empty haversacks, clothes worn out, our little army . . . discouraged and exhausted." He said his hat and shoes were stolen, "leaving me barefoot and bareheaded. . . . Several of the boys in our regiment said it was 'no use going any further,'" and they started out for home. Carroll H. Clark said he "saw them leave and never thought hard of them for leaving." Clark also declared that the men who missed the Georgia and Tennessee campaigns "escaped the hardest part of the war."[44] Lieutenant R. N. Rea would likely have agreed with Clark's assessment. Rea said that "my shoes fell from my feet between Franklin and Columbia and I was forced to march all the way to Tupelo . . . barefooted, in a constant snowstorm and sleet the like of which I never saw before or since."[45]

As the Confederates retreated through Franklin, Private John Pruitt (a member of Company H, Ninth Tennessee, who was on cooking detail) "handed each member of the company a piece of half-baked bread which was soft from the rain. It was the only ration they had had for twenty-four hours previous and would have for thirty-six hours afterwards."[46]

The miserable weather, cold with alternating rain, sleet, and snow, had returned once more, as Lieutenant Rea emphatically reported. Perhaps Rea exaggerated a bit about the awful weather, but many people attested that extreme cold plagued Middle Tennessee. The weather only added to the consternation of defeat. Listening to the conversation of the men who "participated in the recent campaign in Tennessee," wrote the Forty-sixth Mississippi's William P. Chambers, was "enough to discourage the stoutest and most hopeful spirits. . . . They are utterly despondent and would hail with joy, the prospect of peace on any terms. . . ." Chambers estimated that "three-fourths of the Army of Tennessee . . . are in favor of peace on any terms, no matter how ignominious they may be." Chambers also stated that he could "hardly refrain from shedding tears" when he thought of "all the noble lives that have been sacrificed in vain . . . ." Then he concluded that "when it comes to discussing the prosecution of the war," the men are "entirely despondent, being fully convinced that the Confederacy is *gone*. . . . I do not think there is a stand of colors in the Brigade."[47]

Confederate Charles H. Eastman, writing to his sister, significantly cast Southern defeat in terms of slavery. "I am afraid that slavery is doomed, and that we will only gain our independence by consenting to Emancipation," he said. "Without slavery I do not consider the South in [any?] way equal to the North. . . ."[48] Even with defeat staring any realistic Graycoat in the face, there were Confederates who seemed to have no plans for anything other than continued resistance. Sergeant Reuben F. Kolb, in a letter to "My dearest Mother," claimed not to be satisfied "unless I am at the front engaging the enemy. . . . I hate the Yankee race more and more every day and I love to fight them." Kolb went on to declare that "we have plenty of men to fight this thing out yet, if they can only be brought out and will do their duty. . . . With the help of God, I shall remain in the field . . . as long as an armed foe remains."[49] One can only wonder how much of such rhetoric was honest conviction, as opposed to keeping up a positive attitude for the benefit of the home folks.

One would suppose, considering all the evidence presented above, that the retreating Confederates confronted problems sufficient to consume all their energy without creating still more issues. Yet in their stress, strain, and frustration, a fight almost erupted over who—Forrest's cavalry or Cheatham's infantry—would first cross the Duck River. Forrest reportedly became so enraged that he pulled out his revolver and threatened to shoot Cheatham, whereupon Cheatham, according to one source, spurred his horse right up in front of the cavalry commander, saying "Shoot! I am not afraid of any man in the Confederacy!"[50]

The confrontation might have resulted in a tragedy, possibly escalating into an affair that could have seen the death of several men. But someone stepped between the two generals (reports differ as to who it was) and succeeded in preventing senseless bloodshed. The First Arkansas's Private William E. Bevens truthfully remarked that "Forrest was a great officer and a fine cavalry leader, but he was tyrannical and hot-headed." In the interest of proper balance and objectivity, the private might have added that Cheatham too possessed a fiery temper. Bevens did say, in a bit of understatement, "we had troubles enough without fighting each other."[51] As to who eventually crossed the Duck first, reports also differ.

Some of the Rebels experienced difficulty in trying to cross another stream, although the problem was of quite a different nature. The event was at Shoal Creek near Pulaski. Robert A. Jarman of the Twenty-seventh Mississippi Infantry, said about four inches of snow was on the ground when the regiment "arrived at Shoal Creek about the middle of the evening on December 24. . . ." Orders were to wade the creek at once. "Some rolled up their pants," reported Jarman, but "as soon as the icy waters touched their naked legs they came out of it and no persuasion or coaxing could get the brigade in until General [William F.] Brantley's horse stepped on a slick rock in the creek and fell with him, ducking him good." At that sight, said Jarman, "the men took to the water like ducks, laughing as they went. The water was very, very cold, but there was a row of fence fired for us to warm by on the south bank."[52] Thus it was proven once again that there was no substitute in the Civil War for brigadiers, in every circumstance, leading from the front! Only then might they expect the men to follow.

The burning of fences for warmth at Shoal Creek reminds again of how both armies fired fences all over the countryside in their efforts to combat the elements. This, of course, was only one of the ways in which many civilians, innocent or otherwise, suffered at the hands of the military forces. Nimrod

Porter's touching account is again valuable for grasping some measure of understanding about what happened during those trying December days. Naturally the beaten Butternuts rushed on south as fast as possible, leaving little time for foraging and plundering. Not so with the Bluecoats.

"General [Brigadier General John T.] Croxton's headquarters is in our house, with his whole brigade camped all over the yard, lots, lanes and everywhere they can get near enough a fence to keep them in wood," wrote Porter on December 24. "With reluctance the General ordered the provost guard to station out their guards all around the house, but it only gave the guards a better opportunity for marauding than the common soldiers, and they made the best of it." He said that they took all of the apples out of the cellar. They also "broke the weatherboarding off the house for fires, burnt the yard fence, went in our smoke house and took the meat, . . . cooked the last old gobbler and all the chickens over a fire in the yard." As for how the Yankees treated the slaves, Porter declared that "they even took the boots off the blacks. Considerable fuss over that. They should not rob the blacks."[53]

Continuing to supply details, he stated that there "is great tribulation in the country; stealing horses, mules, hogs, breaking in houses. The soldiers are very insulting and impose on everybody. . . . Nothing is safe, no help is anywhere. . . . All that we have is nearly gone." Venting his wrath, Porter wished for "a river of fire a mile wide between the North and the South that would burn with unquenchable fury forever more and that it never could be passed to the endless ages of eternity by any living creature!"[54]

As the Graycoats tramped southward, the Twentieth Tennessee's W. J. McMurray reported that somewhere near Pulaski, "the roads were muddy and crowded, and every soldier was pulling along as best he could," when General Hood and his staff came riding through the troops. McMurray said Hood and the other riders "were about to crowd an old soldier out of the road," when the man struck up a parody of a popular song, "The Yellow Rose of Texas," and quite loudly to assure that General Hood would hear it:

> "You may talk about your dearest maid,
> And sing of Rosa Lee,
> But the gallant Hood of Texas
> Played Hell in Tennessee."[55]

On Christmas Day the Confederates began crossing the Tennessee River near Florence. On December 28, Forrest and the last of the Southern rear guard managed to escape across the stream. There had been great concern that Union gunboats might destroy the pontoon bridge and block the army's passage, but the Federal river force presented no serious challenge and was driven off by the Rebel artillery. After the river crossing, the men turned westward into Mississippi, and the retreat finally ground to a halt at Tupelo. The Yankee pursuit had ceased at the river. Efforts by the Richmond government to learn the truth about the campaign from General Hood were unsuccessful until Lieutenant General Richard Taylor visited the army on January 9.

Only then was it learned that Hood had no more than fifteen thousand infantrymen (an absolute maximum figure) present with the Army of Tennessee. Of this number fewer than half were still equipped and considered effective. There could be no gainsaying the fact that the campaign had miserably failed. When General Beauregard arrived at Tupelo on January 14, the army was virtually without food. No winter clothing and very few blankets were on hand to protect the men from the unusually cold winter. The day before Beauregard arrived, Hood requested that he be relieved of command of the troops. Richmond at once instructed Beauregard to place General Taylor in temporary command. "It was Hood's tragedy," wrote one of his biographers, "that he was such an excellent soldier, but such a poor general."[56]

And so the Army of Tennessee, one of the Confederacy's two major armies, had essentially ceased to exist. And Robert E. Lee's Army of Northern Virginia lay under siege at Petersburg, with no realistic hope of succor. Several thousand of the Confederates at Tupelo would soon head east to reinforce General Joseph E. Johnston in trying to stand off Sherman in the Carolinas. That too was hopeless. In less than four months from the time General Hood requested to be relieved of command, the war was over. Lee formally surrendered to Grant on April 12, and Johnston gave up to Sherman before the month was out. Across five Aprils, almost to the day in the case of Lee's surrender, the war had raged, lasting far longer and entailing far more deaths—approximately 622,000 in a country with a total population less than today's California—than anyone had originally anticipated. Even the legendary old warrior Winfield Scott and William T. Sherman, who, in Sherman's words, expected "a long war, much longer than any politician thinks," had not foreseen anything akin to what actually occurred. Understandably, some people, but certainly not all, wanted to put the war out of their mind and attempted to do so.

It would not be until the year 1883 that Frank Cheatham returned to the Franklin battlefield. Pointing out troop positions to those who accompanied him, reflecting upon "what might have been," and claiming to have "talked more of the events of the war to-day than during all the past . . . years," Cheatham reportedly also remarked that "It is all over now."[57] In a fundamental sense Cheatham was correct. The bloodshed and killing, the campaigning, the war—indeed it was all over. In another sense, however, the war had continued; and would long continue.

Although arguably much had been achieved during the conflict—the doctrine of secession beaten down on the battlefield, the union of the states preserved, the institution of slavery destroyed—a bitter, emotional division plagued the North and the South for decades to come. The South recognized it was beaten, yes. In the post-bellum South there existed a keen awareness of Northern might, but the South was never convinced that it had been in the wrong. The Confederate cause, many Southerners believed, had been just. The bitter feelings between the sections were reflected in many ways. National politics clearly evidenced the deep-seated animosities, as the GAR (Grand Army of the Republic), an organization of Union veterans staunchly supporting the Republican Party, continually "waved the bloody shirt," an expression for keeping alive the memories of the war; campaigned for people to "vote as you shot"; and assured the populace that "if you scratch a Democrat, you will find a rebel underneath."

When Democrat President Grover Cleveland, in a gesture of good will during his first administration, as well as for political reasons, ordered the return of captured Confederate battle flags to the Southern states, the GAR rose up as if "Old Grover" were some kind of dirty, rotten traitor to the nation. The commander of the GAR, doubtless for political reasons also, loosed upon Cleveland his heaviest rhetorical artillery: "May God palsy the hand that wrote that order," he said. "May God palsy the brain that conceived it, and may God palsy the tongue that dictated it." Cleveland, who had already angered Union veterans by vetoing many pension bills he considered unwarranted, backed off on the flag order, having discovered that an earlier act of Congress had provided that only Congress could return the flags. (They would not be returned until the twentieth century.)

Also the South found itself economically subservient to the North, a status the section had feared was developing in the years immediately before the conflict. To some degree because of that threat the South had gone to war; and afterward, of course, the subservience was both fully realized and became yet another reason for continuing hatred of the North. And, most pertinent for this account, the veterans, even the victors, long engaged in an orgy of second-guessing, charges, and counter-charges, often punctuated with cynical, deeply cutting insults. Now it was Federal against Federal and Confederate against Confederate. In that regard the 1864 Middle Tennessee campaign drew the full attention of both sides.

General Thomas, as already noted, experienced tremendous pressure from Washington in the days before the Battle of Nashville. He never knew the true and full story until sometime later. At one point General Grant seemed ready to replace Thomas with Schofield. Then he actually ordered John A. "Black Jack" Logan, on leave from Sherman's army, to entrain for Nashville with authorization to take over from Thomas. Louisville would constitute the point of determination. If, when Logan arrived in that city, Thomas had attacked, "Black Jack" was to proceed no farther. Otherwise the general would continue to Nashville and relieve "the Rock of Chickamauga," and initiate the attack. Finally Grant, hundreds of miles removed from the scene and seemingly placing no credence in the explanations of delay that Thomas sent him, actually decided that he himself should take command in the West, packed his bag, and started to Nashville. His journey did not take him beyond Washington, where he received news that Thomas had attacked and driven the Southerners back on December 15. Wiring Thomas to "Push the enemy and give him no rest until he is entirely destroyed," Grant also telegraphed Logan: "You need not go farther."[58] Thomas had escaped removal by the proverbial "skin of his teeth."

In 1870 the *Cincinnati Gazette* and the *Louisville Courier-Journal* published the orders of General Grant concerning the replacement of Thomas before the Battle of Nashville. An accompanying editorial declared that such a move would have been disastrous. Soon a letter appeared on the front page of the *New York Tribune* of March 12, 1870, of anonymous authorship, severely criticizing Thomas's conduct of the Nashville campaign, and implying that Schofield should have received credit which went to Thomas.

Specifically, the writer stated that it would "have been quite as easy for Schofield to continue to command after the junction with Thomas at Nashville, or to resume it after a few days, as it was to exercise it at and before Nashville." The letter was critical of Thomas's first plan of battle, alleging a "mistake" in not using Schofield's corps properly, instead placing it in the left center where only a feint was to be made, rather than in position to support Smith's corps that was making the real attack on the right. Additionally the critic alleged that Thomas, completely convinced that the enemy had retreated at the close of the first day of battle, issued no orders to continue operations the next day, instead ordering a pursuit of an enemy actually still in position. The *Tribune* letter closed with reference to Thomas's generalship in an arrogantly dismissive manner, as "a common subject of pleasant conversation and jest among officers." The writer said too that "if his special friends had been so discreet as to 'let well enough alone,' 'Old Pap' Thomas might have died in the happy enjoyment of a reputation for generalship as well as for patriotism and heroic combat in battle." The letter was signed, "One who fought at Nashville."

Thomas was sure the anonymous critic was Schofield. From the style of the author, and the information at his disposal, it seemed evident that the writer had been a highly placed officer at Nashville. And Schofield was the officer most hurt by the opinions that he could not have successfully taken Thomas's place. In essence, Thomas was correct. From a letter which Schofield later wrote to Jacob Cox, October 18, 1881, it appears that William M. Wherry, adjutant general to Schofield, actually wrote the letter from notes which Schofield had provided, publishing it with Schofield's consent.

After the appearance of the *New York Tribune* letter of March 1870, General Thomas informed Colonel Alfred L. Hough that he was beginning to examine his papers on the Battle of Nashville, and would prepare an answer that would bring to light all the surrounding circumstances. That very day, March 28, 1870, as fate would have it, General Thomas suffered a severe stroke and died about seven thirty in the evening. (His weight is said to have risen above three hundred pounds since the end of the war.) On the desk at which he had been working when stricken was a partially completed account of his conduct of the Battle of Nashville. After the death of Thomas, Schofield refrained from any public criticism of his commander's conduct of the Battle of Nashville until he published his autobiography in 1897. In it Schofield, who survived until 1906, dwelt at length on several points of criticism.[59]

As for the Confederates, General Hood lived until 1879. It is hardly surprising that he never married Sally "Buck" Preston. The general did eventually marry Anna Marie Hennen of Louisiana. During eleven years of marriage, the couple had eleven children, before both husband and wife died in New Orleans of yellow fever.[60] Unlike General Thomas, who deserved a better fate, Hood lived long enough to write his memoir, *Advance and Retreat,* which set off a fresh round of recriminations and second-guessing. The memoir contained mistakes and misrepresentations (whether the latter were intentional or resulted from misunderstandings and carelessness has long been debated), and various persons, including some generals who served under Hood, delighted in pointing them out. As long as the old soldiers (of both armies) survived, the campaign arguments continued with varying degrees of intensity.

In the years following World War I, a major conflict in which soldiers from North and South once more marched and fought as comrades, a Nashville Battlefield Monument was prepared and appropriately dedicated on Armistice Day, November 11, 1927. The monument is a beautiful work of art which the sculptor Giuseppe Moretti is believed to have considered the crowning glory of all his endeavors. The symbolism of the work, which the author came to understand only after he was grown, is thoughtful and appealing. Two charging

Battle of Nashville monument.
Photograph by John Hursh.

steeds are held in check by a young man. The steeds represent the North and the South, once separated, but then brought together by the younger generation of the World War. Thus the monument is dedicated not alone to the Confederate soldier, but to the Union soldier as well.

When the monument was first unveiled, the dedicatory address was given by Colonel Luke Lea, a well-known figure in the history of Nashville and Tennessee, and a veteran of the Great War. He said that the monument was in memory not only of "the matchless deeds of the Confederate soldier." Also, he continued, it is "erected . . . as an expression of the South's admiration for the Union soldier who fought, bled and died upon this hallowed ground in order that this nation, the pride and hope of both the North and South today, might be preserved." According to Lea, "For the first time in history a sovereign state has contributed . . . to construct a monument as a memorial not only to its own soldiers, but also to the soldiers of the conqueror."

Whether or not this was indeed the first time in history, as Lea claimed, the tribute to both Confederate and Union does make the monument something quite special. Later in his remarks, Lea said: "This monument typifies not only the immortality of the Blue and the Gray. . . . It will tell to the ages the story of the stirring days of 1917 and 1918, when the Stars and Stripes became recognized throughout the world, the emblem of justice, freedom and equality."[61] Standing beside the Franklin Pike for well over forty years, the monument then suffered major damage when a tornado ripped across the former battlefield area. After several years it eventually was restored, rededicated, and placed—because of the manner in which Nashville's transportation arteries had developed—at a different site in the late 1990s.

Only a few years after the tornado's destructive rampage, in December 1977, grave robbers (who were never apprehended) opened the tomb of Colonel William Shy. Finding a solid body, thanks to the effective embalming fluid of arsenic that had been employed well over one hundred years earlier, the robbers left a headless torso sticking straight out of the iron coffin. The head was discovered nearby. Because the Colonel's remains were so well preserved, investigators initially thought a recent murder victim had been discovered; a victim that someone had tried to stuff into an old coffin. Of course the macabre puzzle was eventually solved, and Colonel Shy reburied with appropriate dignity in 1978.

The Civil War soldiers have long been gone. With their voices silenced and their pens forever stilled in death, all memoirs have appeared, all explanations have been made, and all charges and counter-charges examined and re-examined. Colonel Shy rests once more in the yard of his old home place on Del Rio Pike, close to Franklin, while his original coffin is now held at the Carter House Museum in Franklin. With the Battle of Nashville Monument restored and appropriately placed facing the Granny White Pike, perhaps finally, as the general said, "It is all over now."

Organization of the Union Army

At the Battle of Nashville, December 15–16, 1864.

Taken from *Battles and Leaders of the Civil War*, ed. Clarence C. Buel and Robert U. Johnson, vol. 4, pp. 472–74.

Major General George H. Thomas, Commanding

Fourth Army Corps
Brig. Gen. Thomas J. Wood

First Division
Brig. Gen. Nathan Kimball

First Brigade
Col. Isaac M. Kirby

Twenty-first Illinois: Capt. William H. Jamison
Thirty-eighth Illinois: Capt. Andrew M. Pollard
Thirty-first Indiana: Col. John T. Smith
Eighty-first Indiana: Maj. Edward G. Mathey
Ninetieth Ohio: Lt. Col. Samuel N. Yeoman
One Hundred First Ohio: Lt. Col. Bedan B. McDonald

Second Brigade
Brig. Gen. Walter C. Whitaker

Ninety-sixth Illinois: Maj. George Hicks
One Hundred Fifteenth Illinois: Col. Jesse H. Moore
Thirty-fifth Indiana: Lt. Col. Augustus C. Tassin
Twenty-first Kentucky: Lt. Col. James C. Evans
Twenty-third Kentucky: Lt. Col. George W. Northup
Forty-fifth Ohio: Lt. Col. John H. Humphrey
Fifty-first Ohio: Lt. Col. Charles H. Wood

Third Brigade
Brig. Gen. William Grose

Seventy-fifth Illinois: Col. John E. Bennett
Eightieth Illinois: Capt. James Cunningham
Eighty-fourth Illinois: Lt. Col. Charles H. Morton
Ninth Indiana: Col. Isaac C. B. Suman
Thirtieth Indiana: Capt. Henry B. Lawton
Thirty-sixth Indiana: Lt. Col. John P. Swisher
Eighty-fourth Indiana: Maj. John C. Taylor
Seventy-seventh Pennsylvania: Lt. Col. Thomas E. Rose

Second Division
Brig. Gen. Washington L. Elliott

First Brigade
Col. Emerson Opdycke

Thirty-sixth Illinois: Maj. Levi P. Holden
Forty-fourth Illinois: Capt. Alonzo W. Clark
Seventy-third Illinois. Capt. Wilson Burroughs
Seventy-fourth and Eighty-eighth Illinois: Lt. Col. George W. Smith
One Hundred Twenty-fifth Ohio: Maj. Joseph Bruff
Twenty-fourth Wisconsin: Capt. William Kennedy

Second Brigade
Col. John Q. Lane

One Hundredth Illinois: Lt. Col. Charles M. Hammond
Fortieth Indiana: Lt. Col. Henry Leaming
Fifty-seventh Indiana: Lt. Col. Willis Blauch
Twenty-eighth Kentucky: Maj. George W. Barth
Twenty-sixth Ohio: Capt. William Clark
Ninety-seventh Ohio: Lt. Col. Milton Barnes

Third Brigade
Col. Joseph Conrad

Forty-second Illinois: Lt. Col. Edgar D. Swain
Fifty-first Illinois: Capt. Albert M. Tilton
Seventy-ninth Illinois: Col. Allen Buckner
Fifteenth Missouri: Capt. George Ernst
Sixty-fourth Ohio: Lt. Col. Robert C. Brown
Sixty-fifth Ohio: Maj. Orlow Smith

Third Division
Brig. Gen. Samuel Beatty

First Brigade
Col. Abel D. Streight

Eighty-ninth Illinois: Lt. Col. William D. Williams
Fifty-first Indiana: Capt. William W. Scearce
Eighth Kansas: Lt. Col. John Conover
Fifteenth Ohio: Col. Frank Askew
Forty-ninth Ohio: Maj. Luther M. Strong

Second Brigade
Col. P. Sidney Post

Fifty-ninth Illinois: Maj. James M. Stookey
Forty-first Ohio: Lt. Col. Robert L. Kimberly
Seventy-first Ohio: Lt. Col. James H. Hart
Ninety-third Ohio: Lt. Col. Daniel Bowman
One Hundred Twenty-fourth Ohio: Lt. Col. James Pickands

Third Brigade
Col. Frederick Knefler

Seventy-ninth Indiana: Lt. Col. George W. Parker
Eighty-sixth Indiana: Col. George F. Dick
Thirteenth Ohio: Maj. Joseph T. Snider
Nineteenth Ohio: Col. Henry G. Stratton

Artillery
Maj. Wilbur F. Goodspeed

Twenty-fifth Indiana: Capt. Frederick C. Strum
First Kentucky: Capt. T. S. Tomasson
First Michigan, Battery E: Capt. Peter De Vries
First Ohio, Battery G: Capt. Alexander Marshall
Sixth Ohio: Lt. Aaron P. Baldwin
Pennsylvania, Battery B: Capt. Jacob Ziegler
Fourth U.S., Battery M: Lt. Samuel Canby

Twenty-third Army Corps
Maj. Gen. John McAllister Schofield

Second Division
Maj. Gen Darius N. Couch

First Brigade
Brig. Gen Joseph A. Cooper

One Hundred Thirtieth Indiana: Col. Charles S. Parrish
Twenty-sixth Kentucky: Col. Cicero Maxwell
Twenty-fifth Michigan: Capt. Samuel L. Demarest
Ninety-ninth Ohio: Lt. Col. John E. Cummins
Third Tennessee: Col. William Cross
Sixth Tennessee: Lt. Col. Edward Maynard

Second Brigade
Col. Orlando H. Moore

One Hundred Seventh Illinois: Capt. John W. Wood
Eightieth Indiana: Lt. Col. Alfred D. Owen
One Hundred Twenty-ninth Indiana: Col. Charles A. Zollinger
Twenty-third Michigan: Col. Oliver L. Spaulding
One Hundred Eleventh Ohio: Lt. Col. Isaac R. Sherwood
One Hundred Eighteenth Ohio: Maj. Edgar Sowers

Third Brigade
Col. John Mehringer

Ninety-first Indiana: Lt. Col. Charles H. Butterfield
One Hundred Twenty-third Indiana: Col. John H. McQuiston
Fiftieth Ohio: Lt. Col. Hamilton S. Gillespie
One Hundred Eighty-third Ohio: Col. George W. Hoge

Third Division
Brig. Gen. Jacob D. Cox

First Brigade
Col. Charles C. Doolittle

Twelfth Kentucky: Lt. Col. Laurence H. Rousseau
Sixteenth Kentucky: Capt. Jacob Miller
One Hundredth Ohio: Lt. Col. Edwin L. Hayes
One Hundred Fourth Ohio: Col. Oscar W. Sterl
Eighth Tennessee: Capt. James W. Berry

Second Brigade
Col. John S. Casement

Sixty-fifth Illinois: Lt. Col. W. Scott Stewart
Sixty-fifth Indiana: Lt. Col. John W. Hammond
One Hundred Twenty-fourth Indiana: Lt. Col. John M. Orr
One Hundred Third Ohio: Capt. Henry S. Pickands
Fifth Tennessee: Lt. Col. Nathaniel Witt

Third Brigade
Col. Israel N. Stiles

One Hundred Twelfth Illinois: Maj. Tristan T. Dow
Sixty-third Indiana: Lt. Col. Daniel Morris
One Hundred Twentieth Indiana: Maj. John M. Barcus
One Hundred Twenty-eighth Indiana: Lt. Col. Jasper Packard

Artillery

Fifteenth Indiana: Capt. Alonzo D. Harvey
Nineteenth Ohio: Capt. Frank Wilson
Twenty-third Indiana: Lt. Aaron A. Wilber
First Ohio: Capt. Giles J. Cockerill

Army of the Tennessee (detachment)
Maj. Gen. Andrew Jackson Smith

First Division
Brig. Gen John McArthur

First Brigade
Col. William L. McMillen

One Hundred Fourteenth Illinois: Capt. John M. Johnson
Ninety-third Indiana: Col. DeWitt C. Thomas
Tenth Minnesota: Lt. Col. Samuel P. Jennison
Seventy-second Ohio: Lt. Col. Charles G. Eaton
Ninety-fifth Ohio: Lt. Col. Jefferson Brumback
Illinois Artillery (Cogswell's): Lt. S. H. McClaury

Second Brigade
Col. Lucius F. Hubbard

Fifth Minnesota: Lt. Col. William B. Gere
Ninth Minnesota: Col. Josiah F. Marsh
Eleventh Missouri: Lt. Col. Eli Bowyer
Eighth Wisconsin: Lt. Col. William B. Britton
Second Iowa Battery: Capt. Joseph R. Reed

Third Brigade
Col. Sylvester G. Hill

Twelfth Iowa: Lt. Col. John H. Stibbs
Thirty-fifth Iowa: Maj. William Dill
Seventh Minnesota: Col. William R. Marshall
Thirty-third Missouri: Lt. Col. William H. Heath
Second Missouri (Battery I): Capt. Stephen H. Julian

Second Division
Brig. Gen. Kenner Garrard

First Brigade
Col. David Moore

One Hundred Nineteenth Illinois: Col. Thomas J. Kinney
One Hundred Twenty-second Illinois: Lt. Col. James F. Drish
Eighty-ninth Indiana: Lt. Col. Hervey Craven
Twenty-first Missouri (detachment of Twenty-fourth Missouri attached):
    Lt. Col. Edwin Moore
Ninth Indiana Battery: Lt. Samuel G. Calfee

Second Brigade
Col. James I. Gilbert

Fifty-eighth Illinois: Maj. Robert W. Healy
Twenty-seventh Iowa: Lt. Col. Jed Lake
Thirty-second Iowa: Lt. Col. Gustavus A. Eberhart
Tenth Kansas: Capt. William C. Jones
Third Indiana Battery: Lt. Thomas J. Ginn

Third Brigade
Col. Edward H. Wolfe

Forty-ninth Illinois: Col. Phineas Pease
One Hundred Seventeenth Illinois: Col. Jonathan Merriam
Fifty-second Indiana: Lt. Col. Zalmon S. Main
One Hundred Seventy-eighth New York: Capt. John B. Gandolfo
Second Illinois (Battery G): Capt. John W. Lowell

Third Division
Col. Jonathan B. Moore

First Brigade
Col. Lyman M. Ward

Seventy-second Illinois: Capt. James A. Sexton
Fortieth Missouri: Col. Samuel A. Holmes
Fourteenth Wisconsin: Maj. Eddy F. Ferris
Thirty-third Wisconsin: Col. Frederick S. Lovell

Second Brigade
Col. Leander Blanden

Eighty-first Illinois: Lt. Col. Andrew W. Rogers
Ninety-fifth Illinois: Lt. Col. William Avery
Forty-fourth Missouri: Lt. Col. Andrew J. Barr

Artillery
Fourteenth Indiana: Capt. Francis W. Morse
Second Missouri (Battery A): Lt. John Zepp

Provisional Detachment
Maj. Gen. James B. Steedman

Provisional Division
Brig. Gen. Charles Cruft

First Brigade
Col. Benjamin Harrison

Second Brigade
Col. John G. Mitchell

Third Brigade
Col. Charles H. Grosvenor

Miscellaneous

Sixty-eighth Indiana (attached to Third Brigade): Lt. Col. Harvey J. Espy
Eighteenth Ohio: Capt. Ebenezer Grosvenor,
Capt. J. M. Benedict, Lt. Chase Grant

Artillery

Twentieth Indiana: Capt. M. A. Osborne
Eighteenth Ohio: Capt. Charles C. Aleshire

First Colored Brigade
Col. Thomas J. Morgan

Fourteenth USCT: Lt. Col. H. C. Corbin
Sixteenth USCT: Col. William B. Gaw
Seventeenth USCT: Col. William R. Shafter
Eighteenth USCT: (Battalion): Maj. Lewis D. Joy
Forty-fourth USCT: Col. Lewis Johnson

Second Colored Brigade
Col. Charles R. Thompson

Twelfth USCT: Lt. Col. William R. Sellon
Thirteenth USCT: Col. J. A. Hottenstein
One Hundredth USCT: Maj. Collin Ford

Artillery

First Kansas Battery: Capt. Marcus D. Tenney

Post of Nashville
Brig. Gen. John F. Miller

Second Brigade, Fourth Division, Twentieth Corps
Col. Edward C. Mason

One Hundred Forty-second Indiana: Col. John M. Comparet
Forty-fifth New York: Lt. Col. Adolphus Dobke
One Hundred Seventy-sixth Ohio: Lt. Col. William B. Nesbitt
One Hundred Seventy-ninth Ohio: Col. Harley H. Sage
One Hundred Eighty-second Ohio: Col. Lewis Butler

Unattached

Third Kentucky

Twenty-eighth Michigan: Col. William W. Wheeler
One Hundred Seventy-third Ohio: Col. John R. Hurd
Seventy-eighth Pennsylvania (detachment): Lt. Col. Henry W. Torbett
Veteran Reserve Corps: Col. Frank P. Cahill
Forty-fourth Wisconsin (Battalion): Lt. Col. Oliver C. Bissell
Forty-fifth Wisconsin (Battalion)

Garrison Artillery
Maj. John J. Ely

Second Indiana: Capt. James S. Whicher
Fourth Indiana: Capt. Benjamin F. Johnson
Twelfth Indiana: Capt. James E. White
Twenty-first Indiana: Capt. Abraham P. Andrew
Twenty-second Indiana: Capt. Edward W. Nicholson
Twenty-fourth Indiana: Lt. Hiram Allen
First Michigan, Battery F: Capt. Byron D. Paddock
First Ohio, Battery E: Lt. Frank B. Reckard
Twentieth Ohio: Capt. William Backus
First Tennessee, Battery C: Lt. Joseph Grigsby
First Tennessee, Battery D: Capt. Samuel D. Leinart
Second U.S. Colored, Battery A: Capt. Josiah V. Meigs

Cavalry Corps
Brevet Maj. Gen. James H. Wilson
Escort, Fourth U.S.: Lt. Joseph Hedges

First Division
Second and Third Brigades, under Brig. Gen. E. M. McCook, absent
 in Western Kentucky

First Brigade
Brig. Gen. John T. Croxton

Eighth Iowa: Col. James B. Dorr
Fourth Kentucky (mounted infantry): Col. Robert M. Kelly
Second Michigan: Lt. Col. Benjamin Smith
First Tennessee: Lt. Col. Calvin M. Dyer
Illinois Battery: Capt. George I. Robinson

Fifth Division
Brig. Gen. Edward Hatch

First Brigade
Col. Robert R. Stewart

Third Illinois: Lt. Col. Robert H. Carnahan
Eleventh Indiana: Lt. Col. Abram Sharra
Twelfth Missouri: Col. Oliver Wells
Tenth Tennessee: Maj. William P. Story

Second Brigade
Col. Datus E. Coon

Sixth Illinois: Col. John Lynch
Seventh Illinois: Maj. John M. Graham
Ninth Illinois: Capt. Joseph W. Harper
Second Iowa: Maj. Charles C. Horton
Twelfth Tennessee: Col. George Spalding
First Illinois, Battery I: Lt. Joseph A. McCartney

Sixth Division
Brig. Gen. Richard W. Johnson

First Brigade
Col. Thomas J. Harrison

Sixteenth Illinois: Maj. Charles H. Beeres
Fifth Iowa: Lt. Col. Harlan Baird
Seventh Ohio: Col. Israel Garrard

Second Brigade
Col. James Biddle

Fourteenth Illinois: Maj. Haviland Tompkins
Sixth Indiana: Maj. Jacob S. Stephens
Eighth Michigan: Col. Elisha Mix
Third Tennessee: Maj. Benjamin Cunningham

Artillery
Fourth U.S., Battery I: Lt. Frank G. Smith

Seventh Division
Brig. Gen. Joseph F. Knipe

First Brigade
Brevet Brig. Gen. John H. Hammond

Ninth Indiana: Col. George W. Jackson
Tenth Indiana: Lt. Col. Benjamin Q. A. Gresham
Nineteenth Pennsylvania: Lt. Col. Joseph C. Hess
Second Tennessee: Lt. Col. William R. Cook
Fourth Tennessee: Lt. Col. Jacob M. Thornburgh

Second Brigade
Col. Gilbert M. L. Johnson

Twelfth Indiana: Col. Edward Anderson
Thirteenth Indiana: Lt. Col. William T. Pepper
Sixth Tennessee: Col. Fielding Hurst

Artillery

Fourteenth Ohio: Capt. William C. Myers

Organization of the Confederate Army

(Army of Tennessee)
At the Battle of Nashville, December 15–16. 1864

General John Bell Hood, Commanding

Lee's Corps
Lt. Gen. Stephen Dill Lee

Johnson's Division
Maj. Gen. Edward Johnson

Deas's Brigade
Brig. Gen. Zachariah C. Deas

Nineteenth Alabama: Lt. Col. R. Kimbrough
Twenty-second Alabama: Capt. H. W. Henry
Twenty-fifth Alabama: Capt. N. B. Rouse
Thirty-ninth Alabama: Lt. Col. W. C. Clifton
Fiftieth Alabama: Col. J. G. Coltart

Manigault's Brigade
Lt. Col. W. L. Butler

Twenty-fourth Alabama: Capt. T. J. Kimball
Twenty-eighth Alabama: Capt. W. M. Nabors
Thirty-fourth Alabama: Lt. Col. J. C. Carter
Tenth South Carolina: Lt. Col. C. Irvin Walker
Nineteenth South Carolina: Capt. T. W. Getzen

Sharp's Brigade
Brig. Gen. Jacob H. Sharp

Seventh and Ninth Mississippi: Maj. H. Pope
Tenth and Forty-fourth Mississippi and Ninth Mississippi
    Battalion Sharpshooters: Capt. R. A. Bell
Forty-first Mississippi: Capt. J. M. Hicks

Brantley's Brigade
Brig. Gen. William F. Brantley

Twenty-fourth and Thirty-fourth Mississippi: Capt. C. Dancy
Twenty-seventh Mississippi: Capt. S. M. Pegg
Twenty-ninth and Thirtieth Mississippi: Capt. R. W. Williamson
Dismounted Cavalry: Capt. D. W. Alexander

Artillery
Lt. Col. L. Hoxton (Chief of Artillery)

Courtney's Battalion: Capt. J. P. Douglas
Alabama Battery: Capt. S. H. Dent
Alabama Battery: Lt. H. Ferrell
Texas Battery: Lt. Ben Hardin

Stevenson's Division
Maj. Gen. Carter L. Stevenson

Cumming's Brigade
Col. E. P. Watkins

Thirty-fourth Georgia: Capt. R. A. Jones
Thirty-sixth Georgia: Col. Charles E. Broyles
Thirty-ninth Georgia: Capt. W. P. Milton
Fifty-sixth Georgia: Capt. B. T. Spearman

Pettus's Brigade
Brig. Gen. Edmund W. Pettus

Twentieth Alabama: Col. J. N. Dedman
Twenty-third Alabama: Lt. Col. J. B. Bibb
Thirtieth Alabama: Lt. Col. J. R. Elliott
Thirty-first Alabama: Lt. Col. T. M. Arrington
Forty-sixth Alabama: Capt. G. E. Brewer

Clayton's Division
Maj. Gen. Henry D. Clayton

Stovall's Brigade
Brig. Gen. Marcellus A. Stovall

Fortieth Georgia: Col. A. Johnson
Forty-first Georgia: Capt. J. E. Stallings
Forty-second Georgia: Col. R. J. Henderson

Forty-third Georgia: Col. H. C. Kellogg
Fifty-second Georgia: Capt. R. R. Asbury

Gibson's Brigade
Brig. Gen. Randall L. Gibson

First Louisiana: Capt. J. C. Stafford
Fourth Louisiana: Col. S. E. Hunter
Thirteenth Louisiana: Lt. Col. F. L. Campbell
Sixteenth Louisiana: Lt. Col. R. H. Lindsay
Nineteenth Louisiana: Maj. C. Flournoy
Twentieth Louisiana: Capt. A. Dresel
Twenty-fifth Louisiana: Col. F. C. Zacharie
Thirtieth Louisiana: Maj. A. Picolet
Fourth Louisiana Battalion: Capt. T. A. Bisland
Fourteenth Louisiana Battalion Sharpshooters: Lt. A. T. Martin

Holtzclaw's Brigade
Brig. Gen. James T. Holtzclaw

Eighteenth Alabama: Lt. Col. P. F. Hunley
Thirty-second and Fifty-eighth Alabama: Col. B. Jones
Thirty-sixth Alabama: Capt. N. M. Carpenter
Thirty-eighth Alabama: Capt. C. E. Bussey

Artillery Battalion (Eldridge's)
Capt. C. E. Fenner

Alabama Battery: Capt. W. J. McKenzie
Mississippi Battery: Lt. J. S. McCall

Stewart's Corps
Lt. Gen. Alexander P. Stewart

Loring's Division
Maj. Gen. William W. Loring

Featherston's Brigade
Brig. Gen. Winfield S. Featherston

First Mississippi: Capt. O. D. Hughes
Third Mississippi: Capt. O. H. Johnston
Twenty-second Mississippi: Maj. M. A. Oatis

Thirty-first Mississippi: Capt. R. A. Collins
Thirty-third Mississippi: Capt. T. L. Cooper
Fortieth Mississippi: Col. W. B. Colbert
First Mississippi Battalion: Maj. J. M. Stigler

Adam's Brigade
Col. Robert Lowry

Sixth Mississippi: Lt. Col. T. J. Borden
Fourteenth Mississippi: Col. W. L. Doss
Fifteenth Mississippi: Lt. Col. J. R. Binford
Twentieth Mississippi: Maj. T. B. Graham
Twenty-third Mississippi: Maj. G. W. B. Garrett
Forty-third Mississippi: Col. R. Harris

Scott's Brigade
Col. John Snodgrass

Fifty-fifth Alabama: Maj. J. B. Dickey
Fifty-seventh Alabama: Maj. J. H. Wiley
Twenty-seventh, Thirty-fifth, and Forty-ninth Alabama (consolidated):
    Lt. Col. J. D. Weeden
Twelfth Louisiana: Capt. J. T. Davis

Artillery
Lt. Col. S. C. Williams (Chief Corps of Artillery)

Louisiana Battery (Bouanchaud's)
Mississippi Battery (Cowan's)
Mississippi Battery (Darden's)

French's Division (temporarily attached to Walthall's Division)
Maj. Gen. Samuel G. French

Ector's Brigade
Col. David Coleman

Twenty-ninth North Carolina: Maj. E. H. Hampton
Thirty-ninth North Carolina: Capt. J. G. Crawford
Ninth Texas: Maj. J. H. McReynolds
Tenth Texas Cavalry (dismounted): Col. C. R. Earp
Fourteenth Texas Cavalry (dismounted): Capt. R. H. Harkey
Thirty-second Texas Cavalry (dismounted): Maj. W. E. Estes

Sears's Brigade
Brig. Gen. Claudius W. Sears

Fourth Mississippi
Thirty-fifth Mississippi
Thirty-sixth Mississippi
Thirty-ninth Mississippi
Forty-sixth Mississippi
Seventh Mississippi Battalion

Artillery Battalion (Storrs's)
Alabama Battery (Kolb's)
Mississippi Battery (Hoskin's)
Missouri Battery (Guibor's)

Walthall's Division
Maj. Gen. Edward C. Walthall

Quarles's Brigade
Brig. Gen. George D. Johnston

First Alabama: Lt. C. M. McRae
Forty-second, Forty-sixth, Forty-ninth, Fifty-third, and Fifty-fifth
    Tennessee: Capt. A. M. Duncan
Forty-eighth Tennessee: Col. W. M. Voorhies

Cantey's Brigade
Brig. Gen. Charles M. Shelley

Seventeenth Alabama: Capt. J. Bolling Jr.
Twenty-sixth Alabama: Capt. D. M. Gideon
Twenty-ninth Alabama: Capt. S. Abernethy
Thirty-seventh Mississippi: Maj. S. H. Terral

Reynolds's Brigade
Brig. Gen. Daniel H. Reynolds

First Arkansas Mounted Rifles (dismounted): Capt. R. P. Parks
Second Arkansas Mounted Rifles (dismounted): Maj. J. P. Eagle
Fourth Arkansas: Maj. J. A. Ross
Ninth Arkansas: Capt. W. L. Phifer
Twenty-fifth Arkansas: Lt. T. J. Edwards

Artillery Battalion (Truehart's)
Alabama Battery (Lumsden's)
Alabama Battery (Selden's)
Alabama Battery (Tarrant's)

Cheatham's Corps
Maj. Gen. Benjamin F. Cheatham

Brown's Division
Brig. Gen. Mark P. Lowrey

Gist's Brigade
Col. Z. L. Watters

Forty-sixth Georgia: Capt. M. Gillis
Sixty-fifth Georgia and Eighth Georgia Battalion: Capt. W. W. Grant
Second Georgia Battalion Sharpshooters: Capt. W. H. Brown
Sixteenth South Carolina: Capt. J. W. Bolling
Twenty-fourth South Carolina: Capt. W. C. Griffith

Maney's Brigade
Col. H. R. Feild

Sixth, Ninth, and Fiftieth Tennessee: Lt. Col. G. W. Pease
First and Twenty-seventh Tennessee: Lt. Col. J. L. House
Eighth, Sixteenth, and Twenty-eighth Tennessee: Col. J. H. Anderson

Strahl's Brigade
Col. A. J. Kellar

Fourth, Fifth, Thirty-first, Thirty-third, and Thirty-eighth Tennessee:
    Lt. Col. L. W. Finlay
Nineteenth, Twenty-fourth, and Forty-first Tennessee:
    Capt. D. A. Kennedy

Vaughn's Brigade
Col. W. M. Watkins

Eleventh and Twenty-ninth Tennessee: Maj. J. E. Burns
Twelfth and Forty-seventh Tennessee: Capt. C. N. Wade
Thirteenth, Fifty-first, Fifty-second, and One Hundred Fifty-fourth
Tennessee: Maj. J. F. Williamson

Artillery
Col. Melancthon Smith (Chief Corps Artillery)

Artillery Battalion

Alabama Battery (Phelan's)
Florida Battery (Perry's)
Mississippi Battery (Turner's)

Cleburne's Division
Brig. Gen. James A. Smith

Lowrey's Brigade
Brig. Gen. Mark P. Lowrey

Sixteenth, Thirty-third, and Forty-fifth Alabama: Lt. Col. R. H. Abercrombie
Fifth Mississippi and Third Mississippi Battalion: Capt. F. M. Woodward
Eighth and Thirty-second Mississippi: Maj. A. E. Moody

Govan's Brigade
Brig. Gen. Daniel C. Govan

First, Second, Fifth, Thirteenth, Fifteenth, and Twenty-fourth Arkansas:
     Col. P. V. Green
Sixth and Seventh Arkansas: Lt. Col. P. Snyder
Eighth and Nineteenth Arkansas: Maj. D. H. Hamiter

Granbury's Brigade
Capt. E. T. Broughton

Fifth Confederate: Lt. W. E. Smith
Thirty-fifth Tennessee: Col. B. J. Hill
Sixth and Fifteenth Texas: Capt. B. R. Tyus
Seventh Texas: Capt. O. P. Forrest
Tenth Texas: Capt. R. D. Kennedy
Seventeenth and Eighteenth Texas Cavalry (dismounted):
     Capt. F. L. McKnight
Twenty-fourth and Twenty-fifth Texas Cavalry (dismounted):
     Capt. J. F. Matthews
Nutt's (Louisiana) Cavalry Company: Capt. L. M. Nutt

Smith's Brigade
(detached service)

Artillery Battalion (Hotchkiss's)

Alabama Battery (Goldthwaite's)
Arkansas Battery (Key's)
Missouri Battery (Bledsoe's)

Bate's Division
Brig. Gen. William B. Bate

Escort, Capt. J. H. Buck

Tyler's Brigade
Brig. Gen. Thomas Benton Smith

Thirty-seventh Georgia: Capt. J. A. Sanders
Fourth Georgia Battalion Sharpshooters: Maj. T. D. Caswell
Second, Tenth, Twentieth, and Thirty-seventh Tennessee:
    Lt. Col. W. M. Shy

Finley's Brigade
Maj. Jacob A. Lash

First and Third Florida: Capt. M. H. Strain
Sixth Florida: Capt. A. McMillan
Seventh Florida: Capt. R. B. Smith
First Florida Cavalry (dismounted) and Fourth Florida Infantry:
    Capt. G. R. Langford

Jackson's Brigade
Brig. Gen. Henry R. Jackson

First Georgia Confederate and Sixty-sixth Georgia: Lt. Col. J. C. Gordon
Twenty-fifth Georgia: Capt. J. E. Fulton
Twenty-ninth and Thirtieth Georgia: Col. W. D. Mitchell
First Georgia Battalion Sharpshooters: Lt. R. C. King

Artillery Battalion
Capt. R. T. Beauregard

Louisiana Battery (Slocomb's)
South Carolina Battery (Ferguson's)
Tennessee Battery (Mebane's)

Cavalry Division
Brig. Gen. James R. Chalmers

Escort, Capt. C. T. Smith

Rucker's Brigade
Col. E. W. Rucker
Lt. Col. R. R. White

Seventh Alabama
Fifth Mississippi
Seventh Tennessee
Fourteenth Tennessee
Fifteenth Tennessee
Twenty-sixth Tennessee Battalion

Biffle's Brigade
Col. J. B. Biffle

Ninth Tennessee
Tenth Tennessee

At the time of the Battle of Nashville, Gen. Forrest, with Jackson's and Buford's divisions, was operating near Murfreesboro, acting upon the orders of General Hood.

Abbreviations

ALDAH State of Alabama, Dept. of Archives and History, Montgomery

CWD Mark Mayo Boatner III, *Civil War Dictionary* (New York, 1959)

FCHS Filson Club Historical Society, Louisville, Ky.

GDAH State of Georgia, Dept. of Archives and History, Atlanta

MOLLUS Military Order of the Loyal Legion of the United States

MDAH State of Mississippi, Dept. of Archives and History, Jackson

OR *War of the Rebellion: A Compilation of the Official Records of the Union and Confederate Armies.* 129 vols. Washington, D.C., 1880–1901. All references are to serial 1 unless otherwise noted.

ORN *Official Records of the Union and Confederate Navies in the War of the Rebellion.* 22 vols. Washington, D.C., 1908.

SHC Southern Historical Collection, Univ. of North Carolina, Chapel Hill

TSLA Tennessee State Library and Archives, Nashville

USAMHI United States Army, Military History Institute, Carlisle Barracks, Pennsylvania

Chapter 1 * Making Georgia Howl

1. *Ohio State Journal,* August 12, 1880. *Columbus Evening Dispatch,* August 11, 1880. "Columbus," *Encyclopedia Britannica,* 1966 ed., vol. 6: 116.

2. *Ohio State Journal,* August 12, 1880. *Columbus Evening Dispatch,* August 13, 1880.

3. *Columbus Evening Dispatch,* August 11, 1880.

4. Ibid., August 12, 1880. *Ohio State Journal,* August 12, 1880.

5. *Ohio State Journal,* August 12, 1880. *Columbus Evening Dispatch,* August 12, 1880.

6. Lloyd Lewis, *Sherman: Fighting Prophet* (New York, 1932), 631. John F. Marszalek, *Sherman: A Soldier's Passion for Order* (New York, 1993), 449.

7. Actually, upon several occasions, Sherman had said in essence that "war is hell." He had used similar words, or the exact words that he spoke in Columbus, but they never before received as much attention. Basil H. Liddell Hart, *Sherman: Soldier, Realist, American* (1929; reprint, New York, 1958), 310. Marszalek, *Sherman,* 477.

8. Marszalek, *Sherman*, 4. Shelby Foote, *The Civil War: A Narrative*, 3 vols. (New York, 1958–75), 3:320.

9. William T. Sherman, *Memoirs of General William T. Sherman*, 2 vols. (1875; reprint, New York, 1984), 2:26, 27.

10. Marszalek, *Sherman*, 260–61.

11. Gilbert E. Govan and James W. Livingood, *A Different Valor: The Story of General Joseph E. Johnston, C. S. A* (1956; reprint, Westport, Conn., 1973), 317.

12.. James L. McDonough, *Schofield: Union General in the Civil War and Reconstruction* (Tallahassee, 1972), 88. Govan and Livingood, *Johnston*, 322. Sherman, *Memoirs*, 2:72.

13. *Atlanta Appeal*, July 20, 1864.

14. Albert Castel, *Decision in the West: The Atlanta Campaign of 1864* (Lawrence, Kans., 1992), 412, 381.

15. James M. McPherson, *Ordeal by Fire: The Civil War and Reconstruction*, 2nd ed. (New York, 1992), 434.

16. McPherson, *Ordeal*, 434.

17. James Lee McDonough and Thomas L. Connelly, *Five Tragic Hours: The Battle of Franklin* (Knoxville, 1983), 19.

18. David S. Heidler and Jeanne T. Heidler, eds., *Encyclopedia of the American Civil War: A Political, Social and Military History*, 5 vols. (Santa Barbara, Calif., 2000), 4:1767–68.

19. McDonough and Connelly, *Five Tragic Hours*, 19.

20. *OR* 39, pt. 2: 413.

21. Sherman, *Memoirs*, 2:146.

22. Clarence C. Buel and Robert U. Johnson, eds. *Battles and Leaders of the Civil War*, 4 vols. (New York, 1887–88), 4:441. *OR* 39, pt. 3: 135.

23. Lewis, *Sherman*, 426. Sherman, *Memoirs*, 2:153.

24. Sherman, *Memoirs*, 2:145.

25. Ibid., 2:153–54.

26. *OR* 39, pt. 3: 358.

27. Sherman, *Memoirs*, 2:152.

28. McDonough and Connelly, *Five Tragic Hours*, 20. Sherman, *Memoirs*, 2:166.

29. McDonough and Connelly, *Five Tragic Hours*, 20. Sherman, *Memoirs*, 2:168.

30. *OR* 39, pt. 3: 359.

31. Heidler and Heidler, *Encyclopedia of the Civil War* 4:1768.

32. Ibid., 4:1770.

33. Ibid., 4:1940–41.

34. McDonough and Connelly, *Five Tragic Hours*, 20–21. Peter Cozzens, *No Better Place to Die: The Battle of Stones River* (Urbana and Chicago, 1990), 23.

35. James Lee McDonough, *Stones River—Bloody Winter in Tennessee* (Knoxville, 1980), 160.

36. Francis F. McKinney, *Education in Violence: The Life of George H. Thomas* (Detroit, 1961), 252.

37. Foote, *Civil War*, 2:754.

38. Freeman Cleaves, *Rock of Chickamauga: Life of General George H. Thomas* (Norman, Okla., 1948), 208. In addition to Cleaves and McKinney, other studies of Thomas consulted in preparing this portrait are Richard O'Connor, *Thomas: Rock of Chickamauga* (New York, 1948); Wilbur Thomas, *General George H. Thomas: The Indomitable Warrior* (New York, 1964); Thomas B. Van Horn, *The Life of Major General George H. Thomas* (New York, 1882); Henry Coppee, *Great Commanders, General Thomas* (New York, 1895); Don Piatt, *General George H. Thomas: A Critical Biography* (Cincinnati, 1893); John Lee Yargan, "Stone River," *MOLLUS*, Indiana Commandery, Indianapolis, 1898.

39. McDonough and Connelly, *Five Tragic Hours*, 21.

40. Sherman, *Memoirs*, 2:162–63.

41. *Official Register of the Officers and Cadets of the U.S. Military Academy* (West Point, 1850–54), 1853, p. 7. McDonough, *Schofield*, 2.

42. David S. Stanley, *Personal Memoirs of Major General David S. Stanley, United States Army* (Cambridge, Mass., 1917), 214, quoting John Pope.

43. George W. Nichols, *The Story of the Great March* (New York, 1865), 288.

44. Wiley Sword, *Embrace an Angry Wind: The Confederacy's Last Hurrah: Spring Hill, Franklin, and Nashville* (New York, 1992), 99.

45. *St. Louis Daily Missouri Democrat*, August 20, 1861.

46. McDonough, *Schofield*, 29–39.

47. JMS to Henry Halleck, November 18, 1862, John M. Schofield Manuscripts, Library of Congress.

48. James L. McDonough, "John McAllister Schofield," *Civil War Times Illustrated* (August 1974), 13–14. McDonough, *Schofield*, 29–69.

49. Reid Smith, *Majestic Middle Tennessee* (Prattville, Ala., 1975), 62.

50. McDonough, *Schofield*, 130–37.

51. *OR* 45, pt. 1: 340, 1085. Jacob D. Cox, *The Battle of Franklin, Tennessee, November 30, 1864* (New York, 1897), 21ff.

52. Thomas L. Livermore, *Numbers and Losses in the Civil War in America, 1861–1865* (New York, 1969), 131. *OR* 45, pt. 1: 52, 970. Jacob D. Cox, *The March to the Sea, Franklin and Nashville* (New York, 1882), 18.

53. Thomas Robson Hay, *Hood's Tennessee Campaign* (New York, 1929), 78.

54. McDonough and Connelly, *Five Tragic Hours*, 27–28.

55. John Wesley McDonough to Ecloey, Nov. 8, 1864, in McDonough Letters, in possession of John Henry James.

56. McDonough, *Schofield*, 102. Heidler and Heidler, *Encyclopedia of the Civil War* 4:1848.

57. Stanley, *Memoirs*, 214.

58. Buel and Johnson, *Battles and Leaders*, 4:441, 442. General Hatch thought Hood was advancing as early as November 8. Continual rumors of an enemy advance clouded the Federals' intelligence. *OR* 39, pt. 3: 708, 768.

59. *OR* 45, pt. 1: 885. John M. Schofield, *Forty-six Years in the Army* (New York, 1897), 167.

60. *OR* 45, pt. 1: 956.

61. Ibid., 957, 958.

62. Ibid., 957, 958, 974, 1020.

Chapter 2 ✶ My Face Is towards Tennessee

1. J. P. Cannon diary, September 15, 1864, filed under "History of the 27th Alabama Infantry," ALDAH.

2. Norman D. Brown, ed., *One of Cleburne's Command: The Civil War Reminiscences and Diary of Capt. Samuel T. Foster, Granbury's Texas Brigade, CSA* (Austin, 1980), 129. Ben Robertson to "Dear Sister," September 4 and 7, 1864, in the William and Ben Robertson Papers, MDAH. Carroll H. Clark Memoirs, 44, in Confederate Collection, TSLA. Hugh Black to "Dear Wife," July 20, 1864, in Captain Hugh Black Letters, Special Collections, Florida State University, Tallahassee.

3. Anne J. Bailey, *The Chessboard of War* (Lincoln, Nebr., 2000), 12, 14. A. T. Holiday to wife, August 4, 1864, Atlanta Historical Society, Georgia. Henry D. Jamison Jr. and Marguerite Jamison McTigue, eds., *Letters and Recollections of a Confederate Soldier (Robert David Jamison), 1860–1865* (Nashville, 1964), 173.

4. Edgar W. Jones, "History of the 18th Alabama Infantry," 21, ALDAH. John W. DuBose, "History of the 19th Alabama Infantry," 37, ALDAH. George E. Brewer, "History of the 23rd Alabama Infantry," 40, ALDAH. Samuel R. Watkins, *"Co. Aytch," Maury Gray's, First Tennessee Regiment* (Jackson, Tenn., 1952), 242.

5. James Lee McDonough, *War in Kentucky: From Shiloh to Perryville* (Knoxville, 1994), 80, 310–13.

6. Allan Nevins, *The War for the Union*, 4 vols. (New York, 1960), 2:289. Joseph H. Parks, *General Edmund Kirby Smith, C.S.A.* (Baton Rouge, 1962), 241–47.

7. McDonough, *Stones River*, 35, 37, 46, 47. Thomas L. Connelly, *Autumn of Glory: The Army of Tennessee, 1862–1865* (Baton Rouge, 1971), 38, 39, 41, 42. *OR* 20, pt. 2: 435–38, 459–60. Frank E. Vandiver, *Their Tattered Flags: The Epic of the Confederacy* (New York, 1970), 181–86. Frank E. Vandiver, *Rebel Brass: The Confederate Command System* (1956; reprint, New York, 1969), 57–59.

8. G. Moxley Sorrel, *Recollections of a Confederate Staff Officer*, ed. Bell I. Wiley (Jackson, Tenn., 1958), 191.

9. Stanley F. Horn, *The Army of Tennessee* (1941; reprint, Norman, Okla., 1952), 286–89. Davis later claimed that he did not bring up the matter of Bragg's capability to command, but Longstreet, Buckner, Hill, and Cheatham all wrote that he did. *OR* 31, pt. 3: 651. Robert S. Henry, *The Story of the Confederacy* (New York, 1931; reprint, 1957), 314–15.

10. *OR* 39, pt. 2: 21, 829, 826–27, 832. Nathaniel C. Hughes Jr., *General William J. Hardee; Old Reliable* (Baton Rouge, 1965), 240–44.

11. *OR* 39, pt. 2: 835.

12. Gilbert E. Govan and James W. Livingood, *The Story of General Joseph E. Johnston, C.S.A.* (New York, 1956; reprint, 1973), 14–15.

13. Vandiver, *Rebel Brass*, 56.

14. William I. Hair, *The Kingfish and His Realm: The Life and Times of Huey P. Long* (Baton Rouge, 1991), 21–22.

15. T. Harry Williams, *P. G. T. Beauregard: Napoleon in Gray* (Baton Rouge, 1954), 240.

16. *OR* 39, pt. 2: 846.

17. Williams, *Beauregard*, 165.

18. Ibid., 242.

19. Ibid.

20. Alfred Roman, *The Military Operations of General Beauregard in the War Between the States, 1861–1865*, 2 vols. (New York, 1884), 2:277–78.

21. Ibid., 2:278. John Bell Hood, *Advance and Retreat* (New Orleans, 1880; reprint, 1985), 246–47, 254.

22. Hood, *Advance and Retreat*, 253. J. P. Cannon diary, September 26, 1864.

23. Horn, *Army of Tennessee*, 372.

24. S. J. McMurry to cousin, September 24, 1864, Confederate Collection, TSLA.

25. Bailey, *Chessboard*, 21, 22.

26. Hay, *Hood's Tennessee Campaign*, 23.

27. Brown, ed., *One of Cleburne's Command*, 135.

28. Ibid., 136.

29. Ibid., 137.

30. Christopher Losson, *Tennessee's Forgotten Warriors: Frank Cheatham and His Confederate Division* (Knoxville, 1989), 89–90. See Losson's excellent work for a full evaluation of the general.

31. Irving A. Buck, *Cleburne and His Command*, ed. Thomas R. Hay (New York, 1908; reprint, 1987), 186–200, 360–62. Craig L. Symonds, *Stonewall of the West: Patrick Cleburne and the Civil War* (Lawrence, Kans., 1997), 183–91. For more information on Cleburne, consult Howell and Elizabeth Purdue, *Pat Cleburne, Confederate General: A Definitive Biography* (Hillsboro, Tex., 1973).

32. Foote, *Civil War*, 3:356–57. Horn, *Army of Tennessee*, 333. On Stewart see Sam Davis Elliott, *Soldier of Tennessee: General Alexander P. Stewart and the Civil War in the West* (Baton Rouge, 1999).

33. Horn, *Army of Tennessee*, 360. On Lee see Herman Hattaway, *General Stephen D. Lee* (Jackson, Miss., 1976).

34. Marszalek, *Sherman*, 290–92. Foote, *Civil War*, 3:612. Bailey, *Chessboard*, 32–33. Winston Groom, *Shrouds of Glory: From Atlanta to Nashville: The Last Great Campaign of the Civil War* (New York, 1995), 66–69. *Songs of Inspiration* (Nashville, 1949), 198.

35. Nathaniel Cheairs Hughes Jr., ed., *The Civil War Memoir of Philip Daingerfield Stephenson, D.D.* (Conway, Ark., 1995), 253. Kenneth W. Noe, ed., *A Southern Boy in Blue: The Memoir of Marcus Woodcock, 9th Kentucky Infantry* (Knoxville, 1996), 299.

36. Daniel E. Sutherland, ed., *Reminiscences of a Private: William E. Bevens of the First Arkansas Infantry, C.S.A.* (Fayetteville, Ark., n.d.), 199.

37. Jones, "History of the 18th Alabama Infantry," 28.

38. Hughes, *Philip Daingerfield Stephenson*, 255.

39. Bailey, *Chessboard*, 37. Hughes, *Philip Daingerfield Stephenson*, 255.

40. Sutherland, *Reminiscences of a Private*, 199, 200, 201. OR 39, pt. 1: 717–23, 803–10.

41. *Charleston Mercury*, October 24, 1864, quoted in Bailey, *Chessboard*, 38. Hughes, *Philip Daingerfield Stephenson*, 256.

42. Brown, ed., *One of Cleburne's Command*, 140.

43. Williams, *Beauregard*, 243. Hood, *Advance and Retreat*, 264. Roman, *Beauregard*, 2:280, 281, 286, 599, 600.

44. Roman, *Beauregard*, 1:242.

45. Ibid., 2:287. Williams, *Beauregard*, 244.

46. Williams, *Beauregard*, 244–45.

47. Hezekiah M. McCorkle diary, October 18, 1864, Civil War Miscellaneous File, GDAH. Hughes, *Philip Daingerfield Stephenson*, 261–62.

48. William Barry Letters, in the Dr. Benjamin F. and William Robert Collection, MDAH. Hughes, *Philip Daingerfield Stephenson*, 262.

49. Jones, "History of the 18th Alabama Infantry," 32.

50. Charles T. Quintard diary, October 25, November 2, November 9, 1864, DuPont Library, University of the South, Sewanee, Tennessee. Also see Moultrie Gerry, *Men Who Made Sewanee* (Sewanee, Tenn., 1981), 35, 47.

51. John Johnston Memoirs, 129, Confederate Collection, TSLA.

52. Hughes, *Philip Daingerfield Stephenson*, 266. McCorkle diary, November 13, 1864. John Crittenden to wife, October 31, 1864, Auburn University Archives, Alabama.

53. Barry to sister, November 16, 1864, Barry Letters. Johnston Memoirs, 129. James Porter Crane to "Dear Pa," November 17, 1864, Atlanta Historical Society, Georgia. John Crittenden to wife, November 10, 1864, Auburn University Archives.

54. John Crittenden's last letter, November 1864 (the day is not clear), Auburn University Archives.

55. Brown, ed., *One of Cleburne's Command*, 145.

56. Foote, *Civil War*, 3:654. J. W. Harmon Memoirs, 55, Confederate Collection, TSLA. Thomas Hopkins Davenport diary, 29, 31, Confederate Collection, TSLA.

57. Hughes, *Philip Daingerfield Stephenson*, 276.

58. McDonough and Connelly, *Five Tragic Hours*, 18. To fully evaluate Hood see also John P. Dyer, *The Gallant Hood* (Indianapolis and New York, 1950); Richard M. McMurry, *John Bell Hood and the War for Southern Independence* (Lexington, Ky., 1982); Richard O'Conner, *Hood: Cavalier General* (New York, 1949); and of course Hood, *Advance and Retreat*.

59. Robert A. Jarman, "History of Co. K, 27th Mississippi Infantry," 41, in Jarman MSS, MDAH.

60. Quintard diary, November 22 and 23, 1864.

61. Hughes, *Philip Daingerfield Stephenson*, 277. McCorkle diary, November 26, 1864. Johnston Memoirs, 135. Brown, ed., *One of Cleburne's Command*, 146.

62. McDonough, *Schofield*, 104.

63. Ibid., 105.

64. Nimrod Porter diary, December 14, November 24, and December 11, 1864, SHC. The Confederacy repealed the right to furnish a substitute in December 1863.

Chapter 3 * A Run of Luck in Our Favor

1. Smith, *Majestic Middle Tennessee*, 59.

2. Ibid., 62. David E. Roth, "The Mysteries of Spring Hill, Tennessee," *Blue & Gray Magazine* 2 (October–November 1984): 14.

3. Smith, *Majestic Middle Tennessee*, 62.

4. Ibid., 61. David E. Roth, "The General's Tour of Spring Hill, Tennessee," *Blue & Gray Magazine* 2 (October–November 1984): 37–38. Wyemouth T. Jordan, *George Washington Campbell of Tennessee: Western Statesman* (Tallahassee, 1955), 152, 198–99.

5. Bruce Catton, *Never Call Retreat* (New York, 1965), 409.

6. Smith, *Majestic Middle Tennessee*, 58.

7. Frank H. Smith, *History of Maury County, Tennessee* (compiled by the Maury County Historical Society, 1969), 238.

8. J. D. Remington, "The Cause of Hood's Failure at Spring Hill," *Confederate Veteran*, 21 (1913): 569–70.

9. Stanley F. Horn, "The Spring Hill Legend," *Civil War Times Illustrated* 8 (April 1969): 20–32.

10. Hay, *Hood's Tennessee Campaign*, 102.

11. Hood, *Advance and Retreat*, 283.

12. Quintard diary, November 27, 28, 29, 1864.

13. Connelly, *Autumn of Glory*, 492. OR 45, pt. 1: 720.

14. OR 45, pt. 1: 712, 687, 693, 720.

15. Hood, *Advance and Retreat*, 283.

16. Clement Evans, ed., *Confederate Military History*, 12 vols. (Atlanta, 1889), 8:302–4. Joe Spence diary, 1861–62, Confederate Collection, TSLA. Christopher Losson, "Major General Benjamin Franklin Cheatham and the Battle of Stone's River," *Tennessee Historical Quarterly* 41 (fall 1982): 278–92. Ezra Warner Jr., *Generals in Gray: Lives of the Confederate Commanders* (Baton Rouge, 1959), 47–48.

17. Smith, *Majestic Middle Tennessee*, 38. Hay, *Hood's Tennessee Campaign*, 103.

18. OR 39, pt. 2: 442. Edward G. Longacre, *From Union Stars to Top Hat: A Biography of the Extraordinary James Harrison Wilson* (Harrisburg, Pa., 1972), 155, 144.

19. Bruce Catton, *Grant Takes Command* (Boston, 1969), 499. James H. Wilson, *Under the Old Flag*, 2 vols. (New York, 1912), 2:115, 116.

20. Robert S. Henry, *"First with the Most" Forrest* (Indianapolis, 1944), 388.

21. Hay, *Hood's Tennessee Campaign*, 103. *OR* 45, pt. 1: 1089.

22. *OR* 45, pt. l: 558–59, 588. Longacre, *Wilson*, 169–70.

23. Longacre, *Wilson*, 169.

24. Ibid., 168–71. Sword, *Angry Wind*, 103, 105, 110–13. Hay, *Hood's Tennessee Campaign*, 104–9. *OR* 45, pt. 1: 53, 54, 558, 559, 588, 1112, 1144–46, 1169.

25. *OR* 45, pt. 1: 147, 148, 341, 342, 1108, 1141–43. William M. Wherry, "The Franklin Campaign," Schofield MSS. Hay, *Hood's Tennessee Campaign*, 99. Schofield, *Forty-six Years in the Army*, 214, 215, 230. Cox, *Battle of Franklin*, 27.

26. *OR* 45, pt. 1: 1141.

27. Wherry, "Franklin Campaign."

28. Elizabeth Longford, *Wellington: The Years of the Sword* (New York, 1969), 489.

29. *OR* 45, pt. 1: 113, 148, 1070, 1152. Horn, *Army of Tennessee*, 385. McDonough, *Schofield*, 111. McDonough and Connelly, *Five Tragic Hours*, 44–45.

30. Stanley, *Memoirs*, 195. *OR* 45, pt. 1: 113, 229, 239.

31. Stanley, *Memoirs*, 195. *OR* 45, pt. 1: 113, 148, 230, 239, 250, 255, 275.

32. J. P. Young, "Hood's Failure at Spring Hill," *Confederate Veteran* 16 (1908): 30. In addition to Wagner's division, the One Hundred Third Ohio had arrived earlier, on duty as a train guard; and two hundred men of the Twelfth Tennessee Cavalry were also on hand. Foote placed the artillery pieces at thirty-four (*Civil War*, 3:659). Henry noted that "most of Schofield's artillery" was at Spring Hill, while "the Confederates were virtually without guns" (*Forrest*, 391).

33. Young, "Hood's Failure," 31. Henry, *Forrest*, 389.

34. Henry, *Forrest*, 390. Foote, *Civil War*, 3:658. Hay, *Hood's Tennessee Campaign*, 85. Young, "Hood's Failure," 31. Connelly, *Autumn of Glory*, 494.

35. Smith, *History of Maury County*, 237.

36. Ibid., 238.

37. Ibid., 238, 254.

38. Ibid., 254, 238. Roth, "Mysteries of Spring Hill," 31.

39. Horn, *Army of Tennessee*, 386–87. Young, "Hood's Failure," 31. Hay, *Hood's Tennessee Campaign*, 86. McDonough and Connelly, *Five Tragic Hours*, 45–46. Losson, *Cheatham*, 204. Benjamin F. Cheatham, "The Lost Opportunity at Spring Hill, Tennessee—General Cheatham's Reply to General Hood," *Southern Historical Society Papers* 9 (1881): 524–25. Buck, *Cleburne and His Command*, 265.

40. Young, "Hood's Failure," 32. McDonough and Connelly, *Five Tragic Hours*, 46. Horn, *Army of Tennessee*, 387. Hay, *Hood's Tennessee Campaign*, 87–88. *OR* 45, pt. 1: 114.

41. *OR* 45, pt. 1: 742. Buck, *Cleburne and His Command*, 267.

42. *OR* 45, pt. 1: 742. Losson, *Cheatham*, 205. Smith, *History of Maury County*, 238.

43. Young, "Hood's Failure," 33–34. Hay, *Hood's Tennessee Campaign*, 89–90. Horn, *Army of Tennessee*, 388. McDonough and Connelly, *Five Tragic Hours*, 48. Buck, *Cleburne and His Command*, 268.

44. *OR* 45, pt. 1: 712. Young, "Hood's Failure," 39. Horn, *Army of Tennessee*, 388–89. Connelly, *Autumn of Glory*, 497.

45. Campbell Brown's record of his "remarkable conversation" with Isham Harris, May 5 and August 14, 1868, in the Campbell Brown–Richard S. Ewell Papers, TSLA.
46. McDonough and Connelly, *Five Tragic Hours*, 48–49. Connelly, *Autumn of Glory*, 497. Cheatham, "Lost Opportunity," 535. Young, "Hood's Failure," 39.
47. Young, "Hood's Failure," 39.
48. Ibid.
49. *OR* 45, pt. 1: 713. Young, "Hood's Failure," 39. Connelly, *Autumn of Glory*, 499. Henry, *Forrest*, 393.
50. Henry, *Forrest*, 393.
51. Campbell Brown's conversation with Harris, 1868, in the Brown-Ewell Papers.
52. Buel and Johnson, *Battles and Leaders*, 4:438, 439. Henry, *Forrest*, 393–94.
53. McDonough and Connelly, *Five Tragic Hours*, 50–51. Losson, *Cheatham*, 208. Buel and Johnson, *Battles and Leaders*, 4:431, 432, 439.
54. Roth, "Mysteries of Spring Hill," 28.
55. Buel and Johnson, *Battles and Leaders*, 4:439.
56. Samuel G. French diary and autobiography, November 30, 1864, in Samuel G. French Papers, MDAH.
57. Losson, *Cheatham*, 208. Buel and Johnson, *Battles and Leaders*, 4:432, 439. Buck, *Cleburne and His Command*, 274. McDonough and Connelly, *Five Tragic Hours*, 52.
58. *OR* 45, pt. 1: 114, 148, 342. Cox, *Battle of Franklin*, 34.
59. Wherry, "Franklin Campaign." *OR* 45, pt. 1: 148, 342. Cox, *Battle of Franklin*, 5.
60. Roth, "Mysteries of Spring Hill," 21. Sword, *Angry Wind*, 152. *OR* 45, pt. 1: 148.
61. Schofield, *Forty-six Years in the Army*, 173–74. Buel and Johnson, *Battles and Leaders*, 4:447. Cox, *Battle of Franklin*, 34.
62. *OR* 45, pt. 1: 114, 115. Stanley, *Memoirs*, 205.
63. Young, "Hood's Failure," 36.
64. Smith, *Majestic Middle Tennessee*, 59.
65. Hood, *Advance and Retreat*, 286, 290.
66. Connelly, *Autumn of Glory*, 501. Losson, *Cheatham*, 207.
67. Wilson, *Under the Old Flag*, 2:44. Losson, *Cheatham*, 212, 321, see note 45.
68. Elliott, *Soldier of Tennessee*, 234, 235. Young, "Hood's Failure," 39.
69. McDonough and Connelly, *Five Tragic Hours*, 56.
70. Ibid., 57–58.
71. Ibid., 58.
72. Smith, *History of Maury County*, 246.
73. McDonough and Connelly, *Five Tragic Hours*, 58.
74. Losson, *Cheatham*, 325.
75. Smith, *History of Maury County*, 238–39.
76. Roth, "Mysteries of Spring Hill," 28.
77. Buck, *Cleburne and His Command*, 80.
78. Johnston Memoirs, 138.

79. Bailey, *Chessboard*, 88.

80. Hood, *Advance and Retreat*, 290.

81. J. P. Cannon diary, November 29, 1864. *A History of the Seventy-third Illinois Infantry Volunteers* (Springfield, 1890), 475. This book gives the Mississippian's entire account.

82. Alexander P. Stewart letter, February 16, 1886, Lionel Baxter Collections, Civil War Times Illustrated Collection (hereafter cited as CWTI Collection), USAMHI.

83. Stanley, *Memoirs*, 214.

Chapter 4 * General Hood Has Betrayed Us

1. Cox, *Battle of Franklin*, 37, 38. W. W. Gist, "The Battle of Franklin," *Tennessee Historical Magazine* 6 (October 1920): 220. Charles T. Clark, *125th Ohio Volunteer Infantry: Opdycke Tigers* (Columbus, 1895), 332. OR 45, pt. 1: 349, 358, 1107, 1108, 1138. Hay, *Hood's Tennessee Campaign*, 118.

2. Cox, *Battle of Franklin*, 39.

3. Ibid., 39, 49, 50. Clark, *125th Ohio*, 328. L. G. Bennett and W. M. Haigh, *History of the Thirty-sixth Regiment of Illinois Volunteers* (Aurora, Ill., 1876), 647, 648.

4. OR 45, pt. 1: 432. McDonough and Connelly, *Five Tragic Hours*, 80, 81.

5. OR 45, pt. 1: 1117, 1145, 1169.

6. "Williamson County," *The Tennessee Encyclopedia of History and Culture* (Nashville, 1998), 1063.

7. Smith, *Majestic Middle Tennessee*, 68–69.

8. Ibid., 74–75.

9. Arthur B. Carter, *The Tarnished Cavalier: Major General Earl Van Dorn, C.S.A.* (Knoxville, 1999), 174–76.

10. McDonough and Connelly, *Five Tragic Hours*, 96. OR 45, pt. 1: 348–51. Hay, *Hood's Tennessee Campaign*, 118, 119.

11. OR 45, pt. 1: 425, 429–30. Connelly, *Autumn of Glory*, 503. Horn, *Army of Tennessee*, 397. Buel and Johnson, *Battles and Leaders*, 4:449.

12. OR 45, pt. 1: 410, 411, 419, 421, 425. McDonough and Connelly, *Five Tragic Hours*, 81, 119.

13. McDonough and Connelly, *Five Tragic Hours*, 84. OR 45, pt. 1: 240, 320, 326, 330, 334. Horn, *Army of Tennessee*, 397.

14. McDonough and Connelly, *Five Tragic Hours*, 131.

15. Cox, *Battle of Franklin*, 82–84. McDonough and Connelly, *Five Tragic Hours*, 85.

16. OR 45, pt. 1: 240.

17. Ibid., 364, 365, 379, 389. Buel and Johnson, *Battles and Leaders*, 4:449.

18. OR 45, pt. 1: 184, 195, 208.

19. Ibid., 208.

20. Ibid., 195.

21. Ibid., 214.

22. Ibid., 217.

23. Ibid., 223.
24. Ibid., 184.
25. Ibid., 743.
26. McDonough and Connelly, *Five Tragic Hours*, 99.
27. *OR* 45, pt. 1: 115.
28. Cox, *Battle of Franklin*, 68.
29. *OR* 45, pt. 1: 1169, 1170, 1171. Cox, *Battle of Franklin*, 68.
30. *OR* 45, pt. 1: 115, 231, 240, 270, 342, 348, 349, 352, 1174. John K. Shellenberger, "The Battle of Franklin," in *Glimpses of the Nation's Struggle*, series 5, *MOLLUS*, Minnesota Commandery, 1903, 497.
31. Shellenberger, "Battle of Franklin," 497–98.
32. Cox, *Battle of Franklin*, 68, 87.
33. *OR* 45, pt. 1: 1178. Wilson, *Under the Old Flag*, 2:51.
34. *OR* 45, pt. 1: 1170.
35. Lewis, *Sherman*, 426.
36. Hughes, *Philip Daingerfield Stephenson*, 280.
37. Buck, *Cleburne and His Command*, 277–78.
38. Joseph Boyce, "Missourians in the Battle of Franklin," *Confederate Veteran* 24 (1916): 102. J. P. Cannon diary, November 29, 1864.
39. Sword, *Angry Wind*, 178.
40. Foote, *Civil War*, 3:663–64.
41. Horn, *Army of Tennessee*, 397–98.
42. Henry, *Forrest*, 397. John Allan Wyeth, *That Devil Forrest: Life of General Nathan Bedford Forrest* (1899; reprint, New York, 1959), 544. Brian Steel Wills, *A Battle from the Start: The Life of Nathan Bedford Forrest* (New York, 1992), 285.
43. Losson, *Cheatham*, 218.
44. Buck, *Cleburne and His Command*, 280.
45. Horn, *Army of Tennessee*, 398.
46. Losson, *Cheatham*, 218.
47. Liddell Hart, *Sherman*, 123.
48. Losson, *Cheatham*, 219.
49. A. P. Stewart to S. G. French, April 20, 1897, French Papers.
50. Symonds, *Cleburne*, 255.
51. Joe Clark Memoirs, TSLA.
52. Bailey, *Chessboard*, 97.
53. Hood, *Advance and Retreat*, 294.
54. Buck, *Cleburne and His Command*, 290.
55. Ibid., 290.
56. Ibid., 281. David R. Logsdon, ed., *Eyewitnesses at the Battle of Franklin* (Nashville, 1988), 6–7.
57. Buck, *Cleburne and His Command*, 290–91.

58. Sword, *Angry Wind*, 184.
59. Watkins, *"Co. Aytch,"* 234.
60. Logsdon, *Battle of Franklin*, 7–8.
61. Losson, *Cheatham*, 219. Johnston Memoirs, 141. Symonds, *Cleburne*, 256. Boyce, "Missourians," 102. Carey C. Jewell, *Harvest of Death: A Detailed Account of the Army of Tennessee at the Battle of Franklin* (Hicksville, N.Y., 1976), 51.
62. Logsdon, *Battle of Franklin*, 6.
63. R. W. Banks, *The Battle of Franklin* (New York, 1908), 58–59.
64. Boyce, "Missourians," 102.
65. J. P. Cannon diary, November 29, 1864.
66. Hughes, *Philip Daingerfield Stephenson*, 281. Johnston Memoirs, 141.
67. *OR* 45, pt. 1: 737.
68. Boyce, "Missourians," 102.
69. James Lee McDonough, "The Battle at Franklin," *Blue & Gray Magazine* 1 (September 1984): 25.
70. Foote, *Civil War*, 3:667.
71. McDonough and Connelly, *Five Tragic Hours*, 124.
72. Shellenberger, "Battle of Franklin," 498.
73. Groom, *Shrouds of Glory*, 180.
74. Shellenberger, "Battle of Franklin," 500–501.
75. *OR* 45, pt. 1: 353. Brown, ed., *One of Cleburne's Command*, 148–49.
76. McDonough and Connelly, *Five Tragic Hours*, 113.
77. Ibid.
78. *OR* 45, pt. 1: 116, 240, 244, 248, 253, 353, 389–90, 393, 412, 415–16, 418, 421. McDonough and Connelly, *Five Tragic Hours*, 115.
79. *OR* 45, pt. 1: 116.
80. Ibid., 116, 240. *History of the Seventy-third Illinois*, 472.
81. James Lee McDonough, *Chattanooga—A Death Grip on the Confederacy* (Knoxville, 1984), 199–200. *OR* 45, pt. 1: 253. Groom, *Shrouds of Glory*, 189.
82. McDonough and Connelly, *Five Tragic Hours*, 117.
83. *OR* 45, pt. 1: 240, 244.
84. Ibid., 418.
85. McDonough and Connelly, *Five Tragic Hours*, 118. *OR* 45, pt. 1: 116.
86. McDonough and Connelly, *Five Tragic Hours*, 119.
87. *OR* 45, pt. 1: 354.
88. John K. Shellenberger, *The Battle of Franklin* (Cleveland, 1916), 39, 40.
89. James B. Steedman, "Robbing the Dead," *New York Times,* June 22, 1881.
90. Hay, *Hood's Tennessee Campaign*, 126.
91. *OR* 45, pt. 1: 331, 338. Buel and Johnson, *Battles and Leaders*, 4:449.
92. *OR* 45, pt. 1: 720–21.

93. McDonough and Connelly, *Five Tragic Hours*, 121–22.
94. McDonough, "Battle at Franklin," 28.
95. McDonough and Connelly, *Five Tragic Hours*, 150–51.
96. Ibid., 157. McDonough, "Battle at Franklin," 28. This death toll is slightly larger than the Confederates suffered in the two-day battle of Shiloh, where their army was twice as large as at Franklin; and several hundred larger than at Stones River, fought over a three-day period, and also involving a much larger Confederate force.
97. William R. Hartpence, *History of the Fifty-first Indiana Veteran Volunteer Infantry Regiment* (Cincinnati, 1894), 242, 244.
98. *History of the Seventy-third Illinois*, 478–79.
99. Daniel C. Govan to wife, December 4, 1864, Daniel C. Govan Papers, SHC.
100. Virgil S. Murphy diary, 1, 4, 9, SHC.
101. Sword, *Angry Wind*, 302.
102. Jamison and McTigue, eds., *Recollections of a Confederate*, 176.
103. V. H. Rutherford to wife, December 12, 1864. Found by a Federal soldier on the battlefield at Nashville, the letter was published in the *Bucyrus (Ohio) Journal*, February 18, 1865.
104. Brown, ed., *One of Cleburne's Command*, 150–51.
105. *OR* 45, pt. 2: 628.
106. James F. Rusling, *Men and Things I Saw in Civil War Days* (New York, 1899), 86.

Chapter 5 ✦ Fortress on the Cumberland

1. George Rollie Adams and Ralph Jerry Christian, *Nashville: A Pictorial History* (Virginia Beach, 1981), 1, 2.
2. Robert E. Corlew, *Tennessee: A Short History* (Knoxville, 1981), 106. Adams and Christian, *Nashville*, 3. Anita Shafer Goodstein, *Nashville, 1780–1860: From Frontier to City* (Gainesville, 1989), 47."Timothy Demonbreun," *Tennessee Encyclopedia*, 243.
3. "James Robertson," "Nashville," *Tennessee Encyclopedia*, 802, 669. Adams and Christian, *Nashville*, 4.
4. "James Robertson," *Tennessee Encyclopedia*, 802. Corlew, *Tennessee*, 53.
5. Adams and Christian, *Nashville*, 1. Corlew, *Tennessee*, 52. "Charlotte Reeves Robertson," "John Donelson," *Tennessee Encyclopedia*, 801, 255.
6. Corlew, *Tennessee*, 52.
7. Goodstein, *Nashville*, 2.
8. "Charlotte Reeves Robertson," *Tennessee Encyclopedia*, 801. Adams and Christian, *Nashville*, 2, 5.
9. Adams and Christian, *Nashville*, 2. "James Robertson," *Tennessee Encyclopedia*, 803.
10. Goodstein, *Nashville*, 3.
11. "James Robertson," *Tennessee Encyclopedia*, 803. Goodstein, *Nashville*, 9.

12. "Andrew Jackson," *Tennessee Encyclopedia*, 469. Adams and Christian, *Nashville*, 7.

13. Corlew, *Tennessee*, 266.

14. Adams and Christian, *Nashville*, 19.

15. "Nashville," *Tennessee Encyclopedia*, 670. Adams and Christian, *Nashville*, 19.

16. Goodstein, *Nashville*, 190. Adams and Christian, *Nashville*, 19.

17. Charles B. Castner, Ronald Flanary, and Patrick Dorin, *Louisville & Nashville Railroad: The Old Reliable* (Lynchburg, Va., 1996), 1. Kincaid A. Herr, *The Louisville & Nashville Railroad: 1850–1963* (1943; reprint, Lexington, Ky., 2000), 25.

18. Charles Frazier, *Cold Mountain: A Novel* (New York, 1997), 380.

19. "Louisville & Nashville Railroad," "Nashville," *Tennessee Encyclopedia*, 765, 670. Goodstein, *Nashville*, 121.

20. Adams and Christian, *Nashville*, 18–20.

21. James A. Hoobler, *Cities under the Gun: Images of Occupied Nashville and Chattanooga* (Nashville, 1986), 30, 29.

22. Adams and Christian, *Nashville*, 20, 28–29. Hoobler, *Cities*, 99, 29.

23. "The Hermitage," *Tennessee Encyclopedia*, 421. Adams and Christian, *Nashville*, 15.

24. Ridley Wills II, *The History of Belle Meade Mansion, Plantation, and Stud* (Nashville, 1991), 1–54.

25. Adams and Christian, *Nashville*, 29. "Adelicia Acklen," "Belmont Mansion," *Tennessee Encyclopedia*, 1, 60. Mark Grimsley and Todd D. Miller, eds., *The Union Must Stand: The Civil War Diary of John Quincy Adams Campbell, Fifth Iowa Volunteer Infantry* (Knoxville, 2000), 188.

26. Adams and Christian, *Nashville*, 20.

27. Don H. Doyle, *Nashville in the New South, 1880–1930* (Knoxville, 1985), 43.

28. Hoobler, *Cities*, 102.

29. Ibid., 17, 61. Adams and Christian, *Nashville*, 24. Henry McRaven, *Nashville: Athens of the South* (Chapel Hill, N.C., 1949), 93. John H. DeBerry, "Confederate Tennessee" (Ph.D. diss., University of Kentucky, 1967), 212, 236.

30. Adams and Christian, *Nashville*, 24. Thomas P. Lowry, *The Story the Soldiers Wouldn't Tell: Sex in the Civil War* (Mechanicsburg, Pa., 1994), 76.

31. Goodstein, *Nashville*, 141. Adams and Christian, *Nashville*, 20. Lowry, *Soldiers Wouldn't Tell*, 77. David Kaser, "Nashville's Women of Pleasure in 1860," *Tennessee Historical Quarterly* 4 (December 1964): 379–81.

32. Goodstein, *Nashville*, 205.

33. Stephen V. Ash, *Middle Tennessee Society Transformed, 1860–1870: War and Peace in the Upper South* (Baton Rouge, 1988), 64.

34. Heidler and Heidler, "John Bell," *Encyclopedia of the Civil War* 1:205–6. Adams and Christian, *Nashville*, 31.

35. Horn, *Army of Tennessee*, 75.

36. Thomas L. Connelly, *Civil War Tennessee: Battles and Leaders* (Knoxville, 1979), 14.

37. Horn, *Army of Tennessee*, 75. See also Stanley F. Horn, "Nashville during the Civil War," *Tennessee Historical Quarterly* 1 (March 1945): 3–22.

38. J. P. Lesley, *Iron Manufacturer's Guide to the Furnaces, Forges and Rolling Mills of the United States* (New York, 1859), 130–36. J. B. Killebrew, *Middle Tennessee As an Iron Center* (Nashville, 1879), 9–15. Nevins, *War for the Union,* 2:74. Benjamin F. Cooling, *Forts Henry and Donelson: The Key to the Confederate Heartland* (Knoxville, 1987), 45. Thomas L. Connelly, *Army of the Heartland: The Army of Tennessee, 1861–1862* (Baton Rouge, 1967), 8–10.

39. Horn, *Army of Tennessee,* 78. Corlew, *Tennessee,* 305.

40. *CWD,* 63, 932–35, 41.

41. Connelly, *Civil War Tennessee,* 15.

42. Henry, *Story of the Confederacy,* 79.

43. McPherson, *Ordeal by Fire,* 223.

44. George W. Johnson to wife, February 15, 1862, George W. Johnson Papers, Manuscript Department, FCHS.

45. James Lee McDonough, *Shiloh—In Hell Before Night* (Knoxville, 1977), 8.

46. Horn, "Nashville," 8.

47. Horn, *Army of Tennessee,* 100.

48. Horn, "Nashville," 9–10. Adams and Christian, *Nashville,* 32.

49. Horn, "Nashville," 15–16.

50. Adams and Christian, *Nashville,* 41.

51. Horn, "Nashville," 12.

52. McDonough, *Stones River,* 16.

53. John Fitch, *Annals of the Army of the Cumberland* (Philadelphia, 1864), 457.

54. Horn, "Nashville," 16. Stanley F. Horn, "Dr. John Rolfe Hudson and the Confederate Underground in Nashville," *Tennessee Historical Quarterly* 1 (March 1963): 43, 44. Louise Davis, "Box Seat on the Civil War," *Tennessean Magazine* 2 (March–April 1979): 32.

55. McDonough, *Stones River,* 16.

56. Walter T. Durham, *Reluctant Partners: Nashville and the Union, July 1, 1863, to June 30, 1865* (Nashville, 1987), 33, 34.

57. Ibid., 143.

58. Stanley F. Horn, *The Decisive Battle of Nashville* (1956; reprint, Knoxville, 1968), 24.

59. Henry Romeyn, "With Colored Troops in the Army of the Cumberland," *MOLLUS,* District of Columbia, 3 (1904):54–55.

60. Benjamin Franklin Wade, letter to "Brother Samuel," June 23, 1864, Federal Collection, TSLA. McDonough, *Stones River,* 57. Durham, *Reluctant Partners,* 47.

61. Durham, *Reluctant Partners,* 46.

62. Lowry, *Soldiers Wouldn't Tell,* 83.

63. Ibid., 80.

64. Ibid.

65. Durham, *Reluctant Partners,* 47, 48.

66. Lowry, *Soldiers Wouldn't Tell,* 82. Durham, *Reluctant Partners,* 114, 115.

67. Durham, *Reluctant Partners*, 203.

68. *OR* 16, pt. 2: 268.

69. Horn, "Nashville," 13. Adams and Christian, *Nashville*, 38, 34.

70. Hoobler, *Cities*, 111. "Fort Negley," *Tennessee Encyclopedia*, 327. Horn, *Decisive Battle*, 25, 26. Adams and Christian, *Nashville*, 38, 39.

71. Horn, *Decisive Battle*, 24. Heidler and Heidler, "McCooks of Ohio," *Encyclopedia of the Civil War* 3:1279–80.

72. Adams and Christian, *Nashville*, 38.

73. Durham, *Reluctant Partners*, 122–24. McDonough, *Stones River*, 116, 155–57.

74. Durham, *Reluctant Partners*, 122–24, 220–22. Horn, *Decisive Battle*, 28–30. Adams and Christian, *Nashville*, 38.

Chapter 6 * "Siege" at Nashville, Folly at Murfreesboro

1. *OR* 45, pt. 2: 643–44, 650.

2. Livermore, *Numbers and Losses*, 133. Hood, *Advance and Retreat*, 299.

3. Hood, *Advance and Retreat*, 299, 300.

4. *OR* 45, pt. 2: 639, 766.

5. Samuel G. French, *Two Wars: An Autobiography* (Nashville, 1901). 304.

6. Hood, *Advance and Retreat*, 299.

7. Johnston Memoirs, 142. James L. Cooper Memoirs, 50–51, TSLA.

8. McDonough and Connelly, *Five Tragic Hours*, 166.

9. Hughes, *Philip Daingerfield Stephenson*, 289.

10. McDonough and Connelly, *Five Tragic Hours*, 161, 166.

11. James A. McCord to John W. McCord, December 3, 1864, Confederate Collection, TSLA.

12. Logsdon, *Battle of Franklin*, 44.

13. Joseph N. Thompson, "History of the 35th Alabama Infantry," 20, ALDAH.

14. Quintard diary, December 2, 1864.

15. Ibid., December 3, 1864.

16. Buck, *Cleburne and His Command*, 280.

17. Lee to wife, December 6, 1864, James Harrison Papers, SHC.

18. Smith, *Majestic Middle Tennessee*, 78. Robert Brandt, *Touring the Middle Tennessee Backroads* (Winston-Salem, N.C., 1995), 134–36. Virginia McDaniel Bowman, *Historic Williamson County: Old Homes and Sites* (Nashville, 1971), 97.

19. Schofield, *Forty-six Years in the Army*, 226. Schofield to J. D. Cox, December 5, 1881, Schofield MSS. Rusling, *Men and Things I Saw*, 87–88. Livermore, *Numbers and Losses*, 132.

20. *OR* 45, pt. 2: 641.

21. Hughes, *Philip Daingerfield Stephenson*, 319–20.

22. Connelly, *Autumn of Glory*, 508. Steven E. Woodworth, *Jefferson Davis and His Generals: The Failure of Confederate Command in the West* (Lawrence, Kans., 1990), 301.

23. Hay, *Hood's Tennessee Campaign*, 151, 152.

24. Connelly, *Autumn of Glory*, 508.

25. Hay, *Hood's Tennessee Campaign*, 170.

26. Horn, *Decisive Battle*, 36.

27. *OR* 45, pt. 1: 744.

28. Henry, *Forrest*, 403. Hay, *Hood's Tennessee Campaign*, 168. Horn, *Decisive Battle*, 36, 37, 41. Connelly, *Autumn of Glory*, 507. Foote, *Civil War*, 3:677, 678.

29. Sword, *Angry Wind*, 281.

30. McDonough, *War in Kentucky*, 48–53.

31. Edwin Bearss, and Charles Spearman, "The Battle of the Cedars," 1, unpublished account in the Stones River National Military Park files, Murfreesboro, Tennessee.

32. *OR* 45, pt. 1: 755.

33. Milroy to wife, January 1, 1865, in the Robert H. Milroy Papers, Indiana Historical Society, Indianapolis.

34. Milroy to wife, October 23, 1864, Milroy Papers.

35. Robert H. Milroy diary, January 1, 1865, Milroy Papers.

36. *OR* 45, pt. 1: 755.

37. Milroy to wife, January 1, 1865, Milroy Papers.

38. *OR* 45, pt. 1: 746.

39. Ibid.

40. Wyeth, *Forrest*, 487.

41. *OR* 45, pt. 1: 746.

42. Sword, *Angry Wind*, 297.

43. Wyeth, *Forrest*, 488. Herbert S. Norris and James R. Long, "The Road to Redemption," Civil War Times 5 (August 1997): 37.

44. Bearss and Spearman, "Battle of the Cedars," 8. OR 45, pt. l, 756.

45. Milroy to wife, December 26, 1864, Milroy Papers.

46. Milroy to wife, January 1, 1865. Mary to Milroy, December 29, 1864, Milroy Papers.

47. W. S. Carson to Elvira, December 19, 1864, Carson Family Papers, GDAH.

48. *OR* 45, pt. 2: 3.

49. Ibid., 15–16.

50. Ibid., 70, 96.

51. Ibid., 17. U. S. Grant, *Personal Memoirs of U. S. Grant*, 2 vols. (New York, 1886), 2:380.

52. *OR* 45, pt. 2: 84.

53. Ibid., 114.

54. Lucius F. Hubbard, "Minnesota in the Battle of Nashville, December 15–16, 1864," *MOLLUS*, Minnesota, 1909, 6:271. Connelly, *Autumn of Glory*, 508. Horn, *Army of Tennessee*, 410. Foote, *Civil War*, 3:679.

55. Jones, "History of the 18th Alabama Infantry," 45–46. McCorkle diary, December 11, 1864. Cannon diary, December 11, 1864.

56. Brewer, "History of the 23rd Alabama Infantry," 49. Jones, "History of the 18th Alabama Infantry," 45–46.

57. Barry to sister, December 8, 1864, Barry Letters.

58. F. A. Cline to wife, December 12, 1864, Daisy J. Cline Papers, Missouri Historical Society, St. Louis.

59. A. T. Bartlett Reminiscences, 46, Missouri Historical Society, St. Louis.

60. Martin Lewis Hursh diary, Indiana Historical Society, Indianapolis.

61. Nathaniel Cheairs Hughes, *The Pride of the Confederate Artillery: The Washington Artillery in the Army of Tennessee* (Baton Rouge, 1997), 247.

62. *OR* 45, pt. 2: 115.

63. Cleaves, *Rock of Chickamauga,* 259.

64. Van Horn, *Thomas,* 320.

65. Wilson, *Under the Old Flag,* 2:100–102.

66. Schofield, *Forty-six Years in the Army,* 238. Cox, *Franklin and Nashville,* 105.

67. Steedman, "Robbing the Dead."

68. Sanford C. Kellog to David S. Stanley, January 12, 1881, in the West-Stanley-Wright Family Papers, USAMHI.

69. McDonough, *Schofield,* 131–34.

70. Schofield MSS.

71. Schofield, *Forty-six Years in the Army,* 236.

72. *OR* 45, pt. 2: 180.

73. *OR* 45, pt. 1: 37. Livermore, *Numbers and Losses,* 133.

Chapter 7 * A Perfect Slaughter Pen

1. Buel and Johnson, *Battles and Leaders,* 4:457. Henry M. Kendall, "The Battles of Franklin and Nashville," *MOLLUS,* District of Columbia, 2 (1902):369. James Robert Maxwell, *Autobiography of James Robert Maxwell* (1926; reprint, Baltimore, 1996), 266. Horn, *Decisive Battle,* 73. McKinney, *Education in Violence,* 406. Noah Andre Trudeau, *Like Men of War: Black Troops in the Civil War, 1862–1865* (New York, 1998), 341. *OR* 45, pt. 1: 128. Durham, *Reluctant Partners,* 242.

2. Ed Huddleston, "The Civil War in Middle Tennessee," pt. 4, *Nashville Banner,* November 14, 1964, 27.

3. Horn, *Decisive Battle,* 73. Buel and Johnson, *Battles and Leaders,* 4:457. Determining precisely what high ground Thomas occupied during the day of December 15 is not easy. It seems reasonable that he would have spent time on both heights, which together provided the best views of the battle area. To move much more might have made it difficult for staff officers to locate the army's commander.

4. *ORN* 26:650. *OR* 45, pt. 1: 38.

5. *ORN* 26:651. *OR* 45, pt. 1: 38.

6. George R. Lee, "Battle at Nashville," *Brighton (Colorado) Register,* in CWTI Collection, USAMHI.

7. Bobby Lovett, "Negro's Civil War in Tennessee," *Journal of Negro History* 1 (January 1976): 47.

8. Glenn Tucker, *Chickamauga: Bloody Battle in the West* (Dayton, Ohio, 1972), 348.

9. Stanley, *Memoirs*, 191. McKinney, *Education in Violence*, 406.

10. Tucker, *Chickamauga*, 341.

11. Lovett, "Negro's Civil War," 39–43.

12. Thomas Jefferson Morgan, *Reminiscences of Service with Colored Troops in the Army of the Cumberland, 1863–1865* (Providence, 1885), 88. George Washington Williams, *A History of the Negro Troops in the War of the Rebellion, 1861–1865* (New York, 1888), 273.

13. Romeyn, "With Colored Troops," 3:59.

14. McKinney, *Education in Violence*, 404.

15. Lovett, "Negro's Civil War," 42.

16. Trudeau, *Like Men of War*, 277.

17. Ibid., 277, 281.

18. *OR* 45, pt. 1: 504, 527.

19. Ibid., 536.

20. Ibid., 536, 537.

21. Wirt Armistead Cate, ed., *Two Soldiers: The Campaign Diaries of Thomas J. Key, C.S.A., and Robert J. Campbell, U.S.A.* (Chapel Hill, N.C., 1938), 168.

22. Jones, "History of the 18th Alabama Infantry," 28.

23. Charles D. Martin, "Jackson's Brigade in the Battle of Nashville," *Confederate Veteran* 17 (1909): 12.

24. Hughes, *Philip Daingerfield Stephenson*, 320.

25. Martin, "Jackson's Brigade," 12.

26. Hughes, *Philip Daingerfield Stephenson*, 320.

27. Samuel Alonzo Cook Memoir, 7, TSLA.

28. W. J. McMurray, *History of the Twentieth Tennessee Volunteer Infantry* (Nashville, n.d.), 347.

29. Cook Memoir, 7. Martin, "Jackson's Brigade," 12. Cate, ed., *Two Soldiers*, 168.

30. Bennett and Haigh, *Thirty-sixth Illinois*, 675.

31. Lovett, "Negro's Civil War," 48.

32. Durham, *Reluctant Partners*, 243.

33. Hugh Walker, "Blacks Fought in the Battle of Nashville," *Tennessean*, August 1, 1976.

34. Ibid.

35. Hughes, *Philip Daingerfield Stephenson*, 320.

36. Sword, *Angry Wind*, 357, 325, 318.

37. *OR* 45, pt. 1: 527, 504, 739.

38. Ibid., 527. J. M. Benedict, who took command of the Eighteenth Ohio when Captain Grosvenor was killed, said the captain was "pierced by three balls." *OR* 45, pt. 1: 530.

39. *OR* 45, pt. 1: 542–43.
40. Hughes, *Philip Daingerfield Stephenson,* 321–22.
41. Hal Engerud, "Munfordville: The Home of Two Civil War Generals," written for the *Hart County News,* bicentennial edition. Reissued in pamphlet form, February 8, 1974. Copy in files of the Hart County Historical Society. McDonough, *Chattanooga,* 4–8.
42. *OR* 45, pt. 1: 128.
43. Isaac R. Sherwood, *Memories of the War* (Toledo, 1923), 149.
44. *Nashville Dispatch,* December 17, 1864.
45. *OR* 45, pt. 1: 128.
46. Roger Hunt and Jack R. Brown, *Brevet Brigadier Generals in Blue* (Gaithersburg, Mo., 1990), 487.
47. *OR* 45, pt. 1: 289. Wills, *Battle from the Start,* 109–19.
48. *OR* 45, pt. 1: 129.
49. Ibid., 289.
50. McDonough, *War in Kentucky,* 99.
51. *OR* 45, pt. 1: 551, 598–99, 606.
52. Ibid., 765.
53. J. T. Tunnell, "Ector's Brigade in the Battle of Nashville," *Confederate Veteran* 12 (1904): 348–49. *OR* 45, pt. 1: 765.
54. *OR* 45, pt. 1: 765.
55. Ibid., 599.
56. Ibid.
57. Ibid., 600, 765.
58. Ibid., 599–600.
59. Durham, *Reluctant Partners,* 250.
60. *ORN* 26: 651. Horn, *Decisive Battle,* 84.
61. Horn, *Decisive Battle,* 84.
62. James Dinkins, *Personal Recollections and Experiences* (Cincinnati, 1897), 247.
63. *OR* 45, pt. 1: 765.

Chapter 8 * Situation Perilous in the Extreme

1. Maxwell, *Autobiography,* 266.
2. *OR* 45, pt. 2: 628, 690.
3. Ibid., 690–91.
4. Ibid., 692.
5. *OR* 45, pt. 1: 709.
6. *OR* 45, pt. 2: 672.
7. Ibid. Hood, *Advance and Retreat,* 305. Larry J. Daniel, *Cannoneers in Gray: The Field Artillery of the Army of Tennessee, 1861–1865* (Tuscaloosa, Ala., 1984), 167–81.

8. Foote, *Civil War,* 3:694.
9. Ibid.
10. *OR* 45, pt. 1: 722. Maxwell, *Autobiography,* 266. *OR* 45, pt. 2: 691.
11. Maxwell, *Autobiography,* 267. Foote, *Civil War,* 3:693. *OR* 45, pt. 1: 722.
12. *OR* 45, pt. 1: 708–9.
13. Ibid., 709, 722.
14. Ibid., 722.
15. Heidler and Heidler, "James Harrison Wilson," *Encyclopedia of the Civil War* 4:2124.
16. Longacre, *Wilson,* 179–85.
17. *Nashville Daily Union,* December 14, 1864.
18. *OR* 45, pt. 1: 551.
19. Ibid., 561–62.
20. Longacre, *Wilson,* 185.
21. Heidler and Heidler, "Kenner Garrard," *Encyclopedia of the Civil War* 2:814.
22. Heidler and Heidler, "John McArthur," *Encyclopedia of the Civil War* 3:1269–70.
23. *OR* 45, pt. 2: 201.
24. George H. Heafford, "The Army of the Tennessee," *MOLLUS,* Wisconsin, vol. 1 (1888): 317.
25. *OR* 45, pt. 1: 589, 551.
26. Ibid., 589.
27. Ibid., 563, 577, 589, 590, 440.
28. Lewis F. Phillips, *Some Things Our Boys Saw in the War* (Garrity, Iowa, 1911), 70–71.
29. *OR* 45, pt. 1: 589.
30. Ibid., 577, 590.
31. Ibid., 590.
32. Maxwell, *Autobiography,* 268, 269.
33. Ibid.
34. Ibid.
35. Ibid., 271. Daniel, *Cannoneers in Gray,* 233.
36. *OR* 45, pt. 1: 590, 595, 438.
37. Ibid., 590. O. A. Abbott, "The Last Battle of Nashville," *MOLLUS,* Omaha, Nebraska, 1902, 239.
38. Abbott, "Last Battle of Nashville," 239.
39. *OR* 45, pt. 1: 590. Abbott, "Last Battle of Nashville," 239.
40. *OR* 45, pt. 1: 590–91.
41. Ibid., 577, 590.
42. Ibid., 438. A careful examination of the pertinent primary sources, mostly from the *OR* and eleven in number, reveals that Confederate redoubt number four

was the first to be attacked by the Federals, followed by an attack on number five. Most accounts of the battle describe number five as the first to be attacked. That number four actually was first is established by several facts. First, it is clear from the report of Confederate General Walthall, the left of whose command lay directly in the rear of number four, and who was responsible for providing two guns in redoubt five and infantry supports for both five and four, that two guns were in number five and four guns in number four (see *OR* 45, pt. 1: 722). Confederate James Maxwell, a sergeant in charge of a gun in redoubt four, also confirmed that number four had four guns (see Maxwell, *Autobiography*, 267). That four guns were in redoubt four and two guns in five is important in determining which redoubt was attacked first, because nine Federal officers, who were in a position to know what happened, reported that four guns were captured in the first redoubt they attacked, and two guns in the second. Thus the Union forces must have attacked number four first and number five second. General Walthall's report indicates this as well. (See the reports of Generals A. J. Smith, John McArthur, James Wilson, and Edward Hatch; Colonels William McMillen, Lucius Hubbard, Josiah Marsh, and Datus Coon; and Lieutenant Sidney Roberts in the *OR* 45, pt. 1, respectively on pages 433–34, 438, 563, 577, 441, 445, 453, 590, and 595. Walthall's report is on page 722.)

While the author believes the above is decisive, there is yet more evidence. General Smith speaks of the troops, after capturing the initial redoubt, "obliquing to the right" and carrying the second fort. This makes sense if they are moving from number four to number five; if vice versa, that is moving from five to four, then "obliquing to the right" would take them away from number four, which lay north and slightly west (left) of five. General Wilson, after reporting the fall of the first redoubt, "with four guns," said the captured guns "were turned upon the enemy occupying a higher hill"; a hill he further described as "still higher than the one already carried, and with steep sides." Redoubt number five did indeed occupy a higher hill than number four. General Hatch reported that the guns captured in the first redoubt were turned "upon the hill commanding it." To speak of redoubt five as occupying a hill "commanding" number four is accurate, but not vice versa. Colonel McMillen's report says "the enemy was found strongly posted on the side and summit of a high hill, with a four-gun battery in his lower and a two-gun battery in his upper work," another accurate description of redoubt four as positioned lower than five. Colonel Coon's report also supports the second assault as going in against a redoubt on a higher elevation than that of the first that was captured. Finally, Lieutenant O. A. Abbott, Ninth Illinois Cavalry, speaks of attacking a second redoubt "to the right and south of us," which only makes sense if number four was attacked first. If number five were first attacked, Abbott needed to say the second redoubt was "to the left and north of us" (see Abbott, "Last Battle of Nashville," 239).

Lieutenant Colonel John Stibbs, Twelfth Iowa Infantry, did say that redoubt number five was attacked first. This account, however, cannot possibly outweigh all the evidence to the contrary. Furthermore, the account by Stibbs was presented forty-two years later; his regiment was not in the attack on either four or five; he watched the action from a considerable distance; and he noted that the smoke of the guns obscured his view. In his official report, penned only a few days after the battle, he said nothing about the order of the attack. (The *OR* report is in vol. 45, pt. 1: 462–63. The later account is in John H. Stibbs, "McArthur's Division at Nashville As Seen by a Regimental Commander," *MOLLUS,* Illinois, 4:491–92.)

43. *OR* 45, pt. 1: 688.
44. Ibid., 747.
45. Ibid., 688.
46. Ibid., 434.
47. John Keegan, *The Face of Battle: A Study of Agincourt, Waterloo and the Somme* (New York, 1977), 239.
48. *OR* 45, pt. 1: 459.
49. Ibid., 450.
50. Ibid., 446.
51. Horn, *Decisive Battle,* 99, says redoubt number one was the source of the battery. Horn was careful about facts, but I have found no source supporting this statement, and think it more likely the battery came from farther east along Loring's line.
52. *OR* 45, pt. 1: 709. It is difficult to identify this "commanding hill" today. Two or three hills seem possible and to speculate about which seems fruitless.
53. *OR* 45, pt. 1: 577.
54. Ibid., 373.
55. Ibid., 371.
56. Ibid., 371–72.
57. Ibid., 369–70, 577.
58. Ibid., 709.

Chapter 9 ✴ The Final Gamble

1. Hunt and Brown, *Generals in Blue,* 284. Addison A. Stuart, *Iowa Colonels and Regiments* (Des Moines, 1865), 507–12.
2. Stibbs, "McArthur's Division," 492. *OR* 45, pt. 1: 460, 462–63.
3. Stibbs, "McArthur's Division," 492–93.
4. Ibid., 493.
5. Ibid. *OR* 45, pt. 1: 460, 463.
6. Horn, *Decisive Battle,* 100, quoting Carter from an article in the *Confederate Veteran.*
7. *OR* 45, pt. 1: 460, 434, 438, 463, 467. Stibbs, "McArthur's Division," 492. Bartlett Reminiscences, 48.
8. Stibbs, "McArthur's Division," 493.
9. *OR* 45, pt. 1: 460–61.
10. Ibid., 463. Stibbs, "McArthur's Division," 493–94.
11. Stibbs, "McArthur's Division," 494.

12. *OR* 45, pt. 1: 460–61. Stibbs, "McArthur's Division," 494.

13. Hunt and Brown, *Generals in Blue*, 284.

14. Catherine Drinker Bowen, *Miracle at Philadelphia: The Story of the Constitutional Convention, May to September, 1787* (Boston, 1966), 263.

15. *OR* 45, pt. 1: 64–67, 128–29.

16. Ibid., 129.

17. Ibid., 129.

18. Ibid., 180, 155, 129.

19. Ibid., 234, 155, 180, 129.

20. Ibid., 155, 180, 234, 129.

21. Bennett and Haigh, *History of the Thirty-sixth Illinois*, 677–78.

22. Bennett and Haigh, *History of the Thirty-sixth Illinois*, 679, say the man was from the Third Division. But Beatty's Third Division of Wood's corps probably was too far to the east, while men from Hill's Third Division of McArthur's corps entered at about the same time Wood's men did. Horn, *Decisive Battle*, 101–2.

23. *OR* 45, pt. 1: 243.

24. Ibid., 155.

25. Ibid., 190.

26. Horn, *Decisive Battle*, 102.

27. *OR* 45, pt. 1: 155, 156, 243, 441.

28. Sears diary, December 15, 1864, in Claudius W. Sears Papers, MDAH. R. N. Rea, "General C. W. Sears—A Pathetic Incident," *Confederate Veteran* 11 (1903): 327. *OR* 45, pt. 1: 710.

29. *OR* 45, pt. 1: 345.

30. Tunnell, "Ector's Brigade," 348.

31. Hughes, *Philip Daingerfield Stephenson*, 323.

32. Gale to wife, January 19, 1865, Gale Letters, TSLA.

33. Durham, *Reluctant Partners*, 254–55.

34. Gale to wife, January 19, 1865, Gale Letters, TSLA.

35. McDonough and Connelly, *Five Tragic Hours*, 64–67.

36. *OR* 45, pt. 2: 685.

37. *OR* 45, pt. 1: 688, 710.

38. Ibid.

39. Hay, *Hood's Tennessee Campaign*, 156.

40. *OR* 45, pt. 2: 696.

41. *OR* 45, pt. 1: 765, 756.

42. Daniel, *Cannoneers in Gray*, 176.

43. Bennett and Haigh, *History of the Thirty-sixth Illinois*, 682.

44. Huddleston, "Civil War in Middle Tennessee," 34.

45. See the account in Eleanor Graham, ed., *Nashville: A Short History and Selected Buildings* (Nashville, 1974). Paragraph also composed from a brief history of the Longview mansion, based on several sources, written by Martha Riedl, Nashville, and provided to the author.

46. Stibbs, "McArthur's Division," 497.

47. *OR* 45, pt. 1: 109.

48. George R. Lee, memoir article published in the *Brighton (Colorado) Register*, 1906, in CWTI Collection, USAMHI.

49. Charles F. Weller, Memoirs and Letters, letter to "Dear Kate," June 8, 1864. CWTI Collection, USAMHI.

50. *OR* 45, pt. 1: 176, 109, 110.

51. Stephen C. Ayres, "The Battle of Nashville," *MOLLUS*, Ohio, 5:294.

52. Abbott, "Last Battle of Nashville," 240.

53. *Nashville Daily Union*, December 16, 1864.

54. Foote, *Civil War*, 3:696.

55. *OR* 45, pt. 2: 194.

56. Ibid., 195.

57. *OR* 45, pt. 1: 345, 346. Schofield, *Forty-six Years in the Army*, 244.

58. Schofield, *Forty-six Years in the Army*, 244.

59. Cox, *Franklin and Nashville*, 116, 117.

60. Schofield, *Forty-six Years in the Army*, 245.

61. *OR* 45, pt. 1: 39.

Chapter 10 ✦ They Came Only to Die

1. *OR* 45, pt. 1: 694. A Nashville physician said that "the mercury registered sixty-five degrees" at the high point on December 16. John Edwin Windrow, *John Berrien Lindsley: Educator, Physician, Philosopher* (Chapel Hill, N.C., 1938), 81. Also see *OR* 45, pt. 1: 691.

2. *OR* 45, pt. 1: 132, 688, 691, 701, 702, 705.

3. Ibid., 698, 701.

4. Ibid., 695.

5. Isaac Henry Clay Royse, *History of the One Hundred and Fifteenth Illinois Volunteer Infantry* (Terre Haute, Ind., 1900), 241.

6. *OR* 45, pt. 1: 528.

7. Sword, *Angry Wind*, 357.

8. *OR* 45, pt. 1: 131.

9. Ibid., 689, 690, 692, 695, 705.

10. Ibid., 698, 701.

11. J. P. Cannon diary, December 16, 1864.

12. *OR* 45, pt. 1: 131.
13. Ibid., 132.
14. Ibid. Bennett and Haigh, *History of the Thirty-sixth Illinois,* 687. Sword, *Angry Wind,* 355.
15. *OR* 45, pt. 1: 133.
16. Ibid., 132.
17. McDonough, *Chattanooga,* 194.
18. Henry V. Freeman, "A Colored Brigade in the Campaign and Battle of Nashville," *MOLLUS,* Illinois, 1894, 2:416. *OR* 45, pt. 1: 305.
19. *OR* 45, pt. 1: 295.
20. Ibid., 543.
21. Ibid., 528.
22. There is notable variation among the many accounts regarding the time of attack. All factors considered, the time was probably between two and three o'clock; perhaps closer to three.
23. Bailey, *Chessboard of War,* 160.
24. Jones, "History of the 18th Alabama Infantry," 47.
25. Freeman, "Colored Brigade," 416.
26. *OR* 45, pt. 1: 705.
27. Ibid., 133.
28. Ibid.
29. Hunt and Brown, *Generals in Blue,* 487.
30. *OR* 45, pt. 1: 305.
31. Ibid.
32. Ibid., 295, 301.
33. Ibid., 303.
34. Ibid., 299. Hartpence, *Fifty-first Indiana,* 267.
35. *OR* 45, pt. 1: 299. Hartpence, *Fifty-first Indiana,* 265.
36. Bailey, *Chessboard of War,* 160. *OR* 45, pt. 1: 543.
37. *OR* 45, pt. 1: 543.
38. Ibid., 543.
39. Ibid., 543, 528.
40. Ibid., 528.
41. From Pension Records of USCT. Minor pensioners of Henry Dodson, Certificate Number 524230, National Archives, Washington, D.C.
42. From Pension Records of USCT. Widow pensioner of Edward Polk, Certificate Number 822102, National Archives.
43. Benjamin Smith journal, December 16, 1864, MSS Department, Illinois State Historical Library, Springfield, Illinois.
44. *OR* 45, pt. 1: 705, 706. Bailey, *Chessboard of War,* 160.

45. From Pension Records of USCT. Widow pensioner of James C. Babbitt, Certificate Number 785331, National Archives.

46. From Pension Records of USCT. Invalid pensioner Thomas Joyce. Account of Hays Moore is in his testimony on behalf of Thomas Joyce, Certificate Number 624812, National Archives.

47. From Pension Records of USCT. Invalid pensioner Thomas Cross, Certificate Number, 115909, National Archives.

48. *OR* 45, pt. 1: 688.

49. Jones, "History of the 18th Alabama Infantry," 47.

50. Ibid., 47–48.

51. *OR* 45, pt. 1: 705.

52. Horn, *Decisive Battle,* 123. *OR* 45, pt. 1: 688, 698.

53. *OR* 45, pt. 1: 706.

54. Ibid., 133.

55. Sword, *Angry Wind,* 363.

56. Buel and Johnson, *Battles and Leaders,* 4:464.

57. *OR* 45, pt. 1: 508.

58. Walker, "Blacks Fought in the Battle of Nashville." See also Ayres, "Battle of Nashville," *MOLLUS,* Ohio, 5:297, where George H. Thomas is quoted: "This proves the manhood of the negro."

59. Henry A. Norton, "Colored Troops in the War of the Rebellion," *MOLLUS,* Minnesota, 1898, 71–72.

60. *Nashville Daily Union,* December 18, 1864.

61. William D. Evritt to wife, December 18, 1864, in William D. Evritt Papers, Indiana Historical Society.

62. Wiley Sword, "The Battle of Nashville," *Blue & Gray Magazine* 2 (December 1993): 47.

63. S. T. Joshi and David E. Schultz, *Ambrose Bierce: A Sole Survivor, Bits of Autobiography* (Knoxville, 1998), 63.

64. *OR* 45, pt. 1: 134.

65. Ibid., 303, 300, 313.

66. Freeman, "Colored Brigade," 419, quoting Cox. Livermore calculated total Union losses at Nashville as 2,949, with 387 killed, 2,562 wounded, and 112 missing. *Numbers and Losses,* 132–33.

67. *OR* 45, pt. 1: 689.

68. The Battle of Nashville is particularly significant because of the involvement of black combat troops. Only a handful of Civil War battles are distinguished in this manner. Obviously black troops in considerable numbers were fighting for the U.S. army. Were blacks also fighting on the Confederate side at the Battle of Nashville? On December 15, 1993, the 129th anniversary of the battle, an article appeared in the now defunct *Nashville Banner,* in which it was claimed that they did—both slaves and free blacks fighting for the Confederacy. Kwame Leo

Lillard, described in the article as "a civil rights activist," was quoted as saying that "the Confederacy used a lot of black sharpshooters, and they were actually firing at and killing USCT (United States Colored Troops) during the battle." Also quoted was Daris C. Merriweather, referred to as "a lay historian," who claimed that some black sharpshooters were gaining freedom in exchange for dead Yankees. "If they killed 'X' number of Yankees, their master would give them their freedom. If they killed more," said Merriweather, "they might get freedom for their wives or children."

Nothing was revealed in the article about any sources, primary or secondary, that would support such striking claims. Neither in research for this book, nor in researching previous Civil War books over a period of nearly forty years has this author ever found any evidence of such occurrences; not in Confederate or Federal records; not in letters, memoirs, diaries; not anywhere.

Also, Nashville historian Ridley Wills II told the author in a letter of April 27, 1998, that he has never come across any evidence that such things happened. Wills had also consulted Dr. Bobby Lovett, a historian at Tennessee State University in Nashville, who has researched extensively in black history during the Civil War, and he concurred. Historian Walter Durham, in a conversation with the author at the Nashville Public Library on March 26, 2003, affirmed the same observation as Wills and Lovett. If such events happened, given the emotional and racial volatility of the subject, it seems highly likely that some persons who qualified as primary sources would, at the very least, have made mention of the matter.

Chapter 11 * The United States Flag Is on the Hill

1. Connelly, *Autumn of Glory,* 509. Foote, *Civil War,* 3:697.
2. Connelly, *Autumn of Glory,* 508.
3. Hay, *Hood's Tennessee Campaign,* 156, 170.
4. Bailey, *Chessboard of War,* 157.
5. *OR* 45, pt. 1: 442, 418. Stibbs, "McArthur's Division," 497.
6. *OR* 45, pt. 1: 710.
7. Tunnell, "Ector's Brigade," 349. *OR* 45, pt. 1: 722, 748, 749. Horn, *Decisive Battle,* 111.
8. *OR* 45, pt. 1: 740, 748, 749. Foote, *Civil War,* 3:700. Horn, *Decisive Battle,* 111, 121, 126. Both Foote and Horn credit the withdrawal of three of the division's four brigades. But only three were present at Nashville, the fourth being at Murfreesboro. The Confederate situation on the left is very complicated, due in part to so few reports being available. Besides officers who were killed, wounded, or captured, some never filed a report, or the reports were lost.
9. *OR* 45, pt. 1: 723.
10. Larry J. Daniel, *Soldiering in the Army of Tennessee: A Portrait of Life in a Confederate Army* (Chapel Hill, N.C., 1991), 160, 161. *OR* 45, pt. 1: 680, 739, 740, 750. Hubbard, "Minnesota in the Battle of Nashville," 278–79.
11. *OR* 45, pt. 1: 381.

12. Horn, *Decisive Battle,* 115. *OR* 45, pt. 1: 564.
13. Foote, *Civil War,* 3:701. Hughes, *Philip Daingerfield Stephenson,* 328. *OR* 45, pt. 1: 748.
14. *OR* 45, pt. 1: 748, 723. Horn, *Decisive Battle,* 111, 118–19. Connelly, *Autumn of Glory,* 511. Daniel, *Cannoneers in Gray,* 177.
15. *OR* 45, pt. 1: 453. Daniel, *Cannoneers in Gray,* 177. Stibbs, "McArthur's Division," 497. Foote, *Civil War,* 3:701.
16. Stibbs, "McArthur's Division," 497–98.
17. *OR* 45, pt. 1: 749, 723.
18. Ibid., 749.
19. Ibid., 747.
20. Ibid., 748.
21. Ibid., 748.
22. Ibid., 749.
23. Ibid., 749.
24. Ibid., 346, 499.
25. Ibid., 346. *OR* 45, pt. 2: 217, 223, 224.
26. *OR* 45, pt. 2: 214. *OR* 45, pt. 1: 346. Years later, in his memoirs, Schofield struck a different note, as if he could hardly wait to attack, saying "the whole forenoon was passed by me in impatient activity and fruitless efforts to get from General Thomas some orders or authority that would enable us all to act together—that is, the cavalry and the two infantry corps on the right." Schofield, *Forty-six Years in the Army,* 245.
27. *OR* 45, pt. 2: 216.
28. *OR* 45, pt. 1: 435. *OR* 45, pt. 2: 217, 215.
29. Stibbs, "McArthur's Division," 497.
30. *OR* 45, pt. 1: 438.
31. Ibid., 438, 442. Stibbs, "McArthur's Division," 498.
32. Stibbs, "McArthur's Division," 498.
33. Ibid., 499. Hubbard, "Minnesota in the Battle of Nashville," 281.
34. *OR* 45, pt. 1: 442–43.
35. Ibid., 453, 451.
36. Hubbard, "Minnesota in the Battle of Nashville," 281, 283. L. F. Hubbard to aunt, December 21, 1864, in Kenneth Carley, *Minnesota in the Civil War: An Illustrated History* (St. Paul, 2000), 155.
37. *OR* 45, pt. 1: 447, 455.
38. Ibid., 448, 449, 451.
39. Schofield, *Forty-six Years in the Army,* 245–46. Wilson, *Under the Old Flag,* 2:115, 116.
40. Horn, *Decisive Battle,* 130.
41. Van Horn, *Life of Thomas,* 330–32.
42. Cox, *Franklin and Nashville,* 122. Schofield, *Forty-six Years in the Army,* 245–46. Buel and Johnson, *Battles and Leaders,* 4:463–64.
43. *OR* 45, pt. 1: 439.

44. Ibid., 461.

45. Stibbs, "McArthur's Division," 499–500.

46. Ibid.

47. Carley, *Minnesota in the Civil War,* 158–59.

48. Hubbard, "Minnesota in the Battle of Nashville," 282.

49. Hood, *Advance and Retreat,* 303.

50. *OR* 45, pt. 1: 652–56.

51. Cooper Memoirs, 56.

52. Ibid., 57.

53. Watkins, *"Co. Aytch,"* 238–40.

54. *Nashville Tennessean,* December 15, 1963.

55. David E. Roth, "The Death of Colonel William Shy," *Blue & Gray Magazine* 2 (December 1993): 49. Horn, *Decisive Battle,* 127.

56. Louise Davis, "The Battle of Nashville—110 Years Later," *Tennessean Sunday Magazine,* December 5, 1974, 16, 18. Losson, *Cheatham,* 239.

57. Hughes, *Pride of the Confederate Artillery,* 251. Watkins, *"Co. Aytch,"* 240.

58. Cooper Memoirs, 57.

59. Luke W. Finlay, "Another Report on Hood's Campaign," *Confederate Veteran* 15 (1907): 405.

Chapter 12 ∗ It Is All Over Now

1. *OR* 45, pt. 1: 689. Louis F. Garrard, "General S. D. Lee's Part in Checking the Rout," *Confederate Veteran* 12 (1904): 350.

2. *OR* 45, pt. 1: 689.

3. Garrard, "General S. D. Lee's Part," 350. *OR* 45, pt. 1: 689.

4. Garrard, "General S. D. Lee's Part," 350.

5. Ibid., 350

6. Ibid., 351.

7. Losson, *Cheatham,* 238. Horn, *Decisive Battle,* 145–46.

8. Losson, *Cheatham,* 238.

9. J. P. Cannon diary, December 16, 1864.

10. Ibid.

11. Losson, *Cheatham,* 238.

12. Major Joseph B. Cumming War Recollections, 76, SHC.

13. Gale to wife, January 19, 1865, Gale Letters, TSLA.

14. Hughes, *Philip Daingerfield Stephenson,* 332.

15. Wilson, *Under the Old Flag,* 2:122.

16. A Confederate private named John Johnston took part in the battle. In 1905, then a lawyer living in Memphis, Johnston went to Nashville, journeyed to the site of the

fight, drew a map and described the "Battle of the Barricades," as he remembered it. The map and Johnston's reminiscence are in the possession of the Tennessee State Library and Archives. Using Johnston's map and account, two Nashville Civil War enthusiasts, Mr. James D. Kay Jr. and Mr. Fowler Low, spent many hours over a period of several weeks with metal detectors in the area. Finding numerous relics and dropped bullets, they are convinced the barricade across the pike was "just south of Norton Court on a rise in the road." James D. Kay Jr., letters and photocopies to the author, January 22 and February 11, 2003.

17. Wilson, *Under the Old Flag*, 2:122.

18. Henry, *Forrest*, 409. Wilson, *Under the Old Flag*, 2:123.

19. Wilson, *Under the Old Flag*, 2:124. Buel and Johnson, *Battles and Leaders*, 4:469. Tim Burgess, ed., "Reminiscences of the Battle of Nashville, by Private John Johnston," *Journal of Confederate History* 1 (summer 1988): 166.

20. Buel and Johnson, *Battles and Leaders*, 4:469.

21. Burgess, ed., "Reminiscences of Johnston," 167.

22. Ibid., 167, 164.

23. Buel and Johnson, *Battles and Leaders*, 4:467, 470. Longacre, *Wilson*, 186.

24. *OR* 45, pt. 1: 751, 750.

25. *OR* 45, pt. 2: 699.

26. *OR* 45, pt. 1: 40.

27. Martin, "Jackson's Brigade," 12–13.

28. B. F. Thompson, *History of the One Hundred and Twelfth Illinois* (Toulon, Ill., 1885), 288.

29. Bennett and Haigh, *Thirty-sixth Illinois*, 691.

30. Smith journal, December 16, 1864.

31. *OR*, series 2, vol. 8: 19–20. *OR*, series 1, vol. 45, pt. 2: 578–79.

32. Horn, *Decisive Battle*, 141.

33. McMurray, *History of the Twentieth Tennessee*, 348–49.

34. John T. Dowd, *The Pillaged Grave of a Civil War Hero* (Nashville, 1985), 6, 7.

35. *Nashville Daily Union*, December 18 and 20, 1864.

36. Abbott, "Last Battle of Nashville," 241–42.

37. Ayres, "Battle of Nashville," 295–97.

38. Bartlett Reminiscences, 49.

39. Losson, *Cheatham*, 239–40.

40. Quintard diary, December 18 and 19, 1864.

41. Harwood letter to "Dear Rachel," January 14, 1865, Federal Collection, TSLA.

42. James W. Goodwin Diaries and Memoirs, 43, Federal Collection, TSLA.

43. Porter diary, December 17, 1864.

44. Clark Memoirs, 47, 50.

45. From *Military History of Mississippi*, 753, in the Sears-Featherston Sword Research Collection, MDAH.

46. James R. Fleming, *Band of Brothers: Company C, Ninth Tennessee Infantry* (Shippensburg, Pa., 1996), xxi.

47. William Pitt Chambers journal, 150, 155, 159, MDAH.

48. Eastman to sister, December 28, 1864, Charles H. Eastman Papers, TSLA.

49. Kolb to mother, March 9, 1865, in the Kolb-Hume Collection, Auburn University Archives.

50. Sutherland, *Reminiscences of a Private,* 217.

51. Ibid., 219.

52. Jarman, "History of Co. K," 47.

53. Porter diary, December 24, 1864.

54. Ibid.

55. McMurray, *History of the Twentieth Tennessee,* 352. There are differing versions of the parody, and differing accounts of where it took place. For examples, see Horn, *Decisive Battle,* 153, and Bell I. Wiley, *The Life of Johnny Reb* (Indianapolis, 1951), 121. The story, though it has been often repeated, is too good to omit. The author prefers McMurray's version.

56. McDonough and Connelly, *Five Tragic Hours,* 178. McMurry, *Hood,* 191.

57. Losson, *Cheatham,* 230.

58. Catton, *Grant Takes Command,* 400.

59. McDonough, *Schofield,* 136–37. Foote, *Civil War,* 3:1056.

60. McMurry, *Hood,* 195.

61. Portions of Lea's speech taken from the full copy printed in the *Nashville Tennessean,* November 14, 1927. Information about the monument and the sculptor's estimate of it, in various letters and newspapers, was provided to the author by Mr. James Summerville of the Battle of Nashville Preservation Society, May 30, 1998.

BIBLIOGRAPHY

Primary Materials

Records

Official Records of the Union and Confederate Navies in the War of the Rebellion. 22 vols. Washington, D.C., 1908.

Official Register of the Officers and Cadets of the United States Military Academy. West Point, N.Y., 1850–54.

Pension Records of United States Colored Troops. National Archives, Washington, D.C.
    Widow Pensioner of James C. Babbitt
    Invalid Pensioner Thomas Cross
    Minor Pensioners of Henry Dodson
    Invalid Pensioner Thomas Joyce
    Widow Pensioner of Edward Polk

War of the Rebellion: A Compilation of the Official Records of the Union and Confederate Armies. 129 vols. Washington, D.C., 1880–1901.

Collected Works, Diaries, Memoirs, Papers, Reminiscences

Abbott, O. A. "The Last Battle of Nashville." *MOLLUS,* Nebraska, 1902.

Ayres, Stephen C. "The Battle of Nashville." *MOLLUS,* Ohio, vol. 5.

Brown, Norman D., ed. *One of Cleburne's Command: The Civil War Reminiscences and Diary of Capt. Samuel T. Foster, Granbury's Texas Brigade, CSA.* Austin, 1980.

Buck, Irving A. *Cleburne and His Command.* Ed. Thomas R. Hay. New York, 1908.

Buel, Clarence C., and Robert U. Johnson, eds. *Battles and Leaders of the Civil War.* 4 vols. New York, 1887–88.

Cate, Wirt Armistead, ed. *Two Soldiers: The Campaign Diaries of Thomas J. Key, C.S.A. and Robert J. Campbell, U.S.A.* Chapel Hill, 1938.

Cheatham, Benjamin F. "The Lost Opportunity at Spring Hill, Tennessee—General Cheatham's Reply to General Hood." *Southern Historical Society Papers* 9 (1881).

Confederate Veteran. 40 vols. Nashville, 1893–1932. Seven articles, with full citations in the endnotes.

Cox, Jacob D. *The Battle of Franklin, Tennessee, November 30, 1864.* New York, 1897.

———. *The March to the Sea, Franklin and Nashville.* New York, 1882.

Dinkins, James. *Personal Recollections and Experiences.* Cincinnati, 1897.

Fitch, John. *Annals of the Army of the Cumberland.* Philadelphia, 1864.

Freeman, Henry V. "A Colored Brigade in the Campaign and Battle of Nashville." *MOLLUS,* Illinois, 1894.

French, Samuel G. *Two Wars: An Autobiography.* Nashville, 1901.

Grant, U. S. *Personal Memoirs of U. S. Grant.* 2 vols. New York, 1886.

Grimsley, Mark, and Todd D. Miller, eds. *The Union Must Stand: The Civil War Diary of John Quincy Adams Campbell, Fifth Iowa Volunteer Infantry.* Knoxville, 2000.

Heafford, George H. "The Army of the Tennessee." *MOLLUS,* Wisconsin, 1888.

Hood, John Bell. *Advance and Retreat.* New Orleans, 1880.

Hubbard, Lucius F. "Minnesota in the Battle of Nashville, December 15–16, 1864." *MOLLUS,* Minnesota, 1909.

Hughes, Nathaniel Cheairs, Jr., ed. *The Civil War Memoir of Philip Daingerfield Stephenson, D.D.* Conway, Ark., 1995.

Jamison, Henry D., Jr., and Marguerite Jamison McTigue, eds. *Letters and Recollections of a Confederate Soldier (Robert David Jamison), 1860–1865.* Nashville, 1964.

Kendall, Henry M. "The Battles of Franklin and Nashville." *MOLLUS,* District of Columbia, 1902.

Logsdon, David R., ed. *Eyewitnesses at the Battle of Franklin.* Nashville, 1988.

Maxwell, James Robert. *Autobiography of James Robert Maxwell.* 1926. Reprint, Baltimore, 1996.

McMurray, W. J. *History of the Twentieth Tennessee Volunteer Infantry.* Nashville, n.d.

Morgan, Thomas Jefferson. *Reminiscences of Service with Colored Troops in the Army of the Cumberland, 1863–1865.* Providence, 1885.

Nichols, George W. *The Story of the Great March.* New York, 1865.

Noe, Kenneth W., ed. *A Southern Boy in Blue: The Memoir of Marcus Woodstock, 9th Kentucky Infantry.* Knoxville, 1996.

Norton, Henry A. "Colored Troops in the War of the Rebellion," *MOLLUS,* Minnesota, 1898.

Phillips, Lewis F. *Some Things Our Boys Saw in the War.* Garrity, Iowa, 1911.

Roman, Alfred. *The Military Operations of General Beauregard in the War Between the States, 1861–1865.* 2 vols. New York, 1884.

Romeyn, Henry. "With Colored Troops in the Army of the Cumberland." *MOLLUS,* District of Columbia, 1904.

Rusling, James F. *Men and Things I Saw in Civil War Days.* New York, 1899.

Schofield, John M. *Forty-six Years in the Army.* New York, 1897.

Shellenberger, John K. "The Battle of Franklin." *MOLLUS,* Minnesota Commandery, Minneapolis, 1903.

———. *The Battle of Franklin.* Cleveland, 1916.

Sherman, William T. *Memoirs of General William T. Sherman.* 2 vols. New York, 1875.

Sherwood, Isaac R. *Memories of the War.* Toledo, 1923.

Sorrell, G. Moxley. *Recollections of a Confederate Staff Officer.* Ed. Bell I. Wiley. Jackson, Tenn., 1958.

Stanley, David S. *Personal Memoirs of Major General David S. Stanley, United States Army.* Cambridge, Mass., 1917.

Stibbs, John H. "McArthur's Division at Nashville As Seen by a Regimental Commander." *MOLLUS,* Illinois, vol. 4.

Sutherland, Daniel E., ed. *Reminiscences of a Private: William E. Bevens of the First Arkansas Infantry, C.S.A.* Fayetteville, Ark., n.d.

Watkins, Samuel R. *"Co. Aytch," Maury Gray's First Tennessee Regiment.* Jackson, Tenn., 1952.

Wilson, James H. *Under the Old Flag.* 2 vols. New York, 1912.

Wyeth, John Allan. *That Devil Forrest: Life of General Nathan Bedford Forrest.* New York, 1899.

Yargan, John Lee. "Stone River." *MOLLUS,* Indiana Commandery, Indianapolis, 1898.

Unit Histories

Bennett, L. G., and W. M. Haigh. *History of the Thirty-sixth Regiment of Illinois Volunteers.* Aurora, Ill., 1876.

Clark, Charles T. *125th Ohio Volunteer Infantry: Opdycke Tigers.* Columbus, 1895.

Hartpence, William R. *History of the Fifty-first Indiana Veteran Volunteer Infantry Regiment.* Cincinnati, 1894.

A History of the Seventy-third Illinois Infantry Volunteers. Springfield, 1890.

Royse, Isaac Henry Clay. *History of the One Hundred and Fifteenth Illinois Volunteer Infantry.* Terre Haute, Ind., 1900.

Thompson, B. F. *History of the One Hundred and Twelfth Illinois.* Toulon, Ill., 1885.

Manuscripts

Alabama Department of Archives and History, Montgomery
    George E. Brewer, "History of the 23rd Alabama Infantry"
    J. P. Cannon Diary
    John W. DuBose, "History of the 19th Alabama Infantry"
    Edgar W. Jones, "History of the 18th Alabama Infantry"
    Joseph N. Thompson, "History of the 35th Alabama Infantry"

Atlanta Historical Society, Georgia
    James Porter Crane Letters
    A. T. Holiday Letters

Auburn University Archives, Alabama
    John Crittenden Letters
    Kolb-Hume Collection

Filson Club Historical Society, Louisville
    George W. Johnson Papers

Special Collections, Florida State University, Tallahassee
    Captain Hugh Black Letters
Georgia Department of Archives and History, Atlanta
    W. S. Carson Papers
    Hezekiah M. McCorkle Diary
Illinois State Historical Library, Springfield   ·
    Benjamin Smith Journal
Indiana Historical Society, Indianapolis
    William D. Evritt Papers
    Martin Lewis Hursh Diary
    Robert H. Milroy Papers
Library of Congress, Washington, D.C.
    John M. Schofield Papers
John Wesley McDonough Letters in possession of John Henry James, Nashville
Mississippi Department of Archives and History, Jackson
    William Barry Letters in the Dr. Benjamin F. and William Robert Collection
    William Pitt Chambers Journal
    Samuel G. French Papers
    Robert A. Jarman MSS
    William and Ben Robertson Papers
    Sears-Featherston Sword Research Collection
Missouri Historical Society, St. Louis
    A. T. Bartlett Reminiscences
    Daisy J. Cline Papers
Tennessee State Library and Archives, Nashville
    Campbell Brown–Richard S. Ewell Papers
    Carroll H. Clark Memoirs
    Joe Clark Memoirs
    Samuel Alonzo Cook Memoir
    James L. Cooper Memoirs
    Thomas Hopkins Davenport Diary
    Charles H. Eastman Papers
    William Gale Letters
    James W. Goodwin Diaries and Memoir
    J. W. Harmon Memoirs
    J. C. Harwood Letters
    John Johnston Memoirs
    James A. McCord Letters
    S. J. McMurry Letters
    Joe Spence Diary
    Benjamin Franklin Wade Letters
United States Army Military History Institute, Carlisle Barracks, Pennsylvania
    Alexander P. Stewart Letter in the Lionel Baxter Collection, Civil War Times
    Illustrated Collection

Charles F. Weller Memoirs and Letters, Civil War Times Illustrated Collection
West-Stanley-Wright Family Papers
Southern Historical Collection, University of North Carolina, Chapel Hill
Major Joseph B. Cumming War Recollections
Daniel C. Govan Papers
James Harrison Papers
Virgil S. Murphy Diary
Nimrod Porter Diary
University of the South, Sewanee, Tennessee
Charles T. Quintard Diary

Newspapers

Atlanta Appeal
Brighton (Colorado) Register
Bucyrus (Ohio) Journal
Columbus Evening Dispatch
Daily Missouri Democrat (St. Louis)
Hart County News (Munfordville, Kentucky)
Nashville Banner
Nashville Daily Union
Nashville Dispatch
New York Times
Ohio State Journal (Columbus)
The Tennessean (Nashville)

Secondary Materials

Books

Adams, George Rollie, and Ralph Jerry Christian. *Nashville: A Pictorial History.* Virginia Beach, 1981.

Ash, Stephen V. *Middle Tennessee Society Transformed, 1860–1870: War and Peace in the Upper South.* Baton Rouge, 1988.

Bailey, Anne J. *The Chessboard of War.* Lincoln, Nebr., 2000.

Banks, R. W. *The Battle of Franklin.* New York, 1908.

Bowen, Catherine Drinker. *Miracle at Philadelphia: The Story of the Constitutional Convention.* Boston, 1966.

Bowman, Virginia McDaniel. *Historic Williamson County: Old Homes and Sites.* Nashville, 1971.

Brandt, Robert. *Touring the Middle Tennessee Backroads.* Winston-Salem, N.C., 1995.

Carley, Kenneth. *Minnesota in the Civil War: An Illustrated History.* St. Paul, 2000.

Carter, Arthur B. *The Tarnished Cavalier: Major General Earl Van Dorn, C.S.A.* Knoxville, 1999.

Castel, Albert. *Decision in the West: The Atlanta Campaign of 1864.* Lawrence, Kans., 1992.

Castner, Charles B., Ronald Flanary, and Patrick Dorin. *Louisville & Nashville Railroad: The Old Reliable.* Lynchburg, Va., 1996.

Catton, Bruce. *Grant Takes Command.* Boston, 1969.

———. *Never Call Retreat.* New York, 1965.

Cleaves, Freeman. *Rock of Chickamauga: Life of General George H. Thomas.* Norman, Okla., 1948.

Connelly, Thomas Lawrence. *Army of the Heartland: The Army of Tennessee, 1861–1862.* Baton Rouge, 1967.

———. *Autumn of Glory: The Army of Tennessee, 1862–1865.* Baton Rouge, 1971.

———. *Civil War Tennessee: Battles and Leaders.* Knoxville, 1979.

Cooling, Benjamin F. *Forts Henry and Donelson: The Key to the Confederate Heartland.* Knoxville, 1987.

Coppee, Henry. *Great Commanders, General Thomas.* New York, 1895.

Corlew, Robert E. *Tennessee: A Short History.* Knoxville, 1981.

Cozzens, Peter. *No Better Place to Die: The Battle of Stones River.* Urbana and Chicago, 1990.

Daniel, Larry J. *Cannoneers in Gray: The Field Artillery of the Army of Tennessee, 1861–1865.* Tuscaloosa, Ala., 1984.

———. *Soldiering in the Army of Tennessee: A Portrait of Life in a Confederate Army.* Chapel Hill, N.C., 1991.

DeBerry, John H. "Confederate Tennessee." Ph.D. diss., University of Kentucky, 1967.

Dowd, John T. *The Pillaged Grave of a Civil War Hero.* Nashville, 1985.

Doyle, Don H. *Nashville in the New South, 1880–1930.* Knoxville, 1985.

Durham, Walter T. *Reluctant Partners: Nashville and the Union, July 1, 1863 to June 30, 1865.* Nashville, 1987.

Dyer, John P. *The Gallant Hood.* Indianapolis and New York, 1950.

Elliott, Sam Davis. *Soldier of Tennessee: General Alexander P. Stewart and the Civil War in the West.* Baton Rouge, 1999.

Evans, Clement, ed. *Confederate Military History.* 12 vols. Atlanta, 1889.

Fleming, James R. *Band of Brothers: Company C, Ninth Tennessee Infantry.* Shippensburg, Pa., 1996.

Foote, Shelby. *The Civil War: A Narrative.* 3 vols. New York, 1958–75.

Frazier, Charles. *Cold Mountain: A Novel.* New York, 1997.

Gerry, Moultrie. *Men Who Made Sewanee.* Sewanee, Tenn., 1981.

Goodstein, Anita Shafer. *Nashville, 1780–1860: From Frontier to City.* Gainesville, Fla., 1989.

Govan, Gilbert E., and James W. Livingood. *A Different Valor: The Story of General Joseph E. Johnston, C.S.A.* Westport, Conn., 1956.

Graham, Eleanor, ed. *Nashville: A Short History and Selected Buildings.* Nashville, 1974.

Groom, Winston. *Shrouds of Glory: From Atlanta to Nashville, The Last Great Campaign of the Civil War.* New York, 1995.

Hair, William I. *The Kingfish and His Realm: The Life and Times of Huey P. Long.* Baton Rouge, 1991.

Hattaway, Herman. *General Stephen D. Lee.* Jackson, Miss., 1976.

Hay, Thomas R. *Hood's Tennessee Campaign.* New York, 1929.

Heidler, David S., and Jeanne T. Heidler, eds. *Encyclopedia of the American Civil War: A Political, Social and Military History.* 5 vols. Santa Barbara, Calif., 2000.

Henry, Robert S. *"First With the Most" Forrest.* Indianapolis, 1944.

———. *The Story of the Confederacy.* New York, 1931.

Herr, Kincaid A. *The Louisville & Nashville Railroad: 1850–1963.* 1943. Reprint, Lexington, Ky., 2000.

Hoobler, James A. *Cities under the Gun: Images of Occupied Nashville and Chattanooga.* Nashville, 1986.

Horn, Stanley F. *The Army of Tennessee.* 1941. Reprint, Norman, Okla., 1952.

———. *The Decisive Battle of Nashville.* 1956. Reprint, Knoxville, 1968.

Hughes, Nathaniel C., Jr. *General William J. Hardee: Old Reliable.* Baton Rouge, 1965.

———. *The Pride of the Confederate Artillery: The Washington Artillery in the Army of Tennessee.* Baton Rouge, 1997.

Hunt, Roger, and Jack R. Brown. *Brevet Brigadier Generals in Blue.* Gaithersburg, Mo., 1990.

Jewell, Carey C. *Harvest of Death: A Detailed Account of the Army of Tennessee at the Battle of Franklin.* Hicksville, N.Y., 1976.

Jordan, Wyemouth T. *George Washington Campbell of Tennessee: Western Statesman.* Tallahassee, 1955.

Joshi, S. T., and David E. Schultz. *Ambrose Bierce: A Sole Survivor, Bits of Autobiography.* Knoxville, 1998.

Keegan, John. *The Face of Battle: A Study of Agincourt, Waterloo and the Somme.* New York, 1977.

Killebrew, J. B. *Middle Tennessee As an Iron Center.* Nashville, 1879.

Lesley, J. P. *Iron Manufacturer's Guide to the Furnaces, Forges and Rolling Mills of the United States.* New York, 1859.

Lewis, Lloyd. *Sherman: Fighting Prophet.* New York, 1932.

Liddell Hart, Basil H. *Sherman: Soldier, Realist, American.* New York, 1929.

Livermore, Thomas L. *Numbers and Losses in the Civil War in America, 1861–1865.* New York, 1901.

Longacre, Edward G. *From Union Stars to Top Hat: A Biography of the Extraordinary James Harrison Wilson.* Harrisburg, Pa., 1972.

Longford, Elizabeth. *Wellington: The Years of the Sword.* New York, 1969.

Losson, Christopher. *Tennessee's Forgotten Warriors: Frank Cheatham and His Confederate Division.* Knoxville, 1989.

Lowry, Thomas P. *The Story the Soldiers Wouldn't Tell: Sex in the Civil War.* Mechanicsburg, Pa., 1994.

Marszalek, John F. *Sherman: A Soldier's Passion for Order.* New York, 1993.

McDonough, James Lee. *Chattanooga—A Death Grip on the Confederacy.* Knoxville, 1984.

———. *Schofield: Union General in the Civil War and Reconstruction.* Tallahassee, 1972.

———. *Shiloh—In Hell Before Night.* Knoxville, 1977.

———. *Stones River—Bloody Winter in Tennessee.* Knoxville, 1980.

———. *War in Kentucky: From Shiloh to Perryville.* Knoxville, 1994.

McDonough, James Lee, and Thomas L. Connelly. *Five Tragic Hours: The Battle of Franklin.* Knoxville, 1983.

McKinney, Francis F. *Education in Violence: The Life of George H. Thomas.* Detroit, 1961.

McMurry, Richard M. *John Bell Hood and the War for Southern Independence.* Lexington, Ky., 1982.

McPherson, James M. *Ordeal by Fire: The Civil War and Reconstruction.* New York, 1992.

McRaven, Henry. *Nashville: Athens of the South.* Chapel Hill, N.C., 1949.

Nevins, Allan. *The War for the Union.* 4 vols. New York, 1960.

Nichols, George W. *The Story of the Great March.* New York, 1865.

O'Connor, Richard. *Hood: Cavalier General.* New York, 1949.

———. *Thomas: Rock of Chickamauga.* New York, 1948.

Parks, Joseph H. *General Edmund Kirby Smith, C.S.A.* Baton Rouge, 1962.

Piatt, Don. *General George H. Thomas: A Critical Biography.* Cincinnati, 1893.

Purdue, Howell, and Elizabeth Purdue. *Pat Cleburne, Confederate General: A Definitive Biography.* Hillsboro, Tex., 1973.

Smith, Frank H. *History of Maury County Tennessee.* Compiled by the Maury County Historical Society, 1969.

Smith, Reid. *Majestic Middle Tennessee.* Prattville, Ala., 1975.

Songs of Inspiration. Nashville, 1949.

Stuart, Addison A. *Iowa Colonels and Regiments.* Des Moines, 1865.

Sword, Wiley. *Embrace an Angry Wind: The Confederacy's Last Hurrah: Spring Hill, Franklin, and Nashville.* New York, 1992.

Symonds, Craig L. *Stonewall of the West: Patrick Cleburne and the Civil War.* Lawrence, Kans., 1997.

The Tennessee Encyclopedia of History and Culture. Nashville, 1998.

Thomas, Wilbur. *General George H. Thomas: The Indomitable Warrior.* New York, 1964.

Trudeau, Noah Andre. *Like Men of War: Black Troops in the Civil War, 1862–1865.* New York, 1998.

Tucker, Glen. *Chickamauga: Bloody Battle in the West.* Dayton, Ohio, 1972.

Van Horn, Thomas B. *The Life of Major General George H. Thomas.* New York, 1882.

Vandiver, Frank E. *Rebel Brass: The Confederate Command System.* New York, 1956.

———. *Their Tattered Flags: The Epic of the Confederacy.* New York, 1970.

Warner, Ezra, Jr. *Generals in Gray: Lives of the Confederate Commanders.* Baton Rouge, 1959.

Wiley, Bell I. *The Life of Johnny Reb.* Indianapolis, 1951.

Williams, George Washington. *A History of the Negro Troops in the War of the Rebellion, 1861–1865.* New York, 1888.

Williams, T. Harry. *P. G. T. Beauregard: Napoleon in Gray.* Baton Rouge, 1954.

Wills, Brian Steel. *A Battle from the Start: The Life of Nathan Bedford Forrest.* New York, 1992.

Wills, Ridley, II. *The History of Belle Meade Mansion, Plantation, and Stud.* Nashville, 1991.

Windrow, John Edwin. *John Berrien Lindsley: Educator, Physician, Philosopher.* Chapel Hill, N.C., 1938.

Woodworth, Steven E. *Jefferson Davis and His Generals: The Failure of Confederate Command in the West.* Lawrence, Kans., 1990.

Articles, Booklets, Guides, Etc.

Bearss, Edwin, and Charles Spearman. "The Battle of the Cedars." Unpublished account in the Stones River National Military Park files, Murfreesboro, Tenn.

Burgess, Tim, ed. "Reminiscences of the Battle of Nashville, by Private John Johnston." *Journal of Confederate History* 1 (summer 1988).

Davis, Louise. "The Battle of Nashville—110 Years Later." *Tennessean Sunday Magazine,* December 5, 1974.

———. "Box Seat on the Civil War." *Tennessean Magazine* (March–April 1979).

Engerud, Hal. "Munfordville: The Home of Two Civil War Generals." Written for the *Hart County News,* bicentennial edition. Reissued in pamphlet form, February 8, 1974. Copy in files of the Hart County Historical Society, Munfordville, Ky.

Horn, Stanley F. "Dr. John Rolfe Hudson and the Confederate Underground in Nashville." *Tennessee Historical Quarterly* 1 (March 1963).

———. "Nashville during the Civil War." *Tennessee Historical Quarterly* 1 (March 1945).

———. "The Spring Hill Legend." *Civil War Times Illustrated* 8 (April 1969).

Huddleston, Ed. "The Civil War in Middle Tennessee." Part 4. *Nashville Banner,* November 14, 1964.

Kaser, David. "Nashville's Women of Pleasure in 1860." *Tennessee Historical Quarterly* 4 (December 1964).

Losson, Christopher. "Major General Benjamin Franklin Cheatham and the Battle of Stone's River." *Tennessee Historical Quarterly* 3 (fall 1982).

Lovett, Bobby. "Negro's Civil War in Tennessee." *Journal of Negro History* 1 (January 1976).

McDonough, James Lee. "The Battle at Franklin." *Blue & Gray Magazine* 1 (September 1984).

Norris, Herbert S., and James R. Long. "The Road to Redemption." *Civil War Times* 5 (August 1997).

Riedl, Martha. "Brief History of the Longview Mansion." Unpublished paper in possession of Martha Riedl, Nashville, Tenn.

Roth, David E. "The Death of Colonel William Shy." *Blue & Gray Magazine* 2 (December 1993).

———. "The General's Tour of Spring Hill, Tennessee." *Blue & Gray Magazine* 2 (October–November 1984).

———. "The Mysteries of Spring Hill, Tennessee." *Blue & Gray Magazine* 2 (October–November 1984).

Sword, Wiley. "The Battle of Nashville." *Blue & Gray Magazine* 2 (December 1993).

Walker, Hugh. "Blacks Fought in the Battle of Nashville." *Tennessean,* August 1, 1976.

Wilkinson, Jeff. "Blacks Bore Arms on Both Sides in Civil War's Battle of Nashville." *Nashville Banner,* December 15, 1993.

Fredericksburg, Battle of, 137
French Lick (Nashville), 114
French, Samuel G., 35, 36, 70, 96, 98, 108, 136, 184
Fullerton, Joseph H., 71, 72, 204

Gadsden, Alabama, 38, 40, 41
Gale Lane, 142
Gale, William Dudley, 139, 208, 209, 261
Gallatin, Tennessee, 13, 163, 173
Garesche, Julius P., 134
Garfield, James A., 11
Garrard, Kenner, 186
Garrard, Louis F., 258
General Motors Company, 49, 50
Georgia Infantry, First Regiment, 166
Germantown, Battle of, 114
Gettysburg, Battle of, 5, 6, 51, 100
Gibson, Randall L., 218
Gilmer, Jeremy, 125
Gist, States Rights, 107; death, 110, 138
Glen Leven (home), 212
Gone With the Wind, 140
Gordon, George W., 103, 110
Gore, Albert, Jr., 117
Govan, Daniel C., 97, 99, 110, 239
Govan, Gilbert E., 26
Granbury, Hiram, 63, 76; burial, 139; death, 110, 138, 166
Granbury's Brigade (at Nashville), 240
Grand Army of the Republic, 275
Granger, Gordon, 13, 81, 158
Granny White Pike, 141, 142, 143, 156, 182, 207, 208, 210, 237, 238, 243, 256, 259, 262, 263, 264, 268, 279
Grant, U. S., 4, 5, 7, 8, 9, 12, 13, 16, 56, 125, 136, 151, 215, 264, 274, 276; urges Thomas to attack at Nashville, 148–49
Gray, John C., 4
Green Hills (Nashville), 177, 179, 180
Gregory, John, 52, 63, 66, 76, 77
Grierson, Benjamin (Mississippi Raid), 188
Grose, William, 88, 89, 205

Grosvenor, Charles H., 163, 168, 220, 225, 229
Grosvenor, Ebenezer, 168
Guntersville, Alabama, 40

Haddox, Dr. John, 51
Haigh, William, 266
Hair, William I., 28
Hall, William, 205–6
Halleck, Henry W., 7, 9, 14, 15, 34, 145, 148, 149, 153
Hammond, John H., 245
Hand, Katherine Isabella, 41
Hardee, William J., 25, 26, 30, 33
Harding, John and William Giles, 120, 177
Harding Pike, 141, 142, 174, 176, 188
Harding, Selene, 177
Hardison's Mill, 56, 58
Hargrove, Cole, 190
Harmon, J. R., 44
Harper, Joseph W., 191
Harpeth Hills, 237
Harpeth River, 58, 72, 79, 80, 81, 83, 88, 95, 107, 108, 140
Harwood, J. C., 270
Harris, Isham, 30, 66, 68, 70, 128
Harrison House, 82, 83, 94, 138
Harrison, Thomas, 173, 175
Harrison, William, 82
Hartman, John F., 192
Hartpence, William R., 110, 228
Hatch, Edward, 16, 185, 188, 189, 191, 195
Haven, Benny, 26
Hayes, Rutherford B., 2
Hay, Thomas, 52, 53, 142, 238
Hazen, William B., 2
Heafford, George H., 187–88
Heard, J. Theodore, 213
Heiman, Adolphus, 120, 122
Helena, Arkansas, 140
Henderson, John, 15
Hennen, Anna Marie, 277
Henry rifles, 85

United States Infantry, Thirteenth
Regiment, 131
University of Alabama, 183
University of Nashville, 122
Upton, Emory, 2

Vanderbilt University Agrarians, 49
Vanderbilt, University, 134
Vandiver, Frank E., 27
Van Dorn, Earl, 40, 50, 51, 75, 84
Van Dorn, Thomas B., 250
Vicksburg, Campaign of, 4, 7, 24, 186
Virginia Military Institute, 183

Wagner, George D., 60, 61, 65, 89, 90, 94;
advanced position at Franklin,
90–91, 101
Walker, W. H. T., 34
Walthall's Division, 183, 193
Walthall, Edward, 54, 98, 108, 184, 194,
242, 243
War of 1812, 116
Warfield, Amos and Cornelia, 47, 55
Washington, D. C., 9, 132, 215, 276
Washington, George, 10
Waterloo, Battle of, 60
Watkins, Sam R., 97–98, 254–55
Waynesboro, Tennessee, 45
Western & Atlantic Railroad, 8, 30, 35,
38, 171
Western Military Institute, 122
Wherry, William M., 60, 277
Whitaker, Walter C., 88
White, John E., 106

White, William, 138
Williams, T. Harry, 28, 29, 40
Williamson County, Tennessee, 81
Wilson, James H., 8, 16, 71, 73, 148;
advice and reports to Schofield, 58,
91–92; appearance and background,
55, 56, 57, 185; fighting with Forrest,
56, 58, 81; at Nashville, 151–52, 170,
185–88, 194, 240, 245, 250, 259, 262–64
Wilson's Creek, Battle of, 14, 17, 125
Winchester, Virginia, 145
Winstead-Breezy Hill range, 79, 82, 83,
84, 89, 94, 96, 99
Wisconsin Infantry, Eighth Regiment,
195, 249
Wisconsin Infantry, Twenty-fourth
Regiment, 105
Wood, Thomas J., 60, 92, 140, 141, 151,
155, 220; appearance and background,
168, 171; approaches Redoubt number 1, 186, 204; attacks Confederate
right on Dec. 16, 223, 224, 225–26,
234, 235; attacks Montgomery Hill,
169–72; attacks Redoubt number 1,
204–6; instructions from Thomas,
Dec. 16, 222
Woodmont Boulevard, 182, 184
Woodson, Marcus, 36
Woodworth, Steven, 142

"Yellow Rose of Texas," 273
Yeoman, S. N., 206
Young, J. P., 74
Young, R. B., 139

Nashville was designed and typeset on a Macintosh computer system using QuarkXPress software. The body text is set in 9.5/12.5 Palatino, and display type is set in Old Claude and Journal Bold. This book was designed and typeset by Barbara Karwhite and manufactured by Thomson-Shore, Inc.